W9-CIH-863

CRISIS AND LEVIATHAN

CRISIS AND LEVIATHAN

Critical Episodes in the Growth of American Government

Robert Higgs

A *Pacific Research Institute for Public Policy* Book

New York   Oxford
OXFORD UNIVERSITY PRESS
1987

Oxford University Press

Oxford   New York   Toronto
Delhi   Bombay   Calcutta   Madras   Karachi
Petaling Jaya   Singapore   Hong Kong   Tokyo
Nairobi   Dar es Salaam   Cape Town
Melbourne   Auckland

and associated companies in
Beirut   Berlin   Ibadan   Nicosia

Published by Oxford University Press, Inc.
200 Madison Avenue, New York, New York 10016

Oxford is a registered trademark of Oxford University Press

Library of Congress Cataloging-in-Publication Data
Higgs, Robert.
Crisis and leviathan.
"A Pacific Research Institute for Public Policy book."
Bibliography: p.   Includes index.
1. Administrative agencies—United States—History.
2. Bureaucracy—United States—History.   3. Welfare state—History.
4. United States—Politics and government—19th century.
5. United States—Politics and government—20th century.
I. Title.
JK411.H54   1987   353.04′09   86-28536
ISBN 0-19-504967-5

From *The People, Yes* by Carl Sandburg, copyright 1936 by Harcourt Brace Jovanovich, Inc.; renewed 1964 by Carl Sandburg. Reprinted by permission of the publisher.

From "Killers" in *Chicago Poems* by Carl Sandburg, copyright 1916 by Holt, Rinehart and Winston, Inc.; renewed 1944 by Carl Sandburg. Reprinted by permission of the publisher.

From "The Sea and the Mirror" and "In Memory of W. B. Yeats" in *W. H. Auden: Collected Poems*, by W. H. Auden, edited by Edward Mendelson, copyright 1976 by Alfred A. Knopf, Inc., and Random House, Inc. Reprinted by permission of Alfred A. Knopf, Inc., Random House, Inc., and Faber and Faber, Ltd.

From "Cassandra" in *The Selected Poetry of Robinson Jeffers*, by Robinson Jeffers, copyright 1965 by Alfred A. Knopf, Inc., and Random House, Inc. Reprinted by permission of the publisher.

From "Siren Song" by Margaret Atwood. Reprinted by permission of Margaret Atwood from *You Are Happy*, published by Harper & Row, copyright 1974.

From "Guns Before Butter" by Bertolt Brecht, copyright 1976 by Eyre Methuen, Ltd. Reprinted from *Bertolt Brecht Poems, 1913–1956* by permission of the publisher, Methuen, Inc., by arrangement with Suhrkamp Verlag, Frankfurt.

2 4 6 8 10 9 7 5 3 1
Printed in the United States of America

For KSCH

If the gods grant me leave,
    I'll come back as a
    gull over Grayland,
To soar above that sunlit shore
    where we walked in the wind
    and my searching soul
Found a harbor not marked on the map.

Foreword

The literature related to the emergence of Big Government in the United States is vast. Many historians and social scientists have surveyed and interpreted the decline in traditional American values and institutions, but few scholars have attempted to study in depth and empirically the growth of American government: to try to understand how it has happened and to provide the data that underscore the change. By focusing on certain critical episodes in American history, Robert Higgs has documented the remarkable and alarming growth of Big Government. His ambitious work covers the subject in great detail and in a way that will appeal to both scholars and a more general audience.

Surveying the most popular hypotheses advanced to explain the growth of government, Higgs recognizes that Big Government has various sources. But he makes an excellent case for his thesis that it has been nurtured by a succession of crises over the past century: depressions and wars that have occasioned both massive governmental spending and an increased regimentation of American life and thought. Although a crisis eventually subsides, a residue of governmental functions and authority remains; government grows bigger via a ratchet phenomenon of enlarged residual powers following each crisis. Even more alarming, the crises encourage a climate in which government achieves a kind of autonomy. Political officials and bureaucrats can now do almost anything they please, subject only to the political passions of the moment. Traditional limited representative government goes by the boards. In Lord Acton's famous phrase, the passengers exist for the sake of the ship.

For many persons, unfortunately, Big Government has its own fascination. There are, of course, the numerous beneficiaries who in one way or another are on the payroll. Higgs supplies a useful statistical survey of the proliferation of federal agencies, programs, and activities. But more significant than this is the way the ideology of Big Government has captured the popular imagination and obscured reality. Statism has succeeded the older absolutisms of monarchy and church. The warfare state is accepted in the guise of the welfare state. Big Government thus has become a kind of national lottery in which everyone thinks that he or she has a chance to win, and in which no one contemplates losing. The pageantry of Big Government unfolds in Washington, sedulously encouraged by the hero worship with which we surround the Imperial Presidency. Ordinary citizens seldom stop to think that all this is costing money—their money. They complain of taxes but fail to associate those taxes with the trappings and ideology of Big Government.

The conclusion of Higgs's analysis is a thoughtful but disturbing view of American prospects. Whether traditional constitutional restraints or the unique operation of a mixed economy can avert what he and others fear as a march into socialism or fascism no one knows. As we consider the future, Higgs offers enlightenment if not optimism.

Arthur A. Ekirch, Jr.
State University of New York, Albany

Preface

There was a time, long ago, when the average American could go about his daily business hardly aware of the government—especially the federal government. As a farmer, merchant, or manufacturer, he could decide what, how, when, and where to produce and sell his goods, constrained by little more than market forces. Just think: no farm subsidies, price supports, or acreage controls; no Federal Trade Commission; no antitrust laws; no Interstate Commerce Commission. As an employer, employee, consumer, investor, lender, borrower, student, or teacher, he could proceed largely according to his own lights. Just think: no National Labor Relations Board; no federal consumer "protection" laws; no Securities and Exchange Commission; no Equal Employment Opportunity Commission; no Department of Health and Human Services. Lacking a central bank to issue national paper currency, people commonly used gold coins to make purchases. There were no general sales taxes, no Social Security taxes, no income taxes. Though governmental officials were as corrupt then as now—maybe more so—they had vastly less to be corrupt with. Private citizens spent about fifteen times more than all governments combined.

Those days, alas, are long gone. Now, in virtually every dimension, our lives revolve within rigid limits circumscribed by governmental authorities; we are constrained continually and on all sides by Big Government. Regulations clutter the landscape. Governmental spending equals almost four-tenths of the gross national product.

This book is an attempt to explain the rise of that awesome aggregation of forces, programs, and activities we know as Big Government. To understand *why*, over the past century, the United States has developed a Big Government, one must know *how* the government has grown. Knowledge of only the amounts by which governmental spending, taxing, and employment have increased is not sufficient for understanding the process that generated the growth. Besides knowing how much such common measures of the size of government have increased, one must know when; that is, one must pay close attention to the growth profile, for the actual growth was more episodic than smooth and steady. An analysis that ignores timing, sweeping everything into a long-run explanation, leaves out essential aspects of the subject in question.

Further, knowing how the government has grown requires an examination of what, exactly, the government does: the growth of government has resulted not so much from doing more to accomplish traditional governmental functions; rather, it has resulted largely from the government's taking on new functions, activities, and programs—some of them completely novel, others previously the responsibility of private citizens. Evidence of such governmental expansiveness cannot be extracted from aggregative data on spending, taxing, or employment by the government. In fact, many forms of governmental control over the economy and society leave no trace at all in the budget figures, yet they do just as much as the measured activities to determine the allocation and enjoyment of the economy's resources. To comprehend the complete substantive composition of governmental activities and its change over time, one must extract information from laws, regulatory directives, executive orders, court decisions, and similar documents. I have attempted to bring a variety of such evidentiary resources into play in my analysis, in accordance with the conviction that one cannot understand why government has grown unless one understands how it has grown. In comparison with other analyses of the same subject by economists, therefore, mine is less aggregative, more qualitative, and, some might say, less rigorous and elegant. I hope, however, that it gets closer to the heart of the matter.

My account, unlike those typical in the literature, places heavy emphasis—indeed, central emphasis—on how governmental officials and citizens have reacted to national emergencies. For some analysts this approach seems to attribute the outcome to "accidents of history." In a way that is so, but it is nonetheless essential. Accounts of the growth of American government that view it as the inexorable unfolding of a dynamic, closed system (for example, those that say any urbanizing, industrializing economy inevitably gives rise to bigger government) cannot explain the timing of the government's expansion; nor can they explain the substantive composition of that expansion. To illustrate, it was no mere statistical anomaly that federal spending jumped dramatically between 1929 and 1934 and that the bulk of the increased spending was for the relief of farmers and unemployed urban workers. No theory based exclusively on long-run tendencies can explain the timing and content of that change. Nor can such a theory help us to understand the enduring legacies of programs first created to deal with temporary crises.

Chief among the enduring legacies of emergency governmental programs has been ideological change, in particular a profound transformation of the typical American's beliefs about the appropriate role of the federal government in economic affairs. In recent years economists and other social scientists have increasingly recognized the fundamental importance of ideology in the workings of any political economy, but useful models of ideological change are hardly to be found. A novelty of my book is the seriousness with which ideological change is treated: an entire chapter is devoted to examining the nature of ideology in relation to political economy; another chapter is largely devoted to the development of a working hypothesis about how crises—and the government's reactions to them—have generated specific kinds of ideological change in twentieth-century America. This model of ideological change serves to inform and direct much of the historical investigation reported in Chapters 5 through 10. I know of no other extensive study of the growth of government that makes ideological change so central to its explanatory framework. Relations between politico-economic and ideological changes are extraordinarily difficult to identify and test. Probably no other subject in the social sciences is so complex and elusive as the sociology of knowledge—but none is so fundamental either. If my book helps, in some small way, to enhance our understanding of the interplay of politico-economic and ideological changes, I shall be satisfied that my efforts were worthwhile.

Easton, Pa.   R.H.
January 1987

Acknowledgments

While I have been occupied as a full-time professor of economics, I have been preoccupied for the past six years with the research that underlies this book. The growth of American government, properly conceived, is an enormous subject. To understand it one must become familiar with the pertinent materials and findings of several disciplines, including history, law, and several of the social sciences. I could not have made much progress without the assistance of many scholars and several institutions.

For reading and commenting—often at great length and in minute detail—on preliminary versions of one or more of my chapters, I am grateful to Lee Alston, Arthur Ekirch, Price Fishback, Paul Gottfried, John Hughes, Aileen Kraditor, Dwight Lee, Forrest McDonald, Douglass North, William Parker, Murray Rothbard, Andy Rutten, Charlotte Twight, John Wallis, and Gary Walton. The anonymous reviewer for Oxford University Press also gave me some good last-minute advice on revision.

For providing me with copies of published papers and drafts of works in progress, I am grateful to Terry Anderson, Ben Baack, Edward Budd, Jon Elster, Max Hartwell, Michael Hechter, Albert Hirschman, Joseph Kalt, James Kau, Allen Kelley, Gary Libecap, Karl-Dieter Opp, E. C. Pasour, Edward Ray, Joseph Reid, Hugh Rockoff, Richard Rose, David Schap, Harry Scheiber, and Richard Timberlake.

I was fortunate to have many opportunities to present my ideas to groups of scholars. Each occasion taught me something valuable, and I am grateful to the participants in seminars and workshops at the following universities: Washington, Houston, Texas A & M, Duke, Pennsylvania, Georgia, Pennsylvania State, Lehigh, North Carolina State, Miami (Ohio), Arizona State, George Mason, and Rutgers. Also, at the following colleges: Lafayette, Gettysburg, Holy Cross, and Montclair State. Also, at the meetings of the

Economic History Association, the Public Choice Society, the Southern
Economic Association, the Association of Private Enterprise Education, the
Summer Institute on Public Choice Theory (sponsored by the Council for
Philosophical Studies), and the Ninth International Economic History Con-
gress. Finally, at the Greater Washington Area Economic History Seminar
and the Hoover Institution on War, Revolution and Peace.

Early versions of small portions of the book appeared as articles in the
Pathfinder (1982), the *Freeman* (1983), *Continuity: A Journal of History*
(1983), the *Intercollegiate Review* (1984), and *Explorations in Economic History*
(1985). I am grateful to the editors of these journals for giving me the
opportunity to disseminate my ideas and expose them to critical notice.

The Pacific Research Institute for Public Policy has sponsored the project
from its inception. I am grateful to William Mellor, David Theroux, Bruce
Johnson, Charles Baird, and Gregory Christainsen for accommodating me so
graciously and sticking with me in spite of the delays. Not the least of the
Pacific Research Institute's favors was introducing me to the Center for
Libertarian Studies. The Center made a significant financial contribution to
the success of my project by awarding me a Ludwig von Mises Fellowship in
the Humanities and Social Sciences during 1983-1984.

I began the project at the University of Washington and completed it at
Lafayette College. At Washington I learned much from students and colleagues. In particular, discussions with Douglass North over a period of some
fifteen years stimulated my interest in studying the growth of government. In
addition, Doug assisted me in so many other ways that I shall not be able to
repay him. But I shall never forget, nor shall I cease to appreciate deeply, all
he has done for me. At Lafayette, President David Ellis and Provost Sarah
Blanshei generously supported my research. Jerry Heavey, chairman of the
economics department, made exceptional efforts to ease the difficulties of my
relocation. Ron Robbins, Marie Ciofalo, and others at Skillman Library
consistently assisted my scholarship by tracking down fugitive documents,
rushing a book order, or interrupting their daily routine to make copies for
me. Mandy Shane, my student assistant during 1983-1984, aided me considerably. My secretaries, Carol Riffert and Elaine Molchan, have lightened my
burden in countless ways.

After I had, with great relief, completed the final draft and sent it to the
Pacific Research Institute to be readied for publication, Donald McCloskey
read the draft and convinced me that it was not good enough, that I ought to
revise it one more time. For this heartbreaking last-minute intervention I
should thank him? In any event, the reader owes McCloskey a debt; his
painstaking advice on how I could improve the exposition has resulted in a
better book.

Finally, Kathy and Matt, loves of my life, have made my efforts seem worthwhile. They have put up with my obsession, my reading books while eating breakfast, my working until late at night and during weekends, and my constant whining about "not getting any work done." Matt helped me cope with our computer; he also made it draw the graphs in Chapters 2 and 4. Early in the project Kathy worked as my research assistant. Later, when other things occupied her, she never failed to support and encourage me and serve as my sounding board. She knows why the book is dedicated to her. Without her it simply would not have been written.

Contents

Any society that entails the strengthening of the state apparatus by giving it unchecked control over the economy, and re-unites the polity and the economy, is an historical *regression*. In it there is no more future for the public, or for the freedoms it supported, than there was under feudalism.

ALVIN W. GOULDNER

PART ONE

Framework

CHAPTER ONE

The Sources of Big Government:
A Critical Survey of Hypotheses

One of the most striking phenomena of modern times has been the
steady growth of the government sector. Despite the hot political
debates that have greeted the successive steps of government expansion, there is surprisingly little scientific understanding of the forces
tending to bring it about.

J. HIRSHLEIFER

We must have government. Only government can perform certain tasks
successfully. Without government to defend us from external aggression,
preserve domestic order, define and enforce private property rights, few of us
could achieve much. Unfortunately a government strong enough to protect
us may be strong enough to crush us. In recognition of the immense potential
for oppression and destruction, some consider government a necessary evil.
Ludwig von Mises, an arch-libertarian but not an anarchist, disputed this
characterization. "Government as such," he declared, "is not only not an evil,
but the most necessary and beneficial institution, as without it no lasting
social cooperation and no civilization could be developed and preserved."
Like all who inherit the Lockean tradition, Mises believed that a strong but
limited government, far from suffocating its citizens, allows them to be
productive and free.[1]

For more than a century after its formation the United States had a
government that approximated, perhaps as well as any actual government ever
did, the ideal envisioned by Mises: strong but limited. Despite major shortcomings, especially its oppression of blacks and Indians, the government
created a political and legal environment conducive to rapid economic development, fostering what Willard Hurst, the eminent legal historian, has called
a "release of energy."[2] Inventiveness, capital formation, and organizational
innovation flourished as never before. Specialization and trade increased

3

prodigiously. During the nineteenth century the nation became the world's richest and freest society.

The nation's second century, however, has witnessed a decline of the commitment to limited government and extensive private property rights. In 1900 the government still approximated a minimal state. Americans did not practice pure laissez-faire—no society ever did—but they still placed binding constraints on government and allowed relatively few projections of its power into the economic affairs of private citizens. That long-established restraint has largely dissolved during the past seventy years. Government now suffuses every aspect of economic and social life; it may now, as Warren Nutter said, "take and give whatever, whenever, and wherever it wishes." Merely to list its numerous powers would require volumes: farms, factories, and stores; homes, schools, and hospitals; science and technology; even recreation and amusements—all feel its impact. Virtually nothing remains untouched by the myriad influences of governmental expenditure, taxation, and regulation, not to mention the government's direct participation in economic activities.[3] An abbreviated organizational chart for the federal government, shown here as Figure 1.1, suggests the gargantuan scope of modern government, even though it represents only a general outline of the activities undertaken at a single level of government.

How did this momentous transformation of American political, legal, and economic institutions occur? What motives and convictions inspired it? What socioeconomic developments promoted or obstructed it? Who expected to gain, or lose, as a result? What persons, elites, and interest groups played decisive roles? What circumstances allowed them to seize the helm of history? Did the growth of government proceed smoothly or episodically, and what forces shaped the profile of its change? I shall attempt to answer these questions.

My answers necessarily will leave much of the story untold. So many events and influences have had a bearing that nothing less than a comprehensive social, political, legal, and economic history of the past century could begin to answer all the pertinent questions. My objectives are more limited, partly because so much has already been done.

Several explanations of the growth of government have been advanced. Too often, however, the proponent of a particular hypothesis extols it as if no other wheel will roll. But many of the proposed explanations contain valid insights, and they are not necessarily mutually exclusive. Nothing is gained and much is lost by attempts to locate a single source of Big Government.[4] I reject the approach that seeks a monocausal explanation. I shall strive instead to comprehend what the various hypotheses can and cannot explain, applying them selectively and using them as points of departure in developing my own ideas.

Figure 1.1 Organization of the Government of the United States

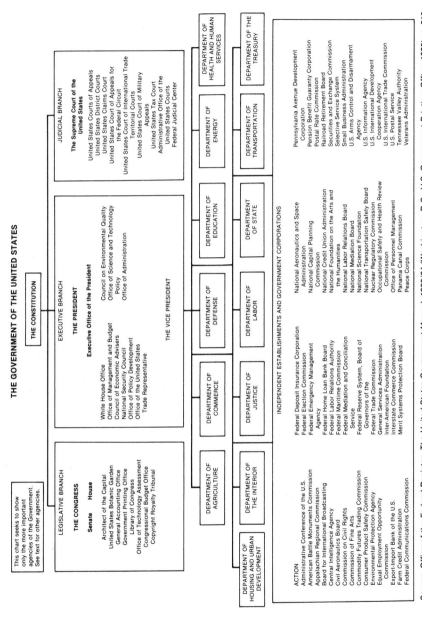

THE GOVERNMENT OF THE UNITED STATES

This chart seeks to show only the more important agencies of the Government. See text for other agencies.

THE CONSTITUTION

LEGISLATIVE BRANCH

THE CONGRESS

Senate   House

Architect of the Capital
United States Botanic Garden
General Accounting Office
Government Printing Office
Library of Congress
Office of Technology Assessment
Congressional Budget Office
Copyright Royalty Tribunal

EXECUTIVE BRANCH

THE PRESIDENT

Executive Office of the President

White House Office
Office of Management and Budget
Council of Economic Advisers
National Security Council
Office of Policy Development
Office of the United States
Trade Representative

Council on Environmental Quality
Office of Science and Technology Policy
Office of Administration

THE VICE PRESIDENT

JUDICIAL BRANCH

The Supreme Court of the United States

United States Courts of Appeals
United States District Courts
United States Claims Court
United States Court of Appeals for the Federal Circuit
United States Court of International Trade
Territorial Courts
United States Court of Military Appeals
United States Tax Court
Administrative Office of the United States Courts
Federal Judicial Center

DEPARTMENT OF HOUSING AND URBAN DEVELOPMENT

DEPARTMENT OF AGRICULTURE

DEPARTMENT OF THE INTERIOR

DEPARTMENT OF COMMERCE

DEPARTMENT OF JUSTICE

DEPARTMENT OF DEFENSE

DEPARTMENT OF LABOR

DEPARTMENT OF EDUCATION

DEPARTMENT OF STATE

DEPARTMENT OF HEALTH AND HUMAN SERVICES

DEPARTMENT OF ENERGY

DEPARTMENT OF TRANSPORTATION

DEPARTMENT OF THE TREASURY

INDEPENDENT ESTABLISHMENTS AND GOVERNMENT CORPORATIONS

ACTION
Administrative Conference of the U.S.
American Battle Monuments Commission
Appalachian Regional Commission
Board for International Broadcasting
Central Intelligence Agency
Civil Aeronautics Board
Commission on Civil Rights
Commission of Fine Arts
Commodity Futures Trading Commission
Consumer Product Safety Commission
Environmental Protection Agency
Equal Employment Opportunity Commission
Export-Import Bank of the U.S.
Farm Credit Administration
Federal Communications Commission

Federal Deposit Insurance Corporation
Federal Election Commission
Federal Emergency Management Agency
Federal Home Loan Bank Board
Federal Labor Relations Authority
Federal Maritime Commission
Federal Mediation and Conciliation Service
Federal Reserve System, Board of Governors of the
Federal Trade Commission
General Services Administration
Inter-American Foundation
Interstate Commerce Commission
Merit Systems Protection Board

National Aeronautics and Space Administration
National Capital Planning Commission
National Credit Union Administration
National Foundation on the Arts and the Humanities
National Labor Relations Board
National Mediation Board
National Science Foundation
National Transportation Safety Board
Nuclear Regulatory Commission
Occupational Safety and Health Review Commission
Office of Personnel Management
Panama Canal Commission
Peace Corps

Pennsylvania Avenue Development Corporation
Pension Benefit Guaranty Corporation
Postal Rate Commission
Railroad Retirement Board
Securities and Exchange Commission
Selective Service System
Small Business Administration
U.S. Arms Control and Disarmament Agency
U.S. Information Agency
U.S. International Development Cooperation Agency
U.S. International Trade Commission
U.S. Postal Service
Tennessee Valley Authority
Veterans Administration

Source: Office of the Federal Register, *The United States Government Manual, 1983/84* (Washington, D.C.: U.S. Government Printing Office, 1983), p. 810.

Unfortunately some explanations of the growth of government deal in abstractions that obscure the very nature of government. Some speak of government as if it were One Big Nonhuman Thing, a gigantic man-eating machine. The Spanish philosopher José Ortega y Gasset, for example, said, "In our days the State has come to be a formidable machine . . . set up in the midst of society . . . anonymous . . . a machine whose existence and maintenance depend on the vital supports around it . . . sucking out the very marrow of society." But for better or worse a government is itself human: it is simply the collectivity of persons who exercise legal authority.[5]

Treating government as One Big Nonhuman Thing, distinct and apart from the people, encourages misleading characterizations of what government is and does. Real governments cannot survive without the sustenance and support, or at least the tolerance, of nongovernmental people. Moreover, some people are always circulating between the rulers and the ruled. The American government includes several levels—federal, state, local, and hybrid; and several branches—legislative, executive, judicial, and hybrid. The sheer number of separate governmental entities belies a conception of government as a coherent institution. There are more than eighty thousand separate governments in the country today, more than sixty thousand with the power to tax.[6] Obviously the multitude of people occupying positions of authority within these varied and numerous governments lack unity of purpose. Conflicts within government may be as common and significant as conflicts between the rulers and the ruled.[7] Because no one in the huge, fragmented domain of authority can simply impose his will on all the others, governmental policies normally result from rivalry and struggle resolved through negotiations, compromises, deals, pulling and hauling. We would do well to bear constantly in mind that the American government is and always has been not One Big Nonhuman Thing but rather many coexisting human institutions of varying function, scope, and authority.[8] My concern in this book is mainly with the widening scope of the legislative, executive, administrative, and judicial powers exercised by the persons who constitute the federal government. One must remember that the growth of the federal government is only part of the story of the growth of government.

EXPLANATIONS OF THE GROWTH OF GOVERNMENT

Modernization

Reading between the lines of many historical works, one encounters the Modernization Hypothesis. It maintains that a modern urban-industrial economy simply must have an active, extensive government; that laissez-faire in the late twentieth century is unimaginable. Declamations about the absurdity of horse-and-buggy government in the Space Age or the impossibility of turning back the clock of history give rhetorical thrust to the idea. Exactly why a modern economy must have Big Government usually remains obscure.

Subscribers to the Modernization Hypothesis sometimes argue that a modern urban-industrial economy must have considerable governmental activity because it is so complex. "That the increased complexities and interrelationships of modern life necessitate this extension of the power of the state," insisted Calvin Hoover, "is no less true because it is such a well-worn cliché."[9] No one denies that the economy has become more complicated. New products, technologies, and industries have proliferated. The population has grown and become more concentrated in urban areas. Interregional and international movements of goods, money, and financial instruments have multiplied. Increased specialization has made individuals less self-sufficient, more dependent on a vast network of exchange.

Yet one cannot correctly infer that, merely because of growing complexities, economic affairs have required more governmental direction for their effective coordination. Many economists, from Adam Smith in the eighteenth century to Friedrich Hayek in the twentieth, have argued that an open market is the most effective system of socioeconomic coordination, the only one that systematically receives and responds to the ever-changing signals transmitted by millions of consumers and producers.[10] This argument turns the Modernization Hypothesis on its head: while the government might be able to coordinate economic activities in a simple economy, it could never successfully do so in a complex one. The artificial shortages and gasoline lines of the United States in the 1970s—not to mention the chronic frustration of consumers in the socialist countries—give force to the critics' argument.

How a market economy operates, of course, depends on the character and degree of the competition that propels it. Some observers believe that the emergence of large corporate firms in the late nineteenth century fundamentally altered the economy's competitiveness, ushering in a new era. "This transformation of competition into monopoly," wrote V. I. Lenin in 1916, "is one of the most important—if not the most important—phenomena of modern capitalist economy." Accepting this claim, one might interpret the growth of government during the late nineteenth and early twentieth centuries as a reaction, a development of "countervailing power," by which the public resisted the higher prices, lower outputs, and distributional distortions that big business would have entailed under unregulated conditions. Representative events include the enactment of antitrust laws and the creation of the Federal Trade Commission and the various industry-specific regulatory commissions such as the Interstate Commerce Commission and the Federal

Communications Commission. In short, according to this interpretation, economic modernization fostered the growth of private monopoly power, and government grew more powerful to hold that pernicious, irresponsible power in check.[11]

The explanation is weak in both theory and fact. Many large corporate enterprises developed during the late nineteenth century, and the turn of the century witnessed a spate of mergers crowned by the creation of such industrial giants as United States Steel, American Tobacco, and International Harvester. But no one has ever established that the economy as a whole became substantially less competitive. Even within specific industries neither huge firms nor high industrial concentration ratios necessarily imply an absence of effective competition. The founders of the big firms sought monopoly power and profits, to be sure, but rarely did they succeed in gaining these objectives for long. The decisive aspects of competition are dynamic—chiefly technological and organizational innovation—and under conditions of dynamic competition neither a firm's bigness nor an industry's high concentration poses a serious threat to the welfare of the public.[12] Furthermore, despite the almost exclusive attention lavished on manufacturing by analysts of the monopoly-power school, manufacturing is not the only important sector of the economy; nor is it in a relevant sense the "dominant" or the most "strategic" sector. Elsewhere—in wholesale and retail trade, for example—competition clearly increased enormously during the decades around the turn of the century. Consider how many local bastions of monopoly power must have been battered down by the advent of the mail-order distributors such as Sears, Roebuck & Company and Montgomery Ward. In many industries the monopolistic proclivities of large firms in concentrated industries were held in check by foreign competitors, actual or potential.

Besides, the government's actions have tended more to preserve weak competitors than to assure strong competition. In this respect the historical performances of the FTC and many of the industry-specific regulatory commissions are notorious. As George Stigler has said, "Regulation and competition are rhetorical friends and deadly enemies: over the doorway of every regulatory agency save two should be carved: 'Competition Not Admitted.' The Federal Trade Commission's doorway should announce, 'Competition Admitted in Rear,' and that of the Antitrust Division, 'Monopoly Only by Appointment.'"[13] The government's regulatory agencies have created or sustained private monopoly power more often than they have precluded or reduced it. This result was exactly what many interested parties desired from governmental regulation, though they would have been impolitic to have said so in public. The "one common conclusion" reached by historians of regulation is that "regulatory politics involved an intricate, complex, struggle among intensely competitive interest groups, each using the machinery of the state whenever it could, to serve particularistic goals largely unrelated to 'public interest' ideology except in the tactical sense."[14] But antitrust activities and the regulation of entry, prices, and services within industries—however one views their motivation and results—constitute a minor part of the multifarious activities of modern government.

Sometimes arguments in support of the Modernization Hypothesis make much of the population's increased crowding. People living cheek by jowl inevitably create spillover costs, which economists call "negative externalities"; outsiders unwillingly share the costs of others' actions. Pollution of air or water is a familiar example. If the legal system fails to define and enforce a private property right over every valuable resource, including clean air and water, then negative externalities may entail an inefficient pattern of production and resource use in the free market. For example, smoke from your factory smokestack may soil the clothing hanging on my clothesline, yet I cannot make you pay for the damages; nor can I effectively constrain or prevent further emissions. From a social point of view the activity of your factory is excessive because a portion of its true cost of operation is shifted without consent or compensation onto outsiders like me, who have no voice in determining how your factory is operated.

Governmental regulation conceivably can ameliorate such conditions. Whether historically it has done so has depended on how the government has framed and enforced its regulations, which has partly determined the magnitudes of the costs and benefits of its interventions. Proponents of the Modernization Hypothesis take for granted that negative externalities historically have been common and significant, that much governmental activity has been motivated by a desire to rectify such conditions, and that the interventions have routinely succeeded in bringing about a more efficient pattern of resource use. Each of the suppositions may be questioned. Some economists doubt that government can or will deal successfully with externalities. As Leland Yeager has said, government is itself "the prototypical sector in which decision makers do *not* take accurate account of all the costs as well as all the benefits of each activity."[15]

No doubt some significant negative externalities have existed and some governmental interventions have been motivated by a desire to rectify baneful conditions. Public health regulations furnish the most compelling examples. Contagious diseases undoubtedly generate external costs: historically they caused tremendous harm; and government's public health regulations were generally framed and enforced to bring about a more efficient condition.[16] In recent decades, antipollution laws and enforcement bureaus such as the Environmental Protection Agency provide examples of the governmental attack on negative externalities, though the framing and enforcement of the environmental regulations raise many questions about their exact intent and about their success when all costs and benefits are taken into account.[17]

In sum, the Modernization Hypothesis has some, but not much, merit as an explanation of the emergence of Big Government. Regulation of industrial competition, public health, and environmental externalities makes up only a small part of what modern governments do. Most governmental activities have no plausible connection with the increased complexity of the economy, maintenance of competition, or the spillover costs that attend population concentration.[18] Especially in application to the federal level, where governmental expansion has been most prodigious in the twentieth century, the Modernization Hypothesis has little to offer.

Public Goods

A related idea—it also involves nonexclusivity or spillover effects—has to do with public goods. In the language of economics a "public good" is not simply or necessarily one supplied by government. Rather, it has the peculiar property of nonrivalry in consumption: its enjoyment by one consumer does not diminish its availability for the enjoyment of another. Once the public good has been produced, its use has no marginal cost, because its enjoyment by additional users requires no further sacrifice of valuable alternatives. National defense is the most familiar example. If more protection from external aggression is provided, all citizens within the protected territory share the benefit of enhanced protection equally. My enhanced security does not entail diminished security for any other citizen.[19]

Public goods create a problem: because all consumers share their benefits fully, each consumer has an incentive to avoid paying for them. Each wishes to be the "free rider." Where private goods are concerned, consumers who won't pay for a good cannot enjoy it, because those who do pay can exclude others from sharing in its benefits. For some public goods, however, the exclusion of nonpaying beneficiaries is either impossible or prohibitively costly. When foreign enemies are deterred from aggression against the United States, every person in the country receives the protection equally; and the all-inclusiveness can scarcely be avoided. Left to provide a nonexclusive public good in the market, people would provide little or nothing. As everyone held back, hoping to be the unexcludable free rider, no provision at all would be made.

Government can break the stalemate created by the free-rider problem. By taxing all—or at least a sufficient number—of the beneficiaries of a public good, it can obtain the funds to pay for the good. Thorny issues remain even after government intervenes, because the appropriate amount of provision and the proper apportionment of the tax burden cannot be determined by any straightforward and practical procedure. In practice the political process determines how much is provided and how the costs are shared by the citizens.[20]

The Public Goods Hypothesis asserts that during the twentieth century the costs of producing nonexclusive public goods—chiefly national defense and the technology associated with modern warfare—have grown and, as only government can assure the production of these goods, government has grown correspondingly. The argument has considerable merit—particularly with reference to the federal government, where the provision of national defense is concentrated. Certainly the twentieth century has witnessed extraordinary international instability and hostility. Two world wars, a host of smaller international conflicts, and the Cold War have elevated the demand for the services of the military establishment far above its nineteenth-century levels. At the same time the development of modern military technology has made the production of national security enormously more costly. Since World War II an ongoing arms race has meant that national security cannot be achieved once and for all, as each round of action and reaction alters the requirements for effective deterrence.

Still, notwithstanding its clear pertinence, the Public Goods Hypothesis provides only a partial explanation of the growth of government. Even at the federal level, most governmental expenditures have no direct relation to national defense. The massive outlays for old-age pensions, unemployment benefits, public housing, job training, medical care, agricultural subsidies, school lunches, and so on—not to mention the hydra-headed regulation of everything from children's pajama fabrics to commodity futures contracts—have no connection with national defense or other nonexclusive public goods.

The Welfare State

The United States has developed not simply a large government but a welfare state. One may employ a variant of the Modernization Hypothesis to explain this aspect of the rise of Big Government. Economic growth and the concomitant socioeconomic transformation have tended in various, often indirect, ways to diminish the social-service roles formerly played by such private institutions as families, churches, and voluntary associations. Victor Fuchs has argued that the "fruits of the market system—science, technology, urbanization, affluence"—have undermined the institutions on which the social order formerly rested. "With the decline of the family and of religion, the inability of the market system to meet such needs becomes obvious, and the state rushes in to fill the vacuum." Bigger government becomes a "substitute for family or church as the principal institution assisting individuals in time of economic or social misfortune."[21] No doubt the substitution of governmental social services for private social services has occurred on a wide front. But Fuchs's remarks stop short of exploring exactly how the wide-ranging substitution has been effected. One needs to know who benefits and who pays, how much and in what ways.

Wilhelm Ropke, like Fuchs and many others, viewed the modern welfare state as "without any doubt, an answer to the disintegration of genuine communities during the last one hundred years." But he also recognized that "[t]oday's welfare state is not simply an improved version of the old institutions of social insurance and public assistance." Rather, it has become "the tool of a social revolution" where "[t]aking has become at least as important as giving," and "it degenerates into an absurd two-way pumping of money when the state robs nearly everybody and pays nearly everybody, so that no one knows in the end whether he has gained or lost in the game."[22] The welfare state has become, if it was not from the beginning, the redistributional state. Governmental policies for the limited purpose of saving the most unfortunate citizens from destitution have merged into governmental policies for the unlimited purpose of redistributing income and wealth among virtually all groups, rich as well as poor.

Political Redistribution

An explanation of how "the state rushes in to fill the vacuum," transforming the welfare state into something far more comprehensive and penetrating, is the Political Redistribution Hypothesis. This argument views government as an instrument for the coercive redistribution of wealth. Often it portrays the voters as highly knowledgeable and narrowly self-interested and the elected officials as sensitively responsive to clear messages sent them by the voters. The argument has taken various forms.

In Allan Meltzer and Scott Richard's version it maintains that Big Government "results from the difference between the distribution of votes and the distribution of income. Government grows when the franchise is extended to include more voters below the median income or when the growth of income provides revenues for increased redistribution."[23] The explanation fits the historical facts poorly. Extensions of the franchise apparently have had no independent effect on the growth of government, and the most dramatic extensions of governmental power have occurred in periods of stagnant or falling real civilian income, during the world wars and the trough of the Great Depression. Furthermore, to assume that government always transfers income to lower-income recipients flies in the face of facts too numerous and familiar to require recitation. As Mancur Olson has observed, governmental redistributions typically "have arbitrary rather than egalitarian impacts on the distribution of income—more than a few redistribute income from lower to higher income people." Many governmental activities are "of no special help to the poor" and many others "actually harm them."[24]

Sam Peltzman's version of the Political Redistribution Hypothesis holds that "governments grow where groups which share a common interest in that growth *and* can perceive and articulate that interest become more numerous." Here governmental growth is seen as driven exclusively by citizen demands, governmental response being taken for granted. Peltzman maintains that "the *leveling* of income differences across a large part of the population . . . has in fact been a major source of the growth of government in the developed world over the last fifty years" because the leveling created "a broadening of the political base that stood to gain from redistribution generally and thus provided a fertile source of political support for expansion of specific programs. At the same time, these groups became more able to perceive and articulate that interest . . . [and] this simultaneous growth of 'ability' served to catalyze politically the spreading economic interest in redistribution."[25]

The apparent sophistication of Peltzman's mathematically specified and econometrically tested model dissolves under close inspection. His approach is to "'treat government spending and taxing as a pure transfer" and to "assume that the amount of spending is determined entirely by majority-voting considerations . . . that political preferences are motivated purely by self-interest . . . [and that] each voter understands costlessly the details of a proposed policy and its implications for his well being." In another version of the model, intended to be more realistic, Peltzman relaxes these stringent conditions slightly, assuming that only one group of voters is fully informed while all the others are completely ignorant and either stay away from the polls or vote randomly. Such assumptions cannot support a convincing explanation of the growth of government. The dubious data and auxiliary assumptions used by Peltzman to implement his econometric tests do nothing to reassure the reader troubled by the highly unrealistic specification of the underlying model.[26]

Unlike the Modernization, Public Goods, and Welfare State Hypotheses, which implicitly assume that government grows automatically in the service of a broad but changing "public interest," the Political Redistribution Hypothesis explicitly views the growth of government as the product of political actions. (Political actions = seeking or wielding the coercive powers of government in order to determine who gets what, when, how.) That perspective is, in any realistic account, indispensable. But in many of its detailed formulations, as we have just seen, the argument characterizes politics in a highly stylized, grotesquely unrealistic way. It usually assumes that the size of government is determined exclusively by elected officials seeking reelection. Where are the Supreme Court and the fundamental restraints of the Constitution and conservative public opinion? What roles are the permanent "civil service" officials of the executive branch and the independent regulatory agencies presumed to play?[27]

Certainly the assumption of fully informed voters is untenable and misleading. To assume that the typical voter is completely ignorant would approximate the truth more closely. An authority on public opinion has reported that Americans can name their astrological sign more readily than they can name their representative in Congress. To suppose that political actors know precisely how an electoral outcome will be linked to a specific policy action and hence to a particular redistribution of wealth is to push the assumption of complete knowledge to an absurdly fictitious extreme. As James Buchanan has observed, "The electoral process offers, at best, a crude disciplinary check on those who depart too much from constituency preferences." Elections occur infrequently. Few citizens possess much accurate information about political issues or the actions of politicians; nor do many citizens have much incentive to inform themselves better. Public choice theorists, the scholars who study politics by using the methods of economics, call this lack of knowledge "rational ignorance." Rational or not, its effect is the same: "almost any politician can, within rather wide limits, behave contrary to the interests of his constituents without suffering predictable harm."[28]

Most likely the politician will behave contrary to the interests of his constituents even if he wants to serve them faithfully. Apart from the heterogeneity of the constituents' interests—and the consequent impossibility of serving all or perhaps even a sizable minority of them—the information problem is simply overwhelming. Political scientists, more often than economists, recognize the problem and emphasize "the practical difficulties legislators experience in discovering what their constituents' interests really are."[29]

The slippage between the interests of constituents and the actions of their elected officials can be readily confirmed, sometimes in an amusing way. Reagan's first budget director, the former congressman David Stockman, provided a charming example in his notorious confessions: "I went around and cut all the ribbons," he said, "and they never knew I voted against the damn programs." Congressman Pete McCloskey made the same point in recalling his first congressional victory. A postelection survey, intended to demonstrate the victorious candidate's mandate, revealed, as McCloskey put it, "that 5% of the people voted for me because they agreed with my views; 11% voted for me even though they disagreed with my views, and 84% didn't have any idea what the hell my views were."[30]

In sum, one has many good reasons to agree with Joseph Schumpeter's assessment: "The freely voting rational citizen, conscious of his (long-run) interests, and the representative who acts in obedience to them—is this not the perfect example of a nursery tale?"[31] Political actions commonly take place in an environment of ignorance, misinformation, posturing, and heated emotions; there are long seasons of lassitude and maneuvering punctuated by brief episodes of frenzied action. In the formulation of detailed policy, the voters at large do not count for much. Strategically placed leaders and interested elites constantly apprised of each moment's political potential are more decisive. Moreover, ideologically motivated actions may drive the course of political events far more than proponents of the Political Redistribution Hypothesis recognize.

Ideology

Many scholars maintain some form of the Ideology Hypothesis to explain the growth of government. The idea is that true believers, committed to a vision of the Good Society, have sought and obtained expanded governmental powers in order to shape social reality in conformity with their ideals. Supporters of the hypothesis make unlikely confederates. They include John Maynard Keynes, the patron saint of modern liberalism, who asserted that "the ideas of economists and political philosophers . . . are more powerful than is commonly understood. Indeed the world is ruled by little else. . . . [S]oon or late, it is ideas, not vested interests, which are dangerous for good or evil."[32] Another firm believer in the force of ideas is Friedrich A. Hayek, perhaps the most celebrated intellectual on the right. He has identified the ultimate cause of the abandonment of the market system as "certain new aims of policy," in particular a conviction that government should "determine the material position of particular people or enforce distributive or 'social' justice" by means of "an allocation of all resources by a central authority."[33] Thus Keynes, who argued in favor of a "somewhat comprehensive socialization of investment," and Hayek, who has devoted a long professional life to combatting socialism of any sort, agree that the growth of government depends ultimately on ideas or, more accurately, ideologies.[34]

Ideology, which some refer to more vaguely as "public opinion," must have played an important part, at least a decisive permissive role. As Ortega y Gasset has said and many others have recognized, "there can be no rule in opposition to public opinion."[35] If people generally had opposed Big Government on principle, free markets could scarcely have been abandoned as they have been during the past seventy years. One can easily document the shift of public opinion toward the left during the twentieth century. Examining evidence from numerous sample-surveys, Herbert McClosky and John Zaller recently confirmed "a virtual turnabout in American attitudes toward laissez-faire over a period of fifty to seventy-five years."[36]

Because ideologies are intangible and difficult to gauge, one must tread lightly in arguing about their effects. Yet much can be established, especially when one recognizes that opinion leaders have the ability to guide the beliefs of the masses. Public opinion, a political scientist has observed, is "often vague, transitory, and inconsistent. . . . In so far as the public is aware of issues, it focuses frequently on issues and topics which have been promoted or popularized by politicians and the media." The views of a Walter Lippmann or a Walter Cronkite, not to mention a Franklin D. Roosevelt, can do more to determine the climate of opinion than the views of millions of less respected and less strategically situated people can do—consider that despite his faltering delivery and often faulty logic, Ronald Reagan gained a reputation as the Great Communicator. "[I]n a mass democracy," Ropke wrote, "policy has to withstand . . . the pressure of . . . mass opinions, mass emotions, and mass passions," but these are "guided, inflamed, and exploited by pressure groups, demagogy, and party machines alike."[37] By concentrating on the ideas disseminated by strategically placed elites and influential persons, one has a more defensible basis for generalizations about the prevailing ideologies that matter. (What has caused the historical twists and turns of ideology among opinion leaders themselves is a separate question.)

Even if the dominant ideologies can be identified, however, one must recognize that a legislature "is not a factory that mechanically converts opinion into statutes."[38] Just as there is much slippage between the economic interests of constituents and the actions of their political representatives, there is much slippage between the opinions or ideologies of constituents and the actions of their political representatives. To understand the discrepancy would be to understand a great deal of the reality of the workings of modern representative democracy. Conceivably it occurs in part because some public officials try to promote the "public interest," which has been described as "broad-gauged, inclusive conceptions of what constitutes the best interests of the societal groups who support them or of society as a whole . . . something other than the summation, processing, or mediation of societal interests."[39] Another part of the slippage may result from nothing more than simple venality, as governmental officials serve the highest bidder. One can only speculate whether the occasional cases of outright bribery that come to light are just the tip of a skunk's tail. Some scholars consider direct bribes a "significant mechanism" in the determination of the actions of governmental agents. Others doubt the importance of direct bribes, mainly because of the "greater ease and legality of bribing policymakers indirectly."[40]

In any event, ideology is not simply an independent variable in the sociopolitical process. Schumpeter perceived this complication when he observed that "whether favorable or unfavorable, value judgments about capitalist performance are of little interest. For mankind is not free to choose. . . .

Things economic and social move by their own momentum and the ensuing situations compel individuals and groups to behave in certain ways whatever they may wish to do—not indeed by destroying their freedom of choice but by shaping the choosing mentalities and by narrowing the list of possibilities from which to choose."[41] Some may object that this declaration goes too far, that it is unjustifiably deterministic, leaving no room at all for ideology as an independent variable.[42] Still, in his provocative formulation of the sociology of knowledge in relation to the growth of government, Schumpeter identified a critical issue and laid down an analytical challenge that any fully satisfying account will have to meet.

Crisis

The final explanation of the growth of government to be considered here is the Crisis Hypothesis. This maintains that under certain conditions national emergencies call forth extensions of governmental control over or outright replacement of the market economy. Supporters of the hypothesis assume that national emergencies markedly increase both the demand for and the supply of governmental controls. "At the time of economic crisis," observed Calvin Hoover, "when critical extensions of governmental power are likely to occur . . . there is little opportunity for a meaningful vote on whether or not, as a matter of principle, the powers of the state should be extended. Instead, there is likely to be an insistent demand for emergency action of some sort and relatively little consideration of what the permanent effect will be."[43]

In American history the most significant crises have taken two forms: war and business depression. At the outbreak of war a suddenly heightened demand for governmental provision of military activities leads immediately to displacement of market-directed resource allocation by greater taxation, governmental expenditure, and regulation of the remaining civilian economy. The larger and longer is the war, the greater is the suppression of the market economy. Modern "total" war, widely regarded as jeopardizing the nation's very survival, also encourages a lowering of the sturdiest barriers—constitutional limitations and adverse public opinion—that normally obstruct the growth of government. In severe business depressions many people come to believe that the market economy can no longer function effectively and that an economy more comprehensively planned or regulated by government would operate more satisfactorily. Hence they give greater support to political proposals for enlarged governmental authority and activity. Though to a lesser degree than during wartime, changes in public opinion during depressions may also stimulate the supply of new governmental interventions by demanding, approving, or at least condoning facilitative reinterpretations of the Constitution. (Note that once constitutional barriers have been lowered during a crisis, a legal precedent has been established giving government greater potential for expansion in subsequent *non*crisis periods, particularly those that can be plausibly described as crises.)

Some scholars have rejected the Crisis Hypothesis completely because by itself it cannot explain all of the growth of government; they have in effect rejected the hypothesis because the evidence appears to show that, although crisis may have been a sufficient condition for governmental expansion, it has not been a necessary condition. Judged by this standard, however, every existing hypothesis would be found wanting. Sometimes the Crisis Hypothesis has been rejected because the growth of government, as measured by a quantitative index such as spending or employment, appears less than perfectly correlated with the sequence of crisis episodes. Such a simpleminded basis for rejection of the hypothesis fails to appreciate the various ways in which crisis may promote the rise of government and ignores the possibility of lags between the occurrence of the crisis and the appearance of some of its effects. Some scholars have rejected the hypothesis because it cannot account for the growth of government in all countries, as if no explanation with less than universal validity has any pertinence at all.

In fact, governmental expansion historically has been highly concentrated in a few dramatic episodes, especially the world wars and the Great Depression. A major virtue of the Crisis Hypothesis, a virtue that it alone appears to possess, is that it conforms fairly well to the most prominent contours of the historical experience. To employ the hypothesis to best advantage, however, one must look beyond the crises themselves. One must discover why the expansions of governmental power during a crisis do not disappear completely when normal socioeconomic conditions return. And one must explain why crises led to upward-ratcheting governmental powers in the twentieth century but not in the nineteenth, which had its own emergencies. Accounting for this difference requires that some of the other hypotheses be brought into play as complements of the Crisis Hypothesis.

CONCLUSIONS

Big Government in the United States has various sources. Not all are equally important, but scholars have yet to develop analytical procedures for determining with precision their relative importance. Given the many intricate interdependencies among the various sources, such a determination may be beyond our grasp conceptually as well as empirically. Ameliorating negative externalities, providing nonexclusive public goods, guaranteeing the livelihood of the most unfortunate citizens, redistributing income and wealth, pursuing the elusive goals of influential ideologies, reacting to crises—such are the activities of modern Big Government. They are related differently to any particular stimulus or obstruction. Only by detailed historical study can one hope to understand the complexities of the growth of American government.

CHAPTER TWO

How Much Has Government Grown?
Conventional Measures and an Alternative View

When you cannot express it in numbers, your knowledge is of a meagre and unsatisfactory kind.

LORD KELVIN

Yes, and when you *can* express it in numbers, your knowledge is of a meagre and unsatisfactory kind.

JACOB VINER

Everyone knows that the government of the United States has grown enormously during the past century, but no one knows exactly how much. Government has many aspects, some of which defy precise measurement.[1] Unfortunately the most readily quantified are not necessarily the most important. Someone who examined only the available quantitative measures, as economists typically do, would be in danger of reaching spurious conclusions. Nevertheless, some attention must be given to such measures. Employed with caution, they can provide valuable information. My objective in examining them is not simply to determine that government is now X times as large as it was at some previous time. Rather, I seek to discover when it grew most rapidly and when it did not grow at all or even shrank. My aim, in short, is to describe the historical profile of the growth of government.

CONVENTIONAL MEASURES OF
THE GROWTH OF GOVERNMENT

Table 2.1, column 1, and Figure 2.1 present a widely used measure: governmental spending (federal, state, and local) for newly produced final goods

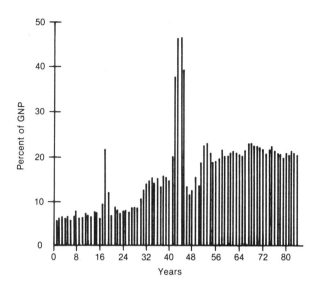

Figure 2.1 Government Spending (Federal, State, and Local, on Budget) for Final Goods and Services as Percentage of Gross National Product, 1900–1984

and services as a percentage of the gross national product (GNP). This has been called "probably the most valid indicator of the relative size of the private versus the public sector."[2] In the early twentieth century it stood at about 6–7 percent, fluctuating only a little from year to year. During World War I the federal government's procurement and mobilization efforts raised the government's share to more than 21 percent of GNP. After the war it descended as rapidly as it has ascended, stabilizing during the 1920s at a level only slightly higher than that of the prewar era.

With the onset of the Great Depression the government's share increased from about 8 percent in the late twenties to a plateau of 14–15 percent during the New Deal era. The initial rise between 1930 and 1932 occurred because GNP fell precipitously while the amount of governmental spending for currently produced goods and services remained roughly the same. After 1933, governmental spending increased but GNP rose at about the same percentage rate; hence the government's share stabilized again. From 1932 to 1940 it was roughly twice as high as it had been during the pre-Depression era, which reflects both the vitality of the New Deal spending programs and the absence of complete economic recovery before the defense buildup.

The massive mobilization of the early forties produced by far the greatest governmental share ever attained. At the peak in 1943–1944 governmental spending for currently produced goods and services commanded more than

Table 2.1
Indexes of the Size of Government, 1900–1984

Year	Government Purchases of Goods and Services as Percent of GNP (1)	Government Budget Expenditures as Percent of GNP (2)	Government Civilian Employees as Precent of Civilian Labor Force (parenthetical figures include "emergency" workers) (3)
1900	6.0		3.9
1901	5.6		
1902	5.7	7.3	
1903	6.2		
1904	6.0		
1905	6.1		
1906	5.6		
1907	6.2		
1908	7.6		4.3
1909	6.0		4.4
1910	6.1		4.4
1911	7.2		4.5
1912	6.8		4.5
1913	6.4	5.7	4.5
1914	7.4		4.6
1915	7.2		4.7
1916	5.9		4.8
1917	8.9		5.0
1918	21.3		6.3
1919	12.0		6.2
1920	6.6		5.7
1921	8.5		5.7
1922	8.0	12.1	5.8
1923	7.2		5.8
1924	7.7		6.0
1925	7.9		6.1
1926	7.5		6.3
1927	8.2	10.6	6.4
1928	8.3		6.5
1929	8.1		6.4
1930	10.2		6.5
1931	12.1		6.6 (7.2)
1932	14.0	21.4	6.4 (7.6)
1933	14.4		6.2 (10.5)
1934	15.1	21.2	6.4 (12.1)
1935	13.9		6.7 (12.6)
1936	14.5	19.5	6.9 (14.0)
1937	13.2		7.0 (12.1)
1938	15.3	18.3	7.1 (13.7)
1939	14.9		7.2 (13.1)
1940	14.2	18.7	7.6 (12.6)
1941	19.9		8.3 (12.3)
1942	37.7	28.1	9.7 (11.3)
1943	46.3		10.9 (11.1)
1944	46.1	47.7	11.1
1945	39.0		11.0
1946	13.1	31.8	9.7
1947	10.9		9.1
1948	12.3	18.4	9.3

22

Table 2.1
(*Continued*)

Year	Government Purchases of Goods and Services as Percent of GNP (1)	Government Budget Expenditures as Percent of GNP (2)	Government Civilian Employees as Precent of Civilian Labor Force (parenthetical figures include "emergency" workers) (3)
1949	14.9		9.6
1950	13.4	23.0	9.7
1951	18.2		10.3
1952	21.7	27.1	10.6
1953	22.5	28.5	10.5
1954	20.7	27.9	10.6
1955	18.8	25.7	10.6
1956	18.8	25.6	10.9
1957	19.6	26.5	11.4
1958	21.1	28.5	11.6
1959	20.0	29.6	11.8
1960	19.8	28.6	12.0
1961	20.6	29.6	12.2
1962	20.9	29.8	12.6
1963	20.7	29.8	12.8
1964	20.4	29.7	13.1
1965	20.0	28.2	13.5
1966	21.0	29.0	14.2
1967	22.5	31.6	14.7
1968	22.8	32.5	15.0
1969	22.1	32.3	15.1
1970	22.2	33.5	15.1
1971	21.8	33.5	15.3
1972	21.3	33.5	15.3
1973	20.4	32.2	15.4
1974	21.2	32.6	15.4
1975	21.9	35.8	15.7
1976	21.1	36.2	15.5
1977	20.6	35.2	15.3
1978	20.1	34.6	15.3
1979	19.6	33.9	15.2
1980	20.4	36.0	15.2
1981	20.2	36.0	14.8
1982	21.2	38.0	14.3
1983	20.7	38.2	14.2
1984	20.4	n.a	14.1

Sources: Column 1 derived from data in John W. Kendrick, *Productivity Trends in the United States* (Princeton, N.J.: Princeton University Press, 1961), pp. 296–297; U.S. Council of Economic Advisers, *Annual Report, 1972* (Washington, D.C.: U.S. Government Printing Office, 1972), p. 195; idem, *Annual Report, 1982* (Washington, D.C.: U.S. Government Printing Office, 1982), p. 233; idem, *Annual Report, 1985* (Washington, D.C.: U.S. Government Printing Office, 1985), pp. 232–233. Column 2 derived from data in U.S. Bureau of the Census, *Historical Statistics of the United States, Colonial Times to 1970* (Washington, D.C.: U.S. Government Printing Office, 1975), Series Y336, Y671, F1; U.S. Council of Economic Advisers, *Annual Report, 1982*, pp. 318, 323, 233; idem, *Annual Report, 1985*, pp. 232, 318, 324. Column 3 derived from data in U.S. Bureau of the Census, *Historical Statistics*, Series D139, Y308, D140, D141, D4; U.S. Council of Economic Advisers, *Annual Report, 1982*, pp. 275, 266; idem, *Annual Report, 1985* (Washington, D.C.: U.S. Government Printing Office, 1985), pp. 266, 275; and Michael R. Darby, "Three-and-a-Half Million U.S. Employees Have Been Mislaid: Or, an Explanation of Unemployment, 1934-1941," *Journal of Political Economy* 84 (Feb. 1976): 7.

46 percent of GNP. Of this, war-related purchases accounted for about nine-tenths. Rapid demobilization dropped the government's share during 1946–1950 to a range of 11 to 15 percent, slightly below the prewar level.

The outbreak of the Korean War led to another steep increase of the government's share, from 13.4 percent in 1950 to 22.5 percent in 1953. Although a few years of retrenchment followed the end of the war, the government's share has remained at a high level, slightly above one-fifth of GNP, since the late fifties. On its postwar plateau it has been approximately three times as large as it was before World War I.

By this measure, significant governmental expansion occurred only twice in the twentieth century: during the early 1930s and the early 1950s. The first episode brought the government's share from about 6–8 percent to about 13–15 percent; the second lifted it to about 19–22 percent. One who accepted this measure of the growth of government as adequate would focus his attention on, first, the Great Contraction and the New Deal and, second, the Korean buildup and the Cold War. By this measure the two world wars had only transitory effects on the relative size of government.

Looking at all governmental expenditures, not just those for currently produced final goods and services, one sees a different pattern (Table 2.1, column 2, and Figure 2.2). This broader measure, which includes the gov-

Figure 2.2   All Government Spending (Federal, State, and Local, on Budget) as Percentage of Gross National Product, 1902–1983

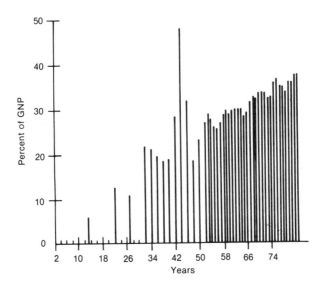

ernment's transfer payments, shows that the government spent at a relatively higher rate after World War I: 10–12 percent of GNP in the twenties, up from 6–7 percent before the war. It shows also a leap in the early thirties— during Hoover's term as President, not Roosevelt's—and a plateau at about 18–21 percent in the late thirties; a huge increase during World War II followed by a complete reversal by 1948; a sharp rise between 1950 and 1953; and, unlike the index previously discussed, an upward trend from the mid-1950s to the mid-1980s, an interval in which the government's budget outlays rose from about 26 percent to about 38 percent of GNP. The increase during the last three decades occurred almost entirely because governmental transfer payments, mainly Social Security outlays, increased faster than GNP.[3]

By the measure under consideration, government has grown about five to six times larger relative to the economy during the twentieth century. Its growth appears more secular, less episodic, than that shown by the previously considered index, though marked and subsequently maintained surges did take place during the era of World War I and during the early thirties. (Lack of complete annual data precludes more precise dating.) By including governmental transfer payments as well as purchases of currently produced final goods and services, one obtains a measure more likely to reveal the growth of the modern welfare state. Not surprisingly this appears fairly sustained over the past seventy years, especially since 1956.

Another commonly employed index of the size of government is its employment share (Table 2.1, column 3, and Figure 2.3). The historical pattern of this measure differs from that of either of the previously examined indexes. Government's civilian employment increased slightly faster than the labor force even before World War I, reaching a share of almost 5 percent on the eve of the war. The share jumped to over 6 percent during the war, fell back slightly in 1920–1921, then drifted slowly upward during the twenties, reaching 6.5 percent in 1930.

Tracing governmental employment during the 1930s, one encounters unusual complications. To tell this tale one must decide what to do about the "emergency workers." These people worked on programs administered by such emergency work-relief agencies as the Civilian Conservation Corps, the National Youth Administration, the Federal Emergency Relief Administration (under which a state relief agency operated in each of the states), the Civil Works Administration, and the Works Progress Administration. At the time they were not considered ordinary governmental employees. Subsequently economic statisticians counted them as unemployed members of the labor force, creating confusion and controversy among economists who study how the labor market operated during the Great Depression.[4]

If one follows the conventional practice, counting the emergency workers

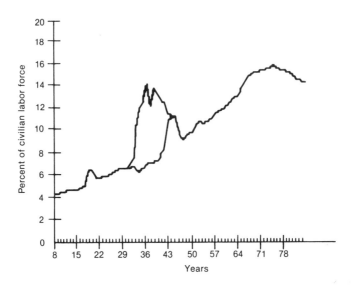

Figure 2.3   All Government Civilian Employees as Percentage of Civilian Labor Force, 1900–1984

as unemployed, then the government's share of the civilian labor force appears to have remained almost constant during the 1930s, falling slightly between 1931 and 1933 before rising slowly to 7.2 percent in 1939. The share increased sharply between 1939 and 1944, reaching an unprecedented 11.1 percent. Thus World War II seems to have stimulated enormous growth of the government's direct participation in the civilian labor market.

If, on the other hand, one counts the emergency workers as governmental employees—and it is certainly more appropriate and revealing to count them as employed by the government than as unemployed—the course of history looks completely different (parenthetical figures in Table 2.1, column 3, and the upper line in Figure 2.3). Now the jump in the government's employment share is seen to have occurred between 1930 and 1936, with especially large increases in 1933 and 1934. At the peak in 1936, governmental workers of all kinds constituted 14 percent of the civilian labor force, more than twice the share in 1930. After 1938, as the ranks of the emergency workers thinned, the government's share diminished. By 1943, when only a handful of emergency workers remained, government employed only about 11 percent of all civilian workers, its share having dropped three full percentage points from the earlier peak. As shown by this more defensible index, the government's increased participation in the labor market grew out of the Great Depression.

Not until 1966, after two decades of steady postwar growth, did the government's employment share exceed that of 1936.

Immediately after World War II the government's employment share fell almost to 9 percent before starting a long march upward. By the late 1960s its growth had become very slow. From the peak of 15.7 percent reached in 1975 it fell slowly, and by the mid-1980s it was down to about 14 percent, equal to the highest share attained during the Great Depression. During the postwar period the greater part of the increase in governmental employment took place at the state and local levels. Between 1947 and 1981 federal employment rose by less than a million workers, while state and local governmental employees added almost ten million to their ranks. Taking a longer view, one sees that the government's relative weight in the civilian labor force has become almost four times greater since the turn of the century.

Simple employment data can be misleading, however, especially in relation to the slow growth of federal employment since World War II. James Bennett and Manuel Johnson have documented that between the late 1950s and the late 1970s the composition of federal employment changed: "specifically, a sizeable shift from blue- to white-collar workers has occurred and, within the white-collar work force, lower-level employees have been displaced by workers in policy-making grades." They note also that "much of the federal labor input is 'invisible' in that millions of individuals are employed indirectly as consultants and contractors on a host of grants, contracts, and programs."[5] Evidently the tendency has been for federal planners and administrators to displace federal clerks and janitors. The trend engages our attention because the meaning of the government's employment share resides entirely in what governmental employees do, especially what they do to or for private citizens.

We could continue to examine quantitative measures of the growth of government (for example, tax revenues, funds borrowed, funds lent, loans guaranteed),[6] but we would gain little additional insight by doing so. Though each such index throws some light on the question at issue, each in a fundamental sense does not tell us what we really want to know. The problem is that the existing quantitative measures of the size of government do not correspond closely—sometimes they do not correspond at all—with the underlying essence of government, which is coercive power.

THE ESSENCE OF BIG GOVERNMENT: AN ALTERNATIVE VIEW

Government can greatly increase its expenditure or employment share and still not become Big Government. What distinguishes the capital-letter leviathan is the wide scope of its effective authority over economic decision-making, that is, the great extent to which governmental officials rather than private citizens effectively decide how resources will be allocated, employed, and enjoyed. As Eric Nordlinger has said, "The mixed-economy welfare state is strong because of the wide scope of its social and economic activities, its enormous regulatory, distributive, and (to a lesser extent) redistributive capacities."[7]

To appreciate the scope of present-day government, consider the table that appears as an appendix to this chapter. It lists by their acronyms some of the agencies, instruments, and functions of the federal government. (Adding entries for state and local governments would extend the list enormously.) I suggest that anyone who maintains a monocausal theory of the growth of government consider each entry in the list and ask: Is the existence of this governmental activity or agency, and the timing of its initiation, explained by my theory? I maintain that every monocausal theory will flunk this test.

The scope of the government's activities has primary importance partly because expanded scope can be, and often is, substituted for greater activity within a fixed scope. Whether the government determines the allocation of resources by ordinary fiscal means—taxing, spending, and employing on its own account—or by other means—requiring private citizens to comply with governmental directives to take actions whose costs appear on private accounts—is economically of secondary importance. (Politically, however, the government's choice of means for achieving its economic objectives is of tremendous importance, as we shall see.)

Under easily imagined conditions the government could be big yet limited. It might have to tax, spend, and employ at high rates merely to protect citizens from foreign foes and from one another. Though it did nothing more, its actions would consume a large share of the economy's resources. Within the constraints of their after-tax incomes, private citizens would remain free to determine the allocation of resources. The heavy tax burden would signal only the high cost of preserving an orderly and free society. Conditions during the Civil War approximated these hypothetical ones, the military draft in the latter part of the war being the most notable deviation.

Modern taxation, of course, is far from a simple governmental taking. It can and frequently does entail the regulation of behavior as well as the capture of resources. Willard Hurst has noted that "[e]specially in the twentieth century tax laws have pervaded entrepreneurial decisionmaking and operated as forms of economic regulation by defining taxable income, setting terms of depreciation allowances, or providing investment tax credits." A government whose taxes consumed a constant share of the national income could easily extend its intrusion into the private economy simply by altering the tax code. It could directly encourage some activities and discourage others by appropriate tax loopholes and penalties. Because of the complexities of tax liability, incidence, and shifting (not to mention the temptation of outright evasion), modern taxation is likely also to produce unintended consequences such as a diversion of resources toward greater use of accountants, lawyers, and investment advisers—diversions that sap the economy's potential to produce goods valued by consumers.[8] The United States government, especially during the forty years after World War II, created increasingly complicated tax laws, giving rise to a multitude of pleas for simplification.

Apart from their inability to reflect the true significance of the government's taxing, spending, and employing, all quantitative indexes of the size of government share a common defect: their changes may indicate either changes in the scope of effective governmental authority or merely changes in the level at which government operates within a constant scope of authority. On the one hand the government might increase its expenditure and employment to extend its regulatory powers over previously unregulated aspects of private economic decision-making. On the other hand it might increase its expenditure and employment to enlarge or improve the judicial system in order to provide quicker and more accurate enforcement of established private property rights. The two cases differ greatly in their implications for the nature and workings of the political economy, yet the standard quantitative measures cannot distinguish them.

Quantitative indexes may register little or no change even when the substance of governmental power changes enormously. The same amount of tax money is required to support the Supreme Court whether the Court's decisions give the owners of private property much or little protection from the depredations of government and other citizens.[9] Many regulatory agencies operate on tiny budgets, yet they exert far-reaching effects on the allocation of resources.[10] American government in the twentieth century has been loath to nationalize industry outright; the regulation of privately owned industry has been the preferred means of governmental control over resource use.[11] In its most important economic effects the continued toleration of nominal private ownership may make little difference; but the accounts look different. When the owners of industrial properties spend billions of dollars at the behest of the Environmental Protection Agency or the Occupational Safety and Health Administration the expenditures are classified as private. The conventional interpretation, that private expenditure signifies voluntary choice, is wholly unwarranted under such conditions.[12] The commonly used quantitative indexes of the size of government completely fail to capture these critical features of economic control under modern Big Government.[13]

Governmental expenditure and employment derive from, but do not themselves constitute, the power of government. Before the government can spend or employ, it must obtain the authority to promote a specified public purpose. If the requisite authority cannot be acquired (a legislative question) and sustained (a judicial question), then the matter is settled: no authority, no program. As Richard Rose aptly observes, authorizing law is the "sine qua non resource of modern government," the absence of which "will keep government at rest."[14]

Because initial authority is critical, a basic imperative in the politics of the mixed economy is to gain official status. As Lance LeLoup has said, agencies "begin modestly and then claim that the program is already going and should not be discontinued. . . . It is easier to defend a program that is already part of the agency's current operations than it is to justify a new program."[15]

With its authority expanded, the government may exercise the newly acquired power at various levels; but using more resources to exercise fixed authority does not in itself widen the scope of governmental activity any further. During the past three decades, for example, Social Security outlays for old-age pensions have increased by billions upon billions of dollars.[16] Yet the upward trend of the expenditures does not signify an accretion of Big Government during the postwar period. The federal government has possessed the authority to make such payments ever since the Social Security Act was passed by the Congress, signed by the President, and upheld by the Supreme Court in the 1930s. The events of the thirties created new potential for this federal activity; subsequent events have determined only the extent to which the potential would be used. Like a limited government, Big Government may operate over a wide range of resource absorption.

RATCHETS: CONVENTIONAL MEASURES
VERSUS FUNDAMENTALS

Many scholars have concluded that conventional measures of the size of government indicate a "ratchet" during the twentieth century: after each major crisis the size of government, though smaller than during the crisis, remained larger than it would have been had the precrisis rate of growth persisted during the interval occupied by the crisis. The data shown in Table 2.1 and Figures 2.1, 2.2, and 2.3 appear generally but not invariably consistent with this characterization. Depending on the index examined and the crisis considered, one may or may not find an evident ratchet. By one measure or another, however, each crisis can be described as displaying this pattern.

Mere visual inspection, however, may not permit a conclusive judgment. Whether or not a measure has reached a higher level than it would have reached in the absence of the crisis turns on how one calculates the counterfactual reference points. Trends can be established by various methods, and the method selected may determine whether one concludes that a ratchet exists. This kind of indeterminacy can lead us into a quagmire of quarreling among statisticians and architects of a world that never was.[17]

Plausible adjustments of the data also may cause the disappearance of what initially appeared to be a ratchet. For example, if one excludes from postcrisis spending the outlays for veterans' benefits and interest on government debt incurred during wartime, on the grounds that the payments are nothing more than the lengthened shadow of a (transitory) crisis, the degree of ratcheting diminishes or disappears entirely after both world wars.[18] Are such exclusions warranted? The answer turns largely on the hypothesis one is testing, especially on whether one is trying to understand the increased scope of governmental activities or the increased determination of individual incomes by government.

Another common practice is to separate federal spending or employment from that of governments at lower levels and—combining the ratchet notion with the idea that crisis causes the centralization of government—to focus exclusively on evidence of federal activity.[19] But ratcheting and centralization need not be linked; either could happen without the other. Besides, it may not matter whether government expands at the federal or a lower level. During the twentieth century the distinction between the levels of government has become ever more difficult to identify. Federal grants to state and local governments have permitted and encouraged them to spend and employ more than they would have without the grants.[20] Also, many activities undertaken by lower-level governments (for instance, state unemployment insurance programs) represent either involuntary compliance with federal requirements or participation in "voluntary" programs that place heavy costs on nonparticipants. When the governments at different levels are so intertwined in their activities and financing, traditional accounting distinctions can become artificial and arbitrary. Jurisdictional fuzziness makes the centralization hypothesis difficult to test and renders questionable a consideration of government at a particular level as if it were independent of governments at other levels. Programs created by Congress are often administered by local governmental employees. Hence the more rapid growth of governmental employment at the lower levels than at the federal level since World War II is neither surprising nor especially significant.[21]

Despite the many defects of the quantitative measures presented in Table 2.1, economists and political scientists, with few exceptions, continue to focus their studies of the growth of government on that kind of evidence. Some are aware of the problems inherent in a reliance on such ambiguous data. Sam Peltzman, for example, begins his study by observing that "to equate government's role in economic life with the size of its budget . . . is obviously wrong since many government activities (for example, statutes and administrative rules) redirect resources just as surely as taxation and spending." Having recognized the problem, however, he immediately dismisses it with the declaration that "the available data leave no other choice."[22] One is reminded of the drunkard searching for his lost keys under the corner street lamp "because the light's better here." Economists are accustomed to empirical research in which disagreements arise from the absence of a direct measure of a theoretically specified variable; hence endless disputes about proxy variables, measurement errors, controls for trend, and so on. Sometimes the econometric wrangling cannot be avoided, because there are no good alternatives.

Fortunately the empirical analysis of the growth of government need not rely exclusively on the standard quantitative indexes—evidence admitted to be ambiguous and incomplete at best and entirely misleading at worst. Other evidence, not only less ambiguous empirically but more germane theoretically, is available. As Rose has observed, "The data are there, if effort is made that the subject warrants."[23] I have argued that high levels of governmental taxing, spending, and employment derive from but are not themselves the essence of Big Government; the essence is a wide scope of effective authority over economic decision-making. Authority comes first: no authority, then no taxing, spending, or employment. Authority arises from executive orders, statutes, court decisions, and the directives of regulatory agencies. All are available for study. That they do not take the form of neat columns of numbers, that they do not lend themselves to ready commensurability and aggregation, that an appreciation of their substance and significance requires more than reading a cardinal scale—none of the difficulties makes them any less fundamental. If the economist is not disposed to analyze such evidence, then perhaps his pretensions in this field of study ought to be abandoned. The keys lost elsewhere will never be found under the lamp post, not even with the aid of the most powerful floodlights. The spectacle of economists bringing their awesome mathematical and statistical techniques to bear on the analysis of irrelevant or misleading data can only disgust those for whom the desire to understand reality takes precedence over the desire to impress their colleagues with analytical pyrotechnics.

By focusing on the fundamental events—the forms and occasions of expanded governmental authority over resource allocation—one can provide a more revealing description of the growth of government. In this approach one seeks evidence of governmental potential. Economists recognize the difference between an economy's potential to produce and the extent to which the potential is realized; they have one branch of study—economic growth theory—dedicated to understanding the former and another branch—macroeconomics—dedicated to understanding the latter. In their studies of government, however, economists and many political scientists as well have proceeded as if one could understand the amount of governmental activity without paying any attention to the underlying potential. But a democratic government cannot do what it lacks the authority to do. Authority is fundamental; activity is secondary and derivative. The long-run growth of output in an economy depends almost entirely on growth of the potential to produce, not on the degree to which the potential is realized at any particular time. Likewise the long-run growth of governmental activity in the U.S. economy has depended mainly on growth of the scope of effective governmental authority over economic decision-making, not on the degree to which existing governmental potential has been realized at any particular time.

When one examines the fundamental events in the growth of the scope of governmental authority over economic decision-making in twentieth-century America, does one discover a ratchet? I believe so. And I doubt that many historians would dispute my conclusion. Persuasive documentation, however, cannot be presented so succinctly as the conventional quantitative measures of governmental growth can be displayed. Compelling illustrations lie all around us: consider the federal government's far-reaching involvement in labor-management relations or social security or agricultural markets or financial institutions or the vast military-industrial complex—all springing from executive orders, legislative enactments, court decisions, and other authoritative actions during past crises. But illustrations are only illustrations. Really persuasive evidence in support of my thesis can be marshalled only by means of extended historical analysis. For the moment the reader is invited to accept my claims only as a plausible point of departure. Plenty of evidence will be presented in due course.

CONCLUSIONS

Relative to the economy, the government has grown enormously during the twentieth century. By conventional quantitative measures it is now three to six times as large as it was before World War I. Much of the growth has occurred during short intervals of national emergency, especially during the wars and the Great Depression. But even the growth that has occurred during normal times can often be traced to sources in preceding crises. National emergency can be seen to have been the fountainhead for the greater part of the growth of government particularly when the growth is viewed as expansion of the effective authority of government over economic decision-making. The ratchet applies not only to many aspects of governmental growth as measured by standard quantitative indexes; even more importantly it applies to the essence of the emergence of Big Government, the rise of government's coercive power over economic life. Could we measure how much the power to effectively allocate resources has been shifted from private citizens to governmental officials during the past seventy years, we might find the growth of government to have been not three- or sixfold but many times more. But no such quantitative measure is available, nor is one likely to be devised. Our study need not halt, however, merely because no unambiguous quantitative measure of a single, simple dependent variable exists. Other evidence, in enormous amounts, is available. The task is to make the available evidence yield robust, significant, and compelling conclusions.

CHAPTER THREE

On Ideology as an Analytical Concept in the Study of Political Economy

Faiths blow on the winds
and become shibboleths
and deep growths
with men ready to die
for a living word on the tongue,
for a light alive in the bones,
for dreams fluttering in the wrists.

CARL SANDBURG

Beliefs matter. In the study of human action, nothing is more fundamental than an appreciation of what the actors believe. For many scholars this methodological observation is a truism. Economists and political scientists, however, often pay little heed to it. In economics the assumption of perfectly informed, completely rational, and narrowly self-interested consumers and producers long served, and often still serves, as a basis for theorizing about markets. In political analysis it is often assumed that the voters know all the pertinent facts about politicians and policies and that the politicians know—and seek to get—exactly what their constituents want. In reality, however, knowledge is always and everywhere a scarce resource, costly to acquire and hence rarely possessed in abundance. Unavoidably, people conduct their affairs in a more or less dense fog of ignorance and uncertainty. Recognition of this reality promotes a more valid comprehension of social behavior and institutions.[1]

To cope with an uncertain social environment, people embrace various forms of belief. Some are as concrete as the everyday facts of place and time (the grocery store on Elm Street opens at 10:00 A.M.) or scientifically tested relations (water can be decomposed into hydrogen and oxygen gases) while

35

others are as vague as philosophical outlooks (we ought to seek virtue) or religious convictions (the meek shall inherit the earth). Between the extremes lie realms of belief where facts, values, and wishful thinking combine in varying proportion. The "softer" forms of knowledge—*knowledge* being understood here as simply what some people believe, whether others agree or not—guide people's behavior as much as, perhaps even more than, the "harder" forms do. Among the most important of the intermediate kinds of belief is ideology.

Convinced that ideology ranks with the prime determinants of human actions, especially the actions of the masses in politics, some scholars have worked hard to comprehend it. For more than a century philosophers, historians, sociologists, and political scientists have tried to understand the nature and significance of ideology and to identify its causes and consequences. Lately even neoclassical economists, who long disdained any resort to such an ambiguous and nonquantitative concept, increasingly have recognized its importance.[2] Notwithstanding all the efforts of scholars, the relation of ideology to the political economy remains an ill-developed and controversial subject.

An understanding of ideology is essential to an understanding of the growth of government. The bare axiom that individuals are, and always have been, self-interested and willing to use government as a means of gaining their personal ends does not suffice for making sense of the political past. It leaves open the critical questions: *What* do people regard as "in their self-interest," and *How* are they willing to use government as a means? Their ideologies give people anwers to these questions. Ideologies therefore determine, at least in part, the form and frequency of the political actions that shape the growth of government.

WHAT IS IDEOLOGY?

Scholars have reached no consensus on precisely how ideology should be conceptualized. Giovanni Sartori has written that "[t]he word ideology points to a black box. . . . [T]he growing popularity of the term has been matched, if anything, by its growing obscurity."[3] Consider some examples of how writers recently have defined ideology:

> [A] distinct and broadly coherent structure of values, beliefs, and attitudes with implications for social policy.[4]

> [A] collection of ideas that makes explicit the nature of the good community. . . . [T]he framework by which a community defines and applies values.[5]

> [A]n economizing device by which individuals come to terms with their environment and are provided with a "world view" so that the decision-

making process is simplified. [It is] . . . inextricably interwoven with moral and ethical judgments about the fairness of the world the individual perceives.[6]

[A] set of ideas and beliefs through which we perceive the outside world and act upon our information. . . . [A] medium through which we try to learn and comprehend the world; but it also generates emotions which hold people together.[7]

[U]nacknowledged dogma that serves social functions. . . . [A] special type of *Weltanschauung*, a constituent part of social psychology.[8]

[T]he complex set of rationales and rationalizations through which a group, class, or nation interprets the world and justifies its actions within it.[9]

Martin Seliger, a careful and incisive student of ideology, has presented a "detailed definition" that fills more than a page of his treatise.[10]

Karl Marx, whose writings have given much of the impetus to the study of ideology, in effect branded as ideology the social thought of all those who did not fully share his views. Such a pejorative ("restrictive") conception of ideology, which need not assume the Marxist form, remains standard for some scholars. It is also the most common usage in ordinary speech. This conception equates ideological thought with "distorted" thought. It suggests fanaticism or ulterior motives.[11] It raises implicitly if not explicitly the possibility that nonideological thought, even the "negation of ideology," can exist for those with "no ideological ax to grind."[12] Despite its widespread use the restrictive conception of ideology is not the most analytically fruitful one. As Seliger has shown, it contains internal contradictions and makes indefensible claims—for instance, that someone does or can know True Reality with certainty.[13] Rejecting the restrictive conception, I shall embrace instead a more general, nonpejorative ("inclusive") view.

By *ideology* I shall mean a somewhat coherent, rather comprehensive belief system about social relations. To say that it is somewhat coherent implies that its components hang together, though not necessarily in a way that would satisfy a logician. To say that it is rather comprehensive implies that it subsumes a wide variety of social categories and their interrelations. Notwithstanding its extensive scope it tends to revolve about only a few central values—for instance, individual freedom, social equality, or national glory.

Ideology has four distinct aspects: cognitive, affective, programmatic, and solidary. It structures a person's perceptions and predetermines his understandings of the social world, expressing these cognitions in characteristic symbols; it tells him whether what he "sees" is good or bad or morally neutral; and it propels him to act in accordance with his cognitions and evaluations as a committed member of a political group in pursuit of definite social objectives. Ideologies perform an important psychological service because without them people cannot know, assess, and respond to much of the vast world of social relations. Ideology simplifies a reality too huge and complicated to be comprehended, evaluated, and dealt with in any purely factual, scientific, or other disinterested way.

Every sane adult, unless he is completely apathetic politically, has an ideology. The notion that ideology is only the distorted, fanatical thought of one's intellectual or political opponents cannot be sustained. Of course, every ideology must deal in part with factual, scientific, and other "hard" knowledge. To the extent that it makes assumptions or claims inconsistent with such well-confirmed, socially tested knowledge one may properly accuse it of "distortion." Some ideologies commit this sin more than others; indeed some thrive on flagrant lies. But all contain unverified and—far more significant— unverifiable elements, including their fundamental commitments to certain values. In relation to these elements, which are neither true nor false, the allegation of distortion has little or no meaning. Ideologies have sources in the guts as well as the mind, and neither logic nor empirical observation can resolve visceral disagreements.

The meaning of ideology differs from that of several terms sometimes used as synonyms. Worldview, a closely related concept, differs in its greater vagueness and its lack of programmatic and solidary aspects. Social or political philosophy is both broader and differently motivated; like worldview, it contains no necessary impulse toward political action nor any implied community membership. Social science or social theory differs in its explicit striving for moral neutrality; relative to ideology, it inclines more toward pragmatism, empirical testing, and avoidance of politics—social theories that espouse the unity of theory and praxis are actually ideologies. Culture denotes a much wider system of symbols, beliefs, and behaviors to which ideologies belong as subsystems.

Most hypotheses about the sources of ideological commitment are either interest theories or strain theories. In interest theories people are assumed to pursue wealth or power, and ideas serve as weapons in the struggle by lending legitimacy to the pursuits. In strain theories people are assumed to flee from anxieties, and ideas bring them comfort and fellowship.[14] Interest theories include the classical Marxian formulation, which maintains that one's (neces- sarily non-Marxist) ideology is simultaneously a reflection of his class situa- tion and a "false consciousness" of true class destinies. (As Seliger puts it, "the [Marxian] assertion of bourgeois misapprehension boils down to the failure—or unwillingness—of the bourgeoisie to fall in with the forecast of its doom.")[15] Aileen Kraditor's recently advanced arguments about ideology exemplify a strain theory. The turn-of-the-century radicals she studied sought, in Seliger's words, "to bridge the gap between the proletariat's imperfect consciousness of its historic destiny (and hence of its unwillingness to achieve it) and the postulated inevitability of its victory."[16] But they undertook the task in pursuit of a solidarity that their would-be comrades had already found elsewhere. Fleeing from anxieties that the masses for the most part did not share, the American socialists could recruit only a minuscule following.[17]

IDEOLOGY AND POLITICAL ACTION

To the extent that the various explanations of the growth of government postulate that individuals or groups take political action—and each of them, implicitly if not explicitly, does so postulate—all rest on a problematical foundation. Each argument posits a benefit that people could enjoy were the government to take an appropriate action: suppression of negative externalities, provision of nonexcludable public goods, income support for the aged and destitute, redistribution of wealth to favored groups, and so forth. To elicit the desired response from government, people take costly actions. They sacrifice valuable time, effort, money, and other resources in order to send letters and telegrams to politicians, campaign and vote for candidates and legislative proposals, make financial contributions to candidates and pressure groups, and act in other ways as members of large political groups. Although such political actions are utterly familiar, the first theorist to inquire seriously whether they are rational concluded that, except under special conditions, they are not.

In his pioneering book *The Logic of Collective Action*, Mancur Olson argued that all group theories of politics commit a fallacy of decomposition. Group theorists "have assumed that, if a group had some reason or incentive to organize to further its interest, the rational individuals in that group would also have a reason or an incentive to support an organization working in their mutual interest." But the assumption, Olson concluded, "is logically fallacious, at least for large, latent groups with economic interests."[18]

To expose the fallacy one need only ask: What are the expected costs and benefits of such political action to the individual political actor? The costs are sufficiently clear and present. Each participant in a political action group must immediately sacrifice his own valuable time, energy, money, or other resources. And the expected benefits? Here is the crux of the problem—a problem inherent in public ("collective") goods available to groups comprising large numbers of people.

The essential fact is that in the large-group case the expected benefits of a collective good do not depend to a significant degree on anything a particular person may or may not do to create them. Whether one does or does not write to one's congressman, that politician will act just the same; a single letter more or less makes no difference. If one does not vote, the same electoral outcome will obtain; one has but a single vote among thousands or even millions, and the likelihood that one's vote will determine the result of the election is very close to nil. If one does not contribute money to a candidate or political pressure group, nothing will differ appreciably; one's few dollars are but a drip in the bathtub. As a single member of a large group, nothing one does or refrains from doing makes any noticeable difference.

And yet, if any collective goods should be created, one will benefit just as much as those who worked at great personal sacrifice to attain them. Even if one were to take no political action at all, one would still benefit from reduced air pollution in one's city, more effective deterrence of foreign enemies, social insurance against destitution, or redistribution of wealth toward groups to which one belongs. It is irrational to bear any cost in an attempt to bring about what will happen no matter what one does. In the large-group context the only rational political action is no action at all. Rational people will always try to be "free riders," enjoying the benefits of collective goods without sharing the costs of their provision.

Of course, when everyone tries to be a free rider there are no rides for anyone: mass collective action, including the collective action that produces or sustains Big Government, just doesn't happen. Olson argues that this Iron Law of Collective Inaction has only two exceptions. The first occurs when selective (excludable) incentives are attached to the collective good, giving it in part the character of a private good. For example, in return for paying dues to the American Medical Association a doctor receives the association's journals; but the AMA uses a portion of the dues to support its lobbying activities aimed at the creation or preservation of collective goods for the medical profession. The second exception occurs when people are coerced to participate in providing the collective good. For example, the government forces citizens to pay the taxes used to finance national defense. But in the absence of selective incentives or coercion the rule holds: a rational person does not take part in large-scale collective action.[19]

The glaring defect of this demonstration is its patent inconsistency with reality. We are crushed, it seems, between irrefutable logic and undeniable facts. As usual in such cases the problem arises from vague concepts and false implicit premises. When the public choice theorist declares that individual political action in a large-group context is "irrational," what exactly does he mean? Is he making debatable implicit assumptions about a person's actual or possible ends and means?

To answer these questions, we must consider what economists call the *utility function*. This is a causal relation between a utility index, U, which measures the person's sense of well-being, and all the variables, $C_1, C_2, \ldots, C_n$, that affect the index; formally,

$$U = f(C_1, C_2, \ldots, C_n).$$

And what are the *C*'s? Economists usually take them to be goods and services purchased in the market and consumed by the person whose utility function we are considering.[20] As noneconomists never tire of remarking, the assumption is an extraordinarily narrow view of the determinants of a typical person's sense of well-being; the idea of *homo oeconomicus*—"something more than Scrooge but a good deal less than the typical human being"—elicits only derision from those acquainted with art, literature, and history, not to mention psychology.[21] Economists respond that for the analysis of many important questions the assumed utility function is quite adequate; changing it would be pointless, merely cluttering the pristine elegance of an admirably parsimonious analytical device. They have a point. Yet one may still ask: Is the standard utility function sufficient for the analysis of political action?

The answer is no, as economists are beginning to recognize. In Amartya K. Sen's words, "The *purely* economic man is indeed close to being a social moron." Sen has urged utility theorists to develop "a more elaborate structure." In the same vein Douglass North has recently written: "Individual utility functions are simply more complicated than the simple assumptions so far incorporated in neoclassical theory. The task of the social scientist is to broaden the theory to be able to predict when people will act like free riders and when they won't. Without a broadened theory we cannot account for a great deal of secular change initiated and carried through by large group actions."[22] Quite so. But how should the orthodox analysis be altered?

North asserts that an understanding of ideology can help us escape from the analytical impasse. "Its fundamental aim," he declares, "is to energize groups to behave contrary to a simple, hedonistic, individual calculus of costs and benefits. This is the central thrust of major ideologies, since neither maintenance of the existing order nor its overthrow is possible without such behavior."[23] Although this observation suggests a way to reconcile economic theory and political fact it leaves the cloud of irrationality hanging over mass political action, the behavior that either directly or by subsequent ratification has brought about the modern growth of government.

Must we conclude that this sequence of great events is the outcome of irrational behavior, that ideologically impelled action and irrational action are only different names for the same reality? I think not. Instead, we can modify the utility function and link it to ideology in a way that simultaneously enhances its psychological plausibility and eliminates the lingering suspicion that mass participation in political action is irrational.[24]

Recall that ideology has four aspects: cognitive, affective, programmatic, and solidary. If it had only the first three, we would have no grounds for identifying ideology as a basis of rational participation in large-group politics. In that event ideology would allow one to perceive and interpret the social world, to impose moral valuations on it, and to conclude that certain political positions or movements deserve support. But one would still lack a personal incentive to take any political action, as explained above. To join rationally in political action in a large-group context, one must expect a benefit that is contingent on one's own participation. Solidarity, the fourth aspect of ideology, is such a contingent benefit.

If a person's utility function were as conventionally postulated by neo-classical economists, solidarity would be worthless—the "economic man" cares only about his own consumption of economic goods and services. But of course most real people also value other things. Certainly one of the most important determinants of a person's sense of well-being is his self-image, which I shall call his (self-perceived) "identity." Russell Hardin gives the example of a young adult American male in 1943, who "might have joined the armed forces because going to war was likely to be the most important experience of his generation of males. We need not assess the costs and benefits of his choice—it is too fundamental to be a matter of costs and benefits . . . ; it is instead a matter of being a male of that generation." With such actions in mind, Richard Auster and Morris Silver have urged economists and other social scientists to recognize that "individuals' levels of satisfaction depend on the extent to which they measure up in their own perceptions to certain ideal types (or images)."[25] Identity need not, as in Hardin's example, have such absolute priority that all trade-offs against economic goods and services are precluded. It is enough for purposes of the present argument that identity be recognized as one of the determinants of a person's utility.[26]

People acquire and sustain their identities within groups by their interaction with other members: first in families, then in various primary and secondary reference groups.[27] Tibor Scitovsky has declared that "the wish to belong, the asserting and cementing of one's membership in the group is a deep-seated and very natural drive whose origin and universality go beyond man and are explained by that most basic of drives, the desire to survive."[28] Although some may dispute Scitovsky's sociobiological reductionism, the urge to belong is itself beyond doubt. The kind of groups to which a person chooses to belong is closely connected with the kind of person he takes himself to be—a matter of prime concern to the typical person. People crave the comfort of association with those they recognize as their "own kind." In the absence of such community membership and involvement in the group's common purposes, people feel alienated and depressed.[29]

To embrace an ideology is to join a community of like-minded people. "Opinions," a political scientist has written, "are the invisible membership cards of society. They tell us who is like us and who may be against us. Opinions held in common are powerful bonds." Not for nothing do Christians call one another "brother" and communists call one another "comrade." Christians and communists, unlike neoclassical economists, have long recognized the importance of identity and its relation to solidarity. It is no coincidence that these two systems of belief have probably mobilized more people for mass political action than any others in history. "As absurd as communist ideology may appear from the outside, it provides a consistent view of history to those who adhere to it and makes even the simplest citizen feel as though his life has meaning, thus fulfilling . . . a basic spiritual need."[30] By internalizing the values and precepts of their communities of shared belief, people not only feel better about themselves but become trustworthy adherents who will act in accordance with their ideology without, or even in opposition to, external material enticement.

We have good reason, then, to rewrite the utility function for purposes of public choice theory as

$$U = f(C_1, C_2, \ldots, C_n, I)$$

where I denotes the degree to which one's self-perceived identity corresponds with the standards of one's chosen (or merely accepted) reference group, that is, with the tenets of the ideology one has embraced.

Clearly, behavior directed toward the maximization of such a utility function cannot properly be called irrational, even though it may sometimes require the sacrifice of one's own consumption of economic goods and services in order to establish or maintain one's identity through solidary activity with like-minded people. Ideological action of this kind is completely rational; the stigma of irrationality need not attach to those who participate in political action even in the large-group case. The truth, as Samuel Bowles has succinctly expressed it, is that "people act politically both to *get* things and to *be* someone."[31]

While the recognition of ideological commitments allows us to explain mass participation in political action, it also helps us to understand why some issues evoke more, and more passionate, political action than others. Obviously many political issues do not inflame the minds and hearts of the populace. Should the local public utility issue bonds of twenty-year or thirty-year maturity? Should the state legislature convene its annual session in January or March? Should the Department of Agriculture or the Department of the Interior manage the federal timber lands? Few citizens care. But other issues, in stark contrast, so excite the citizenry that public consideration of them takes place only with great difficulty, often degenerating into acrimonious displays of mutual distrust and hostility.

When the contentious questions are mainly economic (put aside such inflammatory but mainly noneconomic matters as capital punishment or

abortion) they tend to fall into two grand classes: one relates to the maintenance of the essential character of the economic order (often, capitalism
versus socialism); the other has to do with distributional conflicts within the
economic order (often, the rich versus the poor). The two grand classes of
issues share a common capacity to call forth moral, as opposed to instrumental, considerations. They involve not simply questions of what is technically
better or worse; rather, they are seen to involve good and evil.[32] Those who
propose to deal "pragmatically" with such questions are doomed to fail—
witness as a striking example the failure of neoclassical economists to gain
substantial political support for such "efficient" schemes as lump-sum
transfers of money income to the poor or market incentive (tax/subsidy)
methods of pollution control.[33] One cannot demolish an ideological fortress
with the weapons of neoclassical economics.

Questions about maintenance of the economic order are most likely to be
raised when that order is either seriously threatened by external aggressors or
widely perceived as malfunctioning. Great wars (or the threat of them) and
deep business depressions inevitably provoke Great Debates and hence ideological contention. Those who, like Keynes in 1936, propose to "save
capitalism" by such large extensions of governmental authority and function
as the "socialization of investment" are certain to provoke the resistance of
defenders of the status quo, not so much because the conservatives doubt the
curative powers of the proposed remedies as because they regard large-scale
reform as "revolutionary" and therefore morally reprehensible. To the extent
that the adherents of competing ideologies perceive a political issue as decisive
for determining the essential character of the economic order, they are likely
to consider it on moral rather than instrumental grounds and to plunge into
the struggle full of the political passion appropriate for confrontations at the
barricades. What is at stake, they say, is "civilization itself" or "the very
future of the society."

Distributional struggles within an enduring economic order provoke less
heated responses, yet they also call forth ardent ideological controversy.
When their consequences are greatest, as in disputes over the "progressive"
taxation of incomes, they shade into conflicts over the essential character of
the economic order. (The conflict over the income tax in the 1890s, to be
analyzed later, is a striking example.) But even at less significant levels, as in
arguments about tax loopholes or regulation of public utilities or conservation of natural resources, ideological elements inevitably enter, because different policies have different impacts on the wealth, welfare, and social status
of various groups, and the question of fairness is sure to be raised. Ideologies
deal readily with the question; a belief system that did not, on the other hand,
could not be an ideology (by definition). The oft-lamented failure of the

social sciences to provide guidance for "solving" such distributional problems is actually unavoidable.

IDEOLOGY IN ANALYSIS

If everyone had an ideology but no two persons had the same one, social scientists could make little use of ideology as an applied analytical concept. We could deal with ideology only as economists traditionally have dealt with consumers' tastes: admit that they are profoundly important yet, lacking the capacity to measure or directly observe them, assume that they are constant and therefore can be ignored in causal analysis of changes in consumer behavior. Such an approach (more precisely, nonapproach) is unacceptable in dealing with ideology. As Sartori has said, ideology is "an important variable in explaining conflict, consensus and cohesion . . . [and] the decisive variable in explaining mass mobilization and manipulation."[34] To understand the great events of modern political history, including the growth of government, we must develop an analytical framework for studying ideology.

The theory of ideology, like every other social theory, must make some assumptions. My first, most fundamental assumption is that, trivial differences aside, ideologies do not exist in profusion. Because an ideology is a somewhat coherent, rather comprehensive belief system—that is, an intellectual corpus not readily contrived in every man's sitting room—it is unlikely that more than a few will have much importance in a given time and place.[35]

Second, as Sartori has said, "mass belief publics appear to be dependent variables of elite belief publics."[36] Opinion leaders are the producers and distributors of (a limited number of) ideologies; the masses are mainly consumers. This fact—if indeed the assumption is valid—creates an opportunity to view ideologies. Although one cannot hope to penetrate the minds of the millions, certainly not in much detail, one can ascertain with some reliability the publicly expressed beliefs of the important elite disseminators of ideological messages. An informative recent study of five leading molders of economic policies, for example, rests on the assumption that "'the choice of individuals who not only wielded political power, but also who left an extensive written record of their ideological development, provides an excellent opportunity for analyzing the way in which ideology influenced the evolution of the American political economy. . . . [T]heir lives reflect the crucial point of intersection between ideas and actions."[37]

Curiously, some political scientists deny that ideology shapes the behavior of the masses in American politics. Those who maintain this position usually adopt the restrictive conception of ideology, which denotes doctrinaire beliefs and fanatical behavior; they then contrast ideological politics with the "pragmatic" politics generally taken to be the norm in the United States. But simple confusion is also evident among the political scientists. Robert Dahl declares that "Americans are a highly ideological people." Then, a few pages later, he asserts that "[m]ost Americans . . . simply do not possess an elaborate ideology."[38] Thomas Dye and Harmon Zeigler, following well-known studies by Philip Converse and Herbert McClosky, conclude that "[e]xcept for a small, educated portion of the electorate, the ideological debate between the elites has very little meaning. Since the masses lack the interest and level of conceptualization of the educated, they cannot be expected to possess an ideology. . . . At best, one-third of the electorate can be classified as having an ideology or near ideology."[39] But the findings of virtually all empirical studies by political scientists are consistent with Dahl's conclusion that "the more active a person is in political life, the more likely he or she is to think in ideological terms." It is important to add, as Dahl does, that "it is these very people, the activists and leaders, who more than any others shape not only policies, party platforms, and nominations but constitutional and political norms." So, whatever the ideological status of the masses, ideologies "do have a significant effect on American political life."[40]

Recently William Maddox and Stuart Lilie have argued that the apparently low proportion of ideologically impelled people in the American population reflects not the reality but only the insistence of political scientists and journalists that each person, to qualify as ideological, be located at consistent positions on the liberal-conservative spectrum for various issues. Maddox and Lilie argue that a fourfold categorization reveals more clearly where people actually stand. Their categories—populist, conservative, liberal, libertarian—are formed by the four ways in which people may favor or oppose governmental activism with respect to both economic intervention (say, wage-price controls) and personal noneconomic controls (say, prohibition of abortion). In light of the survey evidence on how people place themselves in the four categories, Maddox and Lilie conclude that "members of the public do have ideological viewpoints and, even though they may not be able to label themselves or articulate those views as well as the political communicators do, their ideological views make sense."[41]

We need not attempt here to resolve the debate over the extent of ideological convictions and behaviors among the masses.[42] For our purposes we can assume either that the elites generally shape the ideologies of the masses (the opinion-leader model) or that the masses have no coherent and persistent ideological commitments (the amorphous-masses model). No matter which model we adopt, our task is to focus on the elites in order to ascertain the ideological commitments that have systematic consequences for political behavior.

My third assumption is that ideologies constrain as well as propel political action. Sartori declares that "ideologies are the crucial lever at the disposal of elites for obtaining political mobilization and for maximizing the possibilities of mass manipulation," but the ideologies embraced by significant elites also limit both the ends sought and the means employed in their political mobilization and manipulation of the masses. Many potentially gratifying ends and many powerful means are patently inconsistent with a particular ideology, and therefore infeasible if not unthinkable. While ideologies serve as levers, they also function as straitjackets. (The constraining role of ideology is evident in Grover Cleveland's defense of the gold standard and in Herbert Hoover's response to the Great Depression, to be described later.) As Alvin Gouldner put it, "Ideologies foster the suppression and repression of some interests, even as they give expression to others."[43]

Fourth, ideology becomes most prominent during social crisis. When the existing order is widely perceived as working poorly, breaking down, or facing serious challenge from foreign or domestic enemies, the incentives for ideological expression are heightened on both sides. On the one hand, supporters of the status quo find it imperative to articulate and disseminate their ideology to shore up threatened institutions. On the other hand, crises provide excellent opportunities for ideological entrepreneurs to find a market for their wares among the growing ranks of the disaffected. As Richard Hofstadter noted, "when a social crisis or revolutionary period at last matures, the sharp distinctions that govern the logical and doctrinaire mind of the agitator become at one with the realities, and he appears overnight to the people as a plausible and forceful thinker."[44] Because crises give rise to a more visible clash of ideologies than one could observe during normal times, they furnish excellent occasions for the historical study of this important social force.

In sum, by identifying the ideological imperatives of political actors we can better understand their actions. The identification can be obtained by an analysis of words (of elite opinion leaders) and deeds (of elites and politically active masses). As Sartori has said, "ideology is crucial to an empirical theory of politics because, and to the extent that, it is conducive to the understanding of *variations* and *varieties*." Ideology is most likely to be decisive during crises, when exceptionally fundamental social choices present themselves, and "unless we are sensitized to the existence of distinctly ideological publics and belief systems we are likely to miss the very nature of 'big conflict.'"[45] Ideology is decisive when it swings policy decisions or other political events that would, on the strength of nonideological influences alone, have gone the other way. An understanding of ideology is most likely to arise from the study of opinion leaders during crises. But what exactly should we look for in the pronouncements of the opinion leaders?

IDEOLOGY AND RHETORIC

The answer is that we must scrutinize their rhetoric. It has been aptly said that "[l]anguage and discourse are not neutral. . . . An ideological position has its own terms of discourse (dismissed as rhetorical by its adversaries) that give meaning to its positions. A change of terms is far more than a semantic shift. It is an imposition of one position over another."[46] Language itself, as some political scientists recognize, is one of the weightiest political resources.[47] Aldous Huxley went even further. "Conduct and character," he asserted, "are largely determined by the nature of the words we currently use to discuss ourselves and the world around us."[48] Successful politicians have always understood the power of words. It should not surprise us that what one politician calls "compassion and humanity" another calls "waste, fraud, and abuse."

Ideological expression aims to persuade, but not in the cool dispassionate manner celebrated by the rational ideal of science and philosophy. Of course it may be rational, at least in part, and it may appeal to indisputable facts. But the persuasive power of ideological expression arises for the most part from neither logic nor facts. It arises mainly from the unabashedly polemical character of the rhetoric employed. Said Lenin: "My words were calculated to evoke hatred, aversion and contempt . . . not to convince but to break up the ranks of the opponent, not to correct an opponent's mistake, but to destroy him." The ideologue wants to convince his listeners not only to accept certain interpretations and valuations of the social world; he wants also to impel them to act politically, or at least not to oppose or interfere with those who do. He knows that the most persuasive argument is not necessarily the most logical or the most factual. "You have to be emotional," says Richard Viguerie, the enormously successful conservative fund-raiser. Another veteran political fund-raiser observes that those who respond most often to political causes are "argumentative, dogmatic and unforgiving. Everything is black and white for them"—that is, they are especially impelled by ideology.[49]

Ideological rhetoric usually takes a highly figurative, quasi-poetic form. Metaphor, analogy, irony, sarcasm, satire, hyperbole, and overdrawn antithesis are its common devices. Ideological thought is expressed "in intricate symbolic webs as vaguely defined as they are emotionally charged."[50] We exaggerate only a little if we say that in ideological expression imagery is everything.

Scientists and (some) philosophers disparage this kind of talk. Metaphor, the most important device for ideological expression, they consider wrong. As a philosopher has put it, metaphor "asserts of one thing that it is something else." Even worse, adds Clifford Geertz, "it tends to be most effective when most 'wrong.'"[51] People who respond to such communication appear to be, at best, intellectually obtuse.

Geertz argues that this assessment of the power of ideological expression, which seems to blame the stupidity of the audience, may itself lack acuity. A "flattened view of other people's mentalities" leads us to choose between two interpretations of the symbol's effectiveness: "Either it deceives the uninformed (according to interest theory), or it excites the unreflective (according to strain theory)." Conceivably, however, its power derives "from its capacity to grasp, formulate, and communicate social realities that elude the tempered language of science." Language may be a far richer resource than scientists and (some) philosophers appreciate, and ideologues may comprehend its richness better than their critics.[52]

Ideologues, hoping to attract those who lack the time or capacity for extended reflection, encapsulate their messages in pithy slogans, mottoes, and self-ennobling descriptions. When these terse war cries produce the desired effect they mobilize large numbers of diverse people. The secret of their success lies partly in their evocative moral appeal and partly in their ambiguity and vagueness, which allow each person to hear them as lyrics suited to his own music. When Marx and Engels declared that "the proletarians have nothing to lose but their chains," they surely understood that revolutionary workers had a good deal to lose—their lives if nothing else—and that workers were not physically tied to their jobs. Yet the image of people confined by chains, suggestive not only of painful and inescapable restraint but of the galling humiliation of the prisoner, had tremendous polemical force. American candidates for the presidency have promised New Freedom, New Deal, Fair Deal, New Frontier, and Great Society, ambiguous images suggestive of great improvements both material and moral. That linguistic purists and political cynics may scoff at the pie-in-the-sky quality of such semantic gimmicks does little to detract from their mass appeal—even educated journalists adopt them, spreading their usage and influence. No one is likely to campaign for the presidency under the feasible banner: Toward a Slightly Improved Society.

All ideologies employ flag words. I call them "flag words" both because they serve as semantic banners under which the faithful rally and because they signal the analyst that ideological expression may be in use. Flag words come in two varieties, discriminating and universalistic. Discriminating flag words are undoubtedly ideological yet call forth entirely different images depending on the ideological predisposition of the perceiver. "Communism" is an example. To a communist it brings to mind such images as human brotherhood, "to each according to his need," and a glorious future when the state will wither away and all people will live according to their true nature. To an anticommunist, in contrast, it connotes ruthless dictatorship, denial of civil liberties, and slave-labor camps. Universalistic flag words, unlike the discriminating ones, have the same moral tilt regardless of the ideological predisposition of the perceiver. "Democracy," for example, now has a positive moral signification for almost everyone, though the empirical referents differ enormously. Democracy in China is not the same as democracy in Canada, even though the Chinese and the Canadians may be equally devoted to democracy in the abstract.[53]

Table 3.1 presents a short list of common ideological flag words. Of course, words often change their meanings over time; the list has been compiled with today's usages in mind. One may note that some words are ideological flags only in combination with certain other words or in a particular context. "Corporate" is not an ideological flag in the expression "corporate accounting systems," but it is in expressions like "corporate economy" or "corporate state."[54]

Ideological flag words often derive their special imagery from their usages in the lexicons of paradigmatic ideologues. Many expressions of today's radical Left, for example, come from Marx, who employed in more or less precise senses such terms as "exploitation," "alienation," "surplus value," "class struggle," "bourgeoisie," and even, as we have seen, the word "ideology" itself.

Despite his (and Engels' and many others') espousal of "scientific" socialism, Marx was an obvious ideologue. Consider the following passage:

Table 3.1
Some Ideological Flag Words

Discriminating	Universalistic
Government intervention	Democracy
Wage labor	Freedom
Class struggle	Self-determination
Profit	Justice
Capitalism	Public interest
Communism	Fairness
Free enterprise	Equality
Socialism	Security
Freedom of choice	Progress
Individualism	Dictatorship
Revolution	Racism
Corporate	Due process of law
Private property	Decency
Welfare state	The people
Imperialism	Oppression
Secular humanism	Coercion
Bourgeoisie	Tryanny

[I]t is self-evident that the labourer is nothing else, his whole life through, than labour-power. . . . [I]n its blind unrestrainable passion, its were-wolf hunger for surplus-labour, capital oversteps not only the moral, but even the merely physical maximum bounds of the working day. . . . It is not the normal maintenance of the labour-power which is to determine the limits of the working day; it is the greatest possible daily expenditure of labour-power, no matter how diseased, compulsory, and painful it may be, which is to determine the limits of the labourers' period of repose. Capital cares nothing for the length of life of labour-power. All that concerns it is simply and solely the maximum of labour-power, that can be rendered fluent in a working day. It attains this end by shortening the extent of the labourer's life, as a greedy farmer snatches increased produce from the soil by robbing it of its fertility.[55]

Without embarrassment, Marx wrote about the capitalists' "were-wolf hunger for surplus-labour" and their "vampire thirst for the living blood of labour."[56] He routinely employed emotionally supercharged language that to a non-Marxist seems hyperbolic and ludicrous. Yet multitudes have found the rhetoric of this "scientific" socialism compelling.

Although Marx supplies excellent examples of ideological expression, we need not single out the ideologies of the Left. Consider, for example, a passage by the great classical liberal, John Stuart Mill:

[T]he strongest of all the arguments against the interference of the public with purely personal conduct, is that when it does interfere, the odds are that it interferes wrongly, and in the wrong place. . . . [I]n these cases public opinion means, at the best, some people's opinion of what is good or bad for other people; . . . very often it does not even mean that; the public, with the most perfect indifference, passing over the pleasure or convenience of those whose conduct they censure, and considering only their own preference. . . . But there is no parity between the feeling of a person for his own opinion, and the feeling of another who is offended at his holding it; no more than between the desire of a thief to take a purse, and the desire of the right owner to keep it. And a person's taste is as much his own peculiar concern as his opinion or his purse.[57]

Here the analogy of a thief and the "right owner" contending over a purse guides the reader insidiously toward agreement with Mill on other, more ambiguous issues within the class under consideration. Notice, too, the parallel between Mill's purse-snatching thief and Marx's fertility-snatching farmer. Evidently the metaphor of theft is so powerful and universally evocative that no ideology can do without it—witness Proudhon's "property is theft" and countless other declarations on all sides of the property question. "Those who want to talk 'ideology,'" said Gouldner, "must also talk 'property.'"[58]

As a final example of ideological rhetoric, drawn from the right side of the political spectrum, consider the following passage from Frank S. Meyer's conservative credo:

> A good society is possible only when both these conditions are met: when the
> social and political order guarantees a state of affairs in which men can freely
> choose; and when the intellectual and moral leaders, the "creative minority,"
> have the understanding and imagination to maintain the prestige of tradition
> and reason, and thus to sustain the intellectual and moral order throughout
> society.[59]

Note especially the critical position in the argument of such ideological flags
as "good society," "moral order," "freely choose," and "creative minority,"
the last of which must have seemed problematical even to Meyer, who
enclosed it in quotation marks.

In sum, one can study the rhetoric of opinion leaders in times of crisis to
determine what the dominant ideologies were and how they changed over
time. We shall see, for example, that the ideology of Grover Cleveland and his
closest associates differed greatly from that of Franklin Roosevelt and his
most trusted advisers, that the ideology of the Supreme Court majority in the
Pollock case (1895) differed enormously from that of the majority in the
Minnesota moratorium case (1934). Clearly ideology and ideological change
are not so vague and shadowy that they defy empirical study. Although we
cannot measure them as we would height or weight, we can learn a good deal
about them qualitatively, and for certain purposes such knowledge may be
adequate.

IDEOLOGY: EXOGENOUS OR ENDOGENOUS?

In the analysis of politico-economic history, one may view ideology as
exogenous, recognizing that it has important consequences for political behavior and hence for economic institutions but simply accepting the ideologies prevailing at any particular time as parametric—that is, outside the
explanatory boundaries of one's analytical framework. Although this approach has obvious shortcomings, it is clearly superior to ignoring ideology
altogether. Economists traditionally have treated the initial distribution of
property rights, the tastes of consumers, and the technologies of production
as parameters of the neoclassical model. If they are justified in doing so,
surely one is just as warranted in making ideology a parameter of a model of
the political economy. In this approach one makes no attempt to explain why
ideological changes occur; one simply recognizes that they do and tries to
understand the consequences.

A priori, viewing ideology as endogenous seems a better approach. As
Peter Berger and Thomas Luckmann have written, "the relationship between
'ideas' and their sustaining social processes is always a dialectical one." They
argue that

theories are concocted in order to legitimate already existing social institutions. But it also happens that social institutions are changed in order to bring them into conformity with already existing theories, that is, to make them more "legitimate." The experts in legitimation may operate as theoretical justifiers of the *status quo*; they may also appear as revolutionary ideologists. Definitions of reality have self-fulfilling potency. Theories can be *realized* in history, even theories that were highly abstruse when they were first conceived by their inventors. . . . Consequently, social change must always be understood as standing in a dialectical relationship to the "history of ideas." Both "idealistic" and "materialistic" understandings of the relationship overlook this dialectic, and thus distort history.[60]

If we accept the validity of this reciprocal relation, our task becomes the identification of the specific ways in which ideology and society are linked.

Attempting to solve this great problem would carry us far beyond the scope of the present book. We can, however, take notice of some factors that scholars have identified as socioeconomic determinants of ideological change.

Marx related "consciousness" to one's position in the class order, though he also imagined discrepancies, the "false consciousness" (actually Engels' term) of the capitalists and the unawakened proletarians. Without accepting the entire Marxist model, one can gain insight from it. Class membership, whether defined by Marxian or other criteria, does have an association with ideological commitments, though the form, strength, and persistence of the association are open empirical questions. As Seliger affirms, "class membership and specific economic conditions are important but not sole factors in the formation of ideological postures."[61]

Others have associated ideology with various nonclass social attributes: occupational, religious, familial, ethnic, and geographic.[62] Eduard Bernstein, the Marxist revisionist who wrote at the turn of the century, anticipated the pluralistic view.[63] As the distribution of occupational, ethnic, and other attributes changes because of industrialization, urbanization, or international migration, a society's ideological composition presumably changes, too, though the causal connections seem nowhere to be spelled out. Merely to propose that we assume "a flexible, competitive and pluralistic configuration of causal determinants" is not very helpful.[64] The explanatory blanks must be filled in.

We must also take into account "beliefs and disbeliefs in their own right."[65] Anyone who has lived among social thinkers knows that ideas have a life of their own, or at least a life that seems unrelated to the positions in the social structure of those who propound, accept, and reject them. Intellectuals, the specialists in the production and distribution of articulate social thought, are subject to fads; from time to time they are carried away by one notion or another for no apparent reason.[66] On the other hand, many ideas have persisted through the ages, proving that whatever the conditions that spawned them, their vitality is independent of their long-extinct social origins. Many aspects of modern ideologies were familiar to Plato and his contemporaries.[67] If ideas are developed autonomously, independent of their enveloping social structures, the dialectic described by Berger and Luckmann does not form a closed system; an element of exogeneity if not of pure randomness intrudes.

How, then, should we think about ideology, as exogenous or as endogenous to the political economy? To assume endogeneity is clearly better if we can specify the connections between ideological and socioeconomic change, that is, if we possess a useful theory of the causes and consequences of ideology. Unfortunately, practitioners of the sociology of knowledge have not produced a useful theory at a level of generality low enough to have much empirical applicability. Propositions like "all social thought is socially conditioned" tell us something, but are too vague and abstract to help us answer the specific questions of the present book. Moreover, if ideological thought has a life of its own—a possibility that cannot be ruled out a priori—any social structural theory of ideology is doomed to remain incomplete. In the next chapter I shall present a partial theory of ideological change, one designed specifically to deepen our understanding of the upward ratcheting growth of government in twentieth-century America. For a general theory of ideological change expressed at an empirically useful level of generality, I can only wait and hope, though I hardly expect my hopes to be fulfilled soon. Except as partially explained in the next chapter, ideological change will be viewed in this book as exogenous to political and socioeconomic change. Even if we do not know much about the causes of ideological change, we can still try to take into account its consequences.

CONCLUSIONS

Beliefs matter, and ideologies are the belief systems of greatest consequence for the political economy. Despite plausible arguments that participation in large-group collective action is irrational, not everyone is paralyzed by the neoclassical economist's Iron Law of Collective Inaction. Many people routinely participate in such large-group political actions as voting or giving money and time to political pressure groups, and they episodically join in mass endeavors to alter society on a grand scale, sometimes in violent attempts to overthrow the government. They take these actions, I have argued, not because they are irrational but because their self-perceived identities are at stake. By acting in concert with others who embrace the same ideology, they enjoy a solidarity essential to the maintenance of their identities. They cannot receive this form of utility without acting; there is no closet solidarity. To behave differently a person would have to be different. Being different would require the internalization of a different ideology. Ideologies give rise to the personal-political complex of identity, solidarity, and political action largely because of their inherent moral content. Ultimately many if not most people treat the choice between right and wrong as more fundamental than the choices they view as purely instrumental.

Ideologies reveal themselves most clearly in the crisis-time pronouncements of opinion leaders. To understand ideology, one must study symbols, paying special attention to rhetoric. How the ideologue expresses himself may be as important as what he says. Imagery holds the key to the identification of ideological motivation and program. Language is an important political resource, at once more delicate and more powerful than hard-nosed people—mathematical economists, for example—generally appreciate. By taking linguistic symbols seriously one opens a window for viewing ideologies in action.

It is, however, a foggy window. Ideological analysis is a necessary part of the study of political economy, but it is an extraordinarily difficult part. Not least of the difficulties is the absence of a full-fledged theory of ideology: a set of relations to characterize at an empirically useful level of generality the interactions of ideology with political and socioeconomic structure. Treating ideological change as exogenous to changes in the political economy creates the potential for a confusion of cause and effect. In addition the likelihood that some ideological dynamics feed only on themselves makes the analysis even more complicated. While the problems of characterization, observation, and qualitative assessment of change are not insuperable, the analysis of ideological change is likely to remain a complex and delicate art.

Unfortunately the artistry raises the odds that ideology will become a deus ex machina drawn into the analysis of change in the political economy when one cannot identify other plausible or convincing causes. The danger cannot easily be avoided. The main safeguard must be the competence and honesty of the analyst (and the critics) throughout the research but especially in the handling of symbolic artifacts. Problems of determining the representativeness of the evidence and resolving ambiguities in its interpretation will plague the study of ideology.

Finally the most fundamental danger must be faced: the analyst may become an ideologue. In social thought a thin line separates ideology from science, "since the latter is very often ideological in both its roots and consequences."[68] But although they border on one another, ideology and social science are not the same thing, and the existence of ideology does not preclude the possibility of social science. As Geertz emphasizes, they employ different symbolic strategies.

Science names the structure of situations in such a way that the attitude contained toward them is one of disinterestedness. Its style is restrained, spare, resolutely analytic: By shunning the semantic devices that most effectively formulate moral sentiment, it seeks to maximize intellectual clarity. But ideology names the structure of situations in such a way that the attitude contained toward them is one of commitment. Its style is ornate, vivid, deliberately suggestive: By objectifying moral sentiment through the same devices that science shuns, it seeks to motivate action.

Social science is diagnostic and critical; ideology is justificatory and apologetic.[69]

David Joravsky has said that "the analysis of ideological beliefs cannot avoid statements that are uncomfortably similar to accusations."[70] Examining people's social values and beliefs moves one insidiously toward *ad hominem* arguments. Still, a real boundary separates the practice of social science and the profession of ideology. The standards of social science include affectively neutral terminology, openness to criticism, empirical testing, welcoming of new (and potentially damaging) evidence. The hallmarks of ideology are retreat to valuational defenses, emotive expression, and a constant orientation toward action. Science, in its pure form, aims simply to understand. Ideology strives above all to call forth political commitment and provoke political action. Hence science and ideology don different costumes. Alertness to their fundamental differences of symbolic style can help to protect the would-be consumer of social science against an acceptance of ideology in its stead.

CHAPTER FOUR

Crisis, Bigger Government, and Ideological Change:
Toward an Understanding of the Ratchet

Be frank about our heathen foe,
    For Rome will be a goner
If you soft-pedal the loud beast;
Describe in plain four-letter words
    This dragon that's upon her:
But should our beggars ask the cost,
    Just whistle like the birds;
Dare even Pope or Caesar know
    The price of faith and honour?

W. H. AUDEN

To understand the rise of Big Government one must study the sequence of critical events through which the scope of effective governmental authority has expanded. Timing lies at the heart of the matter; coercive power is its essence. Increases in governmental revenue, expenditure, and employment are only derivative manifestations subject to variable lags and occasional short-term reversals. The growth path of governmental power over economic decision-making is the core development at issue.

The mixed economy has emerged as the outcome of a political process. Its emergence must therefore be analyzed in a certain way. As Joseph Reid has argued, "timing and motivation cannot be slighted. . . . [T]he explanation of political events must be developed dynamically, not inferred from the outcomes alone." Jerold Waltman agrees that "any model which purports to 'explain' public policy must not ignore the process whereby decisions are reached."[1] To understand how the political economy moved from an initial state (say, its condition circa 1900) to a terminal state (say, its condition circa 1985) one must consider the profile of its changes during the interim.

57

Construed either as a single great leap or as a steady movement along a fixed trend line the whole-period change is but an artifact. By contrast, if the changes during each major segment of the period are understood (1900–1915, 1916–1918, 1919–1931, and so on)—the segments being demarcated by the analytically pertinent events they contain—then the whole-period change is understood *ipso facto* without further ado. An attempt to understand the whole-period change or trend apart from its component segments is not only beside the point; it is positively misleading.

When crisis provoked an extension of governmental powers, the new powers in a fundamental sense never could be merely transitory. Because the postcrisis society inevitably differed in significant ways, crises are properly considered historically critical events; they markedly changed the course of historical development. As William Graham Sumner observed, "it is not possible to experiment with a society and just drop the experiment whenever we choose. The experiment enters into the life of the society and never can be got out again."[2] To understand the sequence of events critical in the emergence of the modern mixed economy in the United States, we must place the emphasis of our study on a handful of decisive crisis episodes, the three most momentous being the two world wars and the trough of the Great Depression.

This methodological perspective differs fundamentally from the quasi-statistical approach of many economists (and a few political scientists) who have studied the growth of government. They generally treat anything that appears to have a monotonic trend—including the time-series of an index of governmental size—as if it were the outcome of a single invariant underlying structure of behavioral relations. They view any short-lived departure from the trend, no matter how large, as transitory or even random, in any event a passing disturbance that leaves the underlying structure intact. Sometimes they simply exclude all information about crisis periods from the analysis.[3] Although the approach *may* be appropriate in studying aggregate investment spending or aggregate household saving or other economic behavior over long periods, it is inappropriate and misleading in studying the rise of Big Government.

The expansion of the scope of governmental power was path-dependent; where the political economy was likely to go depended on where it had been. Those who brought about the growth of government were motivated and constrained at each moment by their beliefs about the potentialities and dangers, the benefits and costs of alternative policies under current consideration. Their beliefs derived in turn from past events as they understood them. A genuine "return to normalcy" was unlikely after a crisis had provoked an expansion of the scope of governmental powers.

The irreversibility obtained not only because of the "hard residues" of crisis-spawned institutions (for example, administrative agencies and legal precedents), few of which necessarily show up in conventional measures of the size of government. More importantly, the underlying behavioral structure could not revert to its prior condition because the events of the crisis created new understandings of and new attitudes toward governmental action; that is, each crisis altered the ideological climate.[4] Though the postcrisis economy and society might, at least for a while, appear to have returned to their precrisis conditions, the appearance disguised the reality. In the minds and hearts of the people who had passed through the crisis and experienced the expanded governmental powers (that is, at the ultimate source of behavioral response to future exigencies), the underlying structure had indeed changed. The experiment, as Sumner recognized, always entered into the life of the society and never could be removed.

The idea of historical path-dependence has been discussed by several scholars in other contexts. Paul David, for example, has argued for it in his studies of technological change. David criticizes "a mechanistic world view that allots to the past at best a transient role in shaping the future." He stresses historical irreversibility, where "previous economic configurations become *irrevocably* lost." As early as 1942 Joseph Schumpeter warned against commission of a mechanistic, trend-imposing "statistical crime": "for any *historical* time series, the very concept of historical sequence implies the occurrence of irreversible changes in the economic structure which must be expected to affect the law of any given economic quantity."[5] Only a few economists have adopted this perspective explicitly in studies of the growth of governmental power over the economy, but among political historians the idea is widely accepted.[6]

A SCHEMATIC VIEW OF THE PROBLEM

As we have seen, several commonly employed indexes of the size of government display a ratchet movement during the twentieth century: government grew suddenly much bigger with the onset of each great crisis; after the crisis it receded but usually not to the precrisis level or even to a level that would have been reached had the precrisis rate of growth persisted instead of being displaced by the events of the crisis. According to at least one standard measure, great crisis produced not only a temporarily bigger government but a permanently bigger government.

Further, we have good reasons to believe that a more informative measure of the size of government, which ideally would gauge the scope of government's effective authority over economic decision-making, would also exhibit the ratchet. In the argument that follows I shall simply take for granted that this has been the pattern of the growth of government in the United States in the twentieth century.

Figure 4.1 presents a schematic representation of the ratchet over a single full episode. Of course, American history since 1900 contains several episodes. Analytically, however, each can be treated in isolation. Though the empirical details differ enormously from one to another and each unfolds in a way that depends in important respects on the specific character of the preceding ones, the process is identical in each, so an explication of the model need focus on only a single episode. Each has five stages: (I) precrisis normality (line segment *AB* in Figure 4.1); (II) expansion (segment *BC*); (III) maturity (segment *CD*); (IV) retrenchment (segment *DE*); and (V) postcrisis normality (segment *EF*). In the figure the vertical axis measures the logarithm of an ideal index of the size of government, and the horizontal axis measures units of time; so the slope of the profile shows the government's rate of growth.

For the figure, government is assumed to grow at the same rate during stages I and V, the normal periods before and after the crisis; it contracts in stage IV about as fast as it expands in stage II; and it does not change at all during stage III, its period of maturity. None of these assumptions is critical, and all are empirically suspect. But nothing in my argument depends on them. They are adopted only for simplicity of presentation, and they can be relaxed without affecting the substance of the argument.

All that I insist on in my analytical representation of the ratchet is: (1)

Figure 4.1   Schematic Representation of the Ratchet

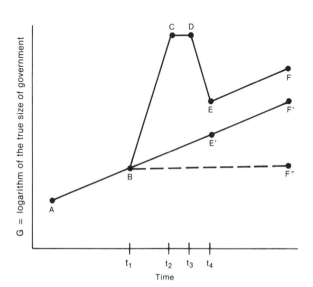

point C lies far above point B, that is, a sudden increase in the true size of government does occur; (2) point E lies far below point D, that is, a genuine retrenchment takes place; (3) point E lies above the counterfactual point E' that it would have reached at time t_4 had the government continued its precrisis rate of growth between t_1 and t_4 (that is, the retrenchment is incomplete); and (4) during the stage of postcrisis normality the rate of growth is sufficiently great that any point such as F lies above its corresponding counterfactual such as F' for an indefinitely long time (presumably until another crisis occurs). The last assumption is critical, for in its absence F could converge toward F' and at the time of their meeting the entire (crisis plus postcrisis) profile described by the points $BCDEF$ could be described as a transitory event in the sense that the true size of government ultimately would be the same as it would have been had the crisis never occurred.

My notion of a ratchet neither maintains nor implies that all governmental growth arises from crisis. Government is assumed to be growing before the crisis. Presumably, in the absence of the crisis it would have continued to grow, as shown by the hypothetical line segment $BE'F'$ in Figure 4.1. As Edward Herman has said, the trend toward bigger government, "which has been evident for many decades and in many countries, surely represents the workings of some very basic social forces and the demands of major interest groups."[7] The Crisis Hypothesis is not necessarily an alternative to the hypothesis that secular forces were producing bigger government. One can most fruitfully view the two approaches to explaining the emergence of the mixed economy as complementary.

Besides permanently increasing the true size of government relative to the size that secular forces alone would have produced, crisis may also affect the operation of the secular forces themselves. After all, the distinction between transitory and secular forces is analytical rather than substantive; it categorizes causal factors according to how persistently they operate, not according to what they are or how they work. Conceivably, without a crisis to break down some of the obstacles to the ongoing growth of government, the secular forces would eventually lose their power to sustain the true growth of government. Several scholars have argued, for example, that high tax rates during the world wars conditioned citizens to accept the enormous levies required to finance the growth of the welfare state after the war.[8] Possibly the growth path in the absence of crisis would have been not $BE'F'$ in Figure 4.1 but rather BF''. Crisis may be necessary to maintain the vitality of what many analysts implicitly assume to be a process of perpetual secular expansion.

Whether or not one views crisis as playing this extraordinarily important role, an explication of the Crisis Hypothesis must answer two questions. First: Why does government grow suddenly much bigger in stage II, especially when crisis takes the form of mobilization for war? Few analysts have considered the question seriously; most simply assume that government *must* expand rapidly under such conditions. They assume not only that government must perform a traditional function (such as the provision of national defense) at a higher level but, more significantly, that it must expand the scope of its effective authority (for example, by replacing to some extent the market economy with a command economy). The assumption is arguably false. Examination of this issue clarifies the Crisis Hypothesis; it also illuminates the nature of government in a modern representative democracy. Second: Why is the postcrisis retrenchment incomplete? Consideration of this question illuminates the character of the modern political economy as well as the relation of ideological change to the growth of government.

WHY STAGE II?
A COST-CONCEALMENT HYPOTHESIS

Why does stage II, the expansion phase of the ratchet, take place? Although answering this question may appear unnecessary, as the rapid growth of government is widely regarded as an inherent aspect of great social crisis, the argument as I have framed it requires that the question be taken seriously. To see why, one must remain aware of what I am striving to explain and not confuse it with something that, I agree, requires little or no explanation.

The difference resides in the distinction I have established between Big Government, which denotes a wide scope of effective governmental authority over economic decision-making, and big government, which denotes many resources employed in the performance of governmental functions, perhaps only traditional protective functions. The ratchet at issue here has to do with the true growth of government, that is, with the growth of government only in the first sense. Obviously, in mobilizing for a great war the government must perform one of its established functions, national defense, at a much higher level of resource consumption. But it need not expand the scope of its effective authority over economic decision-making to accomplish this objective. Government presumably was already taxing, spending, and employing to maintain its peacetime military establishment. It certainly had the authority to take such actions. War requires only that it increase the magnitude of its customary functional and fiscal activities. Such expansion produces bigger government but not Bigger Government.[9]

If the government mobilizes for war not simply by increasing the scale of its traditional activities but by widening the scope of its effective authority over economic decision-making—by drafting men instead of hiring them or by legally preempting the use of raw materials instead of purchasing them in the commodities markets—then a shift toward Big Government occurs. No technical necessity compels the government to expand its true size in response to crisis, not even when the crisis requires mobilization for a great war. There may or may not be what could be termed an economic necessity. In the twentieth century, crisis actually has produced Bigger Government. But the reasons are neither technical nor economic but fundamentally political.

To develop my argument I must make an assumption about the American political system that goes against the grain of both popular mythology and much of the theorizing in political science and public choice analysis: I assume that the government has substantial autonomy in its policy-making. In Peter Navarro's words, "the government is not only the target of special interest pressure but also one of its biggest instigators"; as Samuel Bowles says, it is "capable under some conditions of becoming a major historical actor as opposed to simply a derivative force."[10] The alternative, and more commonly accepted, assumption is that government represents and acts in accordance with the resultant of the various influence-weighted vectors of nongovernmental interests. Depending on the political model adopted, one assumes that governmental actions reflect the desires of the majority of voters, or only well-organized pressure groups, or just big business, or the bourgeoisie, or some other group or class or coalition. But no matter which of these models one adopts, the possibility is ruled out that governmental officials may have and act upon interests of their own, interests not necessarily representative of or in accordance with those of any nongovernmental group.

To assume that the government has substantial autonomy is not to suppose that officials can do anything they please. They face many constraints, which political scientists have studied in detail. Nor does my assumption have any necessarily conspiratorial or malevolent connotations. Public officials may act as they do for the noblest as well as the basest of reasons. It would be naive not to recognize that some form of self-interest enters their calculations, but one need not—and probably should not—assume that narrow material or political self-interest alone impels them. Some governmental officials may act in pursuit of their ideology's conception of the public interest. In doing so they act autonomously to the extent that their conceptions diverge from those of people outside the government. Like Eric Nordlinger, I assume only that "public officials have at least as much independent impact or explanatory importance as any and all private actors in accounting for the public policies of the democratic state," which is "regularly, though by no means entirely, autonomous in translating its preferences into authoritative actions, and markedly autonomous in often doing so even when they diverge from societal preferences."[11]

The autonomy of the government varies with societal circumstances. It is greatest during crises. As Nordlinger says, "during some crisis periods . . . deference to state preferences is overriding."[12] Under conditions widely agreed to constitute a national emergency, especially during great wars or exigencies likened to them in character or seriousness, twentieth-century Americans both expect and desire the government to "do something," and to do it immediately.[13]

Few people outside the government have enough information to identify the precise contours of the emergency or to formulate comprehensive plans for dealing with it. Citizens tend simultaneously to demand (a) more governmental action and (b) less research, public consultation, debate of alternatives, and general "due process" in governmental decision-making. In 1932, a full year before the momentous explosion of New Deal measures enacted during FDR's first hundred days as President, Felix Frankfurter complained that "one measure after another has been . . . hurriedly concocted. . . . [T]hey have been denominated emergency efforts, and any plea for deliberation, for detailed discussion, for exploration of alternatives, has been regarded as obstructive or doctrinaire or both."[14] Involving nongovernmental people in decision-making takes time, and time is extremely scarce in a crisis. Hence the authorities are freer to act according to their own (possibly divergent) preferences. And they do.

It is one thing, however, for governmental officials to select a plan of action, and something else to carry out the plan when it requires widespread compliance or sacrifice by a public that, once aware of what is being done, may object. Policies entail costs. The costs are borne mainly by nongovernmental people, who often must sacrifice heavily. Many draftees, for example, have noticed that wars never take the form of duels between heads of state. They have noticed also the low rate of soldier's pay, the high risks often associated with their involuntary occupation, and their subjection to a peculiar legal code that denies them most of the liberties civilians take for granted. Of course, not everyone is conscripted in a crisis. But substantial pecuniary and other opportunity costs may be imposed on many citizens by the government's policies.

The willingness of citizens to tolerate the costs, which must be borne if the policies are to be carried out, declines as the costs rise. This inverse relation is but a corollary of the economist's Law of Demand. Even the (initially) most popular war loses support as casualties mount, tax burdens rise, and military appetites consume more of the resources needed to produce civilian goods and services.

> Guns on an empty stomach
> Are not to every people's taste.
> Merely swallowing gas
> They say, does not quench thirst
> And without woollen pants
> A soldier, it could be, is brave only in summer.[15]

Governmental officials know that the citizens have limits. Pushing them beyond the limits jeopardizes not only the success of the policies but the very survival of the government.[16]

Obviously, citizens will not react to the costs they bear if they are unaware of them. The possibility of driving a wedge between the actual and the publicly perceived costs creates a strong temptation for governments pursuing high-cost policies during national emergencies. Except where lives are being sacrificed, no costs are so easily counted as pecuniary costs. Not only can each individual count them (his own tax bill); they can be easily aggregated for the whole society (the government's total tax revenue). It behooves a government wishing to sustain a policy that entails suddenly heightened costs to find ways of substituting nonpecuniary for pecuniary costs. The substitution may blunt the citizens' realization of how great their sacrifices really are and hence diminish their protests and resistance.[17]

Students of public finance speak of "fiscal illusion." As Nordlinger has written, this notion "implicitly assumes that public officials periodically prefer to spend larger amounts than does the electorate as a whole, that they frequently increase the proportion of total revenues raised through indirect forms of taxation so as to 'conceal' some of the costs borne by the electorate, and that thereby they come to translate their own preferences into public policy."[18] Thus may a democratic government command more resources than it could if the citizens were all perfectly informed. Fiscal illusion, when facilitated only by such stratagems as payroll withholding of income taxes or inflation-induced "bracket creep," produces only bigger government, not necessarily a move toward Big Government.

Another way to conceal costs, which is to substitute a command economy for a market economy, does generate Bigger Government. Economists have analyzed such cost-concealment in detail in the case of the military draft.[19] Similar analysis can be applied to the full range of contrivances government employs to divert resources to uses of its choosing without bidding for them in open markets.[20]

Many cost concealments go unnoticed because the government makes payments to citizens, ostensibly as a quid pro quo for resources received from them. Even military draftees are paid. But when the government has imposed price controls or otherwise "rigged" the markets—for example, by giving high official priorities to raw materials ordered by favored industries—the prices paid do not reflect the full opportunity costs of the goods and services purchased. By not paying free-market prices, the government in effect gets some of its purchases without paying for them. An implication is that private resource users and suppliers somewhere in the economy bear costs of uncertain magnitude as a result of the governmental taking. (These costs are apart from the "deadweight" costs associated with the "inefficient" allocation of resources when the economy adjusts to a "distorted" structure of relative prices. Only economists appreciate that deadweight costs exist.)[21]

But what of the claim that government has no choice about substituting, at least to some extent, a command (cost-concealing) economy for a market (cost-revealing) economy? It is often alleged that the market economy does not work in a crisis, especially a crisis of vast wartime mobilization. The market, it is said, moves too slowly, and when national survival is at stake it is imperative that mobilization proceed as expeditiously as possible. The market, it is said, will not accept the risks inherent in retooling and otherwise reallocating capital for wartime employments of uncertain duration. The market, it is said, cannot accumulate the vast sums of money that may be required for certain enormous military-industrial undertakings. Therefore the government has no real alternative to displacement of the market economy in the crisis. The ends sought simply could not be attained by pecuniary taxation and expenditure in a free market economy. "To mobilize national resources for war purposes . . . so it was said and believed, the market and its regulatory supplements were hopelessly inadequate. The need was for an adminstrative network with unifying, planning and directive capabilities."[22]

So far as the argument is correct, it says something rather different from what its proponents seem to want it to say. One must recognize—even at the risk of appearing to exalt a tautology—that everything the government accomplishes by means of a command-and-control system does happen; that is, labor, management, capital, and raw materials are actually shifted to producing the newly demanded goods and services on the government's shopping list. That the transformation happens shows that it is possible. Purely technical constraint cannot be the problem.

The revealing question is: Could the government, without coercion or interference in the price system, induce the private owners of the desired resources to supply them voluntarily? The answer is, perhaps. But one thing is certain. The full costs of the government's policy are actually borne. No tricks of deficit or inflationary finance or fiscal deception can alter the fact that the opportunities forgone by the society when real resources are shifted from producing privately favored goods to producing governmentally favored goods are real, immediate, unshiftable costs. Conceivably, were the government to attempt to compensate by acceptable pecuniary payment every soldier, investor, and owner of raw materials, the required payments would exceed the maximum taxable portion of the national income, namely, the portion in excess of the amount needed for the population's subsistence.[23] In that event no feasible fiscal exaction would be sufficient to provide the government enough money to buy what it wants on the open market, where high-speed reallocation of resources and all forms of risk-bearing as well as goods and services themselves must be paid for.[24] So maybe the government could finance the goods and services on its emergency shopping list from tax revenues, in which case the argument for the necessity of the command economy during crisis collapses; or maybe it couldn't.

Inability to levy taxes and then purchase on the open market everything it wishes to use in carrying out its policy shows that the government values the activity more than the citizens, that it takes from them coercively more than they are willing to supply voluntarily at a free-market price. The government might get away with such takings because: (1) its monopoly of substantial force leaves citizens helpless to resist, which seems unlikely in a society with functioning democratic institutions; (2) the costs are distributed so that politically weak people bear the brunt of them, which could be a viable outcome even in a democracy, though it might entail high costs of enforcement; and (3) the costs are concealed so that politically influential citizens fail to appreciate the magnitude of the burden even though they bear much of it. I find the three possibilities more plausible in ascending order. That is, the concealment of the true costs of governmental action in a crisis offers the most compelling explanation of why the command economy tends to displace the market during a national emergency in a democratic society.

To sum up, modern democratic governments expand the scope of their effective authority over economic decision-making during crises because citizens insist that they "do something," and the alternative means of implementing the chosen policies, which is full reliance on pecuniary fiscal and market mechanisms, would reveal the costs of the government's policies so clearly as to threaten the viability of both the policies and the ruling, somewhat autonomous governments themselves. Thus does stage II of the ratchet occur. It is in large measure the product of citizens' imperfect information and understanding and of the statist ideology that underlies the insistence that the government "do something" whenever a problem arises. Surely, with the passage of time, citizens learn about the true costs of governmental policies. Why then do the governmental initiatives undertaken during crises leave any permanent trace?

WHY STAGE IV?
A (PARTIAL) HYPOTHESIS ON IDEOLOGICAL CHANGE

Many scholars view the incompleteness of the postcrisis retrenchment as a product of the politics of governmental bureaucracies, their private clients, and connected politicians. Francis Rourke's succinct explanation is that "bureaucratic services generate constituencies that oppose their liquidation."

Bruce Porter maintains that after a war "the bureaucracy retains much of its growth . . . because Congress lacks the political will to force deep cutbacks in the absence of a pressing need to do so." Jack Hirshleifer refers to the idea that "[w]ars and defense crises that require gigantic budgetary expansions leave in their wake a mass of officeholders, with sufficient political clout to resist budgetary contraction when the crises pass." Friedrich Hayek stresses the strategic position of entrenched bureaucrats who, because of their quasi-monopoly of the expertise needed to assess the costs and benefits of the programs they administer, are well situated to argue persuasively in support of perpetuating whatever they do: Why, all the experts agree![25] In each of its variants the idea is that bureaucracies are easier to create than to destroy; hence bureaus, bureaucrats, and the number of rules they issue all increase irreversibly over time.

The hypothesis has merit. Evidence consistent with it is easily found, and scholars have compiled a lot of such evidence.[26] Still, it cannot account fully for the incompleteness of the postcrisis retrenchment. The emergence of Big Government involves much more than the proliferation of bureaucrats and their decrees. It also involves important changes in judicial interpretations of rights and obligations under the Constitution as well as new statutory constraints placed directly on economic actors by Congress without any new regulatory agencies or additional governmental employees.[27] The hypothesis of bureau-cum-clientele entrenchment tells us nothing about these and other aspects of the growth of government.

The idea seems sometimes to verge on a conspiracy theory. A bureau and its relatively few but passionately interested clients are presumed to extract substantial benefits for themselves, imposing the costs thinly over a much larger group of taxpayers or persons who bear costs indirectly (potential entrants officially denied access to a lucrative industry or occupation, perhaps, or consumers who pay higher prices for goods produced by firms officially shielded from competition). Evidently those who suffer either do not know that they are bearing the costs or consider them too small to justify taking political action in an attempt to eliminate the burden. Without organized political resistance, the bureau maintains or even increases its activities.

No doubt many such quasi conspiracies occur. Their economic logic is certainly ironclad. But we have seen that economic logic, as traditionally understood, is insufficient for understanding political behavior. Perhaps a political entrepreneur could promote his career by publicizing and combatting special-interest "rip-offs" (à la Senator William Proxmire and his Golden Fleece Awards).[28] A big hog feeding at the government trough is hard to hide. If a flow of benefits to a narrow interest group is known to exist and allowed to persist unchallenged, even if only the better informed political actors know about it, then evidently no one considers it a promising political issue. Exposing the largess would produce little or no political "mileage" for the innovative politician publicizing the matter.

One reason for the indifference to such revelations is that people may approve of, or at least not positively oppose, the government's policy notwithstanding its negative (but usually small) impact on them. What Victor Fuchs has written about national health policies may apply as well to other governmental policies: "The constant assertions that this or that regulation or subsidy is irrational and inefficient often fall on deaf ears simply because the majority doesn't see it that way." In a discussion of tax reform, George Shultz and Kenneth Dam observe that advocacy groups "play upon the resentment engendered by the frustration of [established] expectations," thereby becoming "even more effective in resisting the elimination of their tax preferences than they were in obtaining the preferences in the first place." John Mark Hansen argues that, in general, "people are more easily mobilized in response to threats than in response to prospects" because [p]olitical benefits that avoid losses are weighed more heavily than political benefits that promise gains."[29] People are less likely to object to an established policy, complete with an administrative bureaucracy and a group of dependent beneficiaries, than to an equally costly proposed policy. Perhaps they think: "Well, we're all getting more from government nowadays than we used to; and those people deserve their fair share, too."[30]

So far as this ideological position—call it "welfare latitudinarianism" or "vulgar equity"—expresses an attitude more favorable toward established than proposed governmental actions, and to the extent that crises usher in numerous new governmental programs, as argued above, there is a link between crisis and changes in the prevailing ideological posture toward the appropriate scope of governmental action in the economy.

In various ways scholars have affirmed the existence of such a link. Nordlinger declares that past crises "affect the attitudes of current generations," including current public officials. Thomas Dye and Harmon Zeigler write that the Great Depression "undermined the faith of both elites and nonelites in the ideals of the old order" and had "an important impact on the thinking of America's governing elites. . . . Roosevelt's personal philosophy of noblesse oblige—elite responsibility for the welfare of the masses—was soon to become the prevailing ethos of the new liberal establishment. . . . [This was, in part] a tribute to the effectiveness of Roosevelt himself as a mobilizer of opinion among both elites and masses." Dye also maintains that war "conditions citizens to tolerate major increases in government activity, and thus, after the war, government activity remains on a higher plateau than before the war." Barry Karl concludes that "the New Deal transformed . . .

most notably, perhaps, American popular attitudes toward the role of the federal government." Mancur Olson agrees that "[t]he interwar depression, World War II, and other developments led to profound ideological changes that increased the scope of government." Karen Rasler and William Thompson assert that great wars weaken the "general resistance to social and political change." Lawrence Brown observes that "big government is now a fact of life, the battles over welfare state breakthroughs largely over. . . . Postwar generations that have grown up within big government take it for granted and would not do without it."[31]

Although the statements refer variously to changes in popular attitudes, faith, ideals, thinking, philosophy, ethos, opinion, toleration, resistance to change, facts of life, and things taken for granted as well as to ideological change as such, they all pertain to what I call *ideological change*. They all agree that the major crises of twentieth-century America somehow caused changes in ideology and that these in turn somehow facilitated a permanent enlargement of government.

But exactly how does crisis bring about ideological change in the specific sense of a shift in the desire for or toleration of a wider scope of effective governmental authority over economic decision-making? One way to approach the question is by exploiting the many parallels, heretofore unnoticed, between the theory of ideological change and the theory of technological change.[32]

Technology and ideology both have to do with knowledge. Technology pertains to a fairly "hard" form of belief, whereas ideology occupies the zone between such hard knowledge as natural science and such "soft" beliefs as religion and metaphysics; but both pertain to beliefs about how the world works in a certain realm of comprehension. Both forms of belief have great practical effect, one in shaping the techniques of production and the other in shaping sociopolitical organization and activity. Both are difficult to observe directly; in tests of their influence they often appear as "residuals." Thus, improvements in economic productivity that cannot be explained by observed changes in visible inputs are ascribed to technological change; shifts in political behavior that cannot be explained by observed changes in political self-interest (narrowly construed) are ascribed to ideological change.[33] In both cases, qualitative evidence can make the ascription more plausible and allay the suspicion that it is merely giving a name to one's ignorance. Technological change reveals itself in novel formulas, equations, blueprints, diagrams, and the like; ideological change reveals itself in the shifting rhetoric of opinion leaders.

Like any form of knowledge, technology and ideology must be learned. They can be acquired from literary repositories—technical manuals or classics of social thought as the case may be—or from experience. Technology derives heavily from experience with production, ideology from socioeconomic and political experience. Discrete shifts in technological or ideological beliefs are likely to reflect what has been learned from extraordinary events: decisive experiments, deliberate or natural, in the case of technology; societal crisis and the political response to it in the case of ideology. Both realms of belief have their great inventors and entrepreneurs—in technology, such as Whitney, Edison, and Ford; in ideology, such as Smith, Marx, and Keynes—who lead the way toward a radical recasting of beliefs and practices.

Viewed in a broad perspective, both technological and ideological changes appear to evolve within a competitive process. At any time, several alternative modes of belief and practice contend: alternating versus direct currents for electrical transmission; free markets versus collectivist planning for economic organization. Some complexes of belief and practice prove ill suited to survive. Economic or technical conditions may give alternating-current transmission systems an advantage over direct-current systems; demographic or cultural conditions may give collectivism an advantage over the free market. But the direction in which the evolutionary process carries complexes of belief and practice is not random; it is path-dependent.

Consider first the path-dependency of technological change. If capital-intensive techniques of production are commonly used, learning from experience is likely to take the form of advances in capital-intensive techniques. This tendency gives the system a determinate direction. (Of course, any learning process remains ever subject to exogenous or random shocks and may not always produce a single determinate outcome.)[34] If, for example, labor is becoming more expensive relative to capital, producers will tend to substitute more capital-intensive techniques for more labor-intensive techniques. Experience with the new, more capital-intensive techniques leads especially to discoveries of how to make this particular kind of technique work better. The discoveries give even greater advantage to capital-intensive techniques and hence encourage even more substitution in the same direction.[35]

Ideological change can be similarly self-reinforcing. Suppose, for example, that in a great social crisis a command-and-control system displaces the free market. Experience under the new regime will generate learning of several kinds. To some extent government planners and bureaucrats will improve their means of manipulating the economy: new information systems, allocation rules, procedures for resolving disputes between bureaus and reconciling inconsistencies in the overall plan will be devised. These improvements make the controls less obnoxious to aggrieved parties. Meanwhile, learning about how to make the market system work better more or less ceases, as the big payoffs no longer present themselves in this sector.

Citizens also learn that some of their prior beliefs about the impossibilities or dangers of governmental control now appear groundless. The government may decide who can use aluminum, steel, and rubber, what consumer products must not be produced during the crisis, and so on, but it does not deny freedom of worship or nationalize the news media. Popular elections are held as scheduled. Many of the conservatives' stock warnings about the prospective horrors of one thing leading to another are perceived by the masses as well as the elites as overdrawn.

At the same time, many people discover that necessity may be the mother of opportunity. A command economy offers its own avenues for individual advancement, not only in the bureaucracy but in favored parts of the remaining "market" economy. Occupants of privileged positions naturally develop more than an appreciation of the personal advantages; they tend to view the whole apparatus of governmental control as essentially benign. "Handling honey, tar or dung," said Carl Sandburg, "some of it sticks to the fingers."[36] Thus, for various reasons, many people are likely to learn to like, or at least to tolerate without active opposition, socioeconomic and political arrangements that appeared in the beginning as unavoidable—but assuredly temporary—evils necessitated by a great social crisis.[37]

All the while, of course, the government actively strives to justify its policies, magnifying their benefits and virtues while depreciating their costs and vices.

> Political men pour from the barrel
> New lies on the old,
> And are praised for kindly wisdom.[38]

The barrage of propaganda always hits some targets, if only the unsophisticated or devoutly patriotic—possibly a huge throng.[39]

Conceivably, then, ideological learning makes a discrete leap as a result of social crisis and the attendant expansion toward Big Government. This could be the way in which, as Sumner put it, "the experiment enters into the life of the society and never can be got out again."

Of course, countermovements of ideology are possible. Conservatives, seeing their nightmares emerging in the light of day, may redouble their efforts to propagate the Old Time Religion, perhaps with some success. Certainly, egregious examples that support their arguments are easily found. The theory sketched above suggests that the "progressive" movements of ideology overmatch the reactionary ones, but one need not attempt to settle a priori where the balance lies. Historical research can determine which of the opposing forces has weighed more heavily in the American experience.

RECAPITULATION:
WHY THE RATCHET?

To a large extent Big Government has emerged in twentieth-century America during relatively brief episodes of great social crisis, either war or depression. One therefore needs a theory to explain: (1) why government expands the scope of its effective authority over economic decision-making with the onset of a crisis; and (2) why the retrenchment that follows the crisis is incomplete, leaving government permanently Bigger than it would have been had the crisis never occurred. These are essential elements of a theory that views the growth of government not as a mere trend phenomenon but as a path-dependent historical process.

The expansion phase of the ratchet reflects the decisions of a quasi-autonomous government responding to an insistent but ill-defined public demand that the government "do something" about a crisis. Whatever the policy adopted, however, costs must be borne by people outside the government. The greater are the costs, the less willing is the public to tolerate them. When people are burdened too heavily, their resistance jeopardizes not only the policy but, in a normally operating representative democracy, the government itself. Anticipating such reactions, the government takes steps to conceal the true costs of its policies. Most importantly, it substitutes a (cost-hiding) command-and-control system of resource allocation for the (cost-revealing) market system and its utterly visible measuring rod of money.

The incompleteness of the retrenchment phase of the ratchet is usually explained as the product of the politics of entrenched bureaucrats, their clients, and connected politicians—the so-called "iron triangles." The explanation is valid but incomplete. It accounts for only a part of Big Government. It can and should be supplemented by a (partial) theory of ideological change.

This theory pertains to only one aspect of the ideological climate, namely, the beliefs of elites (and presumably of the masses whose beliefs attach to some extent as dependent variables) about the appropriate scope of effective governmental authority over economic decision-making. Crises lead to permanent shifts in the tolerable limits of the true size of government. Crises break down ideological resistance to Big Government by (1) providing occasions for the improvement of command-and-control mechanisms, which renders them less obnoxious; (2) discrediting the conservatives' domino theory, with its implication that all civil and political liberties will be lost in a mixed economy; and (3) creating opportunities for many people both within and without the government to do well for themselves and hence to look more favorably on the new order. In all these respects—strongly reinforced, of course, by ceaseless outpourings of official propaganda—ideological evolution displays a path-dependency of its own, the salient feature of which is the crisis-induced reduction of resistance to Big Government.

THE TASK AHEAD

A study guided by the analytical framework sketched above has an associated program of historical research. For each critical episode, one seeks to understand how socioeconomic and ideological forces caused political actors to expand the scope of governmental power over the economy. At least eight subjects require study: (1) socioeconomic and political conditions before, during, and after the crisis; (2) prevailing ideologies before, during, and after the crisis; (3) leading persons and elites and the interest groups they favor or represent; (4) emergency legislation and executive orders; (5) emergency agencies and their leadership; (6) operation of and reaction to the emergency measures; (7) court challenges, resulting decisions, and innovations of legal—especially constitutional—doctrines; and (8) institutional legacies and perceived "lessons" of the episode. These are the raw materials for an account of the circumstances, actors, motives, and actions that produced and sustained specific accretions of governmental power over economic decision-making during each crisis and its aftermath.

PART TWO

History

CHAPTER FIVE

Crisis under the Old Regime, 1893–1896

When we consider that the theory of our institutions guarantees to
every citizen the full enjoyment of all the fruits of his industry and
enterprise, with only such deduction as may be his share toward the
careful and economical maintenance of the Government which pro-
tects him, it is plain that the exaction of more than this is indefensible
extortion and a culpable betrayal of American fairness and justice.

GROVER CLEVELAND

Except the Civil War, no crisis of the nineteenth century challenged America's political and economic order so profoundly as that of the mid-1890s.
Never before had the economy suffered such deep, pervasive, and sustained
depression. Only in the bloodsoaked breach of the sixties had the polity split
into such venomously hostile factions. Contending parties debated with
unprecedented passion the question of how the government should be involved in the nation's economic affairs. E. L. Godkin, the conservative editor
of the *Nation*, perceived a "craze against property . . . sweeping through the
country." Populism, whose demands made conservatives tremble with apprehension and loathing, spread its influence across the South and the West,
where fire-breathing agitators roared their vituperation to growing throngs
of voters. Soon, perhaps, they would sway the working masses of the East.
"Discontent," said the young historian Frederick J. Turner in 1896, was
"demanding an extension of governmental activity in its behalf."[1]

Having merged their forces with a sympathetic faction of the Democratic
Party, the Populists sent their newly embraced champion, William Jennings
Bryan, into the presidential contest of 1896 pledged to destroy the gold
standard and tear down long-standing limits on the economic powers of
government. The Democratic platform demanded "free and unlimited coinage of both silver and gold at the present legal ratio of 16 to 1," which
would have insured inflation. It called for prohibition of "the issuing of

77

interest-bearing bonds of the United States in time of peace," which would have denied the Treasury an essential means of maintaining its gold reserve and hence the gold standard. It urged "the enlargement of the powers of the Interstate Commerce Commission" and additional restrictions on the business decisions made by railroad companies. Like his Populist supporters, Bryan espoused an income tax. Though he campaigned as a Democrat, he had the exclusive presidential endorsement of the People's Party, which magnified the aura of radicalism that radiated around him. The Populist platform of 1892, besides proposing unlimited coinage of silver and the graduated taxation of incomes, had called for the nationalization of the railroads, telegraph, and telephones and declared support for the organization and objectives of labor unions. Americans of all political persuasions sensed that the future of the political economy lay in the balance. "The election," said newspaperman William Allen White, "will sustain Americanism or it will plant Socialism."[2]

When Bryan and Populism went down in the election of November 1896, their defeat resolved a sociopolitical conflict that had heated up a decade earlier and reached a fever pitch soon after the conservative Democrat Grover Cleveland took office in March 1893. Long before Cleveland left office he had lost the support of his party, most Democrats having moved toward the left while Cleveland stood pat. Except his opposition to protective tariffs, he had little in common with the party's radical candidate of 1896. Repudiated and ridiculed by many of his fellow Democrats, Cleveland nevertheless had achieved some critical policy objectives. For four exasperating years he had struggled to defend the political economy from radical attacks: to save the gold standard, threatened by silverite inflationists; to preserve an orderly and free labor market, jeopardized by unionists, rioters, and proponents of governmental work relief for the unemployed. At the same time the federal judiciary had asserted itself with unprecedented audacity to suppress the disruptive activities of labor unions and to preserve private property rights against attenuation by the taxation of incomes. Therefore, when William McKinley took office, he inherited a political economy with a secure gold standard, labor markets well protected from the most serious union disturbances, and no income tax. Had the dominant ideology of the Cleveland administration and the federal judges been different, McKinley probably would have inherited a markedly different political economy.

Hence my present purpose: to argue that crisis alone need not spawn Bigger Government. It does so only under favorable ideological conditions, and such conditions did not exist in the 1890s. Ideology is for ruling elites not only a lever but a straitjacket. Acting with substantial autonomy, governments even in a representative democracy may seize more power than the majority of citizens wishes to grant them, but they may also refuse to accept or exercise powers that many citizens would thrust upon them. American governments in the twentieth century, impelled by a more "progressive" ideology, readily accepted—indeed eagerly sought—expanded powers. The crisis of the 1890s, the last major battle in which the forces of classical liberalism won a clear victory, serves as an illuminating backdrop against which the crises of the twentieth century stand out in bold relief.

CREATIVE DESTRUCTION
IDEOLOGICALLY SUSTAINED, 1865–1893

When Joseph Schumpeter coined the expression "creative destruction" to describe the dynamics of "relatively unfettered capitalism," he might have had in mind the United States in the late nineteenth century. Certainly the nation's economic development had never been so rapid, nor so erratic and disruptive. The American who studies the statistics of his country's social and economic change, wrote the industrialist Andrew Carnegie in the early 1890s, "becomes almost dizzy at discovering the velocity with which she is rushing on." No doubt Carnegie's own wealth was accumulating at a breath-taking rate. Though few others matched his fabulous achievements, many could boast of substantial success. Yet amid the rush of economic develop-ment, many individuals, some occupations and trades, and even a few entire regions lagged far behind. "Some get an infinitely better and easier living," observed Henry George, "but others find it hard to get a living at all."[3]

After the Civil War the national rates of saving and investment jumped to unprecedented levels and remained there for the rest of the nineteenth cen-tury: more than a fifth of the gross national product took the form of capital goods. Between the war and the end of the century the tangible capital stock grew fourfold, far more than the labor force, which increased by less than 150 percent. Hence tangible capital per worker rose rapidly, by about 80 percent in just three decades.[4] In addition, human capital was accumulated as the average worker became healthier, more educated, and better trained; and intellectual capital was accumulated as inventiveness and the adoption of new techniques of production flourished as never before. The result of all these productivity-enhancing endeavors was economic growth, a process—erratic in the short run but sustained in the long run—that generated rising real income per capita. Between the late sixties and the early nineties, real GNP per capita increased at an average rate of more than 2 percent per year.[5]

Economic growth both caused and in part resulted from ongoing shifts in the relative importance of industries, sectors, and regions. It fed and was nourished in turn by urbanization. In 1870 just 26 percent of Americans lived in incorporated places with populations of more than 2,500; by 1890,

35 percent did. During the interval the number of cities with populations exceeding 100,000 increased from fourteen to twenty-eight. The labor force shifted among sectors. While agricultural employment grew slowly, employment in construction, trade, and transportation surged ahead. Manufacturing employment held at 19 percent of the labor force, but rapid productivity gains raised manufacturing output from 33 percent of all commodity output in 1869 to 53 percent in 1894.[6] The urban-industrial transformation of the socioeconomic structure left few people unaffected. Under these dynamic conditions, to adopt new ways of life and new kinds of production was the road to wealth—or, for the less fortunate, at least an avenue of survival.

The era also witnessed the rise of many giant corporations and the emergence of the "trust question" as a major political issue. The interregional railroads, appearing on the American scene at mid-century, were the first giant enterprises. After the Civil War several transcontinental railroads, all but the Great Northern the beneficiaries of federal land grants, were completed. Chastened by scandals connected with the government's subsidization of these enterprises, Congress made no new railroad land grants after 1871, but in the nostrils of many people the odor of something rotten—corruption and special, unwarranted privilege at the expense of the general public—lingered about the land-grant railroads for decades. After the 1870s, growing numbers of huge manufacturing corporations, including such still-familiar firms as Standard Oil, Bethlehem, American Tobacco, and Armour, achieved prominence. People accustomed to dealing with small locally-owned firms had difficulty in reconciling themselves to an economy in which such corporate behemoths did much of the nation's business.[7]

The great corporations, known to contemporaries as "trusts" though only a few were ever trusts in the strict legal sense, raised the specter of monopoly power in the market. American public opinion and legal tradition had long been hostile toward monopolies. Conspiracies in restraint of trade were unquestionably illegal under the common law.[8] But rarely was a giant corporation the sole supplier of a well-defined product or service. More commonly it was an aggressively innovative firm, supplying improved products and reducing its costs of production and its prices, and increasing its share of the market as a result. Unsuccessful competitors complained bitterly that the "monopolists" were driving them to the wall.[9] Customers frequently objected to real or imagined price discrimination. More than anything else, rate discrimination provoked the outrage of midwestern shippers against the railroads. Often the criticism of a big corporation's alleged monopoly power could be deflected by showing that the firm produced better products or services in growing volumes at ever lower prices.

But this defense, even if appropriate, did nothing to allay the charge that the great corporations subverted the democratic political process. "Corruption," charged the Populists in the preamble to their platform of 1892, "dominates the ballot-box, the Legislatures, the Congress, and touches even the ermine of the bench." Observers of unimpeachable repute agreed. Henry B. Brown, an associate justice of the U.S. Supreme Court, told the Yale law students in 1895 that "[b]ribery and corruption are as universal as to threaten the very structure of society." He averred that "[p]robably in no country in the world is the influence of wealth more potent than in this, and in no period of our history has it been more powerful than now."[10]

No doubt the trusts did make their influence felt in the state legislatures, the halls of Congress, and the courts of law. As Richard Hofstadter put it, "Before business learned to buy statesmen at wholesale, it had to buy privileges at retail. Fabulous sums were spent." Railroad promoters actively lobbied for land grants and other subsidies at every level of government. A chorus of manufacturers continually cried out for tariff protection. Big businessmen routinely resorted to the courts for assistance in their struggle against labor unions. In an age of rough-and-tumble politics and often venal politicians, the owners and managers of big businesses possessed extraordinary ability to sway the political process, and they did so with considerable success. Though the political system never became the unmitigated plutocracy denounced by radical critics, the political activities of the great corporations shook the public's faith in the country's political institutions and embittered a large minority of the citizens.[11] Labor organizations, which achieved their first sustained success in the late nineteenth century, became the implacable foes of big business.

Western farmers, who were far more numerous than organized workers in those days, also contributed heavily to the sentiment against the large manufacturing and railroad corporations. After the Civil War, western settlement had advanced along with the spread of railroad facilities beyond the Mississippi River. Pouring onto the prairies and plains and filling the fertile valleys of the Far West, settlers between 1870 and 1900 more than doubled the country's farm acreage. Unfamiliar conditions in the newly settled farming regions exposed the pioneer farmers to great natural risks. The volatility of national and international markets for staple crops heightened the uncertainties. Remoteness from eastern markets magnified the impact of market fluctuations on their incomes. But when nature or impersonal market forces turned against them, they cursed neither the heavens nor bad luck but identifiable parties with whom they dealt in the markets. Among those they loved to hate, railroads and manufacturers ranked high. All the major agrarian protest movements of the late nineteenth century flourished most where natural and economic uncertainties were relatively great, but the farmers' grievances focused far more on worldly malefactors than on heaven-sent misfortunes.[12]

The farmers' protest movements achieved little success. The state Granger Laws of the early seventies were transitory. Although the U.S. Supreme Court upheld the states' regulatory powers in the famous *Munn* decision of 1877, the railroads' bargaining power in the state legislatures overcame the enthusiasts for regulation, and the regulations were repealed or amended to extract their teeth.[13] *Munn*, so often described as a "landmark," had little visible effect. The Interstate Commerce Act was passed by Congress in 1887, but this vague law, described by Senator Nelson W. Aldrich as "a delusion and a sham," received vacillating enforcement and tended more to stabilize railroad cartels than to protect shippers. By the late nineties the Interstate Commerce Commission had become almost an irrelevancy.[14] The farmers' cultivation of inflationary monetary schemes yielded meager legislative fruit. The Greenbackers, who sought new issues of fiat paper money, met utter defeat. The Bland-Allison Act of 1878 and the Sherman Silver Purchase Act of 1890 required the Treasury to purchase small amounts of silver—the former adding silver dollar coins or equivalent certificates, the latter silver certificates only, to the money stock—but the direct effects on the price level were negligible. The Sherman Antitrust Act of 1890 was a hypocritical sop to public opinion. As Senator Orville Platt said, "the whole effort has been to get some bill headed, 'A bill to punish trusts' with which to go to the country."[15] The law received limited and erratic enforcement, and in the nineties it bore more heavily on labor unions than on the trusts. No doubt the frustration many farmers felt as a result of their political failures in the seventies and eighties contributed to the growing sentiment for Populism in the early nineties.

For the most part the government remained serenely indifferent to the radical winds that swirled around it. Local governments provided police, courts, schools, streets and roads; some of the larger cities added sewers and public water works. The federal government paid veterans' pensions and interest on the Civil War debt; maintained a minuscule military establishment; delivered the mail; chipped away the public domain by various giveaways and sales; kept tariffs high and levied a few excise taxes; and pursued a deflationary monetary policy that allowed during 1865–1878 an approach to the gold standard at the prewar parity and after 1878 the maintenance of that standard and parity. Otherwise, governments did little of much consequence or expense. Though the post–Civil War era did not witness pure laissez-faire in the United States, it did see a limited government and an economy in which people had extensive freedom to enter into economic transactions of their own choosing on terms established by the transactors alone. As the legal historian Lawrence Friedman has expressed it, "Every new law on the statute books, if it dealt with the economy, was a cup of water withdrawn from the oceanic domain of the law of contract."[16]

Notwithstanding the millions who supported Populist and other proposals for expanding the powers of government over the economy, most Americans—including apparently most farmers and laborers—opposed such reform.[17] James Bryce, perhaps the most perspicacious foreign observer of American society in the late nineteenth century, observed that the general public cherished "certain dogmas or maxims" about political, legal, and economic matters. One of the dogmas was the conviction that certain rights of the individual, such as the "right to the enjoyment of what he has earned . . . are primordial and sacred." Moreover, all governmental authorities "ought to be strictly limited" and "the less of government the better. . . . The functions of government must be kept at their minimum."[18]

Employing the concept of "public opinion," Bryce argued in effect that ideology was the fundamental force opposing the extension of governmental powers to redistribute wealth. "[T]he poorer citizens have long been a numerical majority, invested with political power," he wrote. Hence it might have been feared

> that the poor would have turned the tables on the rich, thrown the whole burden of taxation upon them, and disregarded in the supposed interest of the masses what are called the rights of property. Not only has this not been attempted—it has been scarcely even suggested . . . and it excites no serious apprehension. There is nothing in the machinery of government that could do more than delay it for a time, did the masses desire it. What prevents it is the honesty and common sense of the citizens generally, who are convinced that the interests of all classes are substantially the same, and that justice is the highest of those interests. Equality, open competition, a fair field to everybody, every stimulus to industry, and every security for its fruits, these they hold to be the self-evident principles of national prosperity.

One who accepts the veracity of Bryce's description and analysis, which are amply corroborated by many other contemporaries and historians, must conclude that the ultimate check on the growth of government in the late nineteenth century was the dominant ideology. Most people resisted radical pleas for Bigger Government because they believed that such a government would be not only counterproductive but immoral.[19]

A nation largely dedicated to an ideology of limited government elected in 1892 an ideal leader. Grover Cleveland had already proven his devotion to a limited conception of government's role in the economy. The most memorable manifestation of his convictions had occurred in 1887, during his first term as President, after Congress passed the so-called Texas Seed Bill. The act provided for a distribution of seed grain by the U.S. Commissioner of Agriculture to destitute farmers in an area of Texas devastated by drought. Only $10,000, a trifling amount even in those days, was appropriated; and the beneficiaries certainly seemed deserving enough. Yet Cleveland vetoed the bill, because he could "find no warrant for such an appropriation in the Constitution." Further, "A prevalent tendency to disregard the limited mission of [the government's] power and duty should be steadfastly resisted, to the end that the lesson should be constantly enforced that, though the people support the Government, the Government should not support the people."[20] As Robert Wiebe has said, "Cleveland and his close associates, who came from a thoroughly respectable section of the Democratic party, reflected that same deep concern for property, law, and order which was obsessing substantial citizens everywhere. A forceful man, he could be relied upon to resist radical legislation and to intervene promptly wherever the need arose."[21] But as he took office in March 1893 Cleveland could hardly have suspected how difficult it would be to keep the faith through the next four years.

DEPRESSION AND SOCIAL UNREST, 1893–1896

Scarcely had Cleveland settled into the White House when the economy began to collapse. Early in May the failure of the National Cordage Company touched off a panic on the New York Stock Exchange. Several waves of bank failures ensued, creating a temporary liquidity crisis. By midsummer a pervasive depression had set in. The *Commercial and Financial Chronicle* reported a "sudden and striking cessation of industrial activity. . . . [M]ills, factories, furnaces, mines nearly everywhere shut down in large numbers, and commerce and enterprise were arrested in an extraordinary and unprecedented degree. . . . [I]nternal trade was reduced to very small proportions . . . and hundreds of thousands of men thrown out of employment." By the end of the year more than fifteen thousand businesses, several hundred banks, and one-sixth of the country's railroads had gone under.[22]

In 1893 every aspect of macroeconomic performance deteriorated immensely. As usual during the onset of a severe depression, investment spending fell precipitously, this time by over 20 percent (in constant dollars) from the previous year. Real GNP per capita slipped by 7 percent. Unemployment mounted steadily as winter approached, threatening major distress in the industrial cities.

The next year witnessed continued economic decline. Real investment spending fell almost 6 percent further. Real GNP per capita dropped another 5 percent. Unemployment reached an estimated 18 percent of the total labor force. Because about four-tenths of the labor force still worked in agriculture, where workers were almost immune to cyclical unemployment, it is likely that unemployment in the nonagricultural labor force averaged over 30 percent. In the early months of 1894, when joblessness probably reached its peak, perhaps half of those seeking work in manufacturing and construction had no jobs.

For the next four years the economy performed substantially below its potential. A sharp but abbreviated recovery in 1895 failed to erase the bulk of the high unemployment, and a relapse in 1896 pushed the estimated rate of joblessness back over 14 percent of the total labor force. Investment spending rode a roller coaster: up in 1895, down in 1896, up in 1897, down in 1898 before a sustained increase into the new century. Real GNP per capita mirrored the instability of investment, beginning a significant sustained increase and substantially exceeding the level of 1892 only after 1898. For 1893–1898 the estimated rate of unemployment averaged over 14 percent of the total labor force, hence some 20 percent of the industrial labor force.[23]

Only the Great Depression of the 1930s was more severe than the depression of the 1890s. But because the earlier slump began at a much lower level of income—real GNP per capita in 1892 equaled only 55 percent of the corresponding figure for 1929—the collapse in the nineties pushed its victims to a much lower level of economic well-being than that reached at the bottom of the Great Depression. Even at the cyclical trough in 1933, the real GNP per capita exceeded that of the prosperous year 1892 by over 20 percent.[24] Without doubt the mid-nineties witnessed enormous distress and suffering, especially in the large industrial cities during that first terrible depression winter of 1893–1894.

Not surprisingly the dire conditions gave rise to widespread social unrest and protest. In the spring of 1894 popular discontent crystallized in the form of "industrial armies," bands of unemployed men marching to the national capital to present their "petitions with boots on" demanding relief. The best known was Coxey's Commonweal Army, a group of several hundred that Jacob S. Coxey, a radical businessman, led from Ohio to Washington in April. Coxey met an anticlimactic end at a May Day demonstration: Washington police attacked his followers with clubs and arrested him for walking on the grass. More than a dozen other protest groups—one in the West comprising some five thousand men—traversed the country, alternately frightening and amusing the people they encountered. Though many commentators ridiculed the industrial armies and their demands for governmental work relief, others viewed them as manifestations of the potential danger posed by a discontented and increasingly radical working class. Francis Lynde Stetson, a Wall Street lawyer who was a close friend and adviser of Cleveland, warned the President in 1894, "We are on the eve of a very dark night unless a return of commercial prosperity relieves popular discontent."[25]

To brighten that impending dark night, several respectable proponents of reform urged that the government respond to the demands of the ragged industrial armies by expanding public works projects to employ the jobless. In Massachusetts Edward Bellamy, author of the utopian novel *Looking Backward* and inspirer of the collectivist National Clubs, proposed that the state establish workshops for the unemployed. In California a state senator advocated a similar program. Other proposals, including various plans for federal action, surfaced elsewhere—their supporters including the editors of the *Journal of the Knights of Labor* and Samuel Gompers, head of the American Federation of Labor. Benjamin O. Flower, editor of the *Arena* magazine, declared that "[a]n extreme crisis demands prompt and extraordinary measures, and it is the duty of the government to rise equal to the emergency in crises like that through which we are even yet passing." He proposed that the federal government hire the unemployed for such tasks as repairing the levees along the Mississippi River, paying the workers in newly issued fiat paper money. Never before had proposals for governmental work relief received such extensive agitation.[26]

Only a small segment of the public and a handful of politicians responded favorably to the proposals for state or federal public works programs to relieve unemployment. Voicing the dominant ideology, Congressman M. D. Harter declared that "it is not the business of the United States to raise prices, provide work, regulate wages, or in any way to interfere in the private business or personal affairs of the people."[27] Democratic Governor Roswell P. Flower of New York, while lamenting in the autumn of 1893 the "thousands of persons who have been thrown out of employment," asserted that a governmental work-relief program would create "a dangerous precedent for the future, justifying paternal legislation of all kinds and encouraging prodigal extravagance."[28] Senator James H. Berry of Arkansas, an ex-Confederate who had lost a leg in the war, expressed astonishment on the floor of the Senate at the idea "that now, because times are hard, this Government should be more liberal in appropriating money. That is not my theory of the Constitution. My idea is that each individual citizen of the United States should look to himself, and it is not the purpose of this Government to give work to individuals throughout the United States by appropriating money which belongs to other people and does not belong to the Senate."[29] Conforming to the dominant ideology, neither the federal nor the state governments provided any work relief in the 1890s. All help for the unemployed came from the traditional sources, private charities and local governments.

While the jobless languished in the cities, the depression in the countryside took the form of extraordinarily low agricultural prices and incomes. Corn, which had brought about forty cents a bushel in the early nineties, fell to twenty-five cents in 1895 and even less the next year. Wheat, which had sold for more than eighty cents a bushel in 1890–1891, dropped to only about fifty cents during 1893–1895. Cotton plunged in 1894 to less than five cents a pound, the lowest price in memory and scarcely half the value obtained in 1892.[30] As the taxes, interest, and prices paid by farmers had not fallen proportionately, agricultural producers found themselves caught in a painful price-cost squeeze.

Desperately seeking means of extricating themselves, some of the hardest pressed farmers gave their support to Populist panaceas such as silver-fed inflation or stricter regulation of railroad rates. The Populist platform of 1892 also endorsed a subtreasury plan whereby the federal government, on the security of crop deposits, would make loans of fiat currency to farmers at interest rates below those prevailing in the financial markets.[31] (Four decades later a similar scheme was enacted by Congress, and it has played an important part in the government's subsidization of farmers ever since.)

In 1896 a novel proposal to raise the price of wheat appeared from an unexpected source, the Russian minister at Washington. The plan called for the governments of the major wheat-exporting countries to form a cartel to control the international marketing of wheat and maintain its price at a high level. Secretary of State Richard Olney passed along the proposal to the Secretary of Agriculture, J. Sterling Morton, whose response was a paradigm of ideological allegiance to the free market. "In my judgment," he said, "it is not the business of government to attempt, by statutes or international agreements, to override the fixed laws of economics, nor can government repeal, amend, or mitigate the operation of those laws."[32] Of course the United States government did nothing to promote the formation of such a cartel in the 1890s. Doing so would have required that policymakers first escape from severely binding ideological restraints.

SAVING THE GOLD STANDARD

After Reconstruction no national issue (except possibly the tariff) provoked such heated political controversy as the question of monetary standards. While adhering to a de facto gold standard after 1878, the government was not required de jure to maintain that standard. The Bland-Allison Act of 1878 and the Sherman Silver Purchase Act of 1890 kept alive the hopes of silverites. Indeed the act of 1890 had more than symbolic significance. Milton Friedman and Anna Schwartz have concluded that during the fiscal years 1891–1893 "Treasury action was on a scale large enough . . . that . . . if indefinitely maintained, [it] would have driven the United States off the gold standard entirely by its direct effects on the money stock."[33] Many contemporaries appreciated this looming potentiality and reacted by hoarding or exporting gold. The fluctuating prospects of the gold standard and the consequent erratic capital flows threatened wider repercussions. Some observers blamed them for the depression that had become a painful reality by the summer of 1893.

No one embraced this belief more than Cleveland. "Manifestly," said the new President in his inaugural speech of March 4, 1893, "nothing is more vital to our supremacy as a nation and to the beneficient purposes of our Government than a sound and stable currency. . . . [S]o far as the executive branch of the Government can intervene," he promised, "none of the powers with which it is invested will be withheld when their exercise is deemed necessary to maintain our national credit or avert financial disaster."[34]

Throughout 1893 the need for such intervention grew steadily more pressing. Many of the silver certificates issued by the Treasury in accordance with the Sherman Silver Purchase Act, plus many outstanding United States notes ("greenbacks" surviving from the original issue during the Civil War), were being brought to the Treasury for redemption in gold. Since the resumption of convertibility between currency and gold at par in 1879, the Treasury had sought to maintain a gold reserve of at least $100 million. Late in April the reserve for the first time fell below this amount, and apprehension spread that the government would soon be forced to abandon the gold standard. Encouraged by letters from businessmen and bankers, Cleveland decided in June to call a special session of Congress for the express purpose of repealing the Sherman Silver Purchase Act. The session began on August 7. Vigorous opposition by silverites prolonged the deliberations, but finally, late in October, Congress passed a repeal bill, which the President signed into law on November 1. Though economic conditions late in 1893 provided scant cause for cheer, proponents of the gold standard believed that their legislative success augured well both for preservation of the gold standard and for rapid recovery from the depression.

Neither objective was to be achieved so easily. The economy plunged even lower as winter set in, and fears for the gold standard continued to spread. By year's end the gold reserve had fallen to only $81 million, largely because of withdrawals needed to offset the government's unanticipated shortfalls of revenue as the depression deepened. The administration requested authority to use novel means to deal with the deficit, but Congress did not respond. Secretary of the Treasury John G. Carlisle, firmly committed to the maintenance of "sound money," fell back on the only means at his disposal.

On January 17, 1894, he announced the offering of a $50 million bond issue to be sold for gold. The offering at first elicited little response from the public, but negotiations between the Treasury and the leading New York bankers ultimately resulted in disposition of the bonds on reasonably favorable terms. Unfortunately about a third of the gold received by the Treasury was its own; it had been withdrawn in exchange for paper currency and then used to purchase the bonds. Nevertheless the bond sale raised the gold reserve to more than $107 million, providing at least temporary protection of the gold standard against those speculating that it would soon collapse.

Cleveland and Carlisle paid a heavy political price for the bond issue. According to Cleveland's biographer, letters inundated them, "denouncing them as traitors, Judases, tools of the bloated baronage of wealth, friends of financial bloodsuckers." The authors of the letters, sincerely convinced of the miraculous powers of silver-based money, "believed that a coalition with the great bankers to maintain the costly gold dollar was an alliance to crush the poor deeper into the mire."[35]

In view of the vituperative reaction to the bond issue, Cleveland and Carlisle must have deeply regretted the necessity of another issue when the gold reserve dipped to about $60 million in November. A syndicate of New York banks took the entire second issue of $50 million in gold bonds. The government had again sustained the gold standard at enormous cost in political support, especially among Westerners and Southerners.

Still the problem persisted. Unalterably determined to preserve the gold standard and convinced that its abandonment would cause "sudden and catastrophic disaster," Cleveland and Carlisle entered into secret negotiations with the titans of Wall Street, J. P. Morgan and August Belmont. A way had to be found to restore the gold reserve without draining part of the Treasury's initial gold stock in the process. The government also needed to diminish public fears and to discourage the gold hoarding and short-term capital exports of speculators against the dollar. The syndicate headed by Morgan and Belmont promised to achieve these goals by, in effect, controlling the foreign exchange market. In February 1895 the Treasury and the syndicate signed a contract that pledged the government to issue $62 million in 30-year bonds priced to yield 3.75 percent in exchange for about $65 million in gold and the bankers' commitment to protect the Treasury from withdrawals of gold. It worked. For the next five months no gold was withdrawn from the Treasury, and confidence in the government's ability to maintain the gold standard was restored.[36]

Again the hostile spirits raged in reaction. "By the hundreds of thousands," said Allan Nevins, "hard-handed Americans believed that Cleveland and Carlisle had sold the credit of the republic to the Morgans and Rothchilds . . . that bloodsucking Jews and aliens . . . a set of vampires . . . [had] control of our destiny."[37] Anger boiled up within the Western and Southern demagogues and their legions of followers.

Cleveland and Carlisle never doubted that they had done the right thing—right both in the sense of expedient and in the sense of moral. The Morgan-Belmont syndicate made a large profit from its resale of the bonds (purchased from the government on February 8 at 104.5, the bonds were resold to the public on February 20 at 112.25), surprising those who had believed that the public was unwilling to take the bonds on terms acceptable to the government. The emergency, at least in some minds, justified the government's clandestine dealings with the syndicate. "There was," observed the New York *Evening Post*, "no time for prolonged negotiations. . . . If ever there was an emergency in public finance . . . the last week in January [1895] was the time."[38]

At the end of 1895 the Treasury again acted to maintain the gold reserve, issuing $100 million in bonds for direct sale to the public. The sale was an immediate success, and the gold standard soared out of the danger zone. Later the Gold Standard Act of 1900 provided a statutory basis for the monetary standard that the Cleveland administration had fought so desperately to preserve throughout the dark days of the mid-nineties.

The pervasiveness of ideology in the monetary controversies of the late nineteenth century is difficult nowadays to appreciate. Consider, for example, Bryan's famous Cross of Gold speech, which captivated the Democratic National Convention in 1896 and catapulted the orator into the presidential nomination. The speech, regarded as one of the most successful in American history, exhibits as well as anything can the essence of ideological expression. Two powerful metaphors, holy war and Jesus Christ Himself, dominate its rhetoric.

> The humblest citizen in all the land, when clad in the armor of a righteous cause, is stronger than all the hosts of error. I come to speak to you in defense of a cause as holy as the cause of liberty—the cause of humanity. . . . Our war is not a war of conquest; we are fighting in the defense of our homes, our families, and posterity. . . . [I]f [tariff] protection has slain its thousands, the gold standard has slain its tens of thousands. . . . Here is the line of battle. . . . You shall not press down upon the brow of labor this crown of thorns, you shall not crucify mankind upon a cross of gold.[39]

This paradigmatic ideological rhetoric actually related (a modern economist might say) to the federal government's choice of gold or silver as the metal for which it would support the price expressed in units of paper currency. In the minds of contemporaries on both sides, however, fundamental values were at stake. Gold versus silver had come to symbolize an entire complex of issues dividing the polity.

For Cleveland, Carlisle, and their comrades, preservation of the gold standard meant preservation of "sound money." They believed that defeating the proposals for silver-based currency would restore the confidence of investors and propel the economy out of the depression. But sound money meant much more than that to them. As Wiebe has said, Cleveland acted out of "an overriding compulsion to save civilization." Financial probity lay at the heart of his ideology, just as it did with equal but opposite force in the ideology of his opponents. "Gold was the shield of civilized life," and his defense of the gold standard was "pulling society back from the brink of disaster."[40]

MAINTAINING LAW AND ORDER IN THE LABOR MARKET

The rapid technical and organizational changes of the late nineteenth century created a new milieu for employees and employers. More and more employees worked for corporate employers. More and more employers hired huge work forces, supervised by a hierarchy of foremen and salaried managers. The emancipation of the slaves and the enormous influx of immigrants added new racial and ethnic frictions to the already tense transactions of the labor market. The close personal proximity and community institutions that previously had helped to make the linkage of employer and employee more than a "naked cash nexus" were increasingly attenuated. As the old, informally paternalistic relationships declined and a more dynamic, impersonal labor market lurched unpredictably from year to year, misunderstandings and mutual hostility became progressively more common.[41]

Labor unions, with their organizational tactics, attempts at collective bargaining, and episodic strikes, galled employers mightily. Many bosses—and others, including many workers—questioned the legitimacy of unions as representatives of individual workers. Employers resented the challenge to their prerogatives to manage their own private property and contractual affairs. By the second half of the nineteenth century the courts were generally holding that the mere existence and collective-bargaining activities of unions did not violate the law, but important legal questions remained unsettled, especially those pertaining to the permissible bounds of strikes, picketing, and boycotts. With economic and legal conditions in flux, workers and employers often took matters into their own hands, each side attempting to achieve its own objectives at the expense of the other. "Industrial conflict in America," as seen by European visitors at the turn of the century, "was a man-to-man fight, with no quarter asked or given, unmitigated by the tradition of subordination on the one hand, or benevolence and responsibility on the other."[42]

When determined parties on both sides refused to yield, violence frequently ensued. "In the absence of rules and norms, only force can decide a dispute, and . . . labor disputes were particularly violent in the United States in that generation."[43] The great railroad strikes and associated riots in the summer of 1877 caused death and destruction in several areas of the country and were quelled only after federal troops came to the aid of state militias. Though much less costly in lives and property, Chicago's Haymarket riot of

1886 provoked widespread fears for the stability and order of society. In July 1892 a strike at Carnegie's Homestead works near Pittsburgh degenerated into a small war between private armies; casualties mounted to sixteen dead and some sixty wounded before the militia arrived to restore order. Simultaneously, far to the west, striking miners battled strikebreakers in another industrial free-for-all at the silver mines of Coeur d'Alene, Idaho. Again troops had to be called out. At Buffalo in August 1892 thousands of state militiamen intervened in a strike by switchmen. Apprehension of impending anarchy spread across the land.

The public's outrage focused on two aspects of the disorderly industrial relations, especially those involving the railroads: the violence itself, which directly threatened lives and property, and the spillover costs. "The mischievous and outrageous feature of these strikes," observed the Minneapolis *Times*, "is the total disregard of the rights of the public, which is usually the greatest sufferer. . . . [F]or the general disturbance of business and the indirect damage sustained by whole communities, anything like adequate redress is out of the question."[44] To restore order forcibly the state militias and the federal army could be employed, but their intervention in labor disputes, a last resort, signaled that the situation had got frightfully out of hand. Although most people approved the use of troops in extreme circumstances, few wished to rely exclusively on such raw coercion.[45] It seemed far more economical, not to mention civilized, to devise a means of keeping potentially violent labor disputes from reaching the flash point. In quest of such means, private attorneys and federal judges were groping for new legal devices in the early nineties.

The solution they hit upon was to apply an established instrument of equitable relief, the injunction, in a new way. Federal judges began to enjoin railroad workers from abruptly abandoning their employment en masse and from inducing boycotts that would restrain or destroy interstate commerce. District Judge Augustus J. Ricks, recognizing the novelty of this proceeding, maintained that "[e]very just order or rule known to equity courts was born of some emergency to meet some new condition and was therefore in its time without a precedent." U.S. Supreme Court Justice David J. Brewer agreed that "the powers of a court of equity are as vast and its processes and procedure as elastic as all the changing emergencies of increasingly complex business relations and the protection of rights can demand." Aldace F. Walker, a railroad spokesman, argued that the injunctions were only a new means to secure established rights. "The only extension or enlargement perceptible in the recent cases," he said, "is in the use of the mandatory injunction for the enforcement of well-known rights and obligations; this is supported by precedents in other directions and can be employed without objection, being wholly in the direction of the preservation of personal rights and protection of public interests."[46] Despite some reservations about the desirability of such enlarged judicial powers, early reaction to the new application of injunctions was generally favorable. Observers of varied political persuasions hoped that the new legal procedure would help to preserve order and prevent violence from breaking out in industrial disputes.[47]

In 1894 the depression resulted in vast layoffs and sharp wage cuts, causing unprecedented labor unrest. Some 1,400 strikes, involving more than 500,000 workers, took place. In the spring more than 100,000 bituminous coal miners walked off their jobs across the northern coal region. Here and there violence flared. With the arrival of summer, passions got hotter, too.

A labor dispute at the "model town" of Pullman, near Chicago, provided the spark to ignite an enormous conflagration. Workers at the Pullman Palace Car Company, whose wages had been cut but whose rents for company housing had not been reduced, sought the aid of the newly formed American Railway Union. Led by Eugene V. Debs, who would later become the leading American socialist and a frequent candidate for the presidency, members of the ARU had the flush of victory on their faces; in April they had conducted a successful strike against James J. Hill's Great Northern Railway. The ARU decided to boycott, starting June 26, the handling of all trains that included Pullman cars. When the union men did so, they were fired and nonunion replacements were hired by the various railroad companies, whose contracts obliged them to pull the Pullman cars and who were in any event not parties to the Pullman dispute. Soon some sixty thousand railroad workers in Chicago and the entire region to the south and west were on strike. "To the conservative mind of the 1890s, subject to growing fears of unruly majorities and class conflict, the decision of the American Railway Union to press ahead with a boycott and strike, despite all considerations of contractual and property rights and the public necessity, smacked of the most irresponsible radicalism, of 'anarchy' and 'communism.'"[48]

As always the public feared most the potential for violence. Debs publicly exhorted his followers to refrain from violent acts. But many people—certainly most contemporary conservatives—must have agreed with federal Judge James G. Jenkins, who shrilly asserted that "[it] is idle to talk of a peaceable strike. None such ever occurred. The suggestion is impeachment of intelligence. From first to last . . . force and turbulence, violence and outrage, arson, and murder, have been associated with the strike as its natural and inevitable concomitants."[49]

Fearing the violence of strikers and union sympathizers, the conservatives prepared to exert massive counterforce. In Washington during the last days of June, Attorney General Richard Olney was closely monitoring the events at Chicago. He appreciated both the potential usefulness of an injunction—he had previously used one in dealing with "industrial armies" in the West—and the possibility that troops might be required. Basing the federal government's involvement on its responsibility to remove obstructions of interstate commerce, including interstate carriage of the mails, Olney did not intend to wait until local officials requested federal assistance. Illinois Governor John P. Altgeld, a labor union sympathizer, might not ask for federal aid until the situation was out of hand. "I feel," Olney wired his special agent in Chicago, "that the true way of dealing with the matter is by a force which is overwhelming and prevents any attempt at resistance."[50]

By the beginning of July, railroad traffic was disrupted from Chicago to Texas and all the way to the Pacific coast. Movement of trains in and out of Chicago, the hub of the national rail network, had virtually ceased. Livestock, food, fuel, and other vital supplies were no longer reaching their destinations. On July 2 mob violence erupted at Blue Island, south of Chicago.

Federal authorities sprang into action. With authorization by Olney, whose instructions had been approved by the President, the federal district attorney at Chicago asked the federal district court for an injunction. It was immediately issued. Its terms were sweeping. The court ordered several named defendants (Debs and other officers of the ARU)

> and all persons combining and conspiring with them, and all other persons whomsoever, absolutely to desist and refrain from in any way or manner interfering with, hindering, obstructing or stopping any of the business of any of the following named railroads [subsequently listed] . . . ; and from compelling or inducing or attempting to compel or induce, by threats, intimidation, persuasion, force, or violence, any of the employees of any of said railroads to refuse or fail to perform any of their duties as employees of any of said railroads . . . [or] to leave the service of such railroads; and from preventing any person whatever, by threats, intimidation, force, or violence from entering the service of any of said railroads and doing the work thereof.[51]

To make sure that the injunction would be adequately enforced, Olney on July 3 urged the President to send federal troops into Chicago. At least two members of the Cabinet as well as the Army's departmental commander in the West opposed the action at first, but Olney won over the reluctant officials by showing them a telegram from the U.S. Marshall who had faced the mob at Blue Island the previous day. "An emergency has arisen," wired the marshall, pleading for federal troops to assist him in containing the actual and the even greater potential mob violence. Cleveland authorized sending the soldiers, and on July 4 some two thousand troops from Fort Sheridan took up positions in and near Chicago.[52]

Governor Altgeld, who had not asked for the troops, protested in a long wire to the President. "[A]ll these troubles were local in character," he said, "and could easily be handled by the State authorities." Calling the unilateral federal action a "violation of a basic principle of our institutions," he asked for the immediate withdrawal of the troops. Cleveland responded that he had sent them "in strict accordance with the Constitution and laws of the United States" to maintain the free flow of interstate commerce and that he had "no intention of thereby interfering with the plain duty of the local authorities to preserve the peace of the city." When Altgeld sent another long telegram the following day the President, in no mood to continue the exchange of views, responded curtly: "While I am still persuaded that I have neither transcended my authority or duty in the emergency that confronts us, it seems to me that in this hour of danger and public distress, discussion may well give way to active effort on the part of all in authority to restore obedience to law and to protect life and property."[53]

While the federal troops were taking up positions at Chicago, the opposing "commanders" were expressing their divergent expectations. In Washington, Olney told reporters that the country had been brought to "the ragged edge of anarchy." He looked forward to a demonstration that the forces of law and order could restore public peace. At the same time, Debs made an inflammatory declaration to a reporter in Chicago. "The first shots fired by the regular soldiers at the mobs here," he prophesied, "will be the signal for a civil war. . . . Bloodshed will follow, and ninety per cent of the people of the United States will be arrayed against the other ten per cent."[54]

Debs's forecast proved erroneous; but although civil war did not erupt, ferocious mob violence did. Engulfed in what Nevins described as "almost a reign of terror," Chicago became the scene of looting, burning, and vast destruction of property. Gunshots were exchanged. Youths, hoodlums, and overexcited lumpenproletarians plunged into the disorder and magnified it. On July 6, Altgeld finally ordered the state militia into the city. The next day the violence reached its climax. William H. Taft, the future President and Chief Justice, wrote in a personal letter that the "situation in Chicago is very alarming and distressing and until they have had much bloodletting, it will not be better. . . . Word comes tonight that thirty men have been killed by the federal troops. Though it is bloody business, everybody hopes that it is true."[55] The report heard by Taft was somewhat inaccurate, exaggerating the number of deaths. Still, the riot caused great loss of life and property: More than twenty persons were killed, many more wounded, some two thousand railroad cars and much other property destroyed. Eventually the fourteen thousand soldiers in and around Chicago, along with militiamen and federal troops in twenty other states, suppressed the violence and restored order. As railroad workers streamed back to their jobs the strike was broken and the ARU effectively extinguished. By July 13 the trains were again moving freely throughout the country. On July 19 the federal troops withdrew from Chicago.

Public opinion seemed overwhelmingly to approve the Cleveland administration's actions.[56] Even after the inflamed passions of the immediate crisis had cooled, most people approved. Of course the conservatives were happy; but so were many others. Seymour D. Thompson, the "progressive" editor of the *American Law Review*, concluded that "[c]onservative and patriotic opinion everywhere approves the action of the president and rejoices that, at an unusual crisis, we had a president possessing the nerve to take the responsibility. . . . [The railroad companies had] entered upon a struggle with an unknown and appalling force, which threatened to revolutionize the very foundations of society and to reverse all the processes by which our splendid industrial system has been built up. In the stand which they took, they represented the right of every man to manage his own business and to keep his own contracts without dictation from third persons."[57]

The most notorious of the "third persons," Eugene Debs, along with several other leaders of the ARU, was arrested on July 17 for violating the federal injunction. Found guilty of contempt of court, he was sentenced to six months in prison. On May 27, 1895, the U.S. Supreme Court upheld the lower court's approval of the government's actions. Debs's attorney, like Altgeld before him, challenged the authority of the federal government to inject itself uninvited into a "local" affair. The Court rejected the contention. Delivering a unanimous decision, Justice Brewer declared that "there is no such impotency in the national government. The entire strength of the nation may be used to enforce in any part of the land the full and free exercise of all national powers and the security of all rights entrusted by the Constitution to its care. The strong arm of the national government may be put forth to brush away all obstructions to the freedom of interstate commerce or the transportation of the mails. If the emergency arises, the army of the Nation, and all its militia, are at the service of the Nation to compel obedience to its laws."[58]

The labor injunction, conceived in an atmosphere of crisis and established in a genuine national emergency, became a major instrument of federal involvement in the labor markets for almost four decades. Behind the injunction, armed men stood ready to serve as the ultimate enforcers of law and order in labor disputes. Thus did the Debs rebellion and the government's hastily devised response to it have long-enduring consequences.[59]

Though some, particularly in legal circles, worried about the expansion of judicial powers represented by the injunctions and their validation by the Supreme Court in the *Debs* case, most contemporaries approved of these developments. The New York *Voice* reported the bad news: "The decision of the Supreme Court puts into the hands of Federal judges tremendous powers in the case of any future interruption of interstate traffic." The good news was that "a repetition of the scenes of last summer [1894] will be next to impossible hereafter." The New York *Nation's* editor held that the Court's decision "fully indorsing the course taken by the President, and asserting the supreme power of the federal Government in such an emergency" meant that "Debs, Altgeld and Co. have thus unconsciously rendered the country a great service . . . for it is an immense gain to have so important a principle of constitutional construction definitely settled."[60]

STRIKING DOWN THE INCOME TAX

For three decades after the Civil War the federal government faced a fiscal problem now almost beyond comprehension: a chronic surplus of revenue over expenditure. The surplus arose from the combination of rapid economic growth, with its concomitant increase in the volume of imports, and the high-tariff policy of the Republican administrations that ruled almost continuously during that era. In the absence of appreciable political leeway for tariff reduction the government's main response to the embarrassingly routine surpluses was to authorize greater and greater largess for the Civil War veterans and their (ever more distant) dependent relatives. The veterans' pension program, which has been aptly described as the "first large-scale federal welfare system," consumed by 1890 more than a third of the budget.[61] Despite the prodigality of the pensions, the budgetary surpluses persisted, pouring into the Treasury in every fiscal year of the period 1866–1893.

The comfortable condition of the government's postwar finances completely undercut the original *raison d'être* of the income tax law that Congress had enacted first in 1861 and then reenacted several times during and after the war. After taxing the incomes generated in each year of the decade 1862–1871, Congress finally repealed the income-tax law in 1872. But the idea persisted. Congressional proponents of the income tax submitted sixty-eight bills to restore it between 1874 and 1894. They intended to substitute income taxes, which would be borne mainly if not entirely by the rich, for the tariff, which in their judgment burdened mainly if not exclusively the poor. The income tax was seen by proponents and opponents alike as primarily an instrument of redistribution; in the parlance of the time it was "class legislation." Not surprisingly such disaffected groups as the Greenback Party, the Farmers' Alliances, and the Populists formed the vanguard of its supporters.

After two decades of frustration, congressional proponents of the income tax succeeded in adding it to the revenue act of 1894 (often called the Wilson-Gorman Tariff Act after its sponsors, William L. Wilson in the House and Arthur P. Gorman in the Senate). It was not what the President had wanted. Cleveland's major objective, indeed the central plank of his platform, was to reduce tariffs drastically. Recognizing that tariff reduction would diminish federal revenues, the President in his annual message of December 1893 had endorsed as offsets "a few additional internal-revenue taxes, including a small tax upon incomes derived from certain corporate investments"—a far cry from advocacy of a general income tax.[62] Much more comprehensive income-tax provisions found their way into Wilson's bill as a result of dedicated efforts by two of the three members of the House Subcommittee on Internal Taxation: Benton McMillin, a Democrat and longtime proponent of the income tax, and William Jennings Bryan, a Democrat soon to be embraced by the Populists. Though the Senate subsequently removed the sweeping tariff reductions from the Wilson bill, it permitted the income-tax sections to stand. Cleveland, peeved that the law finally enacted by Congress on August 15, 1894, made only slight cuts in the tariffs, allowed it to become law without his signature.

A contemporary analyst observed that "[t]he income tax was not regarded primarily as a fiscal measure. Little was known as to how much it would yield and apparently no one cared very much to know. Almost a year and a half was to elapse from the time of its introduction before its first fruits would flow into the treasury. It could not therefore have commended itself because of its efficiency as an instrument for the immediate relief of the treasury."[63] Clearly the income-tax law was intended primarily to balance the tax burden caused by the existing tariffs, which were generally believed to hurt the poor disproportionately.

The tariffs were also regarded as geographically inequitable, burdening the South and the West while aiding the Northeast, where the protected industries were concentrated. The sectional element revealed itself starkly when the House voted on the internal-revenue amendment to the tariff bill: of 182 votes in favor of the amendment, 177 were cast by representatives from the South and the West. When the Senate voted, not a single senator from the Northeast supported the income tax.[64]

Ignoring the alleged regressivity of the tariff, congressional opponents of the income tax railed against it, calling it a "sop to socialism." Amid the economic, social, and political upheavals of the time—Nevins called the year beginning July 1, 1894, "the *année terrible* of American history between Reconstruction and the World War"— it was inevitable that many would view the income tax as another aspect of a revolutionary undoing of the established order.[65] Speaking to the New York State Bar Association, John F. Dillon, a leading attorney and former federal judge, denounced the new tax as "a forced contribution from the rich for the benefit of the poor. . . . [As such it was] class legislation of the most pronounced and vicious type . . . violative of the constitutional rights of the property owner, subversive of the existing social polity, and essentially revolutionary."[66] Of course, not everyone agreed that the tax was unconstitutional; the Supreme Court would have to decide.

By modern standards the income-tax law of 1894 set a very low rate and affected only a tiny proportion of the population. It exacted from an individual taxpayer 2 percent of the income, defined to include gifts and inheritances, in excess of $4,000. From a corporate taxpayer it took 2 percent of the firm's entire profit; that is, the $4,000 exemption did not apply to corporations. Double taxation of corporate dividends was precluded by an appropriate adjustment to the taxable income of individuals. Many institutions—including charitable, religious, and educational associations, building and loan associations, mutual savings banks, and mutual insurance companies—did not have to pay the tax.

Besides resenting the 2 percent exaction, opponents of the tax saw it as an entering wedge for much greater, perhaps even confiscatory, taxes at a later date. (Indeed many supporters of the tax viewed it similarly.)[67] They hastened therefore to challenge the constitutionality of the law before the Supreme Court. With the cooperation of the U.S. Solicitor General and the use of some questionable legal legerdemain, the case of *Pollock* v. *Farmers' Loan and Trust Company* was expedited directly to the U.S. Supreme Court, where it was consolidated with two other cases, *Hyde* v. *Continental Trust Company* and *Moore* v. *Miller*, for an early hearing. The case was argued from March 7 to March 13 and decided on April 8, 1895.[68]

It was a genuine Great Case. Nevins judged that it "unquestionably excited more feeling than any action by the Supreme Court since the Dred Scott opinion." According to a legal historian it "attracted as much attention in the press of the entire country as any case in the history of the Court." Many newspapers reported each day's arguments in minute detail and at great length.[69] The case received so much attention because it encapsulated much of the socio-political conflict of the time: poor against rich, agriculture against industry, competition against monopoly, rural against urban, the underdeveloped hinterlands against the more developed Northeast. The nation held its collective breath while the contending attorneys argued before the eight supreme justices (one being absent because of illness).

The strictly legal arguments turned mainly on two issues. First, counsel opposing the income tax argued that it was a direct tax and therefore unconstitutional because it was not apportioned among the states according to their populations as required by the Constitution (Article I, Section 2). Second, even if it were not a direct tax, it was still unconstitutional, because its various exemptions violated the constitutional requirement that "all duties, imposts and excises shall be uniform throughout the United States" (Article I, Section 8). The government's lawyers, led by Attorney General Olney, replied that the Supreme Court had always held that only poll taxes and property taxes were direct taxes, and that the uniformity requirement for indirect taxes applied not among classes of taxpayers but among the several states.

In an argument attuned to the conservative legal mentality of the justices, Olney urged that distinctions between direct and indirect taxes propounded by economists and other scholars had no bearing on the case. All that mattered was the Court's own previous decisions, which had never failed to grant plenary powers of taxation to Congress and to define only poll and property taxes as direct. This prior "constitutional exposition" Olney characterized as "practically coeval with the Constitution itself. . . . To reject it after a century's duration is to set a hurtful precedent and would go far to prove that government by written constitution is not a thing of stable principles, but of the fluctuating views and wishes of the particular period and the particular judges when and from whom its interpretation happens to be called for." In conclusion the Attorney General called upon the Court to remain within its proper constitutional domain: the judicial branch of the government should not "supplant the political in the exercise of the taxing power"; it should not "substitute its discretion for that of Congress in respect of the subjects of taxation, the plan of taxation, and all the distinctions and discriminations by which taxation is sought to be equitably adjusted to the resources and capacities of the different classes of society."[70]

Counsel on both sides, especially during the final days of their oral presentations, generated as much ideological heat as legal light. James C. Carter, arguing in favor of the income tax, freely admitted that it was class legislation. He maintained, however, that the existing tax system rested just as squarely on class legislation but "in the wrong direction." He warned that the Court would be unwise to invalidate the income-tax law and that it ought to "accept the voice of the majority as final."[71]

Carter's undisguised resort to majoritarianism provoked opposing attorney Joseph H. Choate to righteous indignation. "I believe," he began his plea, "there are private rights of property here to be protected. . . . The act of Congress which we are impugning before you is communistic in its purposes and tendencies, and is defended here upon principles as communistic, socialistic—what shall I call them—populistic as ever have been addressed to any political assembly in the world." Peering apprehensively into the future, Choate issued an apocalyptic warning to the Court: "There is protection now or never. . . . You cannot hereafter exercise any check if you now say that Congress is untrammelled and uncontrollable."[72]

Choate followed up his ideological jeremiads with an artful argument for designating the income tax a direct tax: the income yielded by property is substantively indistinguishable from the property itself; hence a tax on the income is equivalent to a tax on the property, and thus both are direct taxes. He also attempted to make microscopic distinctions between the issues at hand and those involved in previous decisions, hoping to take the Court off the hook of stare decisis—the doctrine that a court is bound by previous rulings in the same jurisdiction on essentially similar questions.

Choate closed his argument by reminding the justices of the profound importance of the case. "I do not believe," he declared, "that any member of this court ever has sat or ever will sit to hear and decide a case the consequences of which will be so far-reaching as this." The case involved "the preservation of the fundamental rights of private property and equality before the law, and the ability of the people of these United States to rely upon the guarantees of the Constitution." Finally he urged the justices to exercise the authority of judicial review. The Court, he insisted, "*has* the power to set aside an act of Congress violative of the Constitution."[73]

The *Pollock* case placed the Court, especially the more conservative justices, in a difficult position. On the one hand, stare decisis must be accorded respect. The Court's previous decisions, going all the way back to the *Hylton* case of 1796, seemed clearly to call for upholding the power of Congress to levy an income tax without apportionment. On the other hand, following Choate, the Court might decide that none of the previous cases involved precisely the same substantive questions now at issue and that prior judicial pronouncements of direct pertinence were therefore only dicta, not established principles. Olney's legally conservative argument in favor of continuity in the determination of constitutional questions, quite apart from how one chose to characterize the facts involved in previous cases, must have carried considerable weight. However, the more ideologically conservative justices—certainly the venerable Stephen J. Field and his nephew David J. Brewer and probably Chief Justice Melville W. Fuller as well—no doubt shared Choate's dark forebodings about the threat to private property rights should the income-tax law be upheld.

Unable to reconcile the opposing considerations, the Court tried in its decision announced on April 8, 1895, to split the difference. Accepting the logic of Choate's argument but limiting its application, the Court ruled that a tax on the income from real estate, being indistinguishable from a tax on real estate itself, was a direct tax and therefore unconstitutional because it was not apportioned among the states according to population. The decision also held—on this point the justices were unanimous—that Congress had no power to tax the income yielded by the bonds of states or municipalities. On the remaining questions the justices were equally divided and therefore expressed no opinion.

The majority opinion, rendered by Chief Justice Fuller, did not go far enough to satisfy the hoary Justice Field, who had served on the Court since 1863. Decrying the income-tax law as class legislation and denouncing the "gross and arbitrary distinctions" made by it, Field concluded his concurring opinion with the oft-quoted prediction that "[t]he present assault upon capital is but the beginning. It will be but the stepping-stone to others, larger and more sweeping, till our political contests will become a war of the poor against the rich; a war constantly growing in intensity and bitterness."[74] He thought the entire income-tax law should be voided.

Justices Edward D. White and John M. Harlan forcefully dissented. Noting that the Court had overthrown its own long-settled and previously undisputed interpretation, White wrote that the decision was "fraught with danger to the court, to each and every citizen, and to the republic." With what now seems great prescience, he made Olney's argument his own and warned that "[i]f the permanency of [the Court's] conclusions is to depend upon the personal opinions of those who, from time to time, may make up its membership, it will inevitably become a theatre of political strife, and its action will be without coherence or consistency."[75]

The half-loaf dispensed by the Court satisfied no one. Counsel opposing the income tax moved immediately for a rehearing before the full Court (that is, including Justice Howell E. Jackson, who had not participated in the initial proceedings because of illness) to resolve the issues left unsettled. The Attorney General then petitioned that the rehearing consider all the issues anew. The Court accepted the proposal and scheduled limited oral arguments for May 6 through May 8. The rehearing brought forth no new arguments on either side.

On May 20, 1895, by a 5 to 4 majority, the Court declared the entire income-tax law unconstitutional. The Chief Justice, speaking for the majority, explained that "while our former conclusions remain unchanged, their scope must be enlarged by the acceptance of their logical consequences."[76] In fact, all the Court had done was to extend the argument previously used to void the taxation of income from real property so that it applied to the taxation of income from personal (tangible) property as well. Notwithstanding the extension, many forms of income—indeed all payments for the services of labor, whether unskilled, skilled, or professional—might have remained constitutionally vulnerable to taxation. But with so much of the income-tax law invalidated the Court declared that the entire law, not just the provisions explicitly found defective, must fall.

Each of the justices in the minority wrote a strongly worded dissenting opinion. Harlan's filled almost fifty pages of the official report. He prophesied that "a departure by this court from a settled course of decisions on grave constitutional questions, under which vast transactions have occurred, and under which the government has been administered during great crises, will shake public confidence in the stability of the law." The second *Pollock* decision, he feared, "strikes at the very foundations of national authority, in that it denies to the general government a power which is, or may become, vital to the very existence and preservation of the Union in a national emergency." Harlan averred that the American people could not too soon amend the Constitution to nullify the *Pollock* ruling, the effect of which he characterized as "a disaster to the country."[77]

All the dissenting justices deplored the distributional consequences of the decision. In the opinion of the usually moderate Justice Brown, it entailed "nothing less than a surrender of the taxing power to the moneyed class." Brown scoffed at "the spectre of socialism . . . conjured up to frighten Congress from laying taxes upon the people in proportion to their ability to pay them" and hoped that the decision would "not prove the first step toward the submergence of the liberties of the people in a sordid despotism of wealth." Justice Jackson described the majority's decision as "the most disastrous blow ever struck at the constitutional power of Congress." White, who had previously dissented at length, recorded again his repugnance for a decision that in its results "stultifies the Constitution by making it an instrument of the most grievous wrong."[78]

The final *Pollock* decision was both conservative and revolutionary: conservative of the existing structure of private property rights yet revolutionary in the audacity with which the Supreme Court stepped beyond its traditional bounds of constitutional authority to thwart what its majority viewed as a fatal and irrevocable first step toward the political undoing of the established socioeconomic order. The decision had profound consequences. For almost twenty years it staved off the "assault upon capital" dreaded by Justice Field and the millions of substantial property holders for whom he spoke. Not until the ratification of the Sixteenth Amendment in 1913 and the consequent imposition of high tax rates during World War I would Choate's nightmare become a reality. But while they rejoiced, conservative exponents of extensive, secure private property rights might well have entertained some misgivings. For the *Pollock* decision did signal, as Olney and White foresaw, that the Court had jeopardized the permanency of its pronouncements. By making its decision turn so obviously on ideological convictions rather than the traditional doctrine of the Court, the majority led the Court far toward becoming exactly what White feared, "a theatre of political strife." In later times the performances in that theater would often bring less pleasure—indeed much pain—to conservatives in the audience.

CONCLUSIONS

Perhaps it is true that "[t]he clearest instance of the dominant role of ideology is . . . [the behavior of] the independent judiciary."[79] But the other branches of government, though more directly subject to the pressures of political survival and material self-interest, also move in accordance with the attractions and repulsions of ideology. Legislators have considerable leeway to express their ideological convictions. And the actions of the executive branch of government also bear the stamp of ideology, for the pledge to "enforce the laws" can be redeemed in various ways, and the zeal with which the Chief Executive and his subordinates perform their "duties" depends heavily on their operative ideological imperatives.

In the 1890s, ideology decisively influenced the government's response to a multifarious national emergency. The dominant ideology held that less government is better than more *except*—and it is a critically important exception—where extraordinary action is required to maintain law and order, including the monetary order of the economy. The other side of a devotion to strong but limited government is a firm commitment to extensive, secure private property rights. In the late nineteenth century most activities, including virtually all purely economic decision-making, were considered "not the proper business of government"—especially the federal government. There was therefore no ideological contradiction whatever between the government's complete lack of interest in work-relief programs or agricultural price-fixing schemes and its vigorous intervention in the labor disturbances at Chicago and elsewhere.

None of the decisions was preordained; governmental officials did have a choice. Merely counting prospective votes might easily have led the government to provide some aid to the unemployed industrial workers or, even more likely, to the suffering farmers. Cleveland and Carlisle could easily— that is, with political ease—have abandoned the gold standard; Cleveland and Olney could easily have refrained from armed intervention in the Debs riots, at least until state authorities asked for federal assistance.

Yet just as the leaders of the Cleveland administration never seriously considered becoming involved in federal work relief or an international wheat cartel, so they never worried about the political gains or losses of maintaining the gold standard (which indeed cost them dearly in political support) or restoring public order at Chicago and elsewhere in the summer of 1894. Some things a right-thinking person in authority just did not do; other things he just as heedlessly did. In such matters, ideology rather than political expediency was decisive. Nevins subtitled his biography of Cleveland "A Study in Courage," but he could have called it "A Study in Ideology." (A great deal of what historians have described as the courage of statesmen will be found upon close inspection to be behavior more in accordance with ideology than with the material interest or political expediency of the politician in question.)[80]

The federal judiciary also acted in accordance with ideological dictates. For the judges, three ideological imperatives had priority: the rule of law, private property rights and, above all, public peace. All three motivated the innovation of the labor injunction. Judge Jenkins, one of the innovators, expressed in brief the essence of the judicial response to the crisis in labor relations: "it is the duty of the courts to restrain those warring factions [of combined capital and combined labor], so far as their action may infringe the declared law of the land, that society may not be disrupted, or its peace invaded, and that individual and corporate rights may not be infringed."[81] In the *Pollock* case the Supreme Court so feared the attenuation of private property rights that it overturned its own established interpretation after a century of undisturbed rulings upholding the congressional power to levy an income tax without apportionment. Despite the Court's inherent tendency toward legal conservatism, the majority could not resist Choate's ideological plea that "there are private rights of property here to be protected."

At every point, upholders of the dominant ideology clashed with adherents of an opposing ideology. The challengers fervently desired to abandon the gold standard, to redistribute private wealth by income taxation, and to prevent the use of injunctions in labor disputes. In the 1890s the challengers' time had not yet come, as McKinley's crushing defeat of Bryan made plain. But the future belonged to them. Four decades later, in another crisis, they would vanquish the surviving proponents of the classical liberal ideology as completely as the classical liberals had triumphed over them in the crisis of the nineties.

CHAPTER SIX

The Progressive Era:
A Bridge to Modern Times

We are in a temper to reconstruct economic society . . . and political
society may itself undergo a radical modification in the process. No
age was ever more conscious of its task or more unanimously desir-
ous of radical and extended changes in its economic and political
practice.

WOODROW WILSON

The years between the recovery from the depression of the 1890s and
America's entry into World War I are known as the Progressive Era. The
term says as much about the historians who employ it as it does about the
events of the period. Although certain developments of the time, such as
rising levels of living and declining rates of mortality, conform to a general,
unobjectionable conception of "progress," other developments, such as increased governmental regulation, more centralized control of money, and the
taxation of incomes, are "progressive" only in a particular ideological perspective. That almost all historians have applauded the latter aspect of the
progressivism of the pre–World War I period says something about the
prevailing ideology of the historical profession in the twentieth century.[1]

I shall employ the term *Progressive Era* not because I accept the implicit
normative judgment of the period to which it refers but because it seems
inextricably embedded in the vocabulary of historical discourse. The burden
of justification always rests on those who would coin new terms for familiar
ideas. My purposes can be served well enough by the established usage, but
its potential irony may be noted. In an alternative ideological perspective the
Progressive Era, so far as it witnessed expanded politicization of economic
life, brought forth not progress but reaction.

Whatever their own virtues or vices, the economic, political, and ideological changes of the Progressive Era established the context within which the
successive national emergencies of 1916–1918, 1930–1933, and 1940–1945

took place. Emergency alone need not lead to Bigger Government; it does so only under certain ideological conditions. The Progressive Era witnessed the maturation of such conditions.

ECONOMIC DEVELOPMENT AND POLITICAL CHANGE, 1898–1916

After a half-decade in the doldrums, the economy in the late 1890s began one of its most vigorous bursts of expansion. Real GNP per capita is estimated to have grown at an average annual rate of 4 percent between 1898 and 1902. Though this extraordinary pace could not be maintained over a much longer period, the Progressive Era as a whole witnessed remarkable economic growth. Real GNP per capita is estimated to have grown at an average annual rate of 2.5 percent between 1898 and 1912. Growth slowed during the four years preceding America's entry into the war—the available estimates disagree as to whether aggregate output even kept pace with population—but despite its stagnation after 1912, real GNP per capita stood in 1916 about 46 percent above the level of 1898.[2] Judged by this index alone, the economy had performed magnificently.

As always, however, the growth of output was erratic, and the uncertainties and losses associated with business fluctuations made secular progress a mixed blessing. The economy's performance ranged from the spectacular 12 percent annual increases of aggregate real output estimated to have occurred in 1901, 1906, and 1909 to the precipitous drops of 8 percent in 1908 and more than 4 percent in 1914.[3] The extreme annual variance made a mockery of the long-term average rate of increase (3.6 percent). Under such unstable dynamic conditions, business planning could be little more than guesswork, and many workers lost their jobs unexpectedly from time to time. As the relative shift of labor out of agriculture and into the urban-industrial sectors continued apace, the volatility of the economy's performance affected more immediately a growing proportion of the population. Even in the mostly prosperous Progressive Era the problem of the business cycle ranked high as an economic and hence a political concern.

Probably because in those days a financial panic usually accompanied the onset of a business depression, many people subscribed to monetary theories of the economic cycle. During the depression that followed the financial panic of 1907, Congress created a National Monetary Commission to investigate the monetary and banking systems and make recommendations for remedial legislation. The commission made extensive studies, and its report, delivered to Congress in 1912, set in train the deliberations and machinations that culminated in the creation of the Federal Reserve System late in 1913. The

"Fed," as it is commonly called, was an anomalous yet characteristically American institution: a decentralized central bank, its twelve district banks being semiautonomous and its central management relatively powerless. Commercial bankers took comfort from the presence of this "bankers' bank," a source of extra cash reserves in the event of a liquidity crisis. With only a vague notion of how the Fed would operate, the public expected that it would somehow smooth out the fluctuations in the nation's economic growth. The Fed's officers, uncertain of their own capabilities and authority, had scarcely settled into their new offices when the Great War began and the government thrust upon them even more pressing obligations. Attempts to tame the business cycle would have to wait.

As troublesome as the problem of economic fluctuations was the problem of labor relations. After suffering crushing setbacks in the depressed 1890s, labor unions expanded their membership severalfold during the economic boom at the turn of the century. Total union membership surged from less than half a million in 1897 to about two million in 1904, then stabilized for several years before resuming a slow increase after 1909. Not until 1917 did membership reach three million. Unionized workers constituted only a small fraction of the total labor force (never more than a tenth) during the Progressive Era, but they gained significant footholds in two strategic industries, railroads and coal mining, and in the skilled occupations of the construction industry.[4] Militant labor organizations like the Industrial Workers of the World (derisively called the Wobblies) and various socialist organizations never recruited large memberships, but they inspired fears far out of proportion to their visible followings. Both radicals and conservatives, as well as many of those in between, felt that a battle was being fought for the loyalties of the working class. Should many workers fall under the sway of the radicals, drastic consequences were expected to ensue. Forebodings of class warfare haunted many members of the middle and upper classes, giving a sense of crisis to this generally prosperous era.

Despite continued use of injunctions in some of the larger labor disputes, the federal government really had no labor-relations policy, unless standing apart itself be construed as a policy. Labor disputes and the disturbances of the peace that often accompanied them fell within the jurisdictions of local authorities. The actions of local officials varied from sympthetic support for organized labor to brutal suppression. Brutality being more newsworthy, it dominated the public's perceptions and discussions of "the labor problem." Perhaps the most notorious incident took place in 1914 at Ludlow, Colorado, where state troops attacked and burned the tent colony of striking miners, killing men, women, and children and igniting ten days of fierce civil warfare. Such events confirmed the most pessimistic views of this apparently intractable problem. Testifying before a congressional committee in 1912 a witness expressed the prevailing sense of alarm: "There is unrest everywhere. Never before have conditions been so miserably bad. Capital and labor are not satisfied, and we are having clash after clash. The situation looks worse and the future gloomy."[5] To delay venturing into a thorny political thicket, Congress in 1912 created a Commission on Industrial Relations to study the matter. The commission's final report, issued in 1915, did little to allay the widespread anxieties.

Most of the striking miners at Ludlow were recent immigrants who spoke little or no English, a fact symptomatic of the close connection between the labor problem and the immigration problem. Throughout the Progressive Era, enormous numbers of foreigners poured through Ellis Island and the lesser ports of entry. After declining with the economy in the 1890s, the volume of immigration increased rapidly at the turn of the century. During 1901–1914 total immigration averaged almost a million persons annually. (The population of the United States in 1900 was about seventy-six million, so a million immigrants a year had a big effect on the rate of growth of the population. Of course, there was substantial emigration, too.) Predominantly young adult males from southern and eastern Europe, the immigrants supplied much of the muscle to animate the expanding factories, mills, and mines of industrial America. As the events at Ludlow and many other places illustrate, however, integration of the foreign workers into the economy and society created abrasive social frictions. Many native-born citizens and many of the older, now-somewhat-established immigrant groups loathed the newcomers.

Immigrant laborers, however regarded otherwise, certainly augmented the supply of labor. Accordingly their almost totally unimpeded entry into the country pleased most employers and increasingly displeased organized labor. The U.S. Immigration Commission, which conducted an enormous study and delivered its final report to Congress late in 1910, recommended that admission of the "new" immigrants be limited. No limitation was imposed until 1917, when Congress enacted a literacy requirement expected to bear disproportionately on the unpopular groups. Not until the 1920s were effective legal barriers raised. The onset of the war, however, squeezed the torrent of immigration to a trickle during 1915–1920.

While problems of money, banking and the business cycle, labor relations, and immigration attracted widespread public concern, none of them could rival "the trust problem." The question of what to do about big business was without doubt the preeminent public policy issue of the Progressive Era. It was, of course, connected with all the others. One could not talk about banking without considering Morgan and Rockefeller's financial empires and their many links with the great industrial and railroad corporations. Labor relations and immigration could not be dealt with independently of the trusts, where vast and growing throngs of workers, especially the immigrants, found employment. Almost every economic issue had some connection with the trust problem. The corporation, said Woodrow Wilson in 1910, "stands in the forefront of all modern economic questions."[6]

Why was the public obsessed with big business? What indicated the necessity or desirability of *doing anything* about it? And why should the government, the federal government in particular, take the action? Inevitably some firms would be bigger than others. Could the public not see that firms producing on a large scale achieved lower costs per unit as a result of high-volume production and superior organizational structures—economies unattainable by smaller businesses? Was this, in short, a problem more of public misunderstanding than of substance?

In part it *was* a problem of public misunderstanding, fostered by muck-raking journalists and exploited by demagogic politicians. Many people of small means and limited accomplishments resented the rich and successful capitalists (whose conspicuous consumption helped to feed these fires); less successful men relished the idea of cutting the tycoons down to size. A certain species of ambitious politician—Theodore Roosevelt was exemplary—played upon the citizens' envy. "The people," cried Roosevelt, "have but one instrument which they can effectively use against the colossal combinations of business—and that instrument is the government of the United States."[7] Wilson echoed TR's opinion, declaring that "[w]ithout the watchful interference, the resolute interference, of the government, there can be no fair play between individuals and such powerful institutions as the trusts. Freedom today is something more than being let alone. The program of a government of freedom must in these days be positive, not negative merely."[8] It is hardly surprising that power-hungry politicians supported proposals to extend governmental controls over the great corporations.

If the furor had been nothing more than sheer demagoguery, however, it could scarcely have become the focus of such sustained public concern. Many members of the working and middle classes genuinely believed, without any prompting by politicians, that the trusts exerted a pernicious influence over the nation's economic and political life. Their fears of monopoly power in the product markets and monopsony power in the labor markets were not entirely without foundation. At the turn of the century a wave of mergers, capped by creation of the billion-dollar giant, U.S. Steel, heightened public apprehension that the consolidations would drive multitudes of small businesses to the wall. The Sherman Antitrust Act, as interpreted by contemporary courts, seemed powerless to check the growth of monopolies. Roosevelt's successful dismantling of the Northern Securities Company, a Morgan-sponsored railroad consolidation, had greater symbolic than substantive importance. The dissolutions of American Tobacco and Standard Oil ordered by the Supreme Court in 1911 made little difference in the relevant markets. Often the legal and political clamor had to do with public utilities or railroads, industries where so-called natural monopoly conditions prevailed and where therefore the desirability of competition was questionable.[9] Economic survival of the fittest, whatever its meaning and merit elsewhere, had no apparent application to governmentally franchised businesses such as the rapidly growing firms supplying telephone and telegraph service, gas, and electricity—not to mention the railroad industry, a perennial hotbed of controversy.

Apart from the purely economic pros and cons of the trusts, their corruption of the legal and political systems provoked widespread outrage. Here was the most common grist for the muckrakers' mill. In widely circulated magazines, including *McClure's, Collier's,* and *Everybody's,* crusading journalists such as Ida Tarbell, Lincoln Steffens, and Ray Stannard Baker spotlighted the shady deals, illegal actions, political hanky-panky, and assorted unethical practices of railroads, meat-packers, insurance companies, and various other large corporate businesses in league with venal public officials. Steffens exclaimed: "He is a self-righteous fraud, this big business man. He is the chief source of corruption, and it were a boon if he would neglect politics. . . . [T]he 'corruption which breaks out here and there and now and then' is not an occasional offense, but a common practice, and . . . the effect of it is literally to change the form of our government from one that is representative of the people to an oligarchy, representative of special interests."[10]

According to the traditional interpretation of Progressivism, the corruption unearthed by the muckrakers stimulated the citizenry to rise up in righteous indignation and restore lost virtue in the political economy by such means as the Bureau of Corporations (1903), the Clayton Antitrust Act and the Federal Trade Commission Act (both 1914), and major amendments to the Interstate Commerce Act (1903, 1906, 1910). For many years the historians' favorite example was Upton Sinclair's novel *The Jungle,* the revolted readers of which allegedly demanded passage of the Meat Inspection Act and the Pure Food and Drug Act (both 1906).

During the past twenty years historians increasingly have abandoned this simplistic view of the causal relation between the muckrakers' revelations and the landmark Progressive statutes, but in their revisions they have done little to refute the original allegations of widespread corporate corruption. Indeed, one revisionist historian, Gabriel Kolko, has reinterpreted the major political developments of the Progressive Era as, fundamentally, corporate corruption writ large. Turning the traditional interpretation on its head, Kolko characterizes these developments as the "triumph of conservatism," by which he means the attainment of political hegemony by the rich and powerful in general and the great corporations in particular. At his hands even the classic example takes a beating: he argues that the machinations of the large meat-packers, not the uproar that followed publication of Sinclair's book, led to the Meat Inspection Act of 1906.[11] Though the evidence does not support Kolko's thesis across the board, it does support his perspective. Big business-men—and smaller businessmen, too, when they formed effective trade associations—unquestionably wielded significant influence in determining the form and specific content of the Progressive legislation, not only the food and drug laws but the tariff, banking, railroad, antitrust, and trade commission acts as well.[12]

At bottom the conflicts over public policy with respect to the trusts, labor, and banking were struggles over the distribution of national income and wealth. As such, the problems could be "solved" only so far as the various interest groups might come to accept the existing distribution as legitimate. (Even then the problems would not stay solved, because a dynamic economy would inevitably disturb any existing distribution and thereby create new conflicts.)[13] Certainly the Progressive faith in the efficacy of placing "experts" in positions of authority—social engineers to solve social problems—was naive at best. The federal investigatory commissions (Industrial, Monetary, Immigration, Industrial Relations, and others) produced valuable socioeconomic data, but their recommendations for legislative solutions reflected rather than replaced partisan politics. It could hardly have been otherwise, as the experts themselves had material, political, and ideological wars to wage.

More obviously than anything else, tax policy brought political factions directly into the distributional struggle, and here the Progressives achieved their most pregnant triumph: the Sixteenth Amendment to the Constitution. Curiously, in view of its momentousness, the income-tax amendment was the culmination of a somewhat adventitious sequence of political events. Ever since the Supreme Court's *Pollock* decision the Democratic Party had continued to espouse the taxation of incomes. Every session of Congress saw the ritual introduction of income-tax bills, but Congress never acted on them. In 1908 the radicals gained a new ally when Teddy Roosevelt came out in support of an income tax. After William H. Taft's election as President a congressional coalition of Republican Insurgents (reformist lawmakers, most of them from the Midwest and West) and Democrats attempted to add an income-tax amendment to a pending tariff bill. Evidently they expected that, given another opportunity, the Supreme Court would reverse its ruling of 1895 and uphold the law. In an attempt to divert the forces gathering in support of the income tax, Senator Nelson W. Aldrich, leader of the Republican Old Guard (conservatives, most of them from the East) introduced bills providing for a corporation tax and a constitutional amendment giving Congress the authority to tax incomes. Aldrich made no attempt to hide his intentions. "I shall vote for a corporation tax," he declared on the floor of the

Senate, "as a means to defeat the income tax."[14] Both of Aldrich's bills were quickly passed.

The corporation tax, which exacted 1 percent of the net income above $5,000 of all profit-seeking corporations, was immediately challenged in the courts. In a remarkable decision that appeared incompatible with the spirit if not the letter of its *Pollock* decision the Supreme Court upheld the constitutionality of the tax. Skirting the main issue, the Court held that the corporate income tax was not a direct tax but an excise levied on the privilege of doing business as a corporation.[15]

While big businessmen cursed the corporation tax, the income-tax amendment proceeded steadily toward ratification. Aldrich must have been surprised, and profoundly unhappy, that the corporation tax had failed to deflect interest in a general income tax. By early 1913 a sufficient number of state legislatures had approved it, and the amendment became part of the fundamental law.[16] President Wilson immediately convened an emergency session of Congress, which he asked to enact tariff reductions and an income-tax law. Congress complied. On October 3, 1913, a tax "accepted as a natural and inevitable culmination of the constitutional amendment" was approved. The new law resembled that of 1894 in almost every respect except that, unlike the flat 2 percent rate of the old law, its rates were graduated, reaching a top bracket of 7 percent on incomes over $500,000.[17] To all but the very rich the levies were irrelevant—98 percent of the people owed no income tax under the act of 1913—but if ever there was an entering wedge, this was it.

THE IDEOLOGICAL WINDS SHIFT

Progressivism, as historians now understand it, covered a wide range of policy proposals and actions backed by correspondingly diverse individuals and interest groups impelled by a variety of motives. It seems, in short, to be little more than a classificatory umbrella under which historians have gathered virtually all the reformist ideals and programs of the early twentieth century. A notion so utterly comprehensive and hence so subject to internal heterogeneity appears at first glance to signify little besides the identity of the historical time and place to which it pertains. Yet a common element lay beneath the surface diversity of Progressivism.

The big meat-packers who pushed for the Meat Inspection Act, the shippers who fought for amendments to the Interstate Commerce Act, the proponents of trustbusting and the trade commission and the income-tax amendment—all shared a willingness, often an eagerness, to expand the scope of effective governmental authority over economic decision-making. As David Kennedy has written, "the great majority of Progressives saw the central issue of their age as the relation of public to private power, or, more precisely, of the government to the economy. Though they disagreed on specific programs, they were united in rejecting the laissez-faire determinism that had rendered government so unable to control the economic expansion that followed the Civil War." In sum, "a common commitment to the positive state . . . united the men who called themselves Progressives."[18]

When one recognizes, first, that Progressivism was the dominant ideology of economic and political elites on the eve of World War I and, second, that Progressivism was fundamentally at odds with the dominant ideology of ruling elites in the late nineteenth century, it is evident that an ideological turnabout must have taken place around the beginning of the twentieth century. Notwithstanding the gradual tendency toward interventionism at the state and local levels in the late nineteenth century, the dominant ideology of the 1890s—the one embraced by the majority of opinion leaders, governmental officials, and (so far as one can judge) most of the public as well—held that government, especially the federal government, had only a limited mission. Although this was not confined to providing only national defense, domestic order, enforcement of private contracts, and regulation of natural monopolies, it centered on these tasks and a handful of activities, such as street maintenance, education, and sanitation, widely believed to possess the properties of public goods. As Wiebe has noted, "A strikingly different conception of government arrived with the new century, a conception that received at least some support from almost every prominent theorist of the time."[19] The traditional American devotion to limited government did not disappear completely, especially among the middle classes and those who represented them politically, but it lost much of its vitality. After 1900 virtually all important public-policy proposals called for more extensive governmental action, particularly for more extensive action by the federal government.

Perhaps the most striking indication of the ideological transformation was manifested by those who, one might suppose, should have been the staunchest defenders of the old order, the big businessmen. Writing in 1921, Charles Whiting Baker observed that "[d]octrines that were deemed ultra-radical thirty years ago . . . are accepted today without question by railway presidents, financiers and captains of industry." Of course, using the government for their own purposes was nothing new to businessmen. They had always sought—and sometimes got—subsidies, tariffs, favorable legislation to exclude or inhibit competitors, and slanted court rulings to enhance the value of their property rights. But their self-serving efforts to gain governmental aid had usually been justified as special cases and covered by a dense smokescreen of rhetorical devotion to laissez-faire or something akin to it. The novelty of the early twentieth century was the undisguised position taken by a growing number of businessmen (especially among the Eastern elite) that government should intervene more actively in the affairs of business (particularly big corporate business) and that the intervention should be ongoing and institutionalized. Big businessmen's ceremonial obeisance to laissez-faire increasingly fell into desuetude, replaced by a Progressive avowal that government must cease to be only a referee, that it must be a player as well. George W. Perkins, a former executive of the New York Life Insurance Company, a partner of J. P. Morgan and Co., and a director of both U.S. Steel and International Harvester, in 1911 urged the officers of the great corporations to "realize that such concerns are more nearly public institutions than private property."[20] It is hard to imagine anyone in such a position making such a statement in 1895. Yet Perkins, though extreme, was not alone. A growing number of other magnates, including Samuel Insull and Elbert H. Gary, adopted a similar position.

The businessmen, of course, often supported enlarged governmental powers for essentially defensive and strategic reasons. Accepting the inevitability of an enlarged governmental presence in the economy, they sought to shape the statutory authority and administrative mechanisms of the new programs into forms that would yield them the greatest benefit—or at least cut their losses. As Insull put it, the businessman would rather "help shape the right kind of regulation" than have "the wrong kind forced upon him."[21] Yet what was most significant about their position was the belief that greater governmental intervention was inevitable, that not even the immense political resources of big business could calm the raging sea of reform. That Bigger Government had come to be seen as irresistible—only its precise form remained to be worked out—signaled a profound transformation of the ideological environment. The historian is provoked to search for its origins in the views of opinion leaders and disseminators.

The sweeping contemporary claims on behalf of expertise furnish a clue. What now seems a quaint or insincere Progressive faith in socioeconomic experts made a less hollow sound at the time. As never before, fundamental social, political, and economic problems appeared susceptible to expert management, even "solution." Not surprisingly this conviction was embraced most avidly by the would-be experts themselves, that is, by the vastly enlarged and increasingly influential class of intellectuals. The nation's colleges and universities grew rapidly in the early twentieth century. In 1900 the census counted only about seven thousand college presidents, professors, and instructors; twenty years later it found some thirty-three thousand.[22] In addition, growing numbers of journalists, authors, lawyers, social workers, bureaucrats, and free lances sans profession swelled the ranks of the intellectuals. As Joseph Schumpeter observed, "neither the opportunity of attack nor real or fancied grievances are in themselves sufficient to produce, however strongly they may favor, the emergence of active hostility against a social order. For such an atmosphere to develop it is necessary that there be groups to whose interest it is to work up and organize resentment, to nurse it, to voice it and to lead it."[23] Into these tasks the intellectuals of the Progressive Era plunged with gusto, aspiring to tear down the ideological bulwarks of the old order and provide a blueprint for a new one.

Regardless of the specific socioeconomic realm in which the intellectuals sought to carry out their demolition and reconstruction, they expected to work with the same tool: the expanded power of government. Edward A. Ross, whose influential book *Social Control* appeared in 1901, expressed an increasingly popular sentiment when he argued for the efficacy of employing government to solve social problems because it was "an organization that puts a wise minority in the saddle." In an argument that mere facts seem powerless to refute once and for all—it was resurrected in the 1960s by John Kenneth Galbraith—Ross forecasted that a "wise majority" of managers, technicians, planners, and bureaucrats would gain increasing power at the expense of politicians.[24]

Surrounding the intellectual enterprise of the Progressive Era, motivating many of its concerns, framing many of its questions, and establishing the normative context of its analyses, was socialism.

> After 1900, nearly all American reformers, Progressives as well as doctrinaire Marxists, exhibited some socialistic elements in their thinking and ideals. Plainly as an arouser of emotions, if not as a practical political platform, socialism had proved a success in America. Its sentimental aspects were propagated by literary socialists such as William Dean Howells and Upton Sinclair, while its infectious economic doctrines were woven into the social criticism of Henry Demarest Lloyd and Richard T. Ely. Collegiate socialism was in vogue at all the better colleges and universities and colored the thinking of many young radicals, including [Walter] Lippmann and [Randolph] Bourne. Socialism supplied the critique, if not the technique, for much Progressive reform; and though not always recognized, its effect was felt in all social sciences.[25]

Such an intellectual atmosphere suffocated the defenders of the old order. Increasingly exposed and ridiculed as reactionary sycophants of capitalist exploiters and plutocrats, the proponents of the free market and limited government were almost everywhere in retreat.

END AND BEGINNING:
THE RAILROAD LABOR TROUBLES, 1916–1917

The government's response to the railroad labor troubles of 1916–1917 may be seen both as the culmination of Progressivism and as a dress rehearsal for the garrison economy that would be created after the declaration of war. As

Progressive activism, the government's actions simply carried a big step further the long-standing but increasingly extensive federal regulation of the railroad industry. As a precursor of its wartime management of the economy, the government's actions brought about the substitution of a command-and-control system, with its associated concealment and shifting of costs, for the market economy in a time of national emergency. An important legal consequence was the Supreme Court's decision to uphold the exertion of powers previously unclaimed by Congress. (Significantly, Congress laid claim to the powers only at the insistence of the President, to facilitate the conduct of a policy he had chosen.) Though obscured by the Court's simultaneously granting an emergency power and denying that it was doing so, a doctrine of de facto emergency powers began to take shape in this ruling.

The troubles arose early in 1916, when the combined railroad operating brotherhoods failed to reach an agreement with the national bargaining association of the railroad companies.[26] The unions demanded a reduction from ten to eight hours of work per day without any reduction of daily pay and with time-and-a-half rates for overtime work. The employers would not consent to these terms. To resolve the impasse, they proposed binding arbitration. This the unions would not accept. They preferred first mediation and then a nationwide strike if an acceptable deal was not reached. Mediators tried to help, but on August 12 they admitted defeat. The unions prepared to strike, hesitating only to see what President Wilson would do.[27]

Wilson preferred not to become involved, recognizing that anything he might do would make an important interest group angry, but the threat of a disastrous national railroad strike could not be ignored by a President committed to activist government and in sympathy with the cause of organized labor. The imminence of the fall elections may have crossed his mind. (The railroads at that time employed about 1.7 million workers, that is, a host of voters.)[28] Whatever his precise motives, he decided that he must accept the political risks and do something.

Attempting to settle a dispute that the press was describing as "our greatest labor war" and the "greatest attack on capital that has ever been maneuvered in all history," Wilson convened in separate White House meetings the leaders of the two sides.[29] He appealed to the unionists to avoid a strike and to the employers to grant the wage-rate increase that would result from a reduction of the standard day without a change in daily pay. The unions were willing to accept a package that included the (higher paid) eight-hour day but excluded the time-and-a-half rate for overtime work. The employers rejected the package, preferring arbitration of all issues. Wilson tried to persuade the railroad managers by promising to help them gain approval of a general rate hike, perhaps by "packing" the Interstate Commerce Commission with two new members whom he would appoint. He pointedly warned them, however, "If a strike comes, the public will know where the responsibility rests. It will not be upon me."[30] Still the employers refused to accept the President's proposal.

Stymied in his direct intervention, Wilson resorted to Congress. On August 29 he addressed in person the House of Representatives, asking the lawmakers to establish for the railroad industry (1) the eight-hour day without any change of daily pay, (2) a commission to study the new arrangement, and (3) an enlargement of the ICC by two members. Congress hastily responded. The Adamson Act, passed September 2, gave the President everything he wanted except the enlarged ICC.[31] The commission created by the act was to study the new arrangement for six to nine months and report its findings to the President and Congress. Between January 1, 1917, when the law was to take effect, and thirty days after the commission tendered its report, the new, legislatively mandated wage scale was to prevail. Criminal penalties were prescribed for violators.

Lawyers for the railroad companies immediately began to prepare a test case to challenge the constitutionality of the Adamson Act, which the companies resolved to disregard until it had been validated by the Supreme Court. Unwilling to play a waiting game, the unions in mid-November again threatened to strike if the law was not implemented on January 1. In response the companies threatened to seek an injunction against the strike. Meanwhile a federal district court expedited a case, *Wilson* v. *New*, to the Supreme Court. (The Wilson named in the case was not the President but a U.S. District Attorney.) It was argued at Washington January 8 through 10, 1917.[32]

Early in 1917, while the nation awaited the Supreme Court's decision, the unions grew increasingly restive. Finally, on March 12, refusing to allow their own actions to hinge on the Court's ruling with regard to the constitutionality of the Adamson Act, they scheduled a strike for March 17. Later they postponed the walkout until March 20 to allow passengers to complete their journeys. The Wilson administration, using the Secretaries of Labor and Interior as emissaries, desperately sought to persuade the employers to adopt the terms of the law without further delay. On March 19 the companies caved in. No matter: the next day the Court announced its decision upholding the constitutionality of the Adamson Act by a 5 to 4 margin.

The decision, which has been described as marking "the high tide of legal progressivism," rested on an expansive interpretation of congressional authority under the Commerce Clause of the Constitution.[33] Speaking for the Court, Chief Justice Edward D. White argued that the Adamson Act was a legitimate exercise of the legislative will "to the end that no individual dispute or difference might bring ruin to the vast interests concerned in the movement of interstate commerce." He observed that the dispute, "if not remedied, would leave the public helpless, the whole people ruined and all the homes of the land submitted to a danger of the most serious character," and declared that "the power which the act exerted was only exercised because of the failure of the parties to agree and the resulting necessity for the lawmaking will to supply the standard rendered necessary by such failure of the parties to exercise their private right." He stressed that the law "was not a permanent fixing [of wage levels], but in the nature of things a temporary one which left the will of the employers and employees to control at the end of the period if their dispute had then ceased."[34]

The Chief Justice, who repeatedly emphasized the gravity of the circumstances prompting the Adamson Act—"the impediment and destruction of interstate commerce that was threatened" and "the infinite injury to the public which was imminent"—took pains to deny that the emergency per se gave rise to the government's authority under the act. "[A]lthough an emergency may not call into life a [constitutional] power which has never lived," he reasoned, "nevertheless emergency may afford a reason for the exertion of a living power already enjoyed." Furthermore,

[i]f acts which, if done, would interrupt, if not destroy, interstate commerce may be by anticipation legislatively prevented, by the same token the power to regulate may be exercised to guard against the cessation of interstate commerce threatened by a failure of employers and employees to agree as to the standard of wages, such standard being an essential prerequisite to the uninterrupted flow of interstate commerce.[35]

The dissenters took issue on every point. They disputed the majority's contention that wage rates were an aspect of interstate commerce. (The recently decided *Adair* and *Coppage* cases justified the dissenter's conclusion on this point.)[36] Moreover, Justice William R. Day argued that in several respects the act and the circumstances attending its passage denied due process to the railroad companies. Congress, he said,

has in this act itself declared the lack of the requisite information for definite action, and has directed an experiment to determine what it should do, imposing in the meantime an increase in wages peremptorily declared, the expense of which is to be borne entirely by the carrier, without recompense if the investigation proves the injustice or impropriety of the increase.

Such legislation, it seems to me, amounts to the taking of the property of one and giving it to another in violation of the spirit of fair play and equal right which the Constitution intended to secure in the due process clause to all coming within its protection, and is a striking illustration of that method which has always been deemed to be the plainest illustration of arbitrary action, the taking of the property of A and giving it to B by legislative fiat.

Moreover, emergency conditions, however threatening, could not excuse the denial of constitutional rights. Indeed the Constitution was written to protect private rights especially under such conditions.[37] "The suggestion," said Justice Mahlon Pitney in his dissenting opinion, that the act "was passed to prevent a threatened strike . . . amounts to no more than saying that it was enacted to take care of an emergency. But an emergency can neither create a power nor excuse a defiance of the limitations upon the powers of the Government."[38]

Pitney emphasized that the act was "wholly without precedent in either state or national legislation." The fact, he concluded,

> that no law fixing the rate of compensation for railroad employees ever was proposed until this act was brought forward a very few days before its passage, and then only under the coercive influence of a threatened public calamity, is the strongest evidence that in the judgment of executives and legislators, state and national, measures of this sort were not within the bounds of permissible regulation of commerce.[39]

Pitney also perceived that concealment and shifting of costs were inherent in the act. He admitted that the law, viewed as an attempt to prevent a strike, made sense and that the public interest would be served by such prevention. But he asserted that "the emergency conferred no power upon Congress to impose the burden upon the carriers. If the public exigency required it, Congress perhaps might have appropriated public moneys to satisfy the demands of the trainmen. But there is no argument for requiring the carriers to pay the cost, that would not equally apply to renewed demands, as often as made, if made by men who had the power to tie up traffic."[40]

Pitney concluded his dissent with a ringing defense of the rights of private property holders, which he perceived as suffering under the majority's ruling in *Wilson* v *New*:

> Rights of property include something more than mere ownership and the privilege of receiving a limited return from its use. The right to control, to manage, and to dispose of it, the right to put it at risk in business, and by legitimate skill and enterprise to make gains beyond the fixed rates of interest, the right to hire employees, to bargain freely with them about the rate of wages, and from their labors to make lawful gains—these are among the essential rights of property, that pertain to owners of railroads as to others. The devotion of their property to the public use does not give to the public an interest in the property, but only in its use.
>
> This act, in my judgment, usurps the right of the owners of the railroads to manage their own properties, and is an attempt to control and manage the properties rather than to regulate their use in commerce. In particular, it deprives the carriers of their right to agree with their employees as to the terms of employment.[41]

Finally he denied the majority's claims that Congress had a legitimate right to regulate wages temporarily but not permanently and that the legislative power became operative in the absence of agreement by the private disputants. "It is the very essence of the [private] right [to contract] that the parties may remain in disagreement if either party is not content with any term proposed by the other. A failure to agree is not a waiver but an exercise of the right—as much as the making of an agreement." Moveover, "If Congress may fix wages of trainmen in interstate commerce during a term of months, it may do so during a term of years, or indefinitely."[42] By logical extension it could intervene in other labor disputes in other industries to set maximum as well as minimum wages virtually without limit.

Whether or not the dissenters had the better argument, the majority carried the day. The Adamson Act was upheld, the railroads' wage scale was advanced by congressional fiat, and the owners of railroad property bore the cost of preventing a strike that would have imposed immense costs throughout the economy. Thus did the nation embark on what Jonathan Hughes has called a "long and irregular movement away from the ideal of the wage bargain as a sacred bond between the employer and the individual employee."[43]

The potential extension of such governmental action in the future, recognized and feared by Justice Pitney, would quickly become a reality. Soon to be upheld as constitutional "war power" rather than "commerce power," the government's typical course of action would be identical and have virtually the same economic and political effects: "doing something" in response to popular clamor in a national emergency; extending governmental control over previously private economic decision-making; concealing and shifting the costs of its actions on a grand scale; and increasing tremendously the politicization of economic affairs.

CONCLUSIONS

The most significant developments in the political economy during the Progressive Era took two related forms, one institutional, the other ideological. Among the institutional developments the creation of the Fed and the ratification of the Sixteenth Amendment loomed largest, not so much for their immediate impacts, which were slight, but for their immense potentialities—one can scarcely imagine the history of the United States since 1913 without the income tax and the central bank. As great as these and other institutional developments of the period were, however, they pale beside the ideological transformation that occurred. The old Populists must have taken much pleasure in the momentous shift. Not only were several of their most cherished proposals enacted but, more fundamentally, their prayers for the advent of an activist government were decisively answered. The dominant ideology of political and economic elites had now become one that not only tolerated a greatly expanded role for government in economic decision-making; it positively insisted on such activism. Gone forever were the days of Grover Cleveland and his kind. To utter their old-fashioned proverbs as serious guides to policy-making provoked only laughter or disbelief and revealed that one was either making a joke or completely out of touch with the times.

Early in 1917 Big Government seemed firmly ensconced in the United States. The response to the labor troubles of 1916–1917 demonstrated that when the opportunity presented itself the government would not hesitate to exercise unprecedented powers over the economy. We know now, of course, that the Americans of that time, contemplating what seemed to them a largely completed reconstruction of the political economy, had just begun to create the modern mixed economy. They enjoyed but a brief calm before the storm. Active participation in the Great War would do much to open new possibilities and to hasten further developments in the direction already embarked upon.

CHAPTER SEVEN

The Political Economy of War, 1916–1918

[N]ever until World War I did the suppression of freedom enjoy the almost unanimous support of the various agencies of the government—national, state, and local.

ARTHUR A. EKIRCH, JR.

More than anything the Progressives had achieved, war undercut American liberties and fed the growth of Big Government. Notwithstanding the accretions of governmental authority during the Progressive Era, the American economy remained, as late as 1916, predominantly a market system. The next two years, however, witnessed an enormous and wholly unprecedented intervention of the federal government in the nation's economic affairs. By the time of the armistice the government had taken over the ocean shipping, railroad, telephone, and telegraph industries; commandeered hundreds of manufacturing plants; entered into massive economic enterprises on its own account in such varied departments as shipbuilding, wheat trading, and building construction; undertaken to lend huge sums to businesses directly or indirectly and to regulate the private issuance of securities; established official priorities for the use of transportation facilities, food, fuel, and many raw materials; fixed the prices of dozens of important commodities; intervened in hundreds of labor disputes; and conscripted millions of men for service in the armed forces. It had, in short, extensively distorted or wholly displaced markets, creating what some contemporaries called "war socialism."

In this chapter I am concerned with what made such a vast transformation possible and how it was effected; who supported and who opposed the unprecedented measures and for what reasons; how the garrison economy operated; and, most importantly, the legacies that the experience bequeathed to the Americans who survived or came after it.

NEUTRAL PROSPERITY AND THE SHIPPING CRISIS

When the European hostilities erupted in August 1914 the American economy was wallowing in a mild recession. Shocked reactions to the outbreak of war drove the economy down as financial panic spread and export markets floundered. The confusion, however, did not last long. Within a few months the initial uncertainties had subsided, and Americans returned to business as usual in 1915.

Indeed the war seemed almost a blessing to them during 1915 and 1916. European orders for American goods increased prodigiously. In just two years the value of American exports more than doubled. The rate of unemployment sank to 5 percent of the labor force in 1916. Real gross national product reached an all-time high, rising by 8 percent between 1915 and 1916.[1] Incongruously, the mad slaughter and destruction in Europe led to unprecedented prosperity in the United States during its period of neutrality.

The war created many new opportunities for American exporters and their auxiliaries, especially in the Latin American markets vacated by the European belligerents, but profiting from the opportunities hinged on the availability and price of ocean shipping services. Unfortunately such services grew scarcer by the day. German and Austrian merchant ships, fleeing the British navy, were driven into their home ports or interned in foreign harbors. The British, whose ships accounted for about half of the world's steam tonnage, increasingly diverted their merchantmen to military and naval uses. German submarines destroyed many British and French ships. Between early 1914 and early 1916 ocean freight rates increased by a factor of five to ten or more, depending on the commodity and the route. According to a House committee report of May 1916, it was "practically impossible to secure any tonnage either sailing or steam except at exorbitant rates" to carry U.S. exports to South America, Australia, South Africa, and the Far East.[2]

William Gibbs McAdoo, the Secretary of the Treasury, thought that Americans should take advantage of the new opportunities for foreign trade, but he did not think that, even under the high-risk conditions of the war at sea, shippers should have to pay the going rates, which he characterized as "absurdly high" and productive of an "orgy of profiteering." As early as August 1914 he conceived a plan to alleviate the shipping shortage: the government would regulate rates and operate competing ships on its own account. President Wilson gave his blessing to McAdoo's tentative draft of a bill, and friendly legislators introduced it in Congress on August 24, 1914. It was passed by the House early in 1915 but died as a result of a filibuster by Republican opponents in the Senate.[3]

Disappointed but resilient, proponents continued to seek support for the shipping bill. As the public became more concerned about national security, backers of the bill cosmetically altered it to enhance its appeal to the increasingly insecure populace: they represented the proposed fleet of government-operated merchantmen as naval auxiliaries. On a nationwide speaking tour in the fall of 1915 McAdoo "put the idea of naval auxiliaries first, and the merchant marine second." Experience had taught him, he later observed, that "people as a rule are far more interested in fighting, and in preparations for fighting, than they are in any constructive commercial or industrial effort."[4]

Still, when the revamped shipping bill was introduced in Congress on January 30, 1916, strong forces continued to resist it. Opponents included not only all the steamship companies but many business groups and newspaper editors. Some opposed the measure ostensibly on the traditional grounds that the government had no business going into business: "Government competition in any industry," said the Indianapolis *News*, "is always a menace to private enterprise." According to the New York *Herald* the bill was "economically unsound . . . unnecessary and futile." It conjured up in the minds of its opponents "the dread vision of the Government embarked in a socialistic enterprise."[5]

Proponents gained new support in the spring of 1916. The Washington *Post* admired the proposal's promise of "immediate relief" of the shipping shortage. The New York *World* favored the bill as a means of helping Americans gain access to the "almost unlimited commercial opportunities in South America." In testimony before congressional committees the U.S. Chamber of Commerce supported the bill, as did the National Grange, the Farmers Union, the American Federation of Labor, and the seaman's union. The majority report of the House Committee on the Merchant Marine and Fisheries on May 9, 1916, urged passage of the bill, claiming that it "has been framed with the view of encouraging, not to discourage, private enterprise in construction and operation of vessels under the American flag."[6]

Ultimately whatever had restrained Congress from projecting the government into the shipping business gave way before the combined weight of the extraordinary shipping costs, the lure of lucrative trading opportunities, and growing national insecurity. The House passed the bill on May 21, 1916, by a vote of 211 to 161, all the nays being cast by Republicans. The Senate resisted until August 20, when it gave its approval by a vote of 38 (all Democrats) to 21 (all Republicans). After resolution of some differences between the House and Senate versions the bill was signed into law by the President on September 7. As David Kennedy has remarked, "the utility of the emergency of overcoming congressional reluctance about a state-owned shipping corporation suggested just how fruitful a political climate the crisis had created."[7]

The Shipping Act created the U.S. Shipping Board and empowered it to regulate the rates and practices of waterborne common carriers in foreign and interstate commerce and, through a subsidiary, to acquire, construct, and operate merchant vessels. The law authorized $50 million for investment in the subsidiary, subsequently created by the board on April 16, 1917, and known as the Emergency Fleet Corporation. During the war, executive orders, amendments to the act, and related legislation greatly extended the government's authority over the ocean shipping industry. Governmental agencies gained the power to acquire vessels by requisition, commandeering, and seizure, to assign cargoes and routes, to regulate not only shipping and shipbuilding but the wages, hours, and working conditions of laborers in those industries, even to build residential housing, stores, and transport systems for them. By the autumn of 1918 "[g]overnment control of merchant shipping in American service was absolute."[8]

The common denominator of the various governmental powers over the industry was the unwillingness of federal officials to tolerate the continued exercise of private property rights in the provision of shipping services— including the private owners' right to determine the terms on which they would provide the services of their ships—while soaring demands and dwindling supplies combined to produce a large increase in rates. Clearly the rising market price of shipping services during 1914-1916, more than anything else, provoked the conception and passage of the Shipping Act. Subsequent extensions of the government's authority sprang from the same source. When "in the face of leaping costs of shipping" in the summer of 1917 the Shipping Board requisitioned all American ships over 2,500 tons, Edward Hurley, the chairman of the board, said: "There was nothing to do but to own or control every ship that flew the American flag and fix the scale of requisition rates ourselves at some fair level below that prevailing in the market, a level that represented legitimate values."[9] The words "fair" and "legitimate," evoking the medieval notion of a just price, sound suspiciously like ideological rhetoric to clothe a taking of private property. Years later the economic historian George Soule wrote with approval of the "elimination of competition" in the shipping industry during World War I and observed that "all the ships were pooled so that they could be used to best advantage."[10] The revealing question is: To *whose* best advantage?

THE PREPAREDNESS CONTROVERSY AND
NEW GOVERNMENTAL POWERS

To most Americans the outbreak of war in August 1914 was an unwelcome surprise. Dismayed by the breakdown of the balance of power among the world's most economically advanced and "civilized" nations, they viewed the vast bloodletting in Europe as essentially divorced from their own concerns and from the national interest of the United States.

> Under the sun
> Are sixteen million men,
> Chosen for shining teeth,
> Sharp eyes, hard legs,
> And a running of young warm blood in their wrists.
>   And a red juice runs on the green grass;
> And a red juice soaks the dark soil
> And the sixteen million are killing . . . and killing and
>   killing.[11]

Few Americans saw any reason to join in such colossal lunacy. President Wilson ratified the majority's sentiment by hastening to issue an official proclamation of American neutrality and by urging the citizenry to be impartial in both thought and deed.

Acting impartially required delicate judgment, steady nerves, and ample patience. Propagandists for both sides bombarded the country with information and misinformation calculated to sway public opinion. Provocations occurred repeatedly, especially violations by both British blockaders and German submariners of what Americans claimed as their neutral trading rights under international law. The German sinking of the British liner *Lusitania* on May 7, 1915, which caused the deaths of 128 Americans, prompted a change of Wilson's views on the proper defense posture of the United States. Whereas he had previously opposed extraordinary measures to build up the armed forces, the President inclined after mid-1915 toward greater support for military buildup.

Some had endorsed such measures from the start. Led by the perennially bloodthirsty Theodore Roosevelt, who craved another term as President, and his fellow warrior General Leonard Wood, "the official drillmaster for the preparedness crusade," the militaristic faction included such Republican stalwarts as the former Secretaries of War Elihu Root and Henry L. Stimson and the redoubtable Senator Henry Cabot Lodge. They enjoyed the financial backing of some of the country's wealthiest capitalists. (At J. P. Morgan and Company, sole purchasing agent for the British and French governments in the United States, business had never been better; and there was no doubt whose side Morgan and most members of his class were on.) Preparedness lobbies, with the well-heeled National Security League in the van, incessantly beat the drums for a bigger army and navy and for their most cherished proposal, universal military training. These advocates, mostly upper-class northeasterners, represented a minority political position yet one that posed a genuine threat to the President as the electioneering season approached. From early 1915 on, their movement was "mostly preparedness for the presidential election the next year." Seldom did they miss an opportunity to berate the President for his alleged deficiency of martial inclinations.[12]

Goaded by the *Lusitania* disaster and by the preparedness advocates, Wilson adopted a markedly fiercer position in the second half of 1915. On November 4 he publicly endorsed the Army War College's plan to reorganize and enlarge the army. When the proposal encountered stiff opposition in Congress the President set out in January 1916 on an extended speaking tour to rally support for it, focusing his efforts on the Midwest, where pacifism was strongest. On March 24, 1916, the Germans sank an unarmed French vessel, the *Sussex*, causing several American casualties and thrusting the submarine warfare issue again to the forefront. The incident helped to push American public opinion toward acceptance of the President's proposals for strengthening the armed forces.

Meanwhile preparedness efforts were being exerted along other, more directly economic lines. For many years Dr. Hollis Godfrey, the president of Drexel Institute, had been agitating on behalf of industrial preparedness. Howard Coffin, vice president of the Hudson Motor Car Company and a proponent of industrial standardization, and Walter S. Gifford, an AT&T statistician and Coffin's colleague on the Naval Consulting Board, had recently been working to inventory the nation's industrial resources for war. Simultaneously but separately Bernard M. Baruch, a wealthy independent investor, was formulating plans for industrial mobilization. All these volunteer planners agreed on the desirability of establishing a supreme governmental council to oversee and coordinate economic mobilization in the event of war. Early in 1916 the proponents of military buildup incorporated the idea into a proposal for legislative action. General Wood and former Secretary Root lent a hand by advising on how the bill should read. Finally the idea reached Secretary of War Newton D. Baker and the President, who, in collaboration with General Enoch H. Crowder, judge advocate of the army, embodied it in a bill to be introduced in Congress. The various efforts for preparedness culminated in the passage of two landmark statutes in the summer of 1916.[13]

The first was the National Defense Act, which has been called "the most comprehensive piece of military legislation ever passed by Congress." It authorized the President "in time of war or when war is imminent" to place obligatory orders that would "take precedence over all other orders and contracts." Should the owner of the supply facility refuse to fill such orders "at a reasonable price as determined by the Secretary of War" the President was "authorized to take immediate possession of any such plant [and] . . . to manufacture therein . . . such product or material as may be required," while the owner would be "deemed guilty of a felony."[14] The law gave the government extraordinarily sweeping powers. To compel factory owners, by threat of criminal sanctions, to produce munitions for the government at whatever prices the government might choose to pay simply demolished existing private property rights in such facilities; the form of private owner-ship remained, but the substance had been gutted. The act also directed the Secretary of War to make an inventory of all actual or potential munitions plants in the country and to prepare a plan "for transforming each such plant into an ammunition factory." Finally it authorized the President to appoint a Board on Mobilization of Industries Essential for Military Preparedness.[15]

The Army Appropriations Act that became law on August 29, 1916, granted the President additional power to seize private property. Tucked inconspicuously in an act of some fifty pages, between a paragraph authoriz-ing a small expenditure for the replacement of a bridge in Kansas and a paragraph authorizing a small expenditure for the purchase of horses, ap-peared the following extraordinary grant of power:

> The President, in time of war, is empowered, through the Secretary of War, to take possession and assume control of any system or systems of transporta-tion, or any part thereof, and to utilize the same, to the exclusion as far as may be necessary of all other traffic thereon, for the transfer or transportation of troops, war material and equipment, or for such other purposes connected with the emergency as may be needful or desirable.[16]

Sixteen months later this provision would serve as the necessary and sufficient authority for the government's takeover of the nation's privately owned railroads.

In addition the act established a Council of National Defense consisting of six designated cabinet secretaries (War, Navy, Interior, Agriculture, Commerce, and Labor) and an advisory commission of not more than seven persons knowledgeable about industries, public utilities, and natural re-sources. The CND was to investigate and make recommendations "for the coordination of industries and resources for the national security and wel-fare."[17] Authorization of this seemingly powerless council and its advisory commission was the statutory origin of an organizational evolution that eventually resulted in a War Industries Board wielding considerable power over much of the economy in 1918.

As the final winter of American neutrality approached, the advocates of preparedness could feel some satisfaction with their accomplishments. Not that the nation possessed a genuinely potent armed force; it had nothing of the kind. But it now had a President with far-reaching authority to requisi-tion munitions and means of transportation, and it had a high-level Council of National Defense charged with determining how the economy could best be mobilized for war. These developments' had received their impetus partly from sheer militarism, as expressed by the Roosevelt-Wood faction, partly from grasping for war profits, as expressed by Morgan and friends, and partly from certain patriotic engineers' love of technical tidiness and mechanical control, as expressed by Godfrey, Coffin, and Gifford. Free-lancers like Baruch helped to maintain the momentum.

Most of all the crusade for preparedness, especially as it related to the demand for unprecedented governmental powers over the economy, seems to have been inspired by what had been happening in Germany, France, and Britain. There governments had intervened more and more in the market economy in the interest of full-scale mobilization. Even in Britain, the birthplace and long the home of the laissez-faire ideology, free markets eventually had been largely set aside. "As early as 1916, on the advice of a British economist, Sir Walter Layton, Baruch had been persuaded that nothing short of an arbitrary designation of societal priorities would facilitate war mobilization." In Washington "British experience" became the benchmark for discussions of economic mobilization, and "mission after mission crossed the Atlantic to spread information."[18] American planners, therefore, scarcely lacked examples and instruction.

The period of neutrality, said J. M. Clark, was a time of learning, of "mental preparedness." Americans learned, largely by watching the European belligerents and listening to their freely dispensed advice,

> that modern war is the organized mobilization of all the economic resources of a nation; and were ready to apply what were for us unprecedented measures of control; while leaders of industry, in turn, were ready to submit and to cooperate to an extent well-nigh incredible in the light of our individualistic prepossessions. The successful resort to compulsory military service, the control of prices, restriction of consumption and of industrial uses of essential materials: all gained immeasurably from this period of preparation.[19]

No doubt it was so. But Clark's reference to the submersion of "individualistic prepossessions" on the one hand and compulsory military service on the other suggests that the mobilization was not to be entirely a matter of voluntary cooperation with the government's program for war.

WAR AND CONSCRIPTION

Early in 1917, provoked by German resumption of unrestricted submarine warfare, Wilson finally decided to ask Congress for a declaration of war. Congress complied in a Joint Resolution of April 6, declaring that "to bring the conflict to a successful termination all of the resources of the country are hereby pledged." As Grosvenor Clarkson later observed, the pledge "may have amounted in reality to nothing more than a grandiloquent expression of good intentions"—a legal mind might have questioned whether Congress possessed the constitutional authority to direct all the resources of the country—"but in a time when men were not disposed to split hairs it was possible to load it with meaning."[20] The formal declaration of American belligerency made little difference in the course of the war during 1917.

The United States simply had no substantial military might to project. (Of course, American supplies of goods to the Allies continued to be important and even increased in importance after the declaration of war.) On June 30, 1916, military personnel on active duty had numbered only 179,000. Congress had authorized a few additional troops, but enlistments had been insufficient to bring the total up to its newly authorized maximum. Even after the declaration of war, volunteers came forward in a trickle. "Despite all the recruiting appeals of the press and of leaders of opinion, from officials to society women and actresses, the Regular Army had enlisted 4,355 men, an average of 435 a day, in the first ten days after [U.S.] entry into the war." Secretary Baker then announced that volunteers would not have to serve beyond the end of the war, but the promise had little effect. By April 24 only 32,000, just one-sixth of the War Department's quota, had joined.[21] The President and Congress were more eager to send men to war than men were to be sent, given the existing terms of service. Evidently no one in the government ever considered whether the desired number of volunteers could be obtained by making the deal sufficiently sweet. The politicians—and no doubt most of their constituents as well—were averse to paying a market rate for the hire of soldiers.

In fact the President had already decided to seek a draft law. The decision had required a turnabout from his long-standing opposition to conscription. As late as February 1917 both Wilson and his reputedly pacifistic Secretary of War had declared themselves in favor of volunteerism. Military leaders first convinced Baker of the desirability of conscription. General Hugh Scott, Chief of Staff of the Army, asserted that "the country will never be prepared for defense until we do as other great nations do . . . like Germany, Japan, and France." Baker then convinced the President, who approved the draft bill drawn up by the War Department and the General Staff and forwarded it to Congress on April 5, the day *before* the declaration of war.[22]

In Congress the draft proposal ignited a fire storm of outraged opposition, most of it from the President's fellow Democrats, especially those from the South and the West. Congressional rhetoric rose to a shrill pitch as opponents of the draft railed against the attempt to "Prussianize America" with "abject or involuntary servitude," the draft being only "another name for slavery." There was, said Democrat Champ Clark, the Speaker of the House, "precious little difference between a conscript and a convict." Clark's fellow Missourian, Senator James A. Reed, prophesied that "[y]ou will have the streets of our American cities running red with blood on Registration day." The House Military Affairs Committee refused to endorse the draft bill, and the administration suffered the embarrassment of having its proposal supported only in the minority report sponsored by a Republican.[23]

Several weeks of political maneuvering ensued, complicated by Teddy Roosevelt's harebrained scheme to form a volunteer division patterned after his glorious Rough Riders of the Spanish-American War. Roosevelt had enough political friends, many of whom seemed more interested in discomforting Wilson than in TR's prospective military contribution, to keep this ridiculous pot boiling for weeks. Late in April the House, in a bewildering reversal, approved a draft bill by a large majority. (Was the initial opposition merely staged to give the appearance that the legislators had fought a hard but ultimately hopeless fight against conscription? If so, members of Congress would have had the best of both worlds: cheap soldiers but no personal responsibility for the draft.) More time passed while conferees ironed out differences between House and Senate versions of the bill. Finally on May 18, six weeks after the declaration of war, the President signed into law the Selective Service Act.[24]

Wilson now had the legal authority to draft men, but whether he would be able to exercise the authority successfully remained uncertain. The Civil War draft riots had not been forgotten, and Senator Reed's forecast of blood in the streets could not be dismissed lightly. Conscription is always and everywhere unpopular, at least with the conscripts, and the year 1917 in the United States was no exception. The armed forces offered little pay and, as the news from France made clear, considerable risk to life and limb, not to mention the loss of personal freedom, Spartan living conditions, harsh military discipline, and routine humiliation endured by the ordinary soldier. Superpatriots aside, men considered conscription very costly.

It behooved the Wilson administration to conceal the costs or—the other side of the coin—to invent offsetting psychological (fiscally cheap) benefits. In this endeavor Baker proved himself a master. His strategy was first to misrepresent what was being done to the conscripts and second to whip up public emotion to deceive the victims and, should the deception fail, to prompt other citizens to intimidate them into submission. The misrepresentation got off to a good start with the President's explanation that "[i]t is in no sense a conscription of the unwilling: it is, rather, selection from a nation which has volunteered in mass." Proclamation of the registration day, June 5, 1917, when all male Americans aged twenty-one through thirty were to sign up, took the form of a quasi-religious announcement that spoke reverently of "patriotic devotion and obligation" and, as it was published in many newspapers, appeared within a border of American flags, printed in biblical Gothic type.[25] "I am using a vast number of agencies throughout the country," Baker wrote to Wilson, "to make the day of registration a festival and patriotic occasion." Governors, mayors, and chambers of commerce were enlisted to help. On June 5, when almost ten million young men dutifully appeared to register, bands played, flags waved, and the men were made to feel like heroes before they had encountered even a drill sergeant.[26]

Of course, complete reliance could not be placed on patriotic hoopla. "Back of the 'drive' to make registering the 'thing to do' was the reminder that his neighbors were watching every man between twenty-one and thirty-one and might proscribe him as a community outcast if he tried to evade registration; and the cozening velvet glove concealed the reminder of the steel gauntlet to enforce the penalty for failure to register"—namely, a year in prison. To discourage bystanders from obstructing the draft, Congress provided in the Espionage Act of June 15, 1917, that "whoever, when the United States is at war . . . shall willfully obstruct the recruiting or enlistment service of the United States, shall be punished by a fine of not more than $10,000 or imprisonment for not more than twenty years, or both." In addition the Postmaster General, who exercised the government's draconian powers of censorship, warned that "[w]e will not tolerate campaigns against conscription."[27] Still, legal sanctions alone would not do the job; someone had to man the great organization that would select and process the conscripts.

Although Baker kept the top management within the War Department, his supreme coup was to assign the lowest level of administration in the draft system to local civilian boards rather than military personnel. Because the draft law failed to stipulate precise rules with respect to exemptions, each board had wide discretion in deciding whom to induct from the local pool of qualified registrants. Grass-roots administration had enormous utility in focusing effective moral pressure on those selected for induction. In practice the boards were "susceptible to local political pressures . . . and not immune to local prejudices." Southern boards, for example, flagrantly discriminated against blacks. Of course "the obligation of service fell disproportionately on the powerless and the poor"—can one imagine a political process that would not have produced this result?[28]

For top federal officials, however, the rainbow colors of social, ethnic, and political discrimination by the local boards held little fascination. The boards served a fundamental purpose, their rampant corruption notwithstanding, and Provost Marshall General Enoch H. Crowder, who headed the draft system, was remarkably candid in describing that purpose. According to Crowder, the boards served as

> buffers between the individual citizen and the Federal Government, and thus they attracted and diverted, like local grounding wires in an electric coil, such resentment or discontent as might have proved a serious obstacle to war

measures, had it been focussed on the central authorities. Its diversion and grounding at 5000 local points dissipated its force, and enabled the central war machine to function smoothly without the disturbance that might have been caused by the concentrated total of dissatisfaction.[29]

Such frank public admission of Machiavellianism is rare in American history. Clearly the top governmental officials were unmoved by the "concentrated total of dissatisfaction." Their ruling imperative was to feed the war machine whether or not people objected to being fed into it.

Altogether the government drafted 2,820,000 men during 1917 and 1918, or about 70 percent of those who served in the Army. No doubt many of the volunteers, in both the Army and the Navy, came forward only because of the threat of conscription. (Not everyone was frightened into the armed forces by the draft; the rate of evasion was 11 percent.) No resource taken by the government in its war mobilization was more precious, and no one else was so poorly compensated for his sacrifices as the draftee. The basic pay of enlisted men during World War I averaged $417 per year. Though the American Expeditionary Force made a relatively trivial contribution of blood to the overall Allied cause in France, the casualties must have seemed more significant to the 117,000 Americans who died and the 204,000 who were wounded.[30]

Nothing illustrates the expansion stage of the ratchet more clearly than the Wilson administration's conscription program. As Mark Sullivan, a contemporary observer, viewed it,

> this use of immense organized propaganda by government to make the public mind receptive to what the government planned to do, coupled with elaborate, secret, advance preparation of a mechanism which should put the draft in effect, without delay that might permit opposition to generate—this was a new thing in America. Essentially it was a process of causing the mass of the public to move in a direction in which the government wished them to go, a direction which the public, if left alone, would not take. The technique included, as a principle or as a condition that arose in practice, exercise of pressure by the majority to compel the minority to conform. In the case of the draft, any who attempted dissent were called "slackers," and subjected to odium by the public as well as to formal punishment by the government.[31]

Sullivan noted that similar tactics were employed by the government in other areas as the mobilization proceeded: in the Treasury's bond drives, in the efforts of the Food Administration and the War Industries Board to gain compliance with their regulations. Everywhere the underlying rationale was the same. As Kennedy has concluded, "The super-heated patriotism . . . deliberately cultivated by the Wilson administration . . . was a calculated consequence of the administration's reluctance to make the true material costs of the war visible and to lay them explicitly on the people."[32]

MANIPULATING THE MARKET ECONOMY:
THE MAJOR AGENCIES

"Wheat," proclaimed one of the war's most trumpeted propaganda slogans, "will win the war." It was not the whole truth, but it did express the important fact that, as Herbert Hoover put it, "agriculture was really a munitions industry." In Europe the war had simultaneously increased the demand for and decreased the supply of agricultural commodities. The diminished availability of ocean shipping restricted imports from such distant sources of supply as India, Argentina, New Zealand, and Australia. The United States offered a more promising source of additional supplies. American food exports in 1917 and 1918, in tons, were double the annual average for the three prewar years. Prices advanced rapidly.[33]

No one had a better appreciation of the food weapon than Hoover, an engineer-businessman who had served with distinction as head of the Commission for the Relief of Belgium. Early in 1917 Wilson placed him in charge of the Food Administration, an agency without formal powers, created by executive order of the President in May 1917. The agency attempted to alleviate the food shortages by publicizing them and appealing for more production and less consumption. Everyone realized, however, that mere exhortation—even when "[h]alf a million persons went door to door to hand housewives pledge cards that enlisted their patriotic cooperation in the drive to conserve foodstuffs"—could not accomplish all that the government desired.[34]

Legal sanctions were necessary, and the President on May 19 appealed to Congress to provide them in the form he had earlier requested. "Those powers are very great, indeed," said Wilson, "but they are no greater than it has proved necessary to lodge in the other Governments which are conducting this momentous war." He characterized the food controls as strictly emergency measures and promised that they would be removed at the end of the war. "The last thing that any American could contemplate with equanimity would be the introduction of anything resembling Prussian autocracy into the food control in this country."[35]

But Prussian autocracy was precisely what many members of Congress perceived in the requested legislation. "The bare idea of anybody interfering with the food rights of the people," Hoover wrote, "came as a shock" to some lawmakers. The administration's bill stirred up enormous controversy, especially in the Senate, where it was debated for five weeks. Hoover, who had never engaged in this sort of political activity before, lobbied at length for the bill—and came away bloodied. Some opponents objected that the bill did not go far enough: if the government was to fix the prices of wheat and coal, it should also fix the prices of cotton, steel, and various other goods. Other opponents feared the aggrandizement of the President's authority, and some disliked any kind of governmental interference in the market economy. Eventually the administration got most of what it wanted by accepting compromises with various farm interests and with the prohibitionists.[36]

The Lever Act (after Congressman Asbury F. Lever, who sponsored it as a service to the administration), passed by Congress and signed into law on August 10, 1917, was officially entitled "An Act To provide further for the national security and defense by encouraging the production, conserving the supply, and controlling the distribution of food products and fuel."[37] Never before had such sweeping powers of economic control been granted by Congress to the President. He was empowered to require a license of everyone importing, manufacturing, storing, mining, or distributing foods, feeds, fuels, fertilizers, and the equipment used in producing them; to prescribe regulations for the license holders and to revoke the licenses whenever the licensees failed to maintain a "just, reasonable, nondiscriminatory and fair storage charge, commission, profit, or practice" as determined by the President; "to requisition foods, feeds, fuels, and other supplies necessary to the support of the Army or the maintenance of the Navy, or any other public use connected with the common defense, and to requisition, or otherwise provide, storage facilities for such supplies"; "to purchase, to store, to provide storage facilities for, and to sell for cash at reasonable prices, wheat, flour, meal, beans, and potatoes"; "to requisition and take over, for use or operation by the Government, any factory, packing house, oil pipe line, mine, or other plant" producing the designated "necessaries"; to fix a guaranteed price for wheat at not less than $2 per bushel; "to purchase any wheat . . . and to hold, transport, or store it, or to sell, dispose of, and deliver the same"; "to fix the price of coal and coke, wherever and whenever sold, either by producer or dealer" and to requisition these fuels and associated production facilities; "to require any or all producers of coal and coke . . . to sell their products only to the United States through an agency to be designated by the President . . . at such uniform prices . . . as may be determined by said agency to be just and fair." In addition, contrary to Wilson's wishes, the act appeased the prohibitionists by stipulating that "no foods, fruits, food materials, or feeds shall be used in the production of distilled spirits for beverage purposes. . . . Nor shall there be imported into the United States any distilled spirits." Under this law the government could assume virtually complete control over the prices and distribution of foods, feeds, fuels, and fertilizers and over associated equipment suppliers.

On the day that he signed the Lever Act, Wilson established under its authority the United States Food Administration and named Hoover to head it. (In effect, this action merely endowed the previous [powerless] food agency with the statutory powers prescribed by the Lever Act.) The agency attempted, whenever possible by voluntary means, to conserve foodstuffs and to fix the prices of selected commodities. Attaining these objectives sometimes required exertion of its licensing powers and its authority to requisition goods and facilities, though the mere threat of such powerful sanctions usually sufficed. "Price fixing," as a contemporary analyst observed, "was often conducted under the guise of voluntary agreement," but "the various attempts of the Food Administration to limit profits cannot be said to have been thoroughly effective."[38] Congress and the President continued to wrangle over price controls, a major bone of contention being the price of wheat, which the government maintained at $2.20 per bushel in 1917 and 1918, while cotton prices remained free from restraint—a testimony to the power of the Southerners in Congress.[39] Manipulation of wheat prices was effected by a subsidiary, the United States Grain Corporation, whose capital came from the Treasury. Sugar prices were controlled by another subsidiary, the Sugar Equalization Board—a fascinating example of what economists call a "discriminating monopsony."

To implement its far-reaching controls the Food Administration established state, county, and municipal offices staffed by zealous volunteers who exhorted, intimidated, or simply forced their neighbors to comply with numerous food regulations. The pettiness, indeed the silliness, to which the patriotic meddling could descend is illustrated by the following item from a contemporary newspaper:

> Here is your schedule for eating for the next 4 weeks which must be rigidly observed, says S. C. Findley, County Food Administrator:
>
> *Monday:* Wheatless every meal.
> *Tuesday:* Meatless every meal.
> *Wednesday:* Wheatless every meal.
> *Thursday:* Breakfast, meatless; supper, wheatless.
> *Friday:* Breakfast, meatless; supper, wheatless.
> *Saturday:* Porkless every meal; meatless breakfast.
> *Sunday:* Meatless breakfast; wheatless supper.
>
> Sugar must be used very sparingly at all times. Do not put sugar in your coffee unless this is a long habit, and in that case use only one spoonful.

Diners kept watch to make sure that everyone followed the Food Administration's twelve rules for restaurant eating. Retailers had to require every purchaser of wheat to buy an equal amount of another cereal. People were forbidden at different times to kill hens, to eat meat, or to eat more than two pounds of meat a week. Naturally the operation of thousands of petty tyrannies caused unpopular people to suffer harassment at the hands of those who wielded the government's profusely scattered authority.[40]

But a purpose was served. Like the local draft boards, the thousands of local food officials helped to insulate the Wilson administration from popular resentment of and opposition to its pervasive controls. Though Hoover never ceased to distinguish the "voluntary" program of American food controls from its more dictatorial European counterparts, the licensing system through which the Food Administration exerted its powers was patterned after techniques employed in Europe.[41]

Similarly the government's price and physical allocation controls over fuels were "enlightened probably by Great Britain's experience."[42] The proximate cause of the authority over fuels, delegated to the President by the Lever Act, was soaring coal prices: from a range of $1.25 to $1.50 per ton at the mine in the summer of 1916, prices leaped to a range of $7.00 to $8.00 in the summer of 1917. Businessmen as well as governmental officials resented the increase, and hence "vociferous appeal for government control arose from quarters where the contrary is always expected." Making quick use of his new powers the President in late August created the United States Fuel Administration and proclaimed prices in the various mining regions.[43] The dictated prices failed to take account of quality variations in coal, prompting operators to close high-quality mines and produce more coal with high ash content. According to Benjamin Anderson, a contemporary economist, "a great deal of unnecessary disorder arose." In January 1918 the Fuel Administrator, Harry A. Garfield, nearly brought American industry to its knees by ordering all businesses east of the Mississippi not absolutely necessary for war production to reduce their daily fuel usage to customary Sunday quantities during the five days from January 18 through January 22 and on each of the following nine Mondays. By this drastic action, coal shipments were expedited to some 250 munitions-laden ships stalled in eastern ports for want of fuel.[44]

Garfield's fuel holiday and the subsequent "heatless Mondays" vividly dramatized the confusion into which the government's entire program of economic mobilization had fallen in the first winter of the war. "[I]t must be conceded," said Clarkson, "that in the latter part of 1917 and the first part of 1918, the evolution of the basic war control halted and stumbled." The government itself, by its uncoordinated and unrestrained proliferation of purchasing orders, requisitions, and controls, created this chaos; the crisis did not signify, as some have suggested, a breakdown of the market system.

[A]ll Government orders were "rush," and thousands of army and navy officers and flocks of agents of the Emergency Fleet Corporation and the Food and Fuel Administrations goaded the producers to a fury of disordered effort. . . . Even as the deluge grew and the disorder advanced, two-score Government purchasing agencies beat the whirlpool to froth with their bidding and scheming against each other, each obsessed with a mad determination to achieve his own goal. . . . Everything for the Government was preferred until there was no longer a semblance of preference.[45]

For the mobilization to proceed, some means would have to be devised to bring order to the government's uncoordinated and vastly unsettling actions.

Wilson's management of the war economy had attracted many critics from the start, but the crisis of the winter of 1917–1918 provoked them to bring forth extraordinary challenges to his war program and sweeping proposals for its institutional reorganization. Leading the pack was Senator George Chamberlain of Oregon, Chairman of the Committee on Military Affairs. Early in 1918 Chamberlain introduced a bill to create a new department patterned after the British ministry of munitions, to be headed by three civilians with wide and exclusive authority to manage all aspects of the war mobilization, including the procurement functions so jealously guarded by the Army and the Navy. The President, recognizing that the arrangement would effectively transfer authority from him to the proposed ministry, actively opposed it.[46]

To head off Chamberlain's challenge and quiet the critics, Wilson proposed to rearrange and strengthen some existing agencies and to fortify the reorganized bodies with an explicit statutory mandate. Accordingly he wrote and forwarded to Congress a bill giving him authority to rearrange executive departments, their duties, and their jurisdictions without the case-by-case approval of Congress. The bill was introduced by Senator Lee Overman of North Carolina early in February. After extended and heated debate—one senator objected that it would make Wilson a king in everything but name—it became law on May 20, 1918. Thus, according to a historian, "those legislative warriors on the Hill, who had fought many battles with the Chief Executive, had created a dictatorship in the White House."[47]

In reality the Overman Act fell short of making Wilson a dictator, but it did allow him to reorganize the mobilization program. His most important step was to separate from the Council of National Defense the feeble War Industries Board that had been operating since July 1917. He now made it directly responsible to him and delegated to it substantial power. Until its invigoration in March 1918 the WIB had been "a clearing house rather than a directorate." Essentially headless, it had staggered along, attempting without much success to set some priorities, fix a few prices, and coordinate the government's purchases. Government purchasing agents had frequently ignored it. Now the WIB became "a sort of inspector-general of the other war agencies." Baruch, who had headed one of the old board's committees, was placed in charge of the new board. In Clarkson's worshipful hyperbole, "a tired, bored, and discouraged committee had been replaced with an industrial dictator."[48]

In truth the President did not make Baruch a dictator, but he did convey to him clear and significant authority.[49] In his letter of March 4, offering Baruch the appointment as chairman of the WIB, Wilson made plain that "the ultimate decision of all questions, except the determination of prices, should rest always with the Chairman, the other members acting in a cooperative and advisory capacity." (The hypersensitive task of fixing prices was assigned to a separate committee within the WIB directly responsible to the President.) While the chairman "should act as the general eye of all supply departments in the field of industry," he was pointedly instructed to "let alone what is being successfully done and interfere as little as possible with the normal processes of purchase and delivery in the several departments."[50] In other words, the Army, the Navy, the Emergency Fleet Corporation, the Railroad Administration, and all the other governmental agencies purchasing goods and services from private suppliers were to retain their procurement powers. The President did not intend to surrender to Baruch the power he had fought so hard to keep in the struggle over a proposed ministry of munitions. Still, the new WIB would have plenty to do.

The President's letter identified its functions as follows:

(1) The creation of new facilities and the disclosing, if necessary, the opening up of new or additional sources of supply;

(2) The conversion of existing facilities, where necessary, to new uses;

(3) The studious conservation of resources and facilities by scientific, commercial, and industrial economies;

(4) Advice to the several purchasing agencies of the Government with regard to the prices to be paid;

(5) The determination, wherever necessary, of priorities of production and of delivery and of the proportions of any given article to be made immediately accessible to the several purchasing agencies when the supply of that article is insufficient, either temporarily or permanently;

(6) The making of purchases for the Allies.[51]

In pursuit of these diverse objectives the WIB involved itself pervasively in the industrial economy.[52]

Unlike the Shipping Board, the Food Administration, and the Fuel Administration, the WIB had no officially prescribed sanctions to enforce its decisions. Presumably Baruch wielded as delegate the full array of presidential war powers, but exactly what these entailed remained uncertain and open to dispute. Lacking congressionally clarified legal potency the WIB always tried first to gain voluntary cooperation with its decisions. It resorted next to beating recalcitrants with the club of patriotism, empahsizing "the injustice of permitting some at home to profit—and to profiteer—while our boys were away fighting and dying."[53] It could often bring to bear irresistible indirect sanctions by enlisting the Railroad Administration to deny transportation services, the Fuel Administration to withhold fuel, or the War Trade Board to shut off access to international trade. If all else failed, it could ask the War Department or another authorized agency to commandeer the misbehaver's private property, an action these authorities were hardly timid about taking. (Indeed, so anxious were the military authorities to commandeer plants that the WIB was more at pains to restrain than to stimulate the use of this ultimate sanction. The War Department alone made 510 requisitions of goods and issued 996 compulsory production orders.)[54]

"The most important instrument of control," Baruch affirmed, "was the power to determine priority—the power to determine who gets what and when." The significance of establishing priorities, he said, had been impressed on him in 1916 by a British economist, Sir Walter Layton. Again the ubiquitous "British experience" was at work. Setting priorities was "a complex and delicate task":

> Should locomotives go to Pershing to carry his army to the front or should they go to Chile to haul nitrates needed to make ammunition for Pershing's troops? Should precedence be given to destroyers needed to fight the U-boats or to merchant ships whose numbers were being decimated by the German subs? Should nitrates be allocated to munitions or to fertilizer? Should the Railroad Administration or the Fuel Administration get the tank cars both were claiming?

Having more or less set aside the price system, which normally reconciles the multitude of competing demands for resources, the authorities undertook to determine what would best promote the social welfare. "We were not," Baruch admitted, "always as wise as Solomon in deciding these questions."[55] Although official priorities displaced prices in determining the allocation of many resources, prices remained important in determining the distribution of income.

The WIB's price-fixing committee, headed by Robert S. Brookings, a retired lumber merchant, had no legal power to set prices unilaterally. Instead its dollar-a-year men negotiated with selected industrialists—mostly producers of metals, chemicals, construction materials, textiles, and leather goods— to reach voluntary agreements. It was often hard to tell whether government or business had the upper hand in the dealings, and some historians have assailed the board for allowing itself to become an instrument for creating and maintaining de facto cartels.[56]

In an important sense the criticism misses the point. Although businessmen sometimes did use the WIB to acquire cozy cost-plus-a-percentage-of-cost contracts, set favorable prices, or shield themselves from competition, the price system had been rendered largely nugatory as a determinant of resource allocation. "Instead of allowing prices to determine what would be produced and where it would go," said Baruch, "*we decided* [that is, top governmental officials decided] . . . how *our* [that is, everybody's] resources would be employed."[57] This strong assertion needs qualification, to be sure, as the price system did not entirely cease to operate, but it does express the important fact that the WIB exerted genuine power over resource allocation in 1918. While dismissing the idea of "industrial dictatorship" and appreciating the merely political serviceability of the invigorated board in quieting critics of Wilsonian war management, one should not make the mistake of regarding the board as purely cosmetic. The WIB was, all the shakiness of its legal foundations notwithstanding, an enormously powerful agency. Although its mature phase lasted only eight months, it made during that time a profound impact on resource allocation. (And we shall see that it may have had an even greater impact fifteen years later, when people would recall and act upon the "lessons" it had taught them about how to deal with an "economic emergency.")

Despite the immense variety of governmental intrusions into the market system in 1917 and 1918 the economy remained capitalistic in the sense that private capital markets continued to operate. But they did not always operate as the government wished. Some enterprises the government considered essential to its mobilization program—especially in lumbering, coal mining, public utilities, and certain areas of manufacturing—found themselves unable to sell their bonds or to obtain loans from private financial institutions. The problem, like so many others, was actually of the government's own making. Massive governmental borrowing was displacing private borrowing.

To remedy the problem, Treasury Secretary McAdoo recommended the creation of a governmental lending agency to fill the critical gaps opened by the Treasury's gargantuan absorption of loanable funds. Congress responded with an act of April 5, 1918, creating the War Finance Corporation and endowing it with a capital of $500 million and the authority to borrow up to $3 billion by issuing bonds. With McAdoo as ex-officio chairman and Eugene Meyer, a wealthy investor and prewar associate of Baruch, as its managing director, the WFC began business on May 20 as "a rescue mission for essential war-disrupted industries." It lent both to financial institutions making government-approved loans and directly to commodity-producing firms. In the six months that it operated during the war the corporation lent some $71 million. It also took over the big job of stabilizing the market for government bonds, a task previously performed by J. P. Morgan and Company.[58] At the end of the war, as we shall see, the WFC refused to die; at least it would not stay dead for long. So pregnant with political utility was this all-purpose financial rescue mission that it was destined to be revived, not always under the same name, again and again.

The act that created the WFC also gave official status to the Capital Issues Committee, which had operated since early 1918 as an office of the Federal Reserve Board, and authorized it to rule on whether proposed issues of private securities in excess of $100,000 would contribute to what the government regarded as essential war purposes. This official validation lacked decisiveness, however, as Congress had not granted the committee any power to forbid the issues it disapproved. "Fortunately," said McAdoo, "their rulings were observed voluntarily and as a patriotic duty by most of the concerns . . . though there were some rather vicious exceptions."[59] Again the Wilson administration relied on swollen patriotism, a sentiment it ceaselessly animated, to tilt the allocation of private resources in the direction desired by the government.

LABOR PROBLEMS AND THE RAILROAD TAKEOVER

More than any previous federal administration, the Wilson government favored organized labor, and union membership increased rapidly during the war. When the Council of National Defense was organized in the fall of 1916, Samuel Gompers, the venerable president of the American Federation of Labor, was appointed to its Advisory Commission. Organized labor also received representation on many of the war agencies later created, including the Selective Service System, the Food Administration, the Railroad Administration, and the War Industries Board.[60]

More than sympathy for unionists impelled the government: work stoppages posed a serious threat to the war mobilization program. The year 1917 witnessed 4,450 strikes, an all-time high. Sometimes workers could be intimidated into staying on the job—once the President threatened to blacklist striking machinists to deny them war-related work and promised that "the draft boards will be instructed to reject any claim of exemption based on your alleged usefulness on war production"—but usually the government correctly perceived that such heavy-handedness would only prove counterproductive.[61]

The prevailing policy was the more conciliatory one of supporting union organization and compulsory collective bargaining, the eight-hour day, and union work rules. Employers could be indemnified by cost-plus contracts with governmental procurement agencies. To help resolve some of the larger and more threatening labor-management disputes, Wilson in September 1917 created the President's Mediation Commission, whose secretary and legal counsel was Felix Frankfurter, a Harvard law professor destined to exert a great influence on public affairs for a long time to come.[62]

As the government's involvement in labor relations expanded, it grew more and more confused, finally prompting a reorganization in January 1918 that featured the creation by executive order of a War Labor Administration to be headed by the Secretary of Labor, William B. Wilson. The Secretary appointed a National War Labor Board to provide mediation and conciliation in labor disputes and a War Labor Policies Board, headed by Frankfurter, to consider all aspects of wartime labor relations. The WLPB, essentially a clearinghouse, had power only to recommend policies to other governmental agencies. It "never achieved the complete harmony and cooperation among the splintered labor agencies that Frankfurter desired." Though he has been described as the Czar of Labor in World War I, Frankfurter fell far short of his ambitions. A "prowar progressive," he had "an exaggerated belief in the possibilities of social reform through national mobilization made possible by the state of emergency." According to a recent biographer, he "sometimes confused the requirements of mobilization with the demands of justice and sacrificed the immediate interests of ordinary citizens to the enticing vision of a world made safe for democracy."[63]

Nowhere was the labor problem more vexatious than in the railroad industry. Already the threat of a nationwide strike by the operating brotherhoods in the winter of 1916–1917 had compelled the President and a compliant Congress to bring forth, and the Supreme Court to sustain, the Adamson Act. But the effective wage increase produced by the legal imposition of a standard eight-hour day failed to satisfy the unions for long. Toward the end of 1917 they again threatened a nationwide strike. Of course, this would have dealt a mortal blow to the war mobilization program and was completely unacceptable to the Wilson administration. Something had to be done to banish the looming specter.

The railroad companies could do nothing to forestall the strike; they still had their hands tied. If they summarily raised wages substantially without increasing rates and fares, they were sure to incur losses. Yet the shipper-dominated ICC in recent years had repeatedly turned down their requests for general rate hikes. They could not cooperate with one another to effect major improvements in the operating efficiency of the overall railroad system without exposing themselves to the threat of antitrust prosecution. In the circumstances, investors had come to view the industry without enthusiasm, and capital could not be attracted in large amounts except at extraordinary rates of interest. After American entry into the war, massive Treasury borrowing further displaced railroad borrowing, making it even more difficult for the companies to market their debt. Starved for capital to maintain, enlarge, and modernize their facilities, the railroads had suffered a deterioration in the quality of their services. When the war boom created a surge of shipments, the companies were ill-situated to handle the new business expeditiously.

The government's poorly conceived and ill-coordinated mobilization efforts only exacerbated the railroad problems. The draft siphoned off skilled as well as unskilled railroad workers, and war contractors enticed others away with offers of higher pay. The government placed the bulk of its war business with firms in the Northeast, where railroad traffic was already heaviest, and thereby virtually insured that congestion of tracks and terminals would result. Shipments to Europe continued to be routed via the most heavily used eastern ports. The military departments withdrew many Atlantic coastal vessels, diverting still more traffic onto the railroads. Transportation priorities were issued by the military authorities in such thoughtless profusion that they ceased to perform any genuine service in speeding the most urgently needed freight. To make an already desperate situation worse, the winter of 1917–1918 turned out to be the most severe in memory, with heavy snowfalls and bitter cold that further impeded the operations of the railroads. Car shortages and traffic tie-ups threatened to clog the nation's vital arteries of transportation and cripple the entire economy, including the government's mobilization for war. Late in 1917 Wilson was "more disturbed over the condition of the railroads than he was over any other problems of Administration." Governmental officials themselves had tied this Gordian knot and could conceive of only one way to sever it.[64]

The government's solution was to employ the authority granted by the Army Appropriations Act of 1916 and take over the railroads, which the President did by his proclamation of December 26, 1917. "Neither the President nor anybody else in the Administration wanted to take them over," wrote McAdoo. "It was done as an imperative war measure."[65]

The Treasury Secretary was disingenuous, perhaps. He himself had urged the takeover on the President (by this time his father-in-law). As the decisive force behind the earlier passage of the Shipping Act, McAdoo could hardly claim to oppose nationalization on principled grounds. Moreover, knowing that he would probably be put in charge if the railroads were nationalized no doubt whetted his appetite—no one ever accused the Crown Prince of lacking a taste for power. In any event, few people strenuously opposed the takeover, given the sorry situation that had developed. As expected, McAdoo was named Director-General of the United States Railroad Administration, the agency created to manage the commandeered properties. He possessed, as he modestly described it, "an authority that was as nearly absolute as any power can be in America." The government's takeover of the railroads has been portrayed by David Kennedy, a leading historian of World War I, as "without doubt the most drastic mobilization measure of the war. Closing the hand of government over the country's largest and most essential enterprise, Wilson's action had enormous economic scope. It also had rich potential for lasting institutional change."[66]

The Railroad Administration roamed freely where the railroad companies had been economically unable or legally forbidden to go. The entire industry was operated as a unit: "Competition in all its aspects was eliminated." Many services were discontinued or reduced in the interest of "efficiency." (Never was it clearer that the "efficient" allocation of resources depends entirely on who holds the property rights, that is, the effective power to decide how resources will be used.) Passenger service in particular was curtailed. Freight was sent by the shortest route regardless of shipper preferences for longer but cheaper routes. Less-than-carload shipments were restricted. These and many other changes were not, a contemporary analyst observed, "carried out without dissatisfaction to passengers and shippers."[67] But now the government, not the consumer, was sovereign in the market for railroad services.

Likewise in the labor market. To assuage the unions, McAdoo in May ordered wages raised substantially, retroactive to January 1, 1918. "I have never done anything in my life," he later affirmed, "that gave me so much satisfaction." The pay increases were not uniform; rather, they provided larger percentage increases for the lower-paid employees, thereby effectuating the Director-General's personal conception of distributive justice at the expense of shippers and taxpayers. McAdoo also established the eight-hour working day, with time-and-a-half rates of pay for overtime work, for some railroad workers who had not previously enjoyed these terms of employment.[68]

To offset the concessions to labor, McAdoo increased freight rates on the average by about 28 percent and passenger fares by about 18 percent, effective June 25. Although the increases aroused tremendous resentment at the time, they were far too small to compensate for the increased labor costs and for a factor that tended to be ignored in shippers' arguments, namely, the rapidly shrinking purchasing power of money. As Clark recognized some years later, "railroad transportation became relatively cheap, supported by government subsidy," as the government's operation of the industry created a "deficit" that had to be covered by funds from the Treasury.[69] The railroad deficit quickly became the focus of heated controversy.

In the Federal Control Act, passed by Congress on March 21, 1918, the government promised to pay the owners of the commandeered railroad properties an annual rent equal to each company's average net operating income during the three years ending June 30, 1917.[70] At the time, many considered the payment too generous. Because of inflation, however, the guaranteed payment steadily diminished in real value—the consumer price index rose 56 percent between 1917 and 1920—so the railroad owners were hardly getting a good deal. Still, under the government's management, railroad earnings fell short of the rent due the companies; hence the deficit.[71]

To governmental officials the deficit mattered little. "Our first duty," declared McAdoo, "was to keep the trains moving, regardless of costs or profits. . . . [T]he deficit had to be faced as a part of the cost of the war." Clark, a more disinterested observer, agreed that the deficit was part of the war's cost and explained that it "represents simply a shifting to a different group of persons of part of the cost of railroad operation. . . . People paid less freight rates and must ultimately pay more taxes."[72]

Clark's analysis is astute as far as it goes, but in the perspective of political economy it does not go far enough. The deficit shifted costs, to be sure, but not "simply." Indeed the shift was quite cunning. By spreading the railroad deficit across the entire population of taxpayers and purchasers of war bonds, rather than compelling shippers and passengers to pay the full cost of railroad services in the form of higher rates and fares, the government reduced the likelihood of opposition to its policies by making their full costs harder to identify. In the emotional Liberty Bond drives, those who provided the government with the bulk of its general revenues were encouraged, indeed officially agitated, to think of their contributions as arming Johnny in the trenches. That prevailing if largely contrived attitude made it easier for the Wilson administration to accumulate the wherewithal to raise the real wages of railroad workers, subsidize the provision of railroad services, and avoid the hostile political reaction that a policy more honestly matching costs and benefits would have generated.

At the end of the war McAdoo and others, including some Progressive intellectuals and a few populistic farm groups, urged continuation of governmental control over the railroads. In addition the railroad unions, which had opposed nationalization before the war, now saw "the wisdom of a perpetual alliance with the Federal Administration." But the railroad owners pressed hard to recover control of their properties, and most groups of shippers longed to reassert their influence over rate-making through the ICC, which the Railroad Administration had largely set aside after the takeover. Control of the railroads remained up for grabs while the political battles raged for more than a year after the end of the war.

Not until 1920 did the government return the railroads to private management—and then only with strings attached. As we shall see, the latitude allowed railroad owners to manage their own property would never again be as wide as it had been before the war.[73] The Federal Control Act had expressly declared itself to be "emergency legislation enacted to meet conditions growing out of war," adding that "nothing herein is to be construed as expressing or prejudicing the future policy of the Federal Government concerning the ownership, control, or regulation of carriers."[74] Brave words. But after such a vast experiment, reversion to the status quo ante was highly unlikely.

SUPREME COURT RULINGS ON WAR MEASURES

Because many of the actions taken by the government during World War I had no precedent, much less any established constitutionality, court challenges inevitably arose. For the most part the cases were not decided by the

Supreme Court until after the war, when, as a distinguished legal scholar put it, the justices could "only lock the doors after the Liberty Bell [had been] stolen." Nevertheless, the decisions had great significance, because they established precedents for future legal proceedings. In virtually every case the Court upheld the extraordinary powers exercised by the government during 1917–1918.[75]

One set of cases, perhaps the most important of all, did receive expeditious hearing and decision: the military conscription cases.[76] Although men had been conscripted during the Civil War, the Supreme Court had never ruled on the constitutionality of the draft. In 1918 the Court's unanimous decision to uphold the draft found this governmental prerogative implied by the constitutional grant of war powers in combination with the Necessary-and-Proper Clause. Speaking for the Court, Chief Justice Edward White said: "It may not be doubted that the very conception of a just government and its duty to the citizen includes the reciprocal obligation of the citizen to render military service in case of need and the right to compel it." Thus spoke a former Confederate soldier. The Chief Justice could not take seriously the idea that the draft was involuntary servitude and therefore proscribed by the Thirteenth Amendment. He declared that the Court was "unable to conceive upon what theory the exaction by government from the citizen of the performance of his supreme and noble duty of contributing to the defense of the rights and honor of the nation, as the result of a war declared by the great representative body of the people, can be said to be the imposition of involuntary servitude."

Under the prevailing social conditions, permeated by war hysteria, superheated patriotism, and vigilante attacks on "slackers," the ruling was wellnigh inevitable. Men were, after all, being thrown in jail merely for *questioning* the constitutionality of the draft. (The Attorney General went so far as to request the aid of the American Protective League, a private organization of superpatriots, to locate draft resisters. Members of the league conducted numerous "slacker raids," made some forty thousand citizens' arrests, and investigated about three million suspected subversives.) Leon Friedman, an authority on constitutional law, has argued that the draft-law cases "were based upon superficial arguments, disregard of substantial historical evidence, and undue deference to the exigencies of the First World War—in short, that they were incorrectly decided." Nevertheless, he could write in 1969 that "[t]hese decisions have never been seriously challenged, and have been cited repeatedly as determining that question once and for all time." Clearly this institutional legacy of World War I cast a long shadow, as the Court's opinion of 1918 "has survived unchallenged as part of our constitutional doctrine."[77]

A related series of free-speech decisions also upheld the extraordinary reach of the government's wartime powers. The Espionage Act, as indicated above, had "found its real teeth in a provision aimed at willfully obstructing the recruiting or enlistment service." Moreover, "This section was widely used to curtail activities of persons not in sympathy with the conduct of the war."[78] In 1919 and 1920 the Supreme Court ruled against persons who had made antiwar speeches, mailed antidraft pamphlets, and questioned in print the constitutionality of the draft. In the famous *Schenck* decision Justice Oliver Wendell Holmes, Jr., outraged loyal supporters of the First Amendment by declaring: "When a nation is at war, many things that might be said in time of peace are such a hindrance to its effort that their utterance will not be endured so long as men fight and no Court could regard them as protected by any constitutional right."[79] Thus spoke a veteran of Civil War combat for the Union.

The postwar decisions on freedom of speech are now widely regarded as among the most deplorable in American constitutional history. Often overlooked, however, is the common thread that runs through them. Every one of them involved speech perceived by the authorities as threatening the government's successful conscription of men for war. Had the Wilson administration not resorted to a military draft in the first place, it would have had much less to fear from freedom of speech and hence less incentive to suppress it by draconian measures like the Espionage Act and its notorious amendment, the Sedition Act of 1918. In the opinion of a constitutional historian, the free-speech cases that arose from opposition to the draft "left a legal residue available for governmental use more immediate and ominous than in any of the other war power areas."[80]

Having found no fault with the government's suppression of First-Amendment rights, the justices had no qualms about the validation of other extraordinary governmental war measures. In several cases decided in 1919 the Court upheld the constitutionality of the government's takeovers of the railroads, telephone and telegraph lines, and oceanic cables. All the takings were viewed as legitimate exercises of the war powers of the Congress. "[T]he complete and undivided character of the war power of the United States," said the Chief Justice in the railroad decision, "is not disputable."[81]

Whatever the wisdom of placing the government's emergency powers beyond effective legal challenge during the war, the selfsame powers in several instances lingered on, long after the guns had ceased firing in France. As late as the spring of 1921 the Court ruled that a rent-control ordinance that Congress had imposed in late 1919 in the District of Columbia—"its provisions were made necessary by emergencies growing out of the war"— "was not, in the prevailing circumstances, an unconstitutional restriction of the owner's dominion and right of contract or a taking of his property for a use not public." The ruling, which placed great emphasis on the temporariness of the disputed rent controls, seemed to the dissenters to open the door to all kinds of governmental restrictions of the private right of contract. "As a power in government," wrote Justice McKenna, "if it exist at all, it is perennial and universal. . . . [N]ecessarily, if one contract can be disregarded in the public interest every contract can be. . . . [O]ther exigencies may come to the Government making necessary other appeals."[82]

LEGACIES, INSTITUTIONAL AND IDEOLOGICAL

"[N]othing has remained untouched by the war," wrote J. M. Clark in 1931. "Everything that has happened has happened differently because of it."[83] Of course the inevitable postwar revulsion against the great crusade, its sacrifices, and its emotional strains did produce a widespread longing for what presidential candidate Warren Harding called a "return to normalcy." But reversion to the prewar status quo was not to be, could not be. The experience had entered inextricably into the life of the society, with numerous and diverse consequences.

The fiscal activities of the federal government assumed permanently enlarged dimensions. Although the government had concealed many costs by commanding the use of resources at below-market prices, the war had been an enormous financial undertaking. Before the war, federal revenues had never exceeded $762 million in a fiscal year; during the 1920s they were never less than $3,640 million. Before the war, federal expenditures had never exceeded $747 million in a fiscal year; during the 1920s they were never less than $2,800 million. Part of the increase reflected only the higher postwar price level, which was more than 50 percent above the prewar level, but the bulk of it was real. The public debt, which had been slightly more than $1 billion before the war, was over $25 billion at the end of the war and remained almost $17 billion as late as 1929.

After the armistice the more than four million men who had served in uniform became a political rather than a military force. Again and again they would place demands on the peacetime Treasury, as if insisting that the government make restitution for the costs it had imposed on them in 1917 and 1918. Though a war be ever so brief, its veterans survive for decades and form a potent political interest group. The American Legion, founded in 1919, would make its voice heard forever after.

During the war, income-tax rates had been increased enormously, especially for upper-income taxpayers (see Table 7.1). As John F. Witte has observed, "cries of 'ability to pay' and 'war profiteering' drowned out pleas for defense against 'class legislation.'" In 1918 the government made a substantial exaction even on middle-class taxpayers. The tax law as late as 1928 continued to place much greater burdens on upper incomes than it had

Table 7.1
Federal Individual Income Tax Exemptions, and First and Top Bracket Rates, 1913–1928

| Income Year | Personal Exemptions | | Tax Rates | | | |
| | Single | Married, Two Dependents | First Bracket | | Top Bracket | |
			Rate (%)	Income	Rate (%)	Income
1913–1915	$3,000	$4,000	1	$20,000	7	$ 500,000
1916	3,000	4,000	2	20,000	15	2,000,000
1917	1,000	2,400	2	2,000	67	2,000,000
1918	1,000	2,400	6	4,000	77	1,000,000
1919–1920	1,000	2,400	4	4,000	73	1,000,000
1921	1,000	3,300	4	4,000	73	1,000,000
1922	1,000	3,300	4	4,000	73	1,000,000
1923	1,000	3,300	3	4,000	56	200,000
1924	1,000	3,300	1½	4,000	56	200,000
1925–1928	1,500	4,300	1⅛	4,000	25	100,000

Source: U.S. Bureau of the Census, Historical Statistics, p. 1095.

during 1913–1915. The war produced a permanent shift in the sources of federal revenue, away from consumption taxes (including the tariff) and toward income, profit, and estate taxes disproportionately laid on those with high income and wealth. "Without the crisis and the huge financial demands it put upon the government," Kennedy concludes, "that shift in incidence and the accepted legitimacy of such a degree of progression in the tax system might have come about much more slowly, if at all."[84]

Many other wartime innovations survived in the 1920s. The national prohibition of alcoholic beverages, first authorized by the Lever Act, achieved the highest legal sanction with its embodiment in the Constitution. Perhaps in time the prohibitionists would have forced the society to perform the great experiment anyway, but the war hastened the day. Rent controls, which had sprung up during the war in many cities with the active encouragement of federal authorities, gave birth to a political constituency and persisted for years, reducing the expected return on housing investment. Hence the construction of new housing, greatly diminished by severe wartime restrictions on civilian building, had to await revival by "the relaxation or disappearance of the post-war control of rents; coming about finally by a slower process."[85]

Though most of the federal emergency agencies, including the WIB, closed up shop soon after the armistice in compliance with the President's general policy of scrapping them as quickly as possible, some remained in business for months or even years. The Food Administration did not terminate until June 1, 1920. Meanwhile its Grain Corporation continued to guarantee farmers a price of $2.20 per bushel of wheat and marketed the crop of 1919. The Fuel Administration, after having been formally closed on June 30, 1919, was revived in the fall of 1919 to fix fuel prices and did not expire until December 13. The War Trade Board, which had exercised absolute control over international trade during the war, ceased to act as a separate entity on June 30, 1919, but some of its functions and personnel were shifted to the Department of State. Not until May 27, 1921, was it abolished by an act of Congress. Even then a residuum of its controls persisted, being administered for a while longer within the Treasury Department.[86]

The Railroad Administration continued to operate the nation's railroads, losing money all the while, until March 1, 1920, when the properties were officially returned to the management of their owners under the terms of the Transportation Act of 1920. This law, says a legal historian, "stopped only short of nationalization." It gave the Interstate Commerce Commission complete control over rates. In addition it authorized the ICC to regulate the issuance of railroad securities and the expenditure of the proceeds as well as all consolidations and the construction, use, and abandonment of facilities. It created a Railway Labor Board to mediate disputes. Its "recapture" provision required that a portion of a company's earnings in excess of an allowable "fair return" be diverted to railroads with relatively low earnings.[87] After 1920, private property rights in the railroad industry had little substance. Except the most routine administrative actions, almost everything the owners might do was subject to federal regulation or determination. Thereafter, holders of railroad stocks and bonds hardly differed from holders of U.S. government securities, and railroad workers closely resembled governmental employees.

The Shipping Board had been created as a regular governmental agency, so of course it survived the war. The board's biggest postwar problem was the enormous fleet of vessels produced by its Emergency Fleet Corporation, most of which did not reach the water until well after the war had ended. The Merchant Marine Act of 1920 authorized the sale of the ships to American firms on easy terms, including some tax breaks, and provided for subsidies to private operators. It also authorized a governmental Merchant Fleet Corporation to operate shipping lines; hence the EFC lived on under a new name. The shipping business remained depressed during the 1920s, and the government's ventures resulted in chronic losses. By 1929 the Shipping Board had disposed of almost two-thirds of its tonnage. Of the remainder, much lay idle. The country found itself, according to Clark, in "a rather paradoxical situation. The legacy of a huge fleet built for war purposes has precipitated us into a position in which a strong urge toward public assistance has been inevitable in order to give our marine, now that chance has forced one upon us, a tenable economic position. Yet the war-time ships are largely unsuitable to this postwar demand, and fresh construction is called for."[88]

The War Finance Corporation proved hard to kill after the war. Although its wartime mission, assisting essential war industries unable to secure loans through private channels, no longer required attention, its character as a capital-market "rescue mission" suggested to some, especially its astute managing director, Eugene Meyer, that it ought to be assigned new tasks. With the cessation of governmental loans to the Allies after the armistice, European countries found themselves unable to finance a continuing large-scale importation of American commodities. American exporters viewed the situation with understandable horror. To forestall "confusion and despair on both sides of the Atlantic," Meyer proposed to use the WFC to finance American exports, and in March 1919 he nursed through Congress a bill to authorize an expenditure of a billion dollars for this purpose. When the law expired in May 1920, Meyer resigned from the WFC.

But he soon returned. Supported by bankers, businessmen, and journalists concerned about mounting problems in the agricultural economy, Meyer in late 1920 pleaded with congressional committees to revive the WFC. His efforts quickly bore fruit. On December 13, Congress by joint resolution directed the Secretary of the Treasury to resume funding for the WFC's export-financing loans. Wilson vetoed the measure, but Congress overrode the veto by a large margin. After the Senate confirmed Meyer's nomination on March 14, 1921, he was back in business as managing director. Later that year the Agricultural Credits Act officially transformed the WFC into "a rescue mission for the nation's distressed farmers." In this phase the WFC lent large sums to agricultural cooperatives as well as to rural banks. Its lending authority was extended three times.

Not until January 1925 did Meyer liquidate the agency. During its several lives it had lent roughly $300 million for war purposes, $100 million to finance exports, and $300 million directly or indirectly to assist farmers.[89] It had made an impressive mark, especially for a bureau created specifically to deal with a wartime emergency, but, as we shall see, all that the WFC did before 1925 pales by comparison with what it was to do after its revival seven years later under the name Reconstruction Finance Corporation.

A diffuse but still significant legacy of the war was the "associationalism" that flourished during the 1920s. The war had brought thousands of businessmen, many of them working for token compensation as dollar-a-year men, into governmental positions. Especially at the WIB, but to some extent in most of the emergency agencies, former businessmen dealt across the table with active businessmen. Naturally they found it easy to do business; and just as naturally the business they did was often, in effect, a conspiracy against competitors and consumers. (Adam Smith long ago warned that "[p]eople of the same trade seldom meet together . . . but the conversation ends in a conspiracy against the public, or in some contrivance to raise prices. . . . [T]he law . . . ought to do nothing to facilitate such assemblies, much less to render them necessary.") The great scale on which business had been mobilized and brought into contact with powerful but often congenial governmental officials awakened many businessmen to the lucrative possibilities of working more closely with government than they had thought possible or desirable before the war.

To develop and systematize this potentially fruitful "partnership," businessmen during the twenties created or expanded many trade associations. Government, especially the Commerce Department during Hoover's long tenure as Secretary, not only approved of this activity but did much to stimulate and foster it. Provoked by the energetic organizational activity of businessmen, others followed suit: professional groups, farmers, even social workers. The result was

> a marked shift toward corporatism in the nation's business affairs. Entire industries, even entire economic sectors, as in the case of agriculture, were organized and disciplined as never before, and brought into close and regular relations with counterpart congressional committees, cabinet departments,

and Executive agencies. . . . From the war can be dated the origins of the modern practice of massive informal collusion between government and organized private enterprise.[90]

Thus, among the war's most significant legacies was a heightened politicization of the nation's economic life. Landmarks of the ensuing developments included the Air Commerce Act and the Railway Labor Act, both approved in 1926. The former embedded the federal government in the management of an industry just getting off the ground, while the latter extended a bit further the government's intrusion in a long-troubled area of labor relations.

The associationalism of the 1920s intimates the most pregnant of all the war's legacies: ideological change. Because the spirit of the twenties has been so often characterized by historians and others as reactionary, the fundamental ideological shift has been generally overlooked or depreciated. But ample testimony attests to its reality and significance. "[T]he experience of war planning," said Soule, "exerted a permanent influence on the thinking of the economists and engineers who participated in it."[91]

But the economists and engineers were not the only ones affected; many others experienced the same change of views. In particular, many businessmen came away from the war with a new perspective on the relation of government and business. According to Clarkson, who circulated actively in the business community, men who had served as authoritative allocators of resources during the war "meditated with a sort of intellectual contempt on the huge hit-and-miss confusion of peace-time industry. . . . From their meditations arose dreams of an ordered economic world. . . . They beheld the whole trade of the world carefully computed and registered in Washington, requirements noted, American resources on call, the faucets opened or closed according to the circumstances."[92] Of course they envisioned their own hands on the faucet handles.

No one beheld this vision more vividly or more often than Baruch. In his old age he recalled how "men like myself," first brought into the government during World War I, had effected a revolution in the public's attitude toward government:

> The WIB experience had a great influence upon the thinking of business and government. WIB had demonstrated the effectiveness of industrial cooperation and the advantage of government planning and direction. We helped inter the extreme dogmas of laissez faire, which had for so long molded American economic and political thought. Our experience taught that government direction of the economy need not be inefficient or undemocratic, and suggested that in time of danger it was imperative.[93]

Baruch was a deeply interested reporter, and one would be wise to discount somewhat his report of the burial of classical liberal doctrines. The inarticulate commitment of the greater part of the bourgeoisie to these beliefs remained, shaken no doubt yet still animate. Certainly Americans in general felt no urgent need for radical socioeconomic reform in the wake of the war. It would be more accurate to say that the experience of wartime governmental controls "softened up" the middle classes, predisposing them to reforms still to come.

Politically active and articulate leaders on the left learned much from the war. At its end they "hoped to preserve and even extend many of the collectivist practices and much of the state authority that had grown up during the war." Even a more market-oriented Democrat like Secretary of the Navy Josephus Daniels proclaimed the beneficial effect of the war mobilization: "We will not be afraid in peace to do revolutionary things that help mankind, seeing we have become accustomed to doing them in war." He had foremost in mind the governmental control of radio, telephone, and telegraph communications, railroads, and ocean shipping; he also favored peacetime price controls "to protect the public and prevent profiteering." Frankfurter, the former Labor Czar, longed for greater peacetime governmental controls to replace the "chaos of unbridled competition" with the guiding hand of "social scientists and professionally trained experts like himself." He espoused, as did Baruch and Hoover, a continuation of the "cooperation" between labor and management over which he had recently presided in the "rationalized" garrison economy.[94]

Despite the variety of "lessons" people took away from their wartime experience, one thing seems clear: While many viewed the mobilization of the economy as having established both the possibility and the desirability of extended governmental control of economic life, hardly anyone came away from the crisis with an enhanced understanding or appreciation of the market system or greater insight into the inherent cost-imposing, cost-concealing character of a command economy. Of course, many draftees, consumers, businessmen, and others had an ardent self-interested desire to escape from *particular* wartime restrictions bearing on them as individuals; but that is completely different from a revulsion against the command economy *as a system*. Clark spoke wisely when he said: "We have learned things, as men must from any great experience; but too often we seem to have learned the wrong things."[95]

CONCLUSIONS

After the war erupted in Europe its effects on the United States created strong political pressures for the government to "do something." This is not to say that the majority of Americans favored going to war. In fact, there was an overwhelming sentiment to remain neutral. Two years after the outbreak of hostilities, Wilson secured reelection by representing himself as the one who had "kept us out of war." Still, certain war-related problems, such as the rapidly rising costs of ocean shipping and the repeated interferences with or attacks on Americans at sea, led the government in 1916 to enter the shipping business and to give the President sweeping powers over resource allocation in the domestic economy for purposes of war mobilization. Even at this early stage, European examples of the suppression of markets and their replacement by command-and-control systems exerted a strong influence on American thinking.

In early 1917, when the government committed the nation to waging full-scale warfare, it became obvious that raising taxes enough to cover the full market costs of the resources the administration proposed to employ for war purposes would generate immense resistance.[96] For the mobilization to proceed and the government to remain in power the costs had to be at least partially concealed. Accordingly the Wilson administration, with the cooperation of Congress and the Supreme Court, undertook conscription of soldiers, establishment of priorities for the use of transportation, fuel, and manufacturing facilities, price fixing, extensive commandeering, and even outright nationalization of entire industries. To divert attention from the real costs of these actions the government mounted an enormous propaganda compaign to stir up patriotic emotion and encourage citizens to act as monitors and enforcers to suppress those who dared to object or resist. To divide and conquer at the grass-roots level proved an effective tactic to diffuse resistance and insulate the highest authorities from public opposition: witness the thousands of local draft boards, the legion of volunteer food administrators, and the far-flung corps of fuel authorities.

"In time of war," wrote Clark in late 1917, "the movements called for are so huge in quantity and the demand for speed so urgent, that if it were left to the incentives of increased prices and increased wages to bring about these changes, this could only be done at a huge increase in the returns to labor and capital." Precisely. And the increased returns would measure exactly the true social costs of shifting massive amounts of resources to new uses with extraordinary haste. Faster adjustment is in fact socially more costly. It is a fundamental economic fallacy to suppose that compelling people to act more quickly than they are otherwise willing to act "saves time" in the sense of conserving a real resource; it simply shifts the costs of quicker reallocation. But Clark and other contemporaries who rationalized the government's actions did not see it this way. Instead they reasoned: "In such a dilemma the motives of patriotism and the machinery of direct public control can come to the rescue."[97] The question they never raised was: To *whose* rescue?

The problem, in short, was that of "requiring all people to do what but a few people wished."[98] The authorities—President Wilson, Secretary Mc-Adoo, Congressmen Lever and Overman, Chief Justice White, and their confederates in power—wanted people to take certain actions, but they preferred not to jeopardize their own powers and positions by revealing the full costs of the actions and explicitly taxing people enough to compensate fully those who bore the costs. Their first resort was, as economists say, to change people's tastes—by propaganda. Failing that, they would simply command the use of resources, organizing their takings so as to conceal the true value of the resources taken and to diffuse the hostile reactions that might arise.

Evidence on the wartime price controls permits a simple test of the government's motives. Prices were never fixed across the board, but they were fixed for a diverse collection of commodities: soldier's labor, wheat, coal, ammonia, Portland cement, sole leather, burlap, and various others. Why these? Frank Taussig, an eminent economist and a member of the price-fixing committee of the WIB, gave a clear answer:

> The explanation of this great variety of articles—the connecting link between them—is found in the circumstance that all were needed in great quantities by the government. The action of the [price-fixing] Committee in every case had its origin in the circumstance that government purchases were on a great scale and threatened to disturb market prices.[99]

In other words, the objective of the government's price fixing was never to restrain prices in general. Rather, it was specifically to reduce the apparent costs of the goods the government wanted in great abundance for its own purposes and could, by means of the priorities it set or by commandeering, acquire even at below-market prices. As Baruch said, "we decided" what and for whom Americans would produce during the war.

Legacies of wartime collectivism abounded: the corporatism of massive governmental collusion with organized special-interest groups; the de facto nationalization of the ocean shipping and railroad industries; the increased federal intrusion in labor markets, capital markets, communications, and agriculture; and enduring changes in constitutional doctrines regarding conscription and governmental suppression of free speech.

Looming over everything was the ideological legacy. Americans had won the war, or at least they had been on the winning side, and—post hoc, ergo propter hoc—they had won because of the wartime collectivism. Like Baruch, many people had come to believe that however objectionable governmental direction of the economy might be under normal conditions, "in time of danger it was imperative." The future would soon reveal that wartime was not the only time of danger.

CHAPTER EIGHT

The Great Depression: "An Emergency More Serious Than War"

Every collectivist revolution rides in on a Trojan horse of "Emergency." It was a tactic of Lenin, Hitler, and Mussolini. In the collectivist sweep over a dozen minor countries of Europe, it was the cry of the men striving to get on horseback. And "Emergency" became the justification of the subsequent steps. This technique of creating emergency is the greatest achievement that demagoguery attains. The invasion of New Deal Collectivism was introduced by this same Trojan Horse.

HERBERT HOOVER

The Great Depression, owing to the fundamental institutional and ideological changes it provoked or permitted, was the most significant episode of twentieth-century American economic history. The people who lived through it were never the same, for the anxieties and convictions it fostered entered deeply into their attitudes and opinions. The political economy emerged from this wrenching experience altered to its core. Some say that Franklin D. Roosevelt "saved capitalism," while others speak of FDR's "collectivist revolution." Whatever one's terms, no one can reasonably deny that the political economy of 1939 differed hugely from that of 1929. Moreover, many of the institutional innovations of the 1930s remain embedded in the socioeconomic order today: acreage allotments, price supports, and marketing controls in agriculture, detailed regulation of private securities markets, extensive federal intrusion in union-management relations, enormous governmental lending and insurance activities, the minimum wage, national unemployment insurance, Social Security pensions and welfare payments, production and sale of electrical power by the federal government, fiat money wholly without commodity backing—the list goes on and on. All of

159

these familiar politico-economic institutions have functioned continuously since the 1930s.

My thesis is that the institutional revolution of the 1930s depended crucially on the existence of national emergency, a condition that was partly real, partly contrived, enormously exploited for political purposes. My task is to describe how the major events of this historic transformation occurred and to identify their enduring institutional and ideological legacies.

ECONOMIC RISE AND FALL, 1922–1933

The postwar boomlet ended early in 1920, and a short but severe recession ensued. Real gross national product fell by over 2 percent; unemployment rose to 12 percent of the labor force. The most notable aspect of the business contraction was a precipitous deflation: the wholesale price index dropped more than 35 percent in a single year. Then, almost as quickly as it had collapsed, the economy recovered. (The promptness of the recovery was not mere happenstance. A market economy with downwardly flexible prices and wages has great capacity to reestablish a high-employment equilibrium after monetary or other shocks.) By 1923 an all-time high had been reached by real output per capita, and the unemployment rate had fallen to only 3 percent.

For the rest of the decade the economy performed well by historical standards—not spectacularly, as in the myth of the Roaring Twenties, but well. By 1929 real GNP per capita was more than 20 percent above its value in 1919. After the deflation of 1920–1921 the price level remained virtually unchanged until 1930. Whatever else they were, the twenties certainly were not inflationary in the sense that inflation is now understood (namely, a sustained increase in the overall price level). Despite some sick industries—textiles, coal mining, small-scale banking, parts of agriculture—most sectors advanced apace, especially manufacturing, where output almost doubled between the low of 1921 and the high of 1929. Firms producing automobiles, radios, refrigerators, and other innovative consumer durables flourished, as did the construction industry. Although some people complained, as they always do in times of general prosperity, that the rich were getting richer, presumedly at the expense of the poor, the prosperity of the 1920s brought substantial benefits to most Americans.[1]

In such comfortable circumstances it was a joy to be in business. Not only could one rake in the profits; one could also bask in the sunlight of social approval, taking full credit for the prevailing good fortune. People began to call their own time a New Era. With the Federal Reserve System standing ready to offset any extreme deviations from a steady growth path, the business cycle of the past was now, according to many experts, obsolete. The Commerce Department and the Federal Trade Commission actively assisted businessmen in organizing the firms in their industries to eliminate "waste" and "cutthroat competition." Except for this crypto-cartelizing activity—and the wartime holdovers noted above—public policy kept largely within its traditional bounds. H. L. Mencken said of President Calvin Coolidge, who presided over this relatively serene epoch with fitting insouciance, "There were no thrills while he reigned, but neither were there any headaches. He had no ideas, and he was not a nuisance."[2] With such circumspect leadership and such auspicious prospects, Americans began to take progress for granted. But pride, as the proverb says, goeth before destruction.

From mid-1929 onward, most visibly after the stock-market debacle of October, the economy headed downward. Each lull only foreshadowed a more violent storm. Every time people thought that the worst surely must be over, a further collapse ensued. For almost four years—roughly coincident, as it happened, with the unfortunate Herbert Hoover's term as President—production, prices, and profits descended, while idle industrial capacity, unemployment of labor, and human despair ascended.

To say that it was the worst depression is to speak the truth, but hardly begins to suggest how bad the Great Contraction was.[3] Between 1929 and 1933, real GNP per capita fell by more than 30 percent, finally reaching a level about equal to that in the depression year 1908, a quarter of a century before. Wholesale prices dropped by about 30 percent, consumer prices somewhat less. (Recalling how much greater the rate of deflation had been in 1920–1921 is an excellent point of departure for understanding why this economic slide was so much more severe and prolonged in real terms than the earlier contraction.) Production of consumer durables fell by 50 percent, producer durables by 67 percent, new construction by 78 percent, gross private domestic investment by almost 90 percent. Unemployment ultimately reached 25 percent of the labor force, and perhaps one in three of those who still had a job in 1933 was working reduced hours.[4] If all 12,830,000 of the unemployed had formed a line, with the people one yard apart, it could have stretched from New York to Seattle to Los Angeles and back to New York—and still have left more than 280,000 unemployed persons out of the line.

Banks failed in great waves, as panicky depositors swarmed to withdraw their money from institutions already weakened by borrowers' defaults and falling securities markets. More than nine thousand suspended operations during the four years 1930–1933, creating losses of $2.5 billion, over half of which fell on depositors, the rest on other creditors and stockholders. Financial institutions in small towns and rural areas suffered especially heavy mortality.[5] As the financial system disintegrated, the rest of the economy withered because of the credit stringency and the involuntary illiquidity of consumers and businessmen.

While the workers felt more real pain, the capitalists took the greater beating in percentage terms. The net income of corporations didn't just disappear; it became negative. In 1931, 1932, and 1933 the after-tax profits of all corporations added up to less than zero. In 1932, the worst year ever for stockholders, American corporations had net losses of $3.4 billion. Rental and proprietary income fell by more than 60 percent. The stock market, where speculators had made so much easy money in the late 1920s, now took its revenge. The Standard Statistics index of common stock prices dropped more than 80 percent between the peak in 1929 and the trough in 1932. At the end of the twenties the recipients of all forms of property and proprietary income had received 41 percent of the national income; in 1933 they got just 27 percent of a much smaller amount.[6] It was by no means a depression just for poor people.

Farmers suffered disproportionately. While they continued to produce about the same physical amounts, the prices they received for their products plummeted by more than 50 percent. The prices they paid for inputs did not decline nearly so much. Some expenses such as mortgage payments and taxes were fixed in money terms, which meant that their real burden increased greatly as deflation made each dollar more valuable. Threatened with the loss of their farms and homes as well as their livelihoods, farmers reacted with hostility and, on more than a few occasions, with violence. Legislation to delay mortgage foreclosures was sought and obtained by farmers in twenty-five states during 1932–1934.[7] Despite such palliatives, thousands upon thousands of farmers lost their property.

WHAT DID HOOVER DO?

The traditional answer, of course, is nothing. If the man in the street remembers anything about Herbert Hoover it is that his middle name was Laissez-Faire and he did nothing while the American economy went to rack and ruin. As usual the knowledge of the man in the street leaves something to be desired. The popular remembrance of Hoover's quiescence in the face of the depression is a myth. The Great Engineer may have had his faults, but fiddling while the economy burned was not one of them. "Do nothing" was never his motto; his middle name was actually Clark.

Some members of Hoover's administration, led by Secretary of the Treasury Andrew W. Mellon, did favor a hands-off policy. "Liquidate labor, liquidate stocks, liquidate the farmers, liquidate real estate," declared the aged Treasury chief. A bit of depression, he thought, should not be viewed as altogether bad. It could "purge the rottenness out of the system." Hoover insisted that Mellon was not really a hard-hearted man and that the old capitalist's austere recommendation rested on a sincere belief that it would minimize the aggregate of suffering in the long run.[8] Maybe it would have. In Grover Cleveland's day such advice would have been taken, but (ideological) times had changed.

President Hoover rejected completely the liquidationist school of thought. He believed that the federal government could and should take actions to cushion and reverse the economic decline. As time passed and the government's policies failed to arrest the contraction, the Hoover administration intervened more actively. Because later the New Deal went so much further, Hoover's antidepression policies are customarily pilloried as at best "far too little, much too late." Yet no previous administration had done nearly so much to remedy an economic bust.[9] (In the presidential campaign of 1932, candidate Roosevelt criticized Hoover for failing to balance the budget.)

Hoover's first action after the stock market crashed was to make reassuring speeches, a practice he continued throughout his unhappy term in office. This struck him as seemly—after all, if the President himself were to play the role of Chicken Little, what would the public do? It also comported with his theory of recovery. He believed that recovery hinged on a revival of private investment spending, which required an adequately optimistic state of "business confidence." By maintaining a personally sanguine outlook, at least in his public pronouncements, Hoover hoped to encourage investors to pour their money into new factories and equipment. Although he has been ridiculed ever since for his reassuring displays, they could hardly have done much harm.

Hoover next resorted to a series of meetings in November 1929 with the leaders of selected businesses, labor unions, and farm organizations. Ostensibly the parleys produced only choruses to sing in harmony with the President's melody of optimism. (Apparently accomplishing nothing of substance, they inspired J. K. Galbraith to invent the amusing and insightful concept of the "no-business meeting.")[10]

But it is possible—one cannot know for sure—that the meetings did have an important effect, ironically a harmful effect. From the employers attending his conferences the President extracted a promise not to cut wages any faster than the cost of living declined. He believed that real wage cuts, besides being unfair and productive of strife, would reduce consumer purchasing power and thereby exacerbate the recession. Whether because of fidelity to the President or for other reasons, many employers did not reduce money wages much until well into 1931. Meanwhile deflation proceeded apace. Workers who continued to receive the same money wage were getting an increasingly higher real wage. Given the extreme decline of the demand for labor, which happened to be greater in the sectors most refraining from wage cuts, a higher real wage implied a magnified reduction in the quantity of labor that employers would find it worthwhile to hire—that is, the increased real wage caused a great deal of unemployment. Unfortunately, as Lester Chandler has observed, the President "seems to have paid little attention to wage rates as a determinant of costs of production."[11]

Hoover backed various measures to stimulate federal spending and extensions of the government's credit, including increased appropriations for public works and the Federal Land Banks, creation of the Agricultural Credit Banks and the Home Loan Banks, liberalization of the Federal Reserve Banks' lending authority by the Glass-Steagall Act of 1932, and passage of the Emergency Relief and Construction Act of 1932, which allowed the federal government to give (officially, to lend) the state governments funds to use for relief of the unemployed. Hoover also used his discretionary authority to reduce immigration—he supposed that an immigrant would either become a public charge or displace someone else from a job. To quiet the unsettling international disputes over reparations and war debts, he secured a moratorium on intergovernmental payments.[12] None of this suggests a dogmatic adherence to laissez-faire.

Hoover disliked alarmism, but in seeking support for his antidepression policies he did not entirely resist appeals to the emergency rationale or wartime analogies. Arguing for his fiscal proposals in person before the Senate he declared that "an emergency has developed." Later in the address he spoke of "the stress of this emergency" twice in successive sentences. He closed by challenging the senators to show that "democracy has the capacity to act speedily enough to save itself in emergency." Urging support for the Glass-Steagall bill he told the press it was "in a sense . . . a national defense measure."[13] By characterizing the situation as an emergency and likening it to war Hoover sought to stimulate a more insistent public demand for his proposed remedies and hoped to weaken his political opposition. (We shall see that his use of this rhetorical device pales beside its employment by his successor.)

The administration's most important antidepression action, the creation of the Reconstruction Finance Corporation, clearly benefited from the emergency rationale and the wartime analogy. The RFC Act, which became law on January 22, 1932, was officially entitled, "An Act To provide emergency financing facilities for financial institutions, to aid in financing agriculture, commerce, and industry, and for other purposes."[14] The RFC was obviously patterned after the War Finance Corporation. Section 6 of the act evidenced the revivification in the plainest possible way by stating: "Section 5202 of the Revised Statutes of the United States, as amended, is hereby amended by striking out the words 'War Finance Corporation Act' and inserting in lieu thereof the words 'Reconstruction Finance Corporation Act.' " Many of the RFC's first employees had previously worked for the WFC.[15]

Not surprisingly the leading proponent of the RFC Act had been Eugene Meyer, now serving as Governor of the Federal Reserve Board. For some time he had been urging revival of the WFC. After the wave of bank failures associated with the financial stringency that followed Britain's departure from the gold standard in the fall of 1931 Meyer prevailed on Hoover to declare a financial-economic emergency and call a special session of Congress to deal with it. The President resisted the declaration and the special session, but he supported revival of the WFC under a new name, especially after his attempt to marshal financial resources through a voluntary organization of bankers, the National Credit Association, proved futile. Meyer got some officials at the Fed to write a bill, sent the draft to Congress, and testified first in its support. After it was passed he became chairman of the RFC's board of directors, a position that must have felt as familiar to him as his oldest armchair.

The RFC was given $500 million of capital from the Treasury, allowed to borrow up to $1.5 billion more, and authorized to make properly secured loans to financial institutions and railroad companies. (The RFC Act also provided $50 million for the Secretary of Agriculture to lend to farmers "in cases where he finds that an emergency exists.") In July Congress increased the RFC's borrowing authority to $3.3 billion and gave it permission to lend to states for relief purposes. By the time Hoover left office the corporation had lent almost $1.5 billion, most of it to financial intermediaries, about a fifth to railroads, and a smaller fraction to state governments. No doubt it helped somewhat to stem the collapse of the financial system in 1932. Meyer's biographer concluded that "the RFC, like the WFC, both essentially Meyer creations, will stand as a historic precedent for governmental aid, when the economic weather becomes too stormy for private banks and other essential institutions to survive on their own resources." And so it has. Not only did the RFC itself stay in business until the 1950s—through some pretty fair weather as well as foul—but even in the mid-1980s some people were calling for the creation of a new RFC.[16]

At the time, many congressmen and other people objected to the RFC and similar Hoover initiatives because the agencies channeled federal money into large institutions rather than directly into the hands of the suffering masses. Hoover's strategy, as unfriendly wags described it, was to feed the sparrows by feeding the horse; "trickle down" is the epithet that still survives. But Hoover's policies were deliberately designed to conform to his commitment to individualism and the American tradition of federalistic government. As late as August 1932 he said:

> It is not the function of the Government to relieve individuals of their responsibilities to their neighbors, or to relieve private institutions of their responsibilities to the public, or of local government to the states, or of state governments to the Federal Government. . . . It is vital that the programs of the Government shall not compete with or replace any of them but shall add to their initiative and their strength. It is vital that by the use of public revenues and public credit in emergency the Nation shall be strengthened and not weakened. . . . It is only by this release of initiative, this insistence upon individual responsibility, that there accrue the great sums of individual accomplishment which carry this Nation forward.

Had Hoover been a more accomplished politician (the presidency was the only elective office he ever occupied, and "he detested politics and its countless silly indignities"), he would have known that the country was in no mood for a sermon on the virtues of individual responsibility. As the crisis deepened, the cry grew increasingly insistent for a more visibly caring government to take command.[17]

Nothing encapsulated the spiraling sense of emergency, the government's apparent insensitivity to mass misery, and the futility of Hoover's politics so much as the Bonus Army episode. Some fifteen thousand destitute people, mostly veterans and their families, descended on the Capitol in the late spring of 1932, demanding immediate payment of the amounts due on their "adjusted service certificates" scheduled for payment in 1945. (Earlier, in 1931, Congress had authorized over Hoover's veto a partial early redemption sponsored by the American Legion.) The President, still insisting that a restoration of business confidence required balancing the budget, opposed the huge transfer payment. This time the Senate sustained his position, and Congress adjourned late in July without passing a bonus bill. Still, some five thousand members of the so-called Bonus Expeditionary Force remained in Washington, encamped in a shantytown they had thrown up on Anacostia Flats.

At the end of July, when police attempted to clear a construction area blocked by the remnants of the Bonus Army, a riot broke out, and two veterans were killed. Alarmed by the ominous presence of the ragged protesters, Hoover directed General Douglas MacArthur to use troops to disperse them. The general proceeded to do so, a little too forcefully, perhaps. In the ensuing melee the shantytown was burned up, but no one was seriously hurt. Public opinion, however, had been grievously wounded. As the Washington *News* expressed it, "What a pitiful spectacle is that of the great American government, mightiest in the world, chasing unarmed men, women, and children with army tanks." In his memoirs Hoover adduced considerable documentation in an attempt to prove that the Bonus Army was largely communists, criminals, and other ne'er-do-wells.[18] It didn't matter. The

President's treatment of the pathetic group had convinced the public beyond dispute that the Great Humanitarian was actually an ogre.

"No President ever worked harder in the White House than Herbert Hoover," wrote William Leuchtenburg, "but he was never able to convince the nation that he cared deeply how people were suffering and that he shared with them the sorrows and the blighted prospects the depression had brought."[19] No one was surprised when Roosevelt defeated Hoover by an enormous margin in the November election—anyone could have done the same. But after his resounding defeat Hoover still had four months to serve before the victorious FDR could take office. The events of that unfortunate interim were to have a tremendous influence in determining what would happen when the new man finally did take the reins.

INTERREGNUM OF DESPAIR

The winter of 1932–1933 was the darkest hour of the long night of depression.[20] Economic conditions were at their worst: unemployment, idle industrial capacity, and farm foreclosures climbed to their peaks; prices, investment spending, and international trade sank to their troughs. The greatest of all the banking panics beset the financial system. The public's outlook had never been bleaker. "Desperate" is the word used most frequently in contemporary descriptions of the prevailing mood. Hopelessness and despair suffused the emotions of masses and elites alike. Perhaps conditions would continue to deteriorate until wretchedness, ruin, and starvation overwhelmed the nation. A few people agitated for revolution and a larger group feared such an event, but the public at large just endured, not so much rebellious as listless and apathetic.

In Washington the politicians simply floundered. The lame-duck session of Congress that convened in December 1932, though confronted with the most threatening peacetime crisis in American history, produced no important legislation. "We're milling around here," wrote Senator Hiram Johnson, "utterly unable to accomplish anything of real consequence." So notorious did Congress's ineffectuality become that the congressmen themselves lapsed into joking about it in their speeches on the floors of the House and the Senate. In its confusion and unproductiveness Congress mirrored the drift of the country. The legislators, like the public, craved leadership and direction.[21]

Obviously Hoover could not supply the inspiration everyone desired. Always a wooden personality, the repudiated President now plumbed new depths of dourness. A realist, he did not bother to make any grand proposals for congressional action. His distrust of professional politicians remained as strong as ever. Dusting off his veto power to be ready in case the congressmen should rouse themselves, he told his press secretary: "I don't want them to do anything now; whatever they might do would be bad legislation from our point of view."[22]

Still the President did not become inert as he awaited the termination of his term. The economic crisis demanded his attention. He worried especially that fears about FDR's infidelity to the gold standard would provoke speculators at home and abroad to start another run on the banks, demanding gold or foreign exchange in anticipation of future devaluation of the dollar. He thought that the restoration of business confidence, which he continued to regard as the sine qua non of economic recovery, required that the incoming President assure the world that he would balance the budget. In an exchange of letters and personal meetings Hoover and Roosevelt danced around these and related international issues for months, Hoover attempting to get Roosevelt to commit himself publicly to sound money and a balanced budget while Roosevelt refused to be pinned down. FDR was determined to assume office uncontaminated by even the appearance of agreement with the policies of the outgoing, thoroughly repudiated administration.[23]

The futile discussions culminated frantically in the last few days before FDR's inauguration. Financial panic was again spreading fast. By March 3 about half the state governments had imposed banking "holidays," placing various restrictions on the banks' payments to depositors. People revealed what they feared by withdrawing from the banks not just any currency, as in the previous panics, but gold coins and gold certificates. On March 4, banking holidays were declared in twenty-five states, including the major banking states of New York, Illinois, Massachusetts, New Jersey, and Pennsylvania. The day before FDR's inauguration Hoover made one last attempt to enlist Roosevelt's cooperation in an emergency action to calm the financial storm. He proposed "to put into effect [a legally questionable] executive order controlling withdrawals and exchanges if Mr. Roosevelt would approve." But Roosevelt would not approve.[24] The stalemate insured that when FDR assumed office on March 4 the banking system of the United States would be virtually paralyzed.

EMERGENCY, EMERGENCY!

The day after Franklin Delano Roosevelt took the oath of office as President of the United States he issued a proclamation calling Congress into a special session to convene on March 9. His first substantive action, on March 6, was to proclaim a national banking holiday—the very action he had refused to endorse by Hoover just three days earlier. The proclamation referred to withdrawals of gold and speculation in foreign exchange that had "created a national emergency." It claimed the Trading with the Enemy Act of 1917 as its legal authority. "In view of such national emergency and by virtue of the authority vested in me by said Act," Roosevelt directed that during March 6–9 inclusive "all banking transactions shall be suspended."[25] On March 9, observing that "said national emergency still continues," he extended the banking holiday "until further proclamation by the President."[26] Banks were permitted to reopen only after case-by-case inspection and approval by the government, a procedure that dragged on for months.

Hoover and others, including one of FDR's top advisers, regarded the specific form of the banking holiday as a deliberately engineered manifestation of economic collapse and crisis. "Roosevelt did not need to *close* the banks," Hoover argued. He could have simply restricted their dealings in gold and foreign exchange. "But closing the banks would be a sign the country was in the ditch. It was the American equivalent of the burning of the Reichstag to create 'an emergency.'" Others, friendlier toward the new President, have taken a slightly more charitable view. Roosevelt's biographer, Frank Freidel, concludes that during the interregnum FDR followed "the easiest if not the wisest" policy and that the banking panic of March 1933 had little relation to his cooperation with Hoover or the lack thereof. But Raymond Moley, probably the closest of FDR's advisers at the time, later observed that Roosevelt "either did not realize how serious the situation was or . . . he preferred to have conditions deteriorate and gain for himself the entire credit for the rescue operation." Whatever the degree of deliberateness with which he helped to create the panic, Roosevelt certainly seized the opportunity to stamp the emergency label on it. By completely shutting down every bank in the country, he insured that no one could fail to appreciate the gravity of the prevailing economic conditions. A political scientist has shrewdly observed that "there might well have been no crisis in 1933 if President Roosevelt had been required to appoint another to wield the abnormal display of power which he seemed to find so necessary at the moment."[27]

For months the futility of Hoover and the indecisiveness of Congress had contributed to a growing hunger for strong political leadership. To vest dictatorial powers in someone, perhaps the new President, appealed to some people, including some businessmen. While recognizing that "even semi-dictatorships in peace time are quite contrary to the spirit of American institutions," *Barron's* in February 1933 opined that "a mild species of dictatorship will help us over the roughest spots in the road ahead." Mussolini, esteemed in those days for supposedly having made the trains run on time, had an American following. Even so progressive an organ as *The Nation* published an article entitled, "Wanted: A Mussolini." Others looked back with nostalgia on Woodrow Wilson's quasi-dictatorial authority to mobilize resources during World War I. Proposals to revive the authoritative emergency programs of 1917–1918 bloomed like wildflowers.[28]

By the second week of March 1933 an extraordinary conjuncture had developed: (1) a genuine economic crisis, especially the massive unemployment and the pitifully depressed production and consumption; (2) an artificial economic crisis produced by the nationwide banking shutdown; (3) a widespread sense of crisis and a feeling that only extraordinary measures could prevent an even greater catastrophe, sentiments manifested in the numerous and diverse calls to "do something" even if dictatorial powers were required to do it; and (4) a new administration taking office unencumbered by perceived responsibility for past ill fortunes and unchecked by opposition from a partisan Congress eager to obstruct and embarrass the President. "The crisis," John Garraty has written, "justified the casting aside of precedent, the nationalistic mobilization of society, and the removal of traditional restraints on the power of the state, as in war, and it required personal leadership more forceful than that necessary in normal times."[29]

The only ingredient lacking was a strong leader, someone who could seize this pregnant moment and bring to fruition its immense potential. Although many people hoped that Roosevelt would rise to the occasion, he had, before March 4, 1933, hardly established himself as the most auspicious man for the job. He had served as Assistant Secretary of the Navy in the Wilson administration and as governor of New York during 1929–1933. Most noted for his personal charm, his unprincipled propensity to play politics, and his lack of intellectual acuity, he was, in Walter Lippmann's eyes, a "kind of amiable boy scout . . . a pleasant man who, without any important qualifications for the office, would very much like to be President."[30]

Lippmann, along with the many others who shared his opinion, was dead wrong about FDR's capacity to be a strong and effective leader. Roosevelt would prove to be a consummate politician. More significantly he had an uncanny sense of timing. He must have known that the conjuncture that existed in the spring of 1933 would never come again, that he must seize the momentous occasion and harness its vast potential to his purposes.

FDR's inaugural address left no doubt about his commitment to "action, and action now." Best remembered for its cheering if patently false declaration that "the only thing we have to fear is fear itself," the speech emphasized most the existing state of emergency and the extraordinary governmental powers that should be wielded to deal with it. Roosevelt made no attempt to soft-pedal the country's problems: the shrunken prices, the crippled financial system, the mass unemployment. "Only a foolish optimist can deny the dark realities of the moment." (As he spoke, Hoover sat behind him, as glum as ever.) Identifying a public enemy, the new President lashed out at the "unscrupulous money changers" who had brought the nation into such straits and proclaimed that "there must be an end to a conduct in banking and in business which too often has given to a sacred trust the likeness of callous and selfish wrongdoing." Terrible as the country's condition was, however, Americans could extricate themselves by "treating the task as we would treat the emergency of a war." Again and again, sounding like the old Wilsonian that he was, FDR spoke the metaphors of holy war:

> we must move as a trained and loyal army willing to sacrifice for the good of a common discipline. . . . [T]he larger purposes will bind upon us all as a sacred obligation with a unity of duty hitherto evoked only in time of armed strife. . . . I assume unhesitatingly the leadership of this great army of our people. . . . [I]n the event that the Congress shall fail to [act] . . . and in the event that the national emergency is still critical . . . I shall ask the Congress for . . . broad executive power to wage a war against the emergency as great as the power that would be given me if we were in fact invaded by a foreign foe.

The last promise evoked the greatest applause. No doubt Roosevelt perceived correctly that the American people wanted "direct, vigorous action."[31]

For at least two years, cries of "emergency" had emanated from journalists, congressmen, aspiring reformers and would-be revolutionaries, not to mention the legions of poor souls struggling just to survive. Justice Brandeis, dissenting in the *New State Ice* case, had called the depression "an emergency more serious than war." Hoover, with a few exceptions noted above, had generally refrained from describing the situation as an emergency; to have done so would have come uncomfortably close to accepting responsibility for a calamity. Roosevelt, unburdened by such political baggage, had everything to gain by painting the country's condition in the darkest hues. He continued to trumpet the emergency on every occasion. By Hoover's count, FDR based more than two hundred executive orders on emergency grounds and used the word "emergency" more than four hundred times in public statements during 1933–1934. Everyone who had not already jumped on the emergency bandwagon now hastened to do so. Congressment attached the emergency label to almost every bill they enacted. In their rush to legislate, they often conformed to their characterization of the laws they passed. For example, the Emergency Banking Act of March 9, 1933, which validated the President's legally questionable declaration of a national banking closure, was approved by a unanimous shout in the House of Representatives after thirty-eight minutes of debate, even though no member of the House had a copy of the bill. The Speaker of the House was reminded of 1917–1918, when legislators of both parties had given such ready approval to war measures. "Today," he said, "we are engaged in another war, more serious even in its character and presenting greater dangers to the Republic."[32]

By exploiting the emergency rationale and the wartime analogy from the very beginning the Roosevelt administration and the 73rd Congress battered down the normal barriers to sweeping political action. By March 1933 many powerful interest groups had become desperate for governmental measures to ameliorate their plight—that is, the emergency had become for many people quite real. Moreover, FDR's banking closure dramatized, as well as anything could have, the extremities of the occasion, thereby magnifying the already widespread sense of emergency—that is, the feeling of crisis was heightened, perhaps deliberately. Roosevelt's unexpectedly strong leadership provided the final ingredient required to put into motion a sustained political process with enough momentum to overcome the normal inertia of political and governmental interests in conflict or working at cross-purposes. Events unfolded as if the leaders of virtually every major interest group, including those within as well as those outside the government, had simultaneously reached an identical conclusion and each had addressed all the others in unison, saying: We've got to have relief; give us ours and we won't block yours; the people will swallow the whole grasping affair because the times are out of joint. And lest anyone look with too much suspicion on what we are doing, let us never stop repeating that this is an emergency, an emergency, an emergency more serious than war.[33]

PLANTING THE FIRST NEW DEAL:
THE HUNDRED DAYS

The first session of the 73rd Congress, the famous Hundred Days of the New Deal, was a paradigm of "action, and action now." Roosevelt's advisers and governmental subordinates, in close cooperation with leaders of the most powerful private interst groups, fired a barrage of proposed legislation at Congress. Democratic leaders like Joseph Robinson and Robert Wagner in the Senate and Henry Rainey and Sam Rayburn in the House pushed the bills to enactment in record time. By the end of the session, Roosevelt had made believers of all who had doubted his ability to lead. Senator Johnson, a political veteran, exalted that in the White House "there are now courage and boldness and real action."[34] Though the depression persisted, the mood of the country ascended remarkably.

To understand what was wrought by the exhilarating burst of political action, one must appreciate three of its most important aspects: (1) the lack of ideological coherence; (2) the extent to which it revived wartime measures; and (3) the implicit assumption that particular price increases, however generated, would induce—or at least be consistent with—overall economic recovery.

Clearly the New Deal, especially at its beginning, manifested no single coherent ideology. (Of course, the New Dealers, like their Progressive progenitors, shared a common desire to expand the scope of governmental authority.) Within the ranks stood semi-socialist national planners like Rexford Tugwell; semi-fascist members of the pro-business Baruch gang like General Hugh Johnson; labor union leaders like Sidney Hillman; consumerists like Leon Henderson; antitrust enthusiasts like Felix Frankfurter; avowed cartelizers like Donald Richberg; all stripes of agricultural reformers; spending fanatics as well as budget balancers; every species of inflationist and monetary crank; and assorted proponents of panaceas that ranged from spreading the work to building garden cities. The President himself was burdened by few principles, being "flexible rather than doctrinaire, ready to ride congressional movements he favored, and to allow Congress to make significant contributions to the shaping of New Deal legislation."[35]

According to Senator James Brynes the crisis demanded that "principles as well as policies . . . be temporarily subordinated to the necessity of some experimentation in order to preserve the government itself."[36] Experimentation proceeded with a vengeance. Many measures were enacted simply to "try something." Given the large number of conflicting proposals and the corresponding potential for political deadlock, the dominant inclination in the spring of 1933 was to try them all at once. Never mind if they worked largely at cross-purposes. Worry about that later. At the moment the important thing was to "do something," to get one's own foot in the door, to establish a position for subsequent maneuvering.

Many of the institutional arrangements created during the Hundred Days merely reactivated programs and agencies employed during World War I. In his magnificent essay "The New Deal and the Analogue of War" William Leuchtenburg has documented in detail the indebtedness of the early New Deal to the wartime precedents. Such antecedents existed for the foreign exchange controls, the labor laws, the Tennessee Valley Authority, the Civilian Conservation Corps, the securities regulations, the government's housing programs, several of the credit agencies, and the transportation act as well as for the most critical and sweeping measures, the Agricultural Adjustment Act and the National Industrial Recovery Act. Leuchtenburg concludes: "There was scarcely a New Deal act or agency that did not owe something to the experience of World War I." Moreover, the men selected to administer the revised institutions were often those who had played leading roles during 1917–1918, especially in the War Industries Board and the Army.[37] For many the belief that what had worked in the previous (wartime) emergency would also work in the present (depression) emergency held sway. Only in retrospect did the weaknesses of the analogy become transparent.

If the major strategies of the early New Deal had a common denominator or rationale other than simply reinstituting controls like those employed during the war, it was to raise prices. At the time, many people—including virtually all businessmen and farmers—had cause and effect reversed. Not recognizing that prices had fallen because of the depression, they believed instead that depression prevailed because prices had fallen. The obvious remedy: raise prices. And everyone knew how to do so. Whether one had mastered Alfred Marshall's textbook of economics or simply operated a corner grocery, one knew that any price can be raised by sufficiently reducing the quantity of goods supplied to the market. Hence arose the anomalous but widely supported policy proposal to cure the depression, itself a catastrophic decline of real output and employment, by cutting back on production. Once the artificially induced scarcity had increased prices, the argument suggested, everyone would somehow respond with a coordinated increase of production. The scheme is so patently self-defeating that one has difficulty nowadays in accepting that anyone seriously entertained it as a general theory of recovery. (Maybe no one did; maybe it was only an apology mouthed by each interested party seeking higher prices for his own product.) Yet the government certainly proceeded in 1933 as if such a theory undergirded its policies.

Undoubtedly the goofiest application of the theory had to do with the price of gold. The President, even before his election, had embraced the idea made popular by George F. Warren, a Cornell professor, that by raising the dollar price of gold one could cause all other commodity prices to increase roughly in proportion. In a series of steps, starting with the presidential proclamation of March 6, 1933, proceeding through a massive gold-buying program implemented by the RFC, and terminating in the passage of the Gold Reserve Act of January 30, 1934, the government abandoned the gold standard. It nationalized the monetary gold stock, forbade the private ownership of gold (except for jewelry, scientific or industrial uses, and foreign payments), and nullified all contractual promises—whether public or private, past or future—to pay gold. This "act of absolute bad faith" by the government was hard for many people, even some politicians, to swallow. Senator Thomas P. Gore told FDR: "Why, that's just plain stealing, isn't it, Mr. President?" Besides its being theft, it didn't work. Although the price of gold was increased from $20.67 to $35.00 per ounce the desired effect was not achieved. Warren's theory was decisively refuted. Notwithstanding the 69 percent increase in the dollar price of gold the domestic price level increased only about 7 percent between 1933 and 1934, and over the rest of the decade it hardly changed at all.[38] American devaluation and departure from the gold standard did provoke retaliation by other countries, further strangling international specialization and exchange and thereby lowering the world's already depressed level of living.

Farmers, whose prices had fallen disproportionately during the bust, demanded quick relief. The spring plantings of 1933 promised an abundant

and therefore low-priced harvest in the fall. Farm lobbies, officially sponsored during the war and further organized during the hard times that many
farmers experienced in the twenties, had been pushing since the recession of
1920–1921 for governmental relief. They had helped to gain passage of the
Agricultural Marketing Act of 1929, which created the Federal Farm Board
to encourage and supervise a cooperative stabilization scheme; and they had
supported the subsequent establishment of the Agricultural Credit Banks
during Hoover's term. But these institutions had proved to be fragile shelters
against the storm of 1929–1933. The farm groups now demanded more
effective relief, especially from the abysmally low prices and the mass foreclosures.

The New Deal responded with the Agricultural Adjustment Act of May
12, 1933. To make absolutely certain that it would be perceived as an
emergency measure, the legislators employed the word three times in the
official title alone: "An Act To relieve the existing national economic emergency by increasing agricultural purchasing power, to raise revenue for
extraordinary expenses incurred by reason of such emergency, to provide
emergency relief with respect to agricultural indebtedness, to provide for the
orderly liquidation of joint-stock land banks, and for other purposes."[39] The
statute's first section declared an emergency, which it described as "in part the
consequence of a severe and increasing disparity between the prices of agricultural and other commodities." Depressed conditions in agriculture had
"affected transactions in agricultural commodities with a national public
interest," asserted the preamble. Evidently the claim was intended to shore up
the questionable constitutionality of the act's substantive provisions.

The agricultural relief act was a classic case of legislative trade-off, of
something for everybody. (Everybody with political clout, that is. Time
would reveal that it had little or nothing to offer to sharecroppers and other
small fry; indeed it caused the sharecroppers considerable harm, as the program gave some landlords an incentive to evict their tenants.) The President,
who orchestrated the scheming that led to the act, was "determined to avoid
serious division among the farm leaders and ready if need be to experiment
with several devices." Given the farmers' desperation, congressmen felt impelled to bring forth immediate, substantial legislative relief. In the dire
circumstances, leaders of the various farm groups were unusually willing to
put aside their differences. In mid-March Roosevelt's aides, representatives of
the Farm Bureau and the Grange, members of the Baruch gang, some high-
placed agricultural economists, and certain congressmen met to draw up a
bill. After several days of hectic pulling and hauling they emerged with a
proposal "to legalize almost anything anybody could think up."[40]

The House passed the bill after just four hours of debate, but the Senate
pondered it for a couple months. (Already the sense of emergency was
beginning to wane a bit.) Inflationists in the Senate, led by Burton Wheeler of

Montana and Elmer Thomas of Oklahoma, tried to attach their pet monetary measures to the agricultural relief bill. Ultimately Thomas succeeded in part. As finally enacted the bill authorized several means by which the President could at his discretion expand the money stock. The compromise was that the law did not require him to resort to any of them. To Lewis Douglas, the conservative budget director, the authorization to inflate or devalue the currency signaled "the end of Western civilization." But FDR considered acceptance of Thomas's amendment a reasonable price to pay for passage of the farm relief bill.[41]

The Agricultural Adjustment Act authorized the Secretary of Agriculture to intervene extensively in agricultural operations and markets. It provided for acreage and production controls, restrictive marketing agreements, and the regulatory licensing of processors and dealers "to eliminate unfair practices and charges." (The licensing provision was reminiscent of the old Food Administration's main power.) Title II of the act was designated the Emergency Farm Mortgage Act; it empowered several governmental agencies, including the RFC, to lend directly or indirectly to farmers. Farmers who agreed to reduce acreage or production in accordance with a governmentally sponsored program would receive rental or benefit payments. To generate the revenue needed to make the payments, characterized as "extraordinary expenses incurred by reason of the national economic emergency," a tax was levied on processors of agricultural commodities. Marketing agreements received explicit exemption from the antitrust laws. The objective of the law was forthrightly declared to be raising farm commodity prices until they reached the level, relative to nonfarm prices, that had prevailed during a base period of August 1909 to July 1914—an era sometimes called the Golden Age of American Agriculture.

To administer the act, Roosevelt created the Agricultural Adjustment Administration within the Department of Agriculture. After Bernard Baruch declined an offer to head the agency, FDR appointed George Peek, Baruch's longtime lieutenant, a veteran of the WIB, executive of a farm-equipment company, and indefatigable campaigner for governmental aid to agriculture. Peek's wife wrote: "To him, with his war experience, this whole thing clicks into shape, and some of the fine men of the country are coming to his call as they did in 1917, and with the same high purpose." In time the loftiness of the purpose would provoke considerable debate. Perhaps the millions who could hardly feed and clothe their families should be forgiven for questioning the nobility of a program designed to make food and fiber more expensive.

But it was only an emergency measure and, in recognition of the extraordinary conditions that justified it, the lawmakers stipulated that the agricultural controls would terminate "whenever the President finds and proclaims that the national economic emergency in relation to agriculture has been ended." No President ever has so found and proclaimed, and the massive federal intervention in agriculture has remained in place come rain or shine ever since 1933. According to Broadus Mitchell, "Though framers of the act, to overcome congressional objections, presented it as an emergency measure, there is abundant evidence that all along they intended it to be the basis of long-time policy."[42]

In contrast to the title of the agricultural relief act the official title of the National Industrial Recovery Act, enacted on June 16, 1933, did not contain the word "emergency." But the first sentence of its preamble stated: "A national emergency productive of widespread unemployment and disorganization of industry, which burdens interstate and foreign commerce, affects the public welfare, and undermines the standards of living of the American people, is hereby declared to exist." Unlike the AAA, the NIRA was designed to expire after two years "or sooner if the President shall by proclamation or the Congress shall by joint resolution declare that the emergency . . . has ended."[43]

Like the agricultural relief act, the industrial recovery act emerged from a grand compromise. The most prominent parties included businessmen seeking higher prices and barriers to competition, labor unionists seeking governmental sponsorship and protection of their organizational activities and collective bargaining, do-gooders concerned about working conditions and child labor, and proponents of massive governmental spending for public works. The old WIB supplied the prototype for their planning, but amended versions of the wartime agency such as Senator William G. McAdoo's proposed Peace Industries Board or businessman Gerard Swope's well-publicized scheme for industrial self-government by trade associations also figured in the discussions. The one sentiment common to all parties was a revulsion against the market system. As the U.S. Chamber of Commerce's Committee on Continuity of Business and Employment declared in 1931, "A freedom of action which might have been justified in the relatively simple life of the last century cannot be tolerated today. . . . We have left the period of extreme individualism." By 1933, recalled Senator Byrnes, big businessmen were "clamoring for legislation providing government controls."[44]

The proximate background of the NIRA began on April 6, 1933, with a proposal by Senator Hugo Black of Alabama to establish by law a thirty-hour work week. Roosevelt, taken by surprise, directed Secretary of Labor Frances Perkins to develop a workable substitute for Black's proposal. Perkins' efforts elicited a hostile reaction from business interests, who began to prepare a substitute for the substitute. The Chamber of Commerce offered a plan. General Hugh Johnson, a former draft administrator, Army liaison to the WIB, and longtime crony of Baruch, joined the party. Pro-labor interests consolidated around Senator Wagner, with Donald Richberg, a prominent labor lawyer, representing the unions. Under Secretary of Commerce John Dickinson, a veteran of the War Trade Board, had his own plan. On May 10, representatives of the various politically potent interests met with Roosevelt, who characteristically suggested that they lock themselves in a room until they had reached a compromise. They did, and the resulting proposal naturally provided something for each of them. FDR sent the bill to Congress on May 17. It was enacted a month later.[45]

The NIRA empowered the President to approve privately drafted "codes of fair competition" or, lacking an acceptable privately tendered code, to impose one of his own design for every industry. The antitrust laws were explicitly set aside. At his discretion the President could require business licenses or control imports to achieve the vaguely identified objectives of the act. Every code had to contain acceptable provisions setting minimum wages, maximum hours, and decent working conditions. In Section 7(a), the most critical provision for unionists—in the long run the most critical provision for everybody—the act stipulated:

> Every code of fair competition, agreement, and license approved, prescribed, or issued under this title shall contain the following conditions: (1) That employees shall have the right to organize and bargain collectively through representatives of their own choosing, and shall be free from the interference, restraint, or coercion of employers of labor, or their agents, in the designation of such representatives or in self-organization or in other concerted activities for the purpose of collective bargaining or other mutual aid or protection; (2) that no employee and no one seeking employment shall be required as a condition of employment to join any company union or to refrain from joining, organizing, or assisting a labor organization of his own choosing; and (3) that employers shall comply with the maximum hours of labor, minimum rates of pay, and other conditions of employment, approved or prescribed by the President.

In addition the President was authorized to prohibit the transportation in interstate and foreign commerce of "hot oil"—that produced in excess of the amount permitted by recognized state control boards. Title II authorized the President to create a Federal Emergency Administration of Public Works and specified in detail the sorts of construction projects that could be undertaken by the agency and the rules under which it must operate. Finally Congress appropriated $3.3 billion to carry out the purposes of the act. Altogether the NIRA was a tremendous intrusion into the economic life of the country, completely without peacetime precedent. Indeed it went far beyond what had been done during the war by its prototype, the WIB. One congressman thought it made FDR a benign dictator. Another congressman responded, "You might as well talk of a peaceful murderer."[46]

To administer the industrial recovery act—except for the public works program, which was assigned to the Public Works Administration and placed under the control of Secretary of the Interior Harold Ickes—Roosevelt established the National Recovery Administration and named General Johnson to head it. The flamboyant Johnson launched into the task with unrestrained gusto. Calling on the wisdom acquired from his service in the wartime mobilization, he strove to whip up emotion, enthusiasm, even hysteria if possible, to promote the codification of American industry and universal compliance with the codes promulgated.

No one appreciated the importance of symbolism better than Johnson, who attempted to bring about an overnight reversal of many deeply embedded values with regard to the market economy.

> "Competition" became "economic cannibalism," and "rugged individualists" became "industrial pirates." Conservative industrialists, veteran antitrusters, and classical economists were all lumped together and branded "social Neanderthalers," "Old Dealers," and "corporals of disaster." The time-honored practice of reducing prices to gain a larger share of the market became "cutthroat and monopolistic price slashing," and those that engaged in this dastardly activity became "chiselers." Conversely, monopolistic collusion, price agreements, proration, and cartelization became "cooperative" or "associational" activities; and devices that were chiefly designed to eliminate competition bore the euphemistic title, "codes of fair competition." A whole set of favorable collectivist symbols emerged to describe what American law and the courts had previously, under other names, regarded as harmful to society.[47]

At Baruch's suggestion, Johnson adopted an emblem, the famous Blue Eagle, to be displayed by all businesses pledged to comply with the codes.

The NRA organized mass demonstrations of public support, including a parade of 250,000 people in New York. Billboards, posters, buttons, and stickers displayed the NRA's messages. Volunteer boosters, like the Four Minute Men of the wartime Liberty Bond drives, spoke in support of the great crusade. Radio stations and newspapers fell, or were driven, into line. Not since the war had there been anything like the outpouring of hoopla. And like the wartime spectaculars, these had a clear purpose: "rousing patriotic feelings and creating in the public mind the impression of so extensive a support for government policies as to make disagreement appear close to tresason." Again the country resounded with criticism of "slackers" who failed to absorb the government's propaganda and conduct their affairs in accordance with it. The "efforts at mass persuasion" were, according to a prominent historian, "unparalleled among democracies in peacetime." Their only counterpart was the chauvinistic extravaganzas staged by the Nazis in Germany.[48]

Eventually the NRA approved 557 basic and 189 supplementary codes, covering about 95 percent of all industrial employees. Big businessmen dominated the writing and implementing of the documents. Although the codes differed in a multitude of specific features, they generally aimed to suppress competition in any form it might take. Minimum prices, open price schedules, standardization of products and services, advance notice of intent to change prices, and similar anticompetitive provisions figured prominently in them. Having gained the federal government's commitment to stilling the competitive storm, the tycoons looked forward to profitable repose.

But the initial enthusiasm soon evaporated. Small businessmen, labor unionists, consumer representatives, and others discovered that the scheme could not deliver all things to all men. Even big businessmen objected that the NRA interfered too much in their affairs—they had hoped that the NIRA would simply delegate the power of government to them to use as they saw fit without meddlesome interference by snooping bureaucrats. By the time the Supreme Court invalidated the whole undertaking early in 1935 most of its former supporters had lost their taste for it.[49] We shall see, however, that the experiment left permanent legacies.

CULTIVATING AND PRUNING THE FIRST NEW DEAL: THE SUPREME COURT

Legislate as it might, the 73rd Congress still had to get its laws past the courts. For several years the New Deal found the judiciary less than wholeheartedly enthusiastic about approving the emergency measures. By the end of 1936 federal judges had issued about 1,600 injunctions to restrain federal officials from carrying out acts of Congress. Federal courts were also finding many state emergency laws in violation of the U.S. Constitution. If the depression-spawned expansion of the scope of governmental authority was to survive, the Supreme Court, said to "hesitate between two worlds," would have to abandon its old world and embrace the new one.[50] The executive and legislative branches of government, attempting to preserve and expand their powers by creating unprecedented emergency programs, found themselves up against a slow-moving judiciary, the branch of government most insulated from the political currents stirred by the economic crisis.

Much more was at stake, however, than victory in a power struggle among the branches of government. Fundamentally the fate of capitalism was being decided. A market system rests on an indispensable foundation of private property rights. These are the effectively enforced expectations of private citizens that they can: (1) personally own property, including their own bodies and labor power, and exclude all others from deciding how the property shall be used; (2) appropriate the income and enjoy any other benefits yielded by the property; and (3) transfer their rights freely to others by mutually satisfactory contractual agreements. Obviously many New Deal laws and similar state statutes either destroyed or attenuated private property rights.

The U.S. Constitution, especially its Contracts and Due Process clauses but also its various limitations on the powers of the federal government, gave plaintiffs hope that many of the emergency legislative interventions would be found wanting by the courts. But, as usual, everything turned on how the justices chose to read the Constitution. This depended on the court's traditions and precedents, the perceived economic, social, and political exigencies of the time, and the character, courage, and ideologies of the judges. One could never be certain whether the judicial coin would come up heads or tails.

Exceptional uncertainty surrounded the Supreme Court during Roosevelt's first term. In those years the composition of the Court remained fixed. The justices tended to fall into three groups. A "progressive" set, inclined toward allowing considerable experimentation by the legislative branch, comprised Louis D. Brandeis, Harlan F. Stone, and Benjamin N. Cardozo. A "conservative" group, usually staunch in the defense of private property rights and hostile toward governmental intrusion into the market economy, included Willis Van Devanter, James C. McReynolds, George Sutherland, and Pierce Butler; to their many critics they were the "Four Horsemen." Neither the progressives nor the conservatives constituted a majority. Hence the critical power of the remaining two justices, Owen J. Roberts and the Chief Justice Charles Evans Hughes. Because Hughes leaned more toward the progressive position, the most likely "swing man" was Roberts. As his opinion went, so the Court's decision was likely to go. My characterization does not flawlessly describe the variety of voting alignments and underlying ideologies of the judges—the five nonconservatives especially were a mixed lot. Sometimes, as we shall see, the disparate spirits did achieve unanimity. Like the general run of mankind, the nine old men occasionally indulged in the luxury of inconsistency. Nevertheless, the groupings indicated here suggest the rough outlines of their ideologies.

Early in 1934 the Court issued an important decision on the emergency powers of government and the protection to be afforded or withheld from private property rights during the economic crisis. The case involved a legislative moratorium—one of twenty-five such state laws enacted during 1932–1934—on mortgage foreclosures.[51] A statute approved by the government of Minnesota on April 18, 1933, under ominous pressures by indebted farmers, declared an economic emergency and extended temporarily the period during which creditors were prevented from foreclosing on and selling mortgaged real estate. At the discretion of local courts the owners of foreclosed property could be allowed up to two years to redeem their property. During the extended redemption period the mortgagor was required to pay the mortgagee what amounted to rent, but the mortgagee was deprived of control over the property. The Home Building and Loan Association of Minneapolis challenged the law as an unconstitutional impairment of the obligation of contract. Its position was upheld by a county court but overturned by the supreme court of Minnesota, and the case then came before the U.S. Supreme Court on appeal.[52]

The main issue was whether emergency conditions justified the exercise of otherwise unconstitutional powers by a state government. The most compelling precedents for an affirmative answer were *Wilson* v. *New*, wherein the Court had upheld the Adamson Act, and the rent-control cases of 1921, wherein the Court had sustained the postwar rent-control laws of New York and the District of Columbia because of conditions represented as constituting or growing out of emergency. The force of the rent-control decisions was uncertain, however, as Justice Holmes himself had previously said that "they went to the very verge of the law." Counsel for the state of Minnesota conceded that "in normal times and under normal conditions" the state's moratorium law would be unconstitutional. "But these," he urged, "are not normal times nor normal conditions. A great economic emergency has arisen in which the State has been compelled to invoke the police power." The justices would have to decide again whether emergency altered the protections of the Constitution and, if so, what exactly qualified as an emergency. Their decision could have wide repercussions, because virtually all of the important federal statutes enacted during the Hundred Days had appealed to emergency conditions, evidently with an eye toward the Supreme Court.[53]

Although the Court upheld the Minnesota moratorium law, it failed to clarify whether an emergency justified setting aside constitutional protection of private property rights. Perhaps the most important aspect of the decision is simply that state infringement of contractual obligations was validated. Paradoxically, however, the Court denied that it had sustained the Minnesota statute because of emergency. "Emergency does not create power," said Chief Justice Hughes, speaking for the five-man majority. "Emergency does not increase granted power or remove or diminish the restrictions imposed upon power granted or reserved." What could be plainer? Yet, said Hughes, referring to the slippery doctrine enunciated in *Wilson* v. *New*, "While emergency does not create power, emergency may furnish the occasion for the exercise of power." The prohibition of governmental intervention guaranteed by the Contracts Clause, he added, "is not an absolute one and is not to be read with literal exactness like a mathematical formula. . . . The economic interests of the State may justify the exercise of its continuing and dominant protective power notwithstanding interference with contracts." Any doubts about the capaciousness of the police powers of the state government and the implied limitation of the protection of contractual rights, he thought, should have been removed by the rent-control decisions, where "the relief afforded was temporary and conditional . . . sustained because of the emergency." The Chief Justice declared that "the reservation of the reasonable exercise of the protective power of the State is read into all contracts." In apparent contradiction of his earlier assertion, he concluded: "An emergency existed in Minnesota which furnished a proper occasion for the exercise of the reserved power of the State to protect the vital interests of the community."[54]

Hughes' opinion has been called "a masterpiece both of legal realism and pragmatic readaption of the law to the era." The Chief Justice seemed, however, simply to contradict himself. On the one hand he clearly affirmed that emergency does not create governmental power not already sanctioned by the Constitution. On the other hand—quite apart from the t rute fact of his upholding the Minnesota law and, by extension, all others like it—he maintained that the government possessed "reserved powers" on which it might legitimately draw to override private (and one supposes, constitutionally protected) contracts during an emergency. "The distinction," according to a legal scholar, "while it has an air of legerdemain, is of no small importance."[55]

The dissenting Four Horsemen could not have disagreed more emphatically. "He simply closes his eyes to the necessary implications of the decision," said their spokesman, Justice Sutherland, "who fails to see in it the potentiality of future gradual but ever-advancing encroachments upon the sanctity of private and public contracts." The correct doctrine, they thought, was to be found in the classic decision of *Ex parte Milligan* (1866), which declared constitutional guarantees and restrictions to be absolutely invariant with respect to emergencies or any other social conditions. Quoting from a considerable collection of historical works, Sutherland established that the framers had intended the Contracts Clause to apply "*primarily and especially*" during economic crises; indeed a crisis similar to the current depression had provoked them to add it to the Constitution in the first place. "The present exigency is nothing new."[56] The rent-control decisions were dismissed as too weakly justified at the time and as dealing with a matter too dissimilar to the present one to afford a binding precedent.

The dissenters rejected Hughes' sophistical distinction between genuine emergency powers and reserved powers brought into play by emergency conditions:

> the question is not whether an emergency furnishes the occasion for the exercise of that state power, but whether an emergency furnishes an occasion for the relaxation of the restrictions upon the power imposed by the contract impairment clause; and the difficulty is that the contract impairment clause

forbids state action under any circumstances, if it have the effect of impairing the obligation of contracts. . . . The Minnesota statute either impairs the obligation of contracts or it does not. If it does not, the occasion to which it relates becomes immaterial, since then the passage of the statute is the exercise of a normal, unrestricted, state power and requires no special occasion to render it effective. If it does, the emergency no more furnishes a proper occasion for its exercise than if the emergency were non-existent. And so, while, in form, the suggested distinction seems to put us forward in a straight line, in reality it simply carries us back in a circle, like bewildered travelers lost in a wood.

The dissenting opinion concluded: "If the provisions of the Constitution be not upheld when they pinch as well as when they comfort, they may as well be abandoned."[57] The conservative justices' great fear was that the Court, to facilitate the extraordinary governmental measures being implemented at all levels, had indeed embarked on an abandonment of the Constitution.

Less than two months later the Court struck another blow against private property rights in *Nebbia* v. *New York.*[58] The case involved a New York statute, passed in a crisis atmosphere of violence and farm strikes, establishing a board to regulate the milk industry and fix (that is, raise) the retail price of milk. Because many of the New Deal statutes as well as a multitude of diverse state laws also established means of price fixing and limitations on competition, the Court's decision would have wide repercussions. Again both "swing men" sided with the progressive justices, and the New York statute was upheld by a 5 to 4 margin. The majority opinion has been glowingly described by one commentator as "a resounding assertion of the necessary predominance of the general public interest over all private rights of property and contract."[59] In contrast another legal scholar has noted that the New York law "was inspired by unusual public passions and pressures, and its final form was dictated by lobbyists for farmers and large milk dealers," making it precisely the sort of legislation "that warrants the kind of judicial oversight that the Supreme Court repudiated in this case."[60]

Justice Roberts, speaking for the majority, chose not to make the ruling turn on emergency conditions. He did refer to the "desperate" condition of the families of dairy farmers and noted that the legislature had enacted the law to correct "evils" that "could not be expected to right themselves through the ordinary play of the forces of supply and demand." His argument, however, rested more on whether the regulation, specifically the price-fixing, was a permissible exercise of the police powers. He conceded that "[u]nder our form of government the use of property and the making of contracts are normally matters of private and not of public concern. The general rule is that both shall be free of governmental interference." But he insisted that "neither property rights nor contract rights are absolute." He noted that virtually everyone considered monopolies, public utilities, and governmentally franchised businesses as properly subject to price regulation. To draw a line around these types of business, denying the appropriateness of price regulation outside the boundary, struck the majority as constitutionally unwarranted. Harkening back to the classic doctrine of the *Munn* decision (1877), Roberts declared that "there is no closed class or category of businesses affected with a public interest." Further, "a state is free to adopt whatever economic policy may reasonably be deemed to promote the public welfare. . . . Price control, like any other form of regulation, is unconstitutional only if arbitrary, discriminatory, or demonstrably irrelevant to the policy the legislature is free to adopt, and hence an unnecessary and unwarranted interference with individual liberty."[61]

The dissenting minority viewed the New York price-fixing statute as precisely such an unnecessary and unwarranted interference with individual liberty and hence a deprivation of substantive due process. Their opinion, delivered by Justice McReynolds, denied that the emergency justified the act: "If here we have an emergency sufficient to empower the Legislature to fix sales prices, then whenever there is too much or too little of an essential thing—whether of milk or grain or pork or coal or shoes or clothes—constitutional provisions may be declared inoperative." In the ears of the conservatives the majority's claim about legislative promotion of the public welfare was only noise. To them the statute plainly exemplified redistributionist legislation, and the transfer it effected was by no means from the rich to the poor. (Consider all the poor parents who would have to pay more to get milk for their children.) "The Legislature cannot lawfully destroy guaranteed rights of one man with the prime purpose of enriching another," they affirmed, "even if for the moment, this may seem advantageous to the public"[62]

The majority's victory in *Nebbia* did not destroy the conservatives' cherished doctrine of substantive due process once and for all. As late as June 1936 supporters of the doctrine prevailed when Roberts took a swing toward the conservative position and the Court invalidated a New York minimum-wage law. But *Nebbia* was clearly the beginning of the end for substantive due process so far as it pertains to things economic. The death of the doctrine may be dated from 1937 and the Court's ruling in *West Coast Hotel* v. *Parrish*, another minimum-wage case, which established the *Nebbia* opinion as the permanent standard.[63]

Meanwhile the gold-clause cases had placed in jeopardy the New Deal's monetary policy in general and its abrogation of the gold clauses of contractual obligations in particular.[64] Early in 1935 the Supreme Court, again by a 5 to 4 margin, upheld the government's policies. The historic importance of the decisions can hardly be exaggerated. By validating abandonment of the gold standard, they released the federal government from a powerful restraint on its expansion of the money stock. Not by coincidence has the subsequent half-century been an age of inflation.

Congress's Joint Resolution of June 5, 1933, declared: "the existing emergency has disclosed" that contractual obligations to pay fixed amounts of gold "obstruct the power of the Congress to regulate the value of the money" and therefore "every provision . . . which purports to give the obligee a right to require payment in gold . . . is declared to be against public policy." The prohibition applied to all contracts—public or private, past or future.[65] Because such contractual provisions were and long had been common the resolution amounted to a massive impairment of the obligation of contracts. Naturally it was challenged in court.

Chief Justice Hughes, speaking for the majority, delivered an opinion that has been called "a masterpiece of judicial legerdemain" and "to the layman . . . a Chinese puzzle."[66] In part he simply elevated the constitutional power of Congress to regulate the value of money above the constitutional guarantee of due process to law, which would prohibit arbitrary legislative impairment of the obligation of valid contracts: "If the gold clauses . . . interfere with the policy of the Congress in the exercise of that [monetary] authority they cannot stand." Hughes did not recognize a conflict within the Constitution; he simply took for granted that a constitutional delegation of power to Congress must necessarily override a constitutional protection of individual rights. He acknowledged that "express stipulations for gold payments constitute property" and that "the contestants urge that the Congress is seeking not to regulate the currency, but to regulate contracts, and thus has stepped beyond the power conferred." But he rejected the argument completely, finding it "in the teeth of another established principle":

> Contracts, however express, cannot fetter the constitutional authority of the Congress. Contracts may create rights of property, but when contracts deal with a subject matter which lies within the control of the Congress, they have a congenital infirmity. Parties cannot remove their transactions from the reach of dominant constitutional power by making contracts about them. . . . There is no constitutional ground for denying to the Congress the power expressly to prohibit and invalidate contracts although previously made, and valid when made, when they interfere with the carrying out of the policy it is free to adopt.[67]

In the *Perry* case, which challenged the abrogation of gold clauses specifically in obligations of the United States government, the majority reached the curious conclusion that although "the Congress has not been vested with authority to alter or destroy those obligations," the plaintiff had failed to establish that the government's breach of contract had caused him actual damage and hence that he was legally entitled to a remedy. "[T]he change in the weight of the gold dollar did not necessarily cause loss to the plaintiff," said Hughes. He reached this conclusion by assuming that during 1933–1934 the government could and did legitimately deny Americans recourse to foreign markets for gold and foreign currency linked to gold. In other words, the government's (unconstitutional) abrogation of its obligation to pay gold to bondholders had caused them no determinate harm because access to the markets wherein the value of the damages could have been established had been foreclosed by other (constitutional) governmental restrictions. "Plaintiff demands the 'equivalent' in currency of the gold coin promised. But 'equivalent' cannot mean more than the amount of money which the promised gold coin would be worth to the bondholder for the purposes for which it could legally be used."[68] If ever there was legal legerdemain, this argument was it.

Never had the Four Horsemen been more outraged. Justice McReynolds, who orally delivered the dissenting opinion, repeatedly departed from his text to pour verbal vitriol on the majority opinion and mutter such asides as "the Constitution is gone" and "this is Nero at his worst."[69] The government's gold policies promised to "bring about confiscation of property rights and repudiation of national obligations." The conservative justices denied that the government's actions "were designed to attain a legitimate end." Congressional monetary authority "cannot be so enlarged as to authorize arbitrary action, whose immediate purpose and necessary effect is destruction of individual rights. . . . We are dealing here with a debased standard, adopted with the definite purpose to destroy obligations. Such arbitrary and oppressive action is not within any Congressional power heretofore recognized." As for the majority's ruling on the government's own gold clauses, "This amounts to a declaration that the Government may give with one hand and take away with the other. Default is thus made both easy and safe! . . . The Government may not escape the obligation of making good the loss incident to repudiation by prohibiting the holding of gold." Ultimately the government's actions as sustained by the majority opinion spelled DISHONOR. "Loss of reputation for honorable dealing will bring us unending humiliation; the impending legal and moral chaos is appalling."[70]

Not everything that state and federal governments attempted to do in 1933–1934 got so readily over the judicial hurdle. Late in 1934 the Supreme Court heard arguments challenging the authority of the President under the "hot-oil" provision of the NIRA. With only a single dissenting vote the justices ruled that Congress, having provided no standard or policy to guide the exercise of the executive's authority, had made an unconstitutional delegation of legislative power. Roosevelt, "a political realist with a low opinion of legal technicalities," anticipated that eventually the New Deal controls would be accepted by the Court when the statutes had been rewritten in the "correct language."[71] But the hot-oil ruling foreshadowed a greater defeat a few months later.

On May 27, 1935, in the *Schechter* case the Court unanimously ruled the NIRA unconstitutional.[72] This time, in contrast to his action in the Minnesota moratorium decision, Hughes matched his vote with his declaration that "[e]xtraordinary conditions do not create or enlarge constitutional power." The NIRA had established no standards or rules of conduct; it simply delegated to the President broad authority to approve or impose any code provision he thought would promote the vaguely described objectives of the act. But Congress, said Hughes, "cannot delegate legislative power to the President to exercise an unfettered discretion to make whatever laws he thinks may be needed or advisable for the rehabilitation and expansion of trade or industry." To the progressive Justice Cardozo, who wrote a concurring opinion, Congress's heedless procedure for implementing the NIRA constituted "delegation running riot"; it lacked "standards, ethical or commercial."

Moreover, the justices concluded that the wage-and-hour provisions of the (poultry industry) code in question unjustifiably extended federal jurisdiction. The Court rejected the government's argument that actions in intrastate labor markets had an indirect effect on interstate commerce and hence could legitimately be brought within the scope of federal regulation. A distinction between intrastate and interstate commerce must be preserved, said Hughes. "Otherwise . . . there would be virtually no limit to the Federal power, and for all practical purposes we should have a completely centralized government."[73] Prophetic words: by the time the Chief Justice retired, in 1941, the Court had indeed adopted an interpretation of the Constitution permitting precisely such a completely centralized government wherever economic regulation is concerned; and the interpretation has held sway ever since.

On January 6, 1936, the New Deal's other grand scheme for the displacement of free markets, the AAA, received a fatal blow from the Supreme Court. By a 6 to 3 vote, with only the progressive justices dissenting, the Court invalidated the agricultural relief act, finding its tax on processors constitutionally indefensible. The AAA, said Justice Roberts, speaking for the majority, "invades the reserved rights of the states. It is a statutory plan to regulate and control agricultural production, a matter beyond the powers delegated to the federal government. The tax, the appropriation of the funds raised, and the direction for their disbursement, are but parts of the plan. They are but means to an unconstitutional end." The majority also expressed a fear that such taxes, with proceeds directed exclusively toward the benefit of a privileged class, might proliferate without limit, resulting in "the regulation of all industry throughout the United States." The dissenters could only declaim against the dreaded hypothetical repercussions and the majority's "tortured construction of the Constitution," asserting that "all federal taxes inevitably have some influence on the internal economy of the states."[74]

What may we conclude about the relation of the judicial branch to the surge of governmental intervention during the depths of the Great Depression? It is commonly supposed that the courts overthrew most of the emergency measures enacted by state and federal legislatures during 1933–1934; and indeed the judiciary did put many barriers in the path of the depression-spawned legislation. But by no means were all such measures invalidated. The Minnesota moratorium and *Nebbia* decisions sustained state policies of tremendous importance. The gold-standard rulings allowed the federal government to adopt a monetary policy that has altered the course of history ever since. To be sure, the Court's invalidation of the NIRA and the AAA had major importance, but we shall see that the *Schechter* and *Butler* rulings were not the last word on the permissibility of such anticompetitive, redistributionist schemes. Before long the AAA would be back, expressed in the constitutionally "correct langauge," and the NIRA too would reappear—not all of it but several of its critical parts, especially its regulation of labor-management relations. A balanced evaluation of the New Deal's early encounter with the judiciary must conclude that the New Dealers won some and lost some. They might have done worse, yet they seethed with anger that the courts had denied them anything at all.

LEGACIES, INSTITUTIONAL AND IDEOLOGICAL

Legacies of the Great Depression and the governmental response to it—one hardly knows where to begin. Nothing had a greater effect on the twentieth-century economy, polity, and society of the United States. But one need not argue for what almost everyone already believes. Mine is a narrower thesis. Though the depression persisted for over a decade, the heart of the crisis, the true national emergency part of it, occurred in 1932–1933. To maintain, as I shall, that the events of this brief period left important permanent legacies, one must show either that its institutional and ideological changes themselves persisted indefinitely or that the First New Deal led inexorably to the enduring changes effected by the Second New Deal.

The distinction between the First New Deal (1933–1934) and the Second New Deal (1935–1938) has become a commonplace of historical scholarship. It is believed that during the first period the Roosevelt administration embraced a broad coalition, including the major business interests, as represented by the Chamber of Commerce and the Baruch gang, as well as the organized farmers, the labor unions, and others. The crowning achievements were the NIRA and the AAA; the overriding objective was to raise prices through cartelization and other suppressions of market competition. During the second period, in contrast, the administration is seen as estranged from the business community and more devoted to helping the underdogs and building the welfare state. The jewels of this stage were the Social Security Act, the National Labor Relations Act, and the Fair Labor Standards Act, plus a series of vindictive tax and regulatory statutes aimed at the now-despised "economic royalists." A popular historical text describes the First New Deal as an "experiment in compromise," the Second as "the full flowering of social justice progressivism."[75]

The distinction has substance, but one can easily make too much of it. William Leuchtenburg, a leading historian of the period, has warned against "exaggerating the extent of the shift from 1933 to 1935." In particular he notes that "many of the NRA emphases persisted." Recently Larry Gerber has concluded that the traditional interpretation imposes a sharper distinction than the differences between the actors, events, and ideologies of the two periods justify. He observes also that the most important legislation of the Second New Deal "had its origins" in the First New Deal.[76] Let us consider some of the direct connections of laws, agencies, and programs.

The institutional legacies included some of the most central agencies and programs. The RFC, which the New Deal inherited from Hoover, received expanded resources and a variety of new missions. It remained throughout the 1930s (and long afterward) the federal government's chief spending and lending agency. The Tennessee Valley Authority, created during the legislative rush of the Hundred Days, joined with the massive hydroelectric projects in the West to make the federal government a major producer and seller of electricity—positions it has never relinquished. Federally sponsored work-relief programs—starting with the Federal Emergency Relief Administration, the Civil Works Administration, and others in 1933 and blending into the Works Progress Administration in 1935—established a precedent for making the federal government the "employer of last resort." The commitment was reaffirmed by the Employment Act of 1946 and most recently by the Humphrey-Hawkins Act of 1978. A variety of make-work "training" schemes in the 1960s and the diverse jobs supported under the Comprehensive Employment and Training Act in the 1970s testify to the enduring importance of the welfare-employment first provided by the federal government in 1933.[77]

The agricultural relief program struck down by the *Butler* decision came back to life, without the constitutionally offensive tax on processors, as the Soil Conservation and Domestic Allotment Act of 1936 and the Agricultural Adjustment Act of 1938. These statutes preserved such devices as acreage and production controls, benefit payments to farmers, price supports through nonrecourse loans, and marketing agreements—the mainstays of a subsidy-dependent class of farmers for the past half century. As Lester Chandler notes, "Once the federal government had admitted such responsibilities and taken so many actions" as it had under the first AAA, "a return to its laissez-faire policies of the 1920s proved impossible."[78]

The NIRA spawned even more numerous progeny. The National Labor Relations Act of 1935 "grew directly out of the NRA experience." Immediately after the *Schechter* decision, Senator Wagner moved to reinstate in even stronger form the collective bargaining provisions of the NIRA's Section 7(a). Similarly the Fair Labor Standards Act of 1938 stipulated regulations of minimum wages, maximum hours, and working conditions much like those required under the NRA's codes of fair competition. With the Bituminous Coal Act of 1937 the government effectively reenacted the NRA code for the coal industry, excepting its labor provisions but including its price-fixing features. Using the Connally Act of 1935 and estimates of gasoline demand prepared by the Bureau of Mines, the federal government sanctioned and facilitated through state action the effective cartelization of the oil industry. The cartel functioned successfully until the 1970s, when changing market conditions and an even more potent cartel (the Organization of Petroleum Exporting Countries) ousted it from the seat of privilege. The federal housing program included in the public works provisions of the NIRA achieved permanence under an act of 1937 that created the United States Housing Authority. Other legacies included the Robinson-Patman Act of 1936 and the Miller-Tydings Act of 1937, which salvaged for small retailers certain anticompetitive provisions first enjoyed under the NRA codes.[79]

"The programs of the early New Deal," Ellis Hawley has concluded, "generated a new organization consciousness among previously weak and relatively unorganized groups. . . . [T]he NRA and AAA had been eye openers." Many people recognized that now "the group that could develop sufficient political strength and a plausible ideological rationale [such as conserving natural resources or helping the little guy] could secure governmental intervention" to suppress competition, set aside the price system, or gain subsidies.[80]

Roosevelt's bitter confrontation with the Supreme Court during 1935–1936, when several of the First New Deal's most important programs were invalidated, had the most profound consequences; it led to a constitutional revolution. Buoyed by his landslide reelection in 1936, FDR brought forth his court-packing plan. To his surprise, many people treated it as "a naked bid for dictatorship." Although the ill-considered scheme backfired on him—even the leaders of his own party rose up in opposition—the President ultimately achieved the desired end. Justices Roberts and Hughes, for reasons that can only be conjectured but may well have had something to do with Roosevelt's enormous electoral victory, moved into the progressive camp to stay. A series of decisions in 1937, wherein the Court upheld the constitutionality of the National Labor Relations Act, the Social Security Act, a state minimum-wage law, and a variety of other interventions in the market economy, "launched the Court on its new affirmative course of applying, implementing, and extending positive federal economic power" and made it the "validator of positive governmental regulation of the economy." Aged and beaten men, the Four Horsemen retired from the bench between 1937 and 1941, and the President replaced them with such enthusiastic New Dealers as Hugo Black, Stanley Reed, Felix Frankfurter, and William O. Douglas. Gone forever were the days when due process of law implied the sanctity of private property rights and liberty of contract. As the distinguished constitutional scholar Edward S. Corwin observed, "The change which the views of a dominant section of the American people regarding the purpose of government underwent during this period [1929–1937] was nothing short of revolutionary, and it was accompanied in due course by a corresponding change of attitude toward constitutional values." Afterwards virtually any federal economic regulation whatsoever would be free of constitutional restraint.[81]

The depression and the government's responses to it made a deep impression on the nation's intellectuals, the specialists in the production and distribution of ideologies. Before and during the First New Deal, Roosevelt had his Brains Trust. During the Second New Deal Professor Frankfurter's "boys" seemed to be everywhere, drafting laws and piloting them through Congress and past the courts. Never before had the intellectuals enjoyed such pervasive involvement in the machinations of power politics at the highest levels of government. The experience was intoxicating. The respect for individualism and free markets that had survived to 1929 went quickly into retreat thereafter. Social scientists "discarded old concepts and matured new ones to justify a broad expansion of public authority." Whatever the social or economic problem the cause seemed always to be the same: unfettered capitalism. Hence the universal cure: some form of collectivism. The intellectuals actively debated the specific form the movement should take, but only a few of them doubted the need for a move to the left. Right-wingers in those days were widely presumed to be unregenerate apologists for wealthy vested interests and grasping wicked reactionaries. "Conservative" intellectuals, who ironically now included the defenders of classical liberalism, soon became almost an endangered species. Individualism "gave ground to a new emphasis on social security and collective action."[82]

According to Herbert Stein, the thirties taught intellectuals several lessons that would dominate policy-making for decades. Included were the beliefs that unemployment is the greatest economic problem; that governmental controls and fiscal policies can and should be used to redistribute income to "worthy" groups; that the Constitution places no limits on federal regulatory powers; and that an "activist policy by the President . . . will be appreciated by the public." Obviously all of these beliefs still flourish today. As Nathan Glazer has recently written, even the Reagan administration, which many considered reactionary, "represented the complete acceptance of the New Deal welfare state."[83]

Significantly the ideological shift of the 1930s went far beyond a mere change of fashion among the intellectuals. The masses also joined in it. The old regime of free markets and limited government was deeply and widely discredited. "[T]he public," observed Frank Knight in 1939, "has lost faith, such faith as it ever had, in the moral validity of market values," especially in labor markets. The economic crisis and the governmental responses to it "dissipated the distrust of the state" inherited from the eighteenth and nineteenth centuries. "Even Republicans who protested that Roosevelt's policies were snuffing out liberty voted overwhelmingly in favor of coercive measures." The great majority of Americans, regardless of party affiliation, "accepted and approved the new ideals of social welfare democracy."[84] The nation had weathered its worst storm. Always susceptible to the fallacy of post hoc ergo propter hoc, the masses concluded that Roosevelt and his policies had saved the country. It would never do, they thought, to risk a return to a regime of economic freedom, a regime most people believed responsible for the catastrophe of the Great Depression.

CONCLUSIONS

The bust of 1929–1933 plunged the nation into grave national emergency. Mass unemployment, enormous business losses, widespread tax-delinquency sales and mortgage foreclosures on homes and farms, thousands upon thousands of bank failures, and drastically falling personal incomes brought misery and hardship to tens of millions of people. Few escaped the calamity, and none could banish the fear, as the economic collapse pervasively affected the normally secure middle and upper classes as well as the masses of manual workers and farmers. Continuing for almost four years and driving the economy to nearly unbearable depths, the collapse threatened to totally destroy the economic system. The Hoover administration's responses to the depression, though far bolder than those of any previous administration, failed to stem the decline or even to rally the spirits of the suffering citizens. While Hoover prayed that the economy would hit bottom and bounce back, the American people grew ever more desperate. In the streets and in Congress they longed for strong leadership and direction. All the while their despair only deepened.

When Roosevelt took command in March 1933 a unique conjuncture existed. Its elements included the genuine economic crisis; the artificial and possibly contrived crisis produced by completely closing every bank in the country, America's own "burning of the Reichstag"; a pervasive sense of crisis, which manifested itself in a multitude of pleas to "do something" even if it required the assumption of dictatorial powers; and the freedom and ability of the incoming New Deal government, which controlled the presidency and both houses of Congress, to act swiftly and decisively. FDR's unexpectedly bold and astute leadership supplied the final ingredient needed to overcome the normal deadlocks and inertia of the political and governmental systems and therefore to bring forth a burst of legislative and administrative action without equal before or since.

Almost everything done during the Hundred Days relied on the emergency rationale and the wartime analogy. Many programs employed during World War I were resurrected. Like Hoover's RFC, the New Deal's gold policy, the TVA, the AAA, the NIRA, and many other programs had obvious wartime precedents. The administrators of the programs came largely from the ranks of the veterans of the wartime mobilization. The rhetoric and the symbols harkened back to that glorious occasion of extraordinary national solidarity. Roosevelt declared that the nation could conquer the depression by "treating the task as we would the emergency of a war." In this spirit General Johnson launched his colossal propaganda blitz, aiming to intimidate "slackers" and "chiselers" into supporting the NRA codes. This enormous campaign employed an emotion-laden collectivist symbolism previously unknown outside the dictatorships of Europe.

The judiciary placed some barriers in the path of the New Deal collectivists. Although it upheld some important state interferences with private property rights as well as the federal government's highly significant abandonment of the gold standard, the Supreme Court could not stomach Congress's "delegation running riot" and its invasion of jurisdictions long reserved for state action. The justices therefore struck down the NIRA and the AAA. In the ensuing court fight, Roosevelt took a beating but ultimately won by forfeit. The result was a constitutional revolution, as the doctrine of economic substantive due process disappeared from constitutional jurisprudence and free rein was given to all forms of federal economic regulation whatsoever.

Institutional legacies of those fateful years stand all around us: federal lending for a multitude of purposes, federal production and sale of electricity, federal manipulation of agricultural production, prices, and marketing, federal regulation of virtually every aspect of labor markets, the vast federal social insurance system, a plethora of anticompetitive federal laws, and an uncountably large variety of federal subsidies—the list goes on and on.

The most important legacy of the New Deal, however, is a certain system of belief, the now-dominant ideology of the mixed economy, which holds that the government is an immensely useful means for achieving one's private aspirations and that one's resort to this reservoir of potentially appropriable benefits is perfectly legitimate. To take—indirectly if not directly—other people's property for one's own benefit is now considered morally impeccable, provided that the taking is effected through the medium of the government. Only a vague moral uneasiness sets a limit on such takings. The "regulation of all industry throughout the United States" that Justice Roberts feared in the *Butler* decision has long since become a reality, and even people who neither sought nor approved of this development have adjusted their actions and their thinking to it. The commitment of both masses and elites to individualism, free markets, and limited government suffered a blow in the 1930s from which it is unlikely ever to recover fully. In place of the old beliefs there now prevails a greater toleration of, and even a positive demand for, collectivist schemes that promise social security, protection from the rigors of market competition, and very often—to be blunt—something for nothing. Though its grand promises seem never to be fully delivered, the New Deal ideology, embedded so deeply by the events of the 1930s, remains vital even after a half a century.

CHAPTER NINE

The Political Economy of War, 1940–1945

Of all the time-honored Anglo-Saxon liberties, the freedom of contract took the worst beating in the war.

CLINTON L. ROSSITER

The government's actions during World War II resembled in many ways its actions during World War I. Again, with facilitation by Congress and acquiescence by the Supreme Court, the executive branch of the federal government extended its sway over the economy. Drafting men, allocating materials, fixing prices, building and operating entire industries, federal authorities exercised the same kind of powers they had wielded during 1917–1918. But this time almost everything went far beyond its antecedent. By comparison with the actions taken during 1940–1945, the government's economic management during World War I appears limited, unsystematic, and ineffective. World War II witnessed the creation of an awesome garrison economy. (To gain an impression of the tremendous scope of the government's economic management in World War II, see the list of war agencies in the appendix to this chapter.) If one takes seriously the national accounts statistics, which is especially risky in the absence of a full-fledged system of free-market pricing, it appears that about four-tenths of the nation's total real output and a much larger proportion of its industrial output went toward making war at the peak of the effort in 1943–1944.[1] The remaining civilian economy labored under a plethora of governmental burdens and restraints.

The government controlled and directly participated in the economy more extensively during 1940–1945 for several reasons. One had to do with scale. World War II was, as the military men say, the Big One. The Wilson administration had built up military and naval forces of some four million men by the end of 1918. Roosevelt and his lieutenants commanded more than twelve million in 1945. In World War I the United States had been a belligerent for about a year and half, and most of that time was spent getting ready to fight. The Big One took almost four years, involved American forces in a great deal of combat, and gave rise to ten times more expenditure of dollars.

Different preconditions also had an important effect. Before their entry into the conflict in 1917, Americans had not fought a major war for over half a century. In 1941, on the other hand, memories of the previous world war remained vivid, and many men who had exercised notable authority or influence during the earlier hostilities (Roosevelt, Stimson, Baruch, Frankfurter) still occupied positions of authority or influence. They had definite ideas about what to do, because they had "been there" before. In addition the federal bureaucracy had acquired much power and managerial experience during the New Deal years, and businessmen had become more accustomed to dealing with that bureaucracy. Hence, the development of economic controls during World War II could proceed much faster than it had before. Indeed the government secured many of its powers, including the authority to conscript men, before the country formally entered the war. Although American entry into each world war followed more than two years of formal neutrality, the second entry came on the heels of a prolonged depression, whereas the first had followed a time of relatively high-employment production and economic growth. The military effort early in World War II could call upon unemployed resources far more than the mobilization in 1917 could.

The conditions that provoked a declaration of war also differed. The United States entered World War I when the Germans finally pushed Wilson too far, whereas formal entry into World War II was ostensibly a simple and immediate reaction to Japan's surprise attack on Pearl Harbor. This atrocity produced a tremendous solidarity of the American people. Unlike the Congress of 1917, in which six senators and fifty representatives voted against war, the Congress of 1941 gave virtually unanimous approval to American belligerency. (Only one "nay" was cast against war with Japan, none against war with Germany.) For a time the national sense of outrage facilitated the government's extensions of its economic powers, as widespread approval of the government's end—destruction of the Japanese and German war machines—spilled justification onto its means. Said a contemporary observer, "The number of administrative difficulties and impossibilities which were resolved overnight on December 7, 1941, is spectacular."[2]

The differences of scale, preconditions, and circumstances, taken together, insured that the command economy of World War II would dwarf that of the previous war in scope and penetration. Because it did, its legacies also ran deeper. Moreover, differences in postwar international relations compounded several developments set in motion during the war. Whereas

World War I was followed by relative international calm for the United States, the Big One merged almost immediately into the Cold One—not to speak of Korea, Vietnam, and assorted smaller military adventures around the world during the four decades after 1945. The permanent national emergency prolonged indefinitely the life of the military-industrial complex that had first assumed its modern shape during World War II. This legacy alone would be enough to give the American experience of 1940–1945 lasting importance in the evolution of the modern mixed economy. As we shall see, however, it was but one enduring legacy among many.

World War II, it is often said, was the most popular of all American wars. The claim is probably true. Yet its frequent reiteration has had a soporific effect on students of the war. Many people, including some scholars, hastily conclude that because World War II was a relatively popular war the actions taken by the government in prosecuting it enjoyed well-nigh universal approval and cooperation. Such a characterization fails even to approximate the truth. In fact, various "wars" raged within the war: farmers against nonfarmers, small businessmen against big businessmen, labor unionists against employers and the rest of the public, and so forth. In short, the usual politico-economic conflicts continued. Moreover, the issue of guns versus butter intruded on everybody. Wilson had declared during World War I that "politics is adjourned," and FDR insisted during World War II that Dr. Win-The-War had replaced Dr. New Deal and "politics is out"; but all reports of the death of politics were mistaken. Only where truly overriding national security issues arose did the usual political conflicts abate. A central aspect of the conflicts was the ongoing attempt of each interest group to shift the real costs of the war onto others. Above all, the government itself strove mightily to conceal the true costs of its war program.

DE JURE NEUTRALITY, DE FACTO BELLIGERENCY, 1939–1941

In a sense, World War I did not end until 1945. Perhaps someday historians will view the world wars as only two stages of a single enduring conflict. The Treaty of Versailles, with its harsh impositions on Germany, fostered deep resentment and vindictiveness in the vanquished nation. These conditions facilitated the rise of the Nazis, whose control of the German government after 1933 virtually guaranteed a resumption of armed conflict among the European powers sooner or later. Hitler's predatory adventures in Austria and the Sudetenland in 1938 signaled that, French and British appeasement notwithstanding, Europe stood on the brink of war. Informed people knew it was coming.

> In the nightmare of the dark
> All the dogs of Europe bark,
> And the living nations wait,
> Each sequestered in its hate;
>
> Intellectual disgrace
> Stares from every human face
> And the seas of pity lie
> Locked and frozen in each eye.[3]

But even if war was inevitable in Europe, the nature and extent of American involvement in the imminent conflict remained unresolved questions.

The questions became more pointed after the German invasion of Poland and the ensuing declarations of war between the major powers of Western Europe in September 1939. President Roosevelt immediately issued an official proclamation of American neutrality, but his heart was not in it. "This nation will remain a neutral nation," he declared in his radio broadcast of September 3, "but I cannot ask that every American remain neutral in thought as well."[4] FDR had long detested Hitler and sympathized with the British. He wanted the United States to provide more assistance to those resisting the Nazi onslaught and worked craftily toward this objective. In these efforts he enjoyed the support of his able and politically astute cabinet, most business interests, many intellectuals, and the prevailing public opinion of the Northeast and the South. The great region from Ohio to the Rockies, in contrast, contained a large majority opposed to policies that might result in American participation in the European bloodbath. The President, with his political ear ever to the ground, proceeded erratically, making sure not to get visibly too far in front of the citizenry.

The French defeat in June 1940 provoked a substantial shift of American public opinion. The proportion of respondents polled by the Public Opinion Research Project who considered it "more important to help England than to keep out of war" increased during the second half of 1940 from about 35 percent to about 60 percent. The proportion of respondents "[more] willing to risk war with Japan than let Japan continue her aggressions" also rose steadily between mid-1940 and late 1941. Still, only a small fraction of the people surveyed—about a fifth, as late as October 1941—thought the United States should enter the war, and a large majority indicated they would not vote to go to war against Germany if a national referendum were taken.[5]

With public opinion deeply divided, Roosevelt moved cautiously but relentlessly to project the United States into the conflict; his maneuvers included "back-pedaling, obfuscation, impossible promises, and, occasionally, outright deception." The destroyer deal with the British in September 1940, the lend-lease arrangements given statutory sanction in March 1941, and a series of provocative restrictions on trade with the Japanese edged the country ever closer to war. In the heat of the presidential campaign of 1940 FDR flatly promised the "mothers of America" that "your boys are not going to be sent into any foreign wars." Like Wilson's slogan in 1916 ("He kept us out of war"), Roosevelt's promise enhanced his reelection prospects—this time for an unprecedented third term.[6]

Those who want war often want somebody else to fight it, and 1940 was no exception: there was a tremendous political struggle over conscription. Almost no one took seriously the possibility of raising troops by offering recruits sufficient pay and perquisites. On June 30, 1940, the armed forces had only 458,000 persons on active duty. For the United States to make its presence felt in a shooting war a great mobilization would be required. The leaders of the armed forces, including the venerable Henry L. Stimson, whom FDR had brought out of retirement in July 1940 to head the War Department (and head off the President's Republican critics), had long espoused conscription to mobilize manpower for war. The American Legion—we did our duty, now we'll make certain that you do yours—actively supported the draft. The President himself did not find it politic to come out publicly in support of a draft bill until August.[7]

A national peacetime draft had no precedent in American history, and powerful men vigorously opposed breaking with that tradition. Significantly the opponents were also isolationists. (One has no incentive to conceal the costs of a policy if one opposes the policy in the first place; indeed, one strives to reveal the full costs.) In the Senate Arthur Vandenberg described a peacetime draft as "repugnant to the spirit of democracy and the soul of Republican institutions," while Henry F. Ashhurst opposed "riveting shackles of militarism upon the American people" and Walter F. George worried that Congress could not grant the President such power "and convince the American people that we are not ready and resigned and reconciled to the final, inevitable, short step of actually entering the war." After the French capitulation, however, public and congressional opposition to the draft law diminished. By compromising its terms somewhat and heavily emphasizing its temporary, emergency character, supporters secured its enactment on September 16, 1940.[8]

Soaring in clouds of self-contradiction the Selective Training and Service Act of 1940 declared that "in a *free* society the obligations and privileges of military training and service should be shared generally in accordance with a fair and just system of selective *compulsory* military training and service."[9] It identified "our traditional military policy" with the National Defense Act of 1916 to justify calling the National Guard into active national service. It required that every male aged 21–35 register for the draft and authorized the President "whether or not a state of war exists" to induct into the armed forces "such number of men as in his judgment is required" up to a peacetime maximum of 900,000 in active training or service in the land forces, subject only to a sufficient congressional appropriation. The conscripts were to serve for twelve consecutive months "except that whenever the Congress has declared that the national interest is imperiled, such twelve-month period may be extended by the President to such time as may be necessary in the interests of national defense." The act contained the important proviso, included at the insistence of the isolationists, that the conscripts "shall not be employed beyond the limits of the Western Hemisphere" except in U.S. territories and possessions. It provided for the deferment of public officials, ministers of religion and, at the President's discretion, men with dependents or those employed in essential jobs. It provided for assignment of conscientious objectors to noncombat service. Local civilian boards were to administer the act— the wisdom of World War I had not been forgotten. Failure to comply was punishable by up to five years imprisonment or $10,000 fine.

The act went beyond the draft of soldiers, empowering the President to place obligatory orders for products and materials that would "take precedence over all other orders and contracts." Refusal to comply would be deemed a felony punishable by up to three years imprisonment or a fine of $50,000. Further, the President was authorized to "take immediate possession of any such [noncomplying] plant" and to operate it as he saw fit. Owners would receive "fair and just" compensation when the government took over their property.[10]

After the Selective Service System went into operation in the fall of 1940 the armed forces grew rapidly. By June 30, 1941, about 1,800,000 men were on active duty.[11] But as the conscripts' year of service approached its end, the prospect loomed that the newly formed army would disintegrate unless Congress authorized retaining the draftees. Congressional leaders doubted that extending the term of involuntary service could gain approval, even under the ominous international conditions prevailing in the summer of 1941. Although the act of 1940 provided for extending the term of service whenever Congress declared that "the national interest is imperiled," few politicians wanted to bear the responsibility for what would look like breaking a promise to the conscripts. Again Roosevelt hesitated before sending Congress a strong appeal for extension.

In Congress the opposition mounted fierce resistance, making passage of the extension bill highly uncertain. Congressman Hamilton Fish, the representative of FDR's home district and a man thoroughly despised by the President, characterized the proposed extension of the draft as "part and parcel of a giant conspiracy" to bring the United States into the war. Senator Burton K. Wheeler used his franking privilege to mail a million antiwar postcards, an action that the superpatriotic Stimson considered treasonous.

After the administration accepted some compromises, including a limitation of the extension to eighteen months, Congress on August 14 passed the Draft Extension Act. The margin of victory could not have been slighter: the House vote was 203 in favor and 202 opposed. Conscription was sustained by a single vote![12]

After the United States formally entered the war the draft laws received periodic amendment. The ages of men subject to induction were extended at both ends to cover the span 18–45 inclusive, and the period of service became the duration of the war plus six months. Deferments remained controversial, especially the general exemption of agricultural workers, which the congressional farm bloc used its clout to maintain. All in all, the system worked well enough to please the government.

Of the sixteen million who served in the armed forces during the war, ten million were conscripts. (Popular war?) Further, many of the volunteers came forward only because of the draft, some seeking to avoid uncomfortable and dangerous service in the infantry by joining the Navy. Secretary of War Stimson, like his predecessor in World War I, considered the administration of the draft law by local civilian boards "a triumph of decentralization." Recruitment for the armed forces had brought forth only a trickle of volunteers before passage of the draft law in 1940, but no difficulty was encountered in securing volunteers to staff the draft boards. More than 100,000 persons served in that capacity without pay.[13] Some 6,000 conscientious objectors went to prison rather than submit to either military service or the alternative employments prescribed by the government.[14]

Few scholars have appreciated how much the legitimacy of the entire wartime command economy rested on the existence of military conscription. A passage by the influential economist Wesley C. Mitchell, written in 1943, clearly illustrates the dependence. Mystically imagining that in wartime "virtually all wills become one," Mitchell declared that "[t]he dominant single aim" of military victory "assures general assent to the mobilizing of economic resources under governmental direction." It does so especially when the soldiers are draftees:

> The signal evidence of readiness to pay whatever price may be necessary is the passing of a draft law requiring those fittest for military service to leave their homes and wonted occupations, accept low pay and physical discomforts, and risk their lives in the horrible job of killing others. After common consent has been given to that act, civilians are morally bound to accept the lesser sacrifices war imposes on them.

"When lives themselves are treated as a means [to the end of military victory]," said Mitchell, "so is property."[15] If its premises are accepted, the argument is indeed compelling, and we shall encounter it again and again: when we consider universal service, which became an important political issue later in the war; when we consider the Supreme Court's wartime decisions; and in a variety of other contexts.

If the Roosevelt administration proceeded cautiously in building up the armed forces during 1940–1941, its prewar planning for economic mobilization was even less decisive. In the three years before the attack on Pearl Harbor the planning was, in the words of an economic historian, "mismanaged, confused, and marked by political expediency." In 1939 FDR appointed a War Resources Board, headed by Edward R. Stettinius of U.S. Steel, to study economic mobilization. Many New Dealers, viewing the board as mostly robber barons, and many isolationists, viewing it as a cabal of warmongers, hurried to attack it. Chastened by the reactions, the President disbanded the board and suppressed its report. There followed a series of makeshift commissions and boards charged with planning and coordinating the government's economic mobilization: National Defense Advisory Commission (created May 29, 1940), Office of Production Management (January 7, 1941), Office of Price Administration and Civilian Supply (April 11, 1941), Supply Priorities and Allocations Board (August 28, 1941). None of them enjoyed much genuine power, administrative independence, or effective leadership. All were created by executive action of the President, who carefully refrained from delegating many of his own prerogatives in this politically sensitive area. Defying the laws of administrative science, Roosevelt deliberately divided authority over the OPM between businessman William Knudsen and unionist Sidney Hillman. At the OPACS, Leon Henderson, lacking clear statutory authority for price controls, vainly strove to hold down price increases by jawboning and threatening firms with the loss of government contracts. The last thing the President wanted was an economic "czar" or "dictator" such as Bernard Baruch reputedly had been during World War I. "[M]y constant insistence on one-man control of the defense effort," Baruch later recalled, "annoyed and even angered the President at times." Only after the attack on Pearl Harbor did Roosevelt move in the direction advised by the old war-horse.[16]

In mid-1940 Congress enacted important legislation expanding the powers of the Reconstruction Finance Corporation, still the bailiwick of the politically durable conservative Democrat, Jesse Jones,

> (1) To make loans to, or, when requested by the Federal Loan Administrator with the approval of the President, purchase the capital stock of, any corporation (a) for the purpose of producing, acquiring, and carrying strategic and critical materials as defined by the President, and (b) for plant construction, expansion and equipment, and working capital, to be used by the corporation in the manufacture of equipment and supplies necessary to the national defense, on such terms and conditions and with such maturities as the Corporation may determine; and

(2) When requested by the Federal Loan Administrator, with the approval
of the President, to create or to organize a corporation or corporations, with
power (a) to produce, acquire, and carry strategic and critical materials as
defined by the President, (b) to purchase and lease land, to purchase, lease,
build, and expand plants, and to purchase and produce equipment, supplies,
and machinery, for the manufacture of arms, ammunition, and implements of
war, (c) to lease such plants to private corporations to engage in such manufacture, and (d) if the President finds that it is necessary for a Government
agency to engage in such manufacture, to engage in such manufacture itself.[17]

During the war these powers, which Jones described as "perhaps the broadest
powers ever conferred upon a single government agency," would be exercised
on a grand scale as the federal government became an investor, producer, and
commercial dealer through numerous RFC subsidiaries: Metals Reserve Company, Defense Plant Corporation, Defense Supplies Corporation, Petroleum
Reserves Corporation, Rubber Reserve Company, U.S. Commercial Company, War Emergency Pipelines, Inc., War Insurance Corporation, and others. (See the appendix to this chapter.) Here was wartime socialism in the
strict sense of governmental ownership and (sometimes) management of the
means of production. Jesse Jones was truly an economic czar.[18] (There were
others: Harry Hopkins in charge of Lend-Lease, Donald M. Nelson at the
War Production Board, and eventually above all the rest James F. Byrnes at
the Office of War Mobilization. Of them, more is said later in this chapter.)

When the Japanese bombs rained down on Pearl Harbor the United States
was not totally unprepared for war, nor did the government lack authority to
mobilize the nation's economic resources. The draft law, with its provision
for obligatory orders, gave the government the power to procure human and
material resources at prices below true market costs. The various control
boards, armed with the government's statutory power to set priorities for the
use of essential materials, had developed some expertise in coordinating the
components of the war program. The RFC possessed the authority to enter
directly into a wide variety of economic activities. Still, the nation did not
have a fully mobilized and coordinated garrison economy. The warfare state
had passed beyond its infancy, but its scope remained limited. To achieve
maturity it required that important additional authority be placed in the
hands of the government.

MORE POWERS AND PRICE CONTROLS

On December 9, 1941, in a radio address to the nation, Roosevelt sought to
rally the American people to resist the "sudden criminal attacks" of the
powerful and resourceful gangsters" who had "treacherously violated the

longstanding peace." The news, he admitted, was all bad. Still, like it or not, "every single man, woman and child is a partner in the most tremendous undertaking of our American history." The war would be long and hard, demanding vast amounts of money, materials, work—and lives. But not to worry:

> It is not a sacrifice for any man, old or young, to be in the Army or the Navy of the United States. Rather is it a privilege. It is not a sacrifice for the industrialist or the wage-earner, the farmer or the shopkeeper, the trainman or the doctor, to pay more taxes, to buy more bonds, to forego extra profits, to work longer or harder at the task for which he is best fitted. Rather is it a privilege. It is not a sacrifice to do without many things to which we are accustomed if the national defense calls for doing without.

The President expressed his confidence that the American people would "cheerfully" submit to heavy taxation and to doing without "those material things they are asked to give up."[19]

But he knew that, given the prices the government was willing to pay, the American people would voluntarily supply little of what the government now wanted from them. They would have to be compelled, and the Roosevelt administration hastened to acquire the legal powers necessary to achieve its war goals. Spurred by an alarmed public opinion and an insistent demand that the government act immediately to protect the country from powerful, determined, and cunning foreign aggressors, Congress quickly brought forth legislation to grant the executive branch sweeping war powers.

The First War Powers Act, which became law on December 18, 1941, authorized the President "in matters relating to the conduct of the present war" to redistribute functions, duties, powers, and personnel among existing executive agencies as he saw fit. (Recall how long and hard Woodrow Wilson had to fight to get the Overman Act, which gave him these powers. In 1941 the argument could be made in Congress that the proposed law merely gave FDR the same powers Wilson had been given in the previous war.) Although the act forbade the government's use of cost-plus-a-percentage-of-cost contracts or any violation of existing legal limits on profits, it gave the executive branch a substantially free hand to deal with private suppliers. The President could authorize "any department or agency of the Government exercising functions in connection with the prosecution of the war effort . . . to enter into contracts . . . and to make advance, progress and other payments thereon, without regard to the provisions of law relating to the making, performance, amendment, or modification of contracts whenever he deems such action would facilitate the prosecution of the war." The act amended in several ways the Trading with the Enemy Act of 1917, giving the President far-reaching authority to regulate international financial transactions and the use of foreign-owned property in the United States. It also authorized the censorship of all communications between the United States and *any* foreign country.[20]

The Second War Powers Act, which became law on March 27, 1942, was a collection of miscellaneous enactments, the first four of which involved significant congressional delegations of economic powers. Title I expanded the authority of the Interstate Commerce Commission to regulate motor carriers. The ICC could now require the joint use of equipment, garages, and other facilities and could alter or suspend orders, licenses, and regulations "to the extent necessary to facilitate the prosecution of the war." Title II expanded the power of executive agencies to acquire by purchase or condemnation proceedings any real and associated personal property "that shall be deemed necessary, for military, naval, or other war purposes" and to take immediate possession of the property. Title III authorized the Secretary of the Navy to contract for stipulated goods and services "with or without advertising or competitive bidding upon determination that the price is fair and reasonable" (Josephus Daniels, the Navy Secretary who had fought to retain competitive bidding in World War I, must have shed a tear); to impose priorities on deliveries of contracted goods and service; and to use cost-plus-a-fixed-fee contracts provided the fee did not exceed 7 percent of the estimated cost. In addition this part of the act gave the President tremendous, effectively unrestrained power over resource allocation: "Whenever the President is satisfied that the fulfillment of requirements for the defense of the United States will result in a shortage in the supply of any material or of any facilities for defense or for private account or for export, the President may allocate such material or facilities in such manner, upon such conditions and to such extent *as he shall deem necessary or appropriate* in the public interest and to promote the national defense." No greater economic power was ever delegated by Congress to the President. This provision became the legal foundation for the War Production Board's pervasive control of the economy during the last three years of the war. Title IV of the act liberalized the authority of the Federal Reserve System to purchase government securities "without regard to maturities either in the open market *or directly from*" the Treasury.[21] This allowed the Treasury to use the Fed as a de facto printing press, which it did on an enormous scale to help finance the government's gargantuan deficits.

Even with all the powers provided by the two war powers acts, the government faced the prospect that the resources needed to carry out its ambitious war program—Roosevelt called for sixty thousand planes, forty-five thousand tanks, twenty thousand antiaircraft guns, and eight million tons of merchant ships, among other things, in 1942 alone—could be obtained only by bidding up the prices of military products and their inputs to an embarrassingly obvious and politically threatening extent.[22] The reluctance of the administration and Congress, especially the latter, to collect enough ordinary taxes or sell to the public enough bonds in a free bond market to finance the war program meant that the hidden tax of inflation would have to carry more of the load. But this resort raised problems of its own. Rapidly accelerating inflation, which is a rising tax on the holding of all assets denominated in nominal money units, eventually becomes widely perceived as a "taking"; it comes to be seen as enriching either the government or privileged parties in the private economy. (After all, people who play their cards right can always profit from inflation; and the government, which owes vast amounts of nominal money to the public, always plays the inflation game with a deck stacked in its favor.) Political reactions to a perceived taking encourage the government to conceal the no-longer-hidden tax of inflation by imposing price controls.

The Roosevelt administration appreciated these political realities even before the country formally entered the war. As the prewar mobilization gained impetus in 1941 the price level began to rise by about 1 percent per month, which seemed like enormous inflation to people whose big problems during the past decade had been first *de*flation and then *low* prices. The OPACS (after August 28, 1941, the OPA) tried to hold down selected prices but, lacking effective legal sanctions, had little success. Seeking to strengthen its hand, the administration arranged for a price-control bill to be introduced in Congress at the end of July. According to the sardonic John Kenneth Galbraith, Henderson's chief deputy at the OPA, this legislation was "by a wide margin, the most discussed and the most controversial of World War II." The draft law, which had been vigorously debated in Congress the year before, had "involved only the life and liberty of the subject. Price control involved money and property and thus had to be taken more seriously." After more than three months of hearings and discussion the House passed a price-control bill on November 28. The Senate tarried.[23]

After the attack on Pearl Harbor the senators felt more pressure to pass the pending bill, and they finally did so in January 1942. Unhappy with the amendments that various interest groups had succeeded in getting Congress to make, the President pressured members of the conference committee to retrace their steps. His intervention produced some changes in the ultimate legislation, but the statute signed by the President on January 30, 1942, still did not satisfy the administration. Concessions to agricultural interests especially hobbled the government's power over prices. Senator Alben Barkley called the measure a "farm relief" law.[24]

The Emergency Price Control Act of 1942 declared a long list of purposes, including the prevention of "speculative, unwarranted, and abnormal increases in prices and rents," the elimination and prevention of "profiteering, hoarding, manipulation, speculation, and other disruptive practices," and the protection of "persons with relatively fixed and limited incomes." Perhaps the most revealing declared purpose was "to assure that defense appropriations are not dissipated by excessive prices"—that is, to assure that the government would not have to pay free-market prices to obtain the resources needed to carry out its war program.[25]

The act established the Office of Price Administration as an independent agency, with a Price Administrator as its head, and delegated to it wide-ranging authority to control prices and rents by direct regulation or by the licensing of dealers. It also authorized the administrator to enter into such commercial dealings and to make such subsidy payments "as he determines to be necessary to obtain the maximum necessary production." The act made it unlawful "regardless of any contract, agreement, lease, or other obligation heretofore or hereafter entered into" for anyone to buy or sell in violation of the administrator's rules—adios, freedom of contract. Penalties of one year in prison or $5,000 fine were provided. Anticipating disputes, the act established a procedure for protesting OPA regulations and created an Emergency Court of Appeals with exclusive jurisdiction and subject to review only by the Supreme Court.

Several exclusions were made from the administrator's jurisdiction, including employee compensation (a concession to the labor unions) and the prices charged by common carriers, public utilities, insurance companies, communications businesses, and providers of professional services. The most important exceptions, however, pertained to agriculture. The act stipulated that "no powers or functions conferred by law upon the Secretary of Agriculture shall be transferred to the Office of Price Administration or to the Administrator." It further provided that no maximum price could be established for any agricultural commodity below the highest of the following: (1) 110 percent of the parity price; (2) the market price on October 1, 1941; (3) the market price on December 15, 1941; or (4) the average price during the period from July 1, 1919, to June 30, 1929.[26] This complex exclusionary provision, concocted jointly by the American Farm Bureau Federation and other farm lobbies, the Department of Agriculture, and the congressional farm bloc, left ample room for farm prices to rise.

After a few months of ad hoc price fixing, the OPA on April 28, 1942, issued the General Maximum Price Regulation, which made the highest price charged in March 1942 the legally allowable maximum henceforth for most consumer goods. Eighteen more specific orders, plus a rule imposing rent controls on 323 housing areas, fleshed out the administrator's corpus of commands.[27] At the prices fixed by the government, quantities demanded generally exceeded quantities supplied, and nonprice allocations—selling the available products to friends, to whites, to pretty girls, to those first in line—popped up everywhere, threatening to make many commodities unavailable to persons unfavored by the sellers.

To preclude this politically explosive outcome the government resorted to an official rationing program for "necessities" such as gasoline, tires, coffee, canned foods, shoes, meats, sugar, and typewriters. Taking a page from the Selective Service book, the OPA established some eight thousand local rationing boards to administer the program. As Richard Polenberg has noted, the boards, staffed by solid citizens "who had prestige in the community and whose decisions were difficult to challenge . . . did not always resist community pressures." Customary social discriminations marked the decisions made within this empire of petty tyrannies.[28]

At the upper reaches of the OPA a harried corps of economists, accountants, lawyers, and clerks toiled mightily but in vain to keep up with price control, rent control, rationing, and the hundreds of protests and requests for adjustments that deluged them. "The steady barrage of complicated new rationing programs had baffled and irritated almost everyone," observed Chester Bowles, who headed the OPA during the later years of the war, "and the price and rent regulations, many of which were necessarily intricate, had engulfed many businessmen in a maze of red tape."[29]

Replacing the market system with a governmental price-control bureau gave rise to a welter of newly manifested political conflicts between interest groups: "rural and urban forces clashed over food prices; opposing factions struggled for the upper hand in local rationing boards; Congress resented what it considered the arrogant exercise of power by OPA bureaucrats; and state political machines sometimes fought to prevent OPA patronage from going to Congressmen." Vast profits and losses were at stake, and governmental officials had their hands on the levers that controlled how the mechanism would operate. The politicians, observed Fiorello La Guardia (who knew something about politicians), "are drooling at the mouth and smacking their jowls in anticipation of the pickings once they get their slimy claws into the price administration."[30]

By the end of August 1942 the price-control program faced a deepening crisis. Compliance with the rules was far from universal, especially among small retailers. Since the implementation of "General Max" in May, food prices had risen by more than 1 percent per month, the prices of exempt goods about 3.5 percent per month. With the purchasing power of their earnings falling so fast, workers were increasingly unwilling to hold the line on wages and salaries. But if labor costs were to rise without check, employers would be caught in a cost-price squeeze from which they could escape only by violating the price controls. Unless more pieces of the puzzle were hooked together the whole undertaking threatened to disintegrate.[31]

Finally Roosevelt took matters into his own hands. On September 7, in a speech reminiscent of his first inaugural address, he issued an ultimatum to Congress. He wanted legislation to facilitate more effective price controls, including the effective restraint of wages and farm commodity prices.

> I ask the Congress to take this action by the first of October. Inaction on your
> part by that date will leave me with an inescapable responsibility to the people
> of this country to see to it that the war effort is no longer imperiled by threat
> of economic chaos. In the event that Congress should fail to act, and act
> adequately, I shall accept the responsibility, and I will act.

With elections only two months away, Congress was reluctant to comply, but
the President's threat could not be ignored. On October 2, one day after
FDR's deadline, the legislators passed the Economic Stabilization Act of
1942, amending the Emergency Price Control Act.[32]

The President got most of the additional authority over prices and wages
that he had sought. Agricultural prices still enjoyed a privileged position:
their ceilings could not be set below either the parity level or the highest level
that had prevailed during the period from January 1, 1942, to September 15,
1942. Although the old provision for 110 percent of parity had been eliminated, the Secretary of Agriculture was now required to include farm labor
costs in his calculation of parity, which meant that the farmers had actually
surrendered very little of their high ground. The new act placed a floor under
wages at the highest level achieved between January 1, 1942, and September
15, 1942. The President received open-ended power to make adjustments in
prices and wages "to aid in the effective prosecution of the war or to correct
gross inequities"—that is, to do virtually whatever he wished.[33]

The day after he approved the Economic Stabilization Act Roosevelt
issued an executive order establishing the Office of Economic Stabilization.
James Byrnes, a veteran politician and friend of FDR, resigned from his
recently occupied seat on the Supreme Court to become the Economic
Stabilization Director, the paramount coordinator and arbitrator for all the
governmental agencies involved, directly or indirectly, in controlling prices.
Byrnes was directed to develop "a comprehensive national economic policy
relating to control of civilian purchasing power, prices, rents, wages, profits,
rationing, subsidies, and all related matters."

Roosevelt's order also directed the Price Administrator to set prices that
would prevent "unreasonable or exorbitant" profits, which provoked some
congressmen and businessmen to complain that the government, under the
guise of wartime price control, was attempting to destroy capitalism.[34] The
criticism was apt. Though the Roosevelt administration, essentially opportu-
nistic and guided by political expediency, had no grand design to destroy
capitalism, the fact remains that an economy in which resources are allocated
and prices set largely by governmental directives is not capitalism. After
April 8, 1943, when the President issued his "hold-the-line" order, clamping
down on wage increases and bringing virtually all consumer goods within the
reach of the price controls, the price system had limited significance in
determining what, how, and for whom the economy would produce; the

free-market system remained for the duration of the war in suspended anima-
tion. (The existence of thriving black markets requires a qualification of this
statement, but the qualification is minor. After all, even the Soviet Union has
its black markets, but no one supposes that they make the overall system
capitalistic.) Whether one calls the prevailing political economy "war socialism," "war fascism," or something else is largely a matter of linguistic taste,
but capitalism it definitely was not.

The effectiveness of the price controls and the full range of their consequences remain controversial subjects among economists four decades after
the war.[35] Contemporary economists, many of whom worked for the OPA,
generally praised the program. Their descriptions and accounts, which do
not speak well for the theoretical competence of economists in the 1940s,
unwittingly reveal much about the impetus and rationale of the program.
Seymour E. Harris, who left Harvard to serve as a high-ranking official of the
OPA in 1942–1943, wrote a detailed apology, reproducing all the classical
errors and misconceptions about wartime price controls. In wartime, he
reasoned, the drafting of military manpower makes legitimate the great
sacrifices required of civilians. "No one should be allowed to obtain more
than his fair share," he wrote, serenely oblivious to the difficulties of attach-
ing meaning to the concept of fair share. He considered inflation obviously
unfair and hence price controls justified. Moreover, inflation "adds to the cost
of the war" and accordingly ought to be suppressed. A free price system
would not work in wartime because "the response to a rise of the prices is
slow and unpredictable." Even worse, "uncontrolled prices may well result in
the movement of labor and capital to industries which can be dispensed with
in wartime." (*Who* says they can be dispensed with?) Exclusive reliance on
fiscal measures and the price system to achieve the wartime mobilization
desired by the government "would require a tax program of fantastic proportions."[36] Indeed. The analytical errors embedded in these views have already
been sufficiently exposed. The pervasive statism that infused Harris's analysis, and which infused virtually all other contemporary analyses of governmental economic policy during the war, is remarkable. The United States, at
war against countries where statism had run violently amok, had taken on
much of the enemy's coloration.

THE ARMED FORCES AND THE ECONOMY

In marshalling resources for World War II, as in 1917–1918, the armed forces
jealously guarded what Secretary of War Stimson called "the natural and
traditional procurement functions of the Army and the Navy." Their vast
procurement efforts inevitably brought the military authorities into a variety

of conflicts with the guardians of civilian economic interests. The ensuing "war within a war," the scene of "continuous conflict, acrimony, and bureaucratic infighting as civilian and military agencies clashed in the forwarding of their opposing interests," affords many lessons for students of public administration and politics.[37] My focus, however, is on another aspect of this experience. The great military-industrial mobilization of 1940–1945 created a new institution (or set of connected institutions), the military-industrial complex, pregnant with implications for the character of the postwar political economy. The origins and nature of that complex in World War II are at issue here.

The military-industrial complex denotes the institutionalized arrangements whereby the military procurement authorities, certain large corporations, and certain executive and legislative officials of the federal government cooperate in an enormous, ongoing program to develop, produce, and deploy weapons and related products. (Some writers include the labor unions, research organizations, universities, and others involved in the programs.) Operating in peacetime as well as in wartime, it has no significant antecedents before 1940 except the transitory and limited arrangements of 1917–1918. Between the world wars, as during every other previous period of peace, the American armed forces struggled just to survive. (The naval buildup around the turn of the century was a minor exception to the rule.) Congress normally authorized only the barest essentials of equipment and supply and minimal numbers of officers and men. Traditional apprehension about a peacetime standing army denied respect and high social status to the military profession, which remained a thankless calling until bullets began to fly.

After the capitulation of France in June 1940, these conditions changed marvelously. Abandoning its characteristic frugality in military appropriations, Congress approved the spending of billions, then tens of billions, and ultimately hundreds of billions of dollars; all told more than $300 billion was spent for war goods and services during 1941–1945—a classic case of solving a problem by "throwing money at it." The associated procurement program has been described as a "buckshot operation." Though much of the money was wasted, so much was spent that great things were accomplished anyhow.[38] After 1941 the military procurement agencies operated virtually without a budget constraint.

By more or less surrendering its power of the purse, Congress relinquished effective control over the military to the executive branch, where everything hinged on the President's exercise and delegation of his war powers, including his decisions as Commander in Chief. While Roosevelt gave his military commanders a free hand to deal with military procurement, he had to resolve the consequent conflicts over resource use. In January 1942, finally conceding that all-out economic mobilization would require a czar, he created the War Production Board and named Donald M. Nelson, a former Sears executive, to head it. Nelson was instructed to "exercise general direction over the war procurement and production program" and to "determine the policies, plans, procedures, and methods of the several Federal departments, establishments, and agencies in respect to war procurement and production."[39] More a committee man than a leader, Nelson soon came under attack from all sides.

His biggest problem was that the government's semiautonomous, uncoordinated mobilizers were trying to do more than could possibly be done. In a "procurement free-for-all," government departments and agencies during the first half of 1942 placed contracts valued at more than $100 billion, a demand far outdistancing the economy's capacity to respond. Chaos ensued:

> Merchant ships took steel from the Navy, and the landing craft cut into both. The Navy took aluminum from aircraft. Rubber took valves from escort vessels, from petroleum, and from the Navy. The pipe lines took steel from ships, new tools, and the railroads. And at every turn there were foreign demands to be met as well as requirements for new plants.

The system for assigning priorities broke down completely as a result of "priority inflation." Officially sanctioned claims on resources far exceeded the amount of resources available.[40]

Throughout 1942 and into 1943 the contending forces struggled, each with its own preferred solution, to clean up the organizational mess. How they did clean it up—eventually more or less successfully if one may judge by the sheer volume of physical outputs—is a long and complicated tale, full of political sound and bureaucratic fury. Many men and even more rules were broken along the way. The beleaguered Nelson, miraculously, survived until the summer of 1944, when the President finally eased him out. In 1942, in the face of preposterously large military demands, the WPB had ceased to act as an umpire and had become a player in defense of civilian claims on the economy's limited resources. Congressional support grew for what would have amounted to a civilian ministry of munitions, with authority over procurement, production, labor, and price controls. To head off the challenge to his authority Roosevelt created a new umpire on May 27, 1943, establishing the Office of War Mobilization and elevating Byrnes from the OES to take charge of it. A skillful and respected conciliator who enjoyed the President's full confidence and backing, Byrnes kept the Battle of the Potomac within tolerable bounds thereafter.[41]

In the campaigns on the home front the military departments won most of the battles. They were "not only represented at every point within the [WPB] . . . but were in a position to delay or recommend action, both on top policy decisions and in the smallest details, if the action proposed did not suit their views or desires."[42] When Roosevelt had to choose between soothing a military headache and curing a civilian deficiency disease, he usually selected the medicine prescribed by Dr. Win-The-War.

To procure military goods the Army and the Navy dealt mainly with big businesses. At the insistence of the military authorities, with whom FDR again sided, antitrust prosecutions were placed on the shelf for the duration of the war. There were more than eighteen thousand prime contractors, but a hundred firms got two-thirds of the war business; just thirty-three got about half; and General Motors alone got 8 percent. No grand conspiracy produced the pattern. The military authorities wanted the goods, wanted them fast; price did not much matter to them but quality and reliability did. Big firms had the technical and managerial expertise and the large physical facilities to respond readily to the huge military demands. Besides, it was easier to deal with a few contractors than with many. If the services of smaller businesses were needed, they could be acquired under subcontracts by the prime contractors.[43]

Though most of the big contractors—firms such as General Motors, Ford, Bethlehem, Chrysler, Du Pont, and General Electric—had long enjoyed prominence in American industry, some previously obscure companies rode the wave of war to industrial heights. Aircraft producers, in particular, vaulted from famine to feast. Excellent opportunities existed for "entrepreneurs who were willing to cooperate with the government and bid for contracts, or ally themselves with the major producers." Shipbuilders Andrew Jackson Higgins on the Gulf Coast and Henry J. Kaiser on the West Coast amassed fabulous fortunes by catering to the warlords. Kaiser liked to think of himself as a savior of the free-enterprise system but, as John Morton Blum has noted, "government supplied his capital, furnished his market, and guaranteed his solvency on the cost-plus formula—and so spared him the need for cost efficiency, rewarded speed at any price, and came close to guaranteeing his profits."[44] Higgins, Kaiser, and their brethren in the other big corporations supplying the military had discovered a good thing (at least for themselves), but it was not free enterprise. Their own views notwithstanding, it was the negation of the free-market economy.

Whatever one calls it, it was the wave of the future. Businessmen, many of whom had been hostile toward the New Deal since 1935, increasingly adapted themselves after 1940 to working smoothly with governmental officials. "The attitude of suspicion, of slow, meticulous negotiation, which characterized the relation of government with business at the beginning of the war, gave way very largely to an attitude of mutual confidence as the war went on." The multitude of contacts made and friendships cemented between military officers and corporate executives during the war augured well for a continuation of their genial and mutually beneficial dealings. After 1945 the

Cold War, the development of ever-more-sophisticated weapons systems, and the great migration of retired military officers into corporate employment in the defense industries well-nigh insured that the military-industrial complex would not only survive but prosper, as indeed it has to an almost unbelievable degree during the past four decades. During 1946–1985 federal purchases of goods and services for national defense totaled about $3 *trillion*—that is, the incredible sum of $3,000,000,000,000—making the Pentagon itself one of the world's largest nonmarket systems of resource allocation.[45]

WORK OR FIGHT

When the United States entered the war it had plenty of labor in reserve. As young men were drawn into the armed forces, millions of teenagers, women, and older men came forward to replace them on the production lines. For the first two years of the war the government felt little need to regiment the civilian labor force, as the mere availability of well-paid jobs in the munitions and related industries proved sufficient inducement to attract people into the kinds of employment favored by the government.

The price controllers, however, quickly became involved in the labor markets, because unchecked wage increases threatened the OPA's maintenance of ceilings on the prices of civilian goods and services. Not until the passage of the Economic Stabilization Act in October 1942 and the issuance of FDR's hold-the-line order the following April did the government get a firm grip on hourly straight-time wage rates. Real weekly earnings continued to climb, boosted by overtime pay, upgrading of workers, and enhanced fringe benefits. Between the end of 1940 and the end of 1944, average hourly straight-time earnings increased about 40 percent while weekly earnings went up about 80 percent.[46] The Roosevelt administration, not wishing to offend its many friends in the labor unions, did not worry excessively about the slack in its wage controls.

A much greater concern was work stoppages. Even before the war, during the defense buildup of 1941, strikes had plagued the government's mobilization program. On March 19, 1941, Roosevelt appointed a National Defense Mediation Board to help settle labor-management disputes. The board had some early success but ceased to function in November after its two CIO members resigned in disagreement with a decision by the board not to recommend a union shop in a dispute involving the United Mine Workers and several "captive" coal mines owned by steel companies. In three cases in 1941 the President "settled" disputes by seizing the strike-bound facilities.[47]

Immediately after the United States formally entered the war, Roosevelt acted to gain some control over labor-management relations. On December 17, 1941, he convened a dozen employers and a dozen unionists in Washington. They promised that they would not resort to lockouts or strikes during the war and would submit to governmental intervention in unresolved disputes. On January 12, 1942, the President created the National War Labor Board, patterned after the WLB of World War I, to resolve disputes by mediation or arbitration. The board had the President's war powers behind it and could enforce its decisions through plant seizures in accordance with the draft act of 1940. Eventually dozens of seizures were ordered, some involving entire industries (coal mining and railroads).[48]

The NWLB's most ticklish problem concerned arrangements for union security. Employers generally opposed closed or union shops, while unions desired the tightest possible control of the supply of labor. Strikes frequently occurred not so much over wages as over whether the union or the employer would control the selection and retention of employees. As its standard the board adopted a compromise, a modified form of "maintenance of membership." Where an open shop had existed and the union was demanding a union shop, the board provided that during a fifteen-day "escape period" any worker could resign from the union and retain his job. After the escape period, union members had to remain members and pay dues for the life of the contract, and the union remained the exclusive collective bargaining agent at the workplace no matter how many nonunion workers subsequently became employed there. Employers did not like this; they considered it a union shop in disguise. (They were right: unionists needed to intimidate new employees, to get them to join the union, or existing members, to prevent them from leaving the union, for only fifteen days; afterwards, union membership became a condition of employment—that is, enforced by the employer.) The unions flourished under this regime. During the four years of war, union membership increased by more than four million, or about 40 percent.[49]

Work stoppages continued to occur, the no-strike pledge of December 1941 notwithstanding. The worst year, 1943, witnessed a flurry of strikes, including several in essential war industries. The most notable took place in bituminous coal mining, where John L. Lewis, the flamboyant head of the United Mine Workers, regarded the war as Roosevelt's problem, not his. Lewis knew he occupied a strong bargaining position and pressed demands for wage increases far greater than the government's standard would allow. Provoked by three short strikes of miners in May and June, Roosevelt seized the mines and threatened to end the draft deferments of striking miners. The miners drifted back to work, and the government returned control of the mines to the owners. Lewis remained vociferously uncooperative. (FDR, who loathed Lewis, flippantly promised that he would resign from the presidency if Lewis would just commit suicide.) The dispute persisted. In spite of assorted threats, arrests, intimidations, and another governmental seizure of the mines in the fall, the United Mine Workers had the upper hand. The government had to have the coal to achieve its war aims, and only the miners—who were fiercely loyal to their union leader—could produce it. As Secretary of the Interior Harold Ickes reminded Roosevelt, "a jailed miner produces no more coal than a striking miner." Eventually the miners got a large pay increase, but labor-management relations in the coal industry remained unsettled into 1944.[50] (Steadfastly refusing to kill himself, Lewis outlived Roosevelt by a quarter-century.)

Congress, now dominated by Republicans and conservative Democrats, did not find the confrontation of FDR and Lewis amusing. In June 1943 the lawmakers passed, by large majorities in both houses of Congress, the War Labor Disputes (Smith-Connally) Act. Besides giving the War Labor Board explicit statutory authority, the law expanded the President's power to seize production facilities, made it unlawful to interfere with the operation of seized facilities or to aid anyone so interfering, provided for a thirty-day "cooling-off period" before strikes, required that employees have an opportunity to vote on whether to approve a proposed strike, and forbade political contributions by labor organizations to candidates for federal office. Roosevelt, not wanting to antagonize his many friends in the unions—or to lose their campaign contributions—vetoed the bill, urging that he be authorized instead to draft strikers up to age sixty-five into noncombat military service. Within hours Congress overrode the veto.[51]

The War Labor Disputes Act quickly became a loose cannon on the deck of federal intrusion in the labor markets. In 1944, in a tragicomic dispute over Montgomery Ward's refusal to accept a maintenance-of-membership arrangement, the act served as the ostensible authority for the government to seize the mail-order business. But Montgomery Ward was not a war-related business—it had neither government contracts nor any apparent relation to the government's mobilization program—and hence did not properly fall within the jurisdiction defined by the War Labor Disputes Act. The takeover, which the conservative press exploited to demonstrate the high-handedness of "that man," did illustrate that power tends to be abused, in this instance by the use of a war measure to achieve the altogether separate political ends of those in authority.[52]

As labor became scarcer, the government found its war production program increasingly jeopardized by spot shortages and rapid turnover of workers, especially in the defense production centers of the West Coast, the Northeast, and Midwestern beehives like Detroit and Wichita. By the fall of 1943 the supply of labor had become for the first time a binding constraint. Early in 1942 in anticipation of such problems the President had created the War Manpower Commission and named Paul V. McNutt, the head of the

Federal Security Agency, as its chairman. For six months the commission served only as a powerless forum for policy discussion. Then, during the fall of 1942, the President by several executive orders transformed the WMC into a powerful agency by giving it control over the U.S. Employment Service and the Selective Service System and granting it authority to regulate the hiring and recruitment of workers in areas it designated as critical. In a related action, on December 5, almost all voluntary enlistments in the armed forces were terminated; henceforward the draft would provide personnel for the Navy and the Marines as well as the Army. Although private employers retained their prerogatives to hire and fire (subject, of course, to any restrictions imposed by collective labor contracts), the WMC could now exert a powerful influence on the allocation of labor.[53]

The WMC moved on several fronts. In January 1943 McNutt issued a "work-or-fight" order, threatening men in "nonessential" jobs with conscription. The directive met resistance from the largely autonomous local draft boards, who preferred to make family status rather than occupation the touchstone for deferment. Congress also asserted itself to preserve deferments for farm workers and to exclude fathers from the draft. Late in 1943 control of the Selective Service System was taken away from the WMC altogether. Defeated on this front, the commission moved to implement a system to control labor turnover and allocation. For the labor markets of Seattle, Portland, San Francisco, Los Angeles, and San Diego, manpower priorities were established and workers were referred to designated high-priority employments by the Employment Service. Employers were not to hire anyone without a referral by the Employment Service. Selective Service was supposed to cooperate by deferring men employed in essential war work. This West Coast Manpower Plan, which grew out of an officially requested investigation and recommendations by Bernard Baruch and his associate John M. Hancock, was gradually extended to other areas of the country during the winter of 1943–1944. It was less compulsory than some governmental officials, particularly the military authorities, wanted it to be—an employer received no penalty for disregarding it—and in practice it had no apparent effect on labor turnover. At best it made officials at the Selective Service System, the WPB, and the military procurement agencies more aware of the labor-supply aspects of their decisions about other things.[54]

From the beginning of the war, some had wanted to treat civilian labor as the government treated military labor, by draft. Grenville Clark, a consultant to Stimson and an advocate of preparedness since the days before World War I, organized and headed a Citizens' Committee for a National War Service Act. In 1942 he prepared several versions of a national service bill. McNutt, an aspiring manpower czar, campaigned actively for a national service system of his own design in the fall of 1942. The military departments and of course the American Legion supported the general idea. Stimson, who resented "the incompletely warlike attitude of the nation," thought that national service would "extend the principles of democracy and justice more evenly throughout our population. . . . Certainly the nation has no less right to require a man to make weapons than it has to require another man to fight with those weapons." The President, sensing the absence of a consensus, remained "consistently ambivalent" and refused to offer public support for a draft of civilian labor.[55]

From early 1943 to early 1945 Congress considered several national service bills. On January 11, 1944, Roosevelt surprised most of his advisers by coming out strongly in favor of such a law, "which, for the duration of the war, will prevent strikes, and, with certain appropriate exceptions, will make available for war production or for any other essential services every able-bodied adult in this Nation." The President insisted that "there can be no discrimination between the men and women who are assigned by the Government to its defense at the battle front and the men and women assigned to produce the vital materials essential to successful military operations." But FDR, regarding national service as merely a component of a bundle of desired measures that included greatly increased taxation of high incomes, never put his full political weight behind the proposal. In testimony before congressional committees the main support came from representatives of the Army, the Navy, and the Maritime Commission. Now fearful of losing turf if a universal draft were implemented, spokesmen for the WMC turned lukewarm. The opponents made unlikely confederates: the AFL, the CIO, the National Association of Manufacturers, and the Chamber of Commerce. Stimson, disgusted by the "national refusal to fight an all-out war," observed that "Both labour and management preferred the anarchy of a voluntary system to the imagined perils of Government direction."[56]

In truth the opponents had more self-serving concerns. Unionists, who ranted about "slave labor" and "involuntary servitude," did *not* oppose military conscription—surely a more reprehensible form of involuntary servitude than assignment to a safe, well-paid civilian job. Union leaders knew that national service would put an end to genuine collective bargaining and render them personally superfluous. Philip Murray warned the CIO executive board: destroy collective bargaining "and see how effective you will be with your people back home. You will find out how quick they will tell you to go to hell." Businessmen, of course, wanted to retain control over hiring and firing. They also perceived that drafting civilian labor would lead directly to demands for "conscription of profits"—that is, confiscatory taxation—and governmental takeovers of their production facilities.[57] Stimson and those in his camp had little regard for individual liberty in wartime, but they had at least the virtue of moral (immoral?) consistency. The leaders of the labor unions and the spokesmen for the business interests preferred the hypocrisy of defending their own privileges and property rights while supporting the conscription of men for service in the armed forces. Swayed by the strength of the opposing coalition, Congress never approved a national service law.

THE SUPREME COURT ALSO GOES TO WAR

Toward the end of the war, Edward Corwin summarized the "restrictions that today exist on the property right in consequence of our participation in World War II":

> The government has the right to condemn property for its own wartime uses. It can place mandatory orders, and a manufacturer must make what he is told to make, regardless of the fact that he could earn more profits doing something else. The government can commandeer or requisition any private plant it deems essential to our war program. It can in effect fix prices to be paid by itself for products, and the renegotiation authority—by which several billions were returned to the Treasury first and last—is one of the means. The government absorbs excess profits through taxation. The government controls the flow of raw materials to the manufacturer, thus again limiting what he can earn on his capital. By priorities over transportation it controls the flow of raw materials further. It sets hours of work, fixes wage scales, compels the payment of overtime wages and establishes working conditions. It can withhold manpower from a plant by labeling its product unessential. It dominates the capital market by furnishing on its own terms the vast bulk of war industry financing. Finally, through OPA the government elbows aside the law of supply and demand with mandates of its own, setting maximum prices and rents.[58]

Corwin could have made a much longer list. Of course, an enumeration of the extraordinary economic powers exercised by the government is simultaneously a catalog of private economic rights derogated or destroyed.

Where was the Supreme Court while the government was riding roughshod over the long-established constitutional rights of individuals? The answer is that the justices, almost without exception, had formed themselves into a cheering section for the expansive legislative and executive actions of those bellicose times. None of the government's exceptional exercises of power, not even one, was disapproved by the Supreme Court. (There was, as we shall see, some judicial quibbling over procedural as opposed to substantive issues; but even there the majority of the Court never found anything to disallow.)[59] Perhaps the judicial capitulation should not surprise us. After all, during the war the Court consisted almost entirely of men Roosevelt had appointed. Except Owen J. Roberts, all the justices had the highest regard for the New Deal; most had played leading roles in it. They looked with favor on legislative delegation and executive activism. FDR had been and remained their leader, and none of them hankered to bite the hand that led them.

Formally the Court took its stand on an expansive unqualified interpretation of the constitutional war powers. As Clinton Rossiter observed, "the Court, too, likes to win wars." Corwin, expressing himself with slightly more generosity, noted that "in total war the Court necessarily loses some part of its normal freedom of decision and becomes assimilated, like the rest of society, to the mechanism of the national defense." At the outset, in a case decided on February 16, 1942, the Court revealed the position it would take for the duration of the war. "Congress can draft men for battle service," wrote Justice Hugo Black. "Its power to draft business organizations to support the fighting men who risk their lives can be no less."[60]

For the most part the suppression of individual rights was not even challenged—or, if challenges arose, the Supreme Court considered them unworthy of review. The government's most drastic action, the military draft, generated many cases in the lower courts, but the Supreme Court washed its hands of the question, denying without opinion a petition for certiorari to review a lower court's decision. In many of its wartime decisions, as in the one just quoted, the Court simply took for granted the constitutionality of military conscription.[61] Somehow the justices never found an occasion to rule on the constitutionality of the government's powers to allocate materials and facilities, seize plants in labor disputes, or ration consumer goods.

Price control was the only important wartime power to receive extensive consideration by the Supreme Court. But no one questioned the constitutionality of price control per se. All the cases dealt solely with the constitutionality of the procedures employed by the government to implement the price controls. While procedure was by no means a trivial issue, and some important questions were considered in passing, it did not go to the heart of the matter. The leading case was *Yakus* v. *United States*, decided March 27, 1944.[62] The majority opinion upheld the government on every contested point: the Emergency Price Control Act did not make an unwarranted delegation of legislative power, nor did the procedure it provided for appeals violate due process in any way.

Justice Roberts, the "swing man" of the Court in the 1930s, now swung against the government in a strongly worded dissenting opinion. In his view the act did make an unconstitutional delegation of legislative power to the Price Administrator, because it established no genuine standards to guide the administrator's wide-ranging decisions. "Reflection will demonstrate," said Roberts, "that in fact the Act sets no limits upon the discretion or judgment of the Administrator." Nor did the procedure for appeals afford a protestant due process. He "must carry an unsupportable load, . . . [and] in truth, the court review is a solemn farce in which the Emergency Court of Appeals, and this court, on certiorari, must go through a series of motions which look like judicial review but in fact are nothing but a catalogue of reasons why, under the scheme of the Act, the courts are unable to say that the Administrator has exceeded the discretion vested in him." Roberts found it unsurprising that the Emergency Court of Appeals had dismissed twenty-eight of the thirty-one complaints it had considered against the administrator. He worried that the lawmaking power had in reality been "surrendered to an autocrat whose 'judgment' will constitute the law."[63]

Justices Wiley B. Rutledge and Frank Murphy also dissented, objecting that the act denied due process because of its asymmetrical provisions for criminal prosecution and defense. The government could prosecute violators in ordinary federal and state courts, but those accused of violations were forbidden to challenge the validity of the regulations in the same courts. Anyone who protested the regulations in the only permissible forum, the Emergency Court of Appeals, had to lodge the complaint within sixty days in order to receive legal consideration. Rutledge and Murphy regarded these provisions as inadequate. "Even war," they asserted, "does not suspend the protections which are inherently part and parcel of our criminal process."[64]

On the same day that it handed down the *Yakus* decision the Court ruled on a related case pertaining to the OPA's control of residential rents, *Bowles* v. *Willingham.* Again the majority could find no constitutional defect in the authorizing legislation: "no grant of unbridled administrative discretion as appellee argues," no lack of adequate standards, no excessive delegation, no unconstitutional taking of property. Speaking for the majority, Justice William O. Douglas rested his argument on the fundamental theorem of the garrison economy: "A nation which can demand the lives of its men and women in the waging of that war is under no constitutional necessity of providing a system of price control on the domestic front which will assure each landlord a 'fair return' on his property." Further, "where Congress has provided for judicial review after the regulations or orders have been made effective it has done all that due process under the war emergency requires." Douglas denied that the government must implement its rent controls so that they impinge uniformly on the affected individuals. He readily conceded that "[a] member of the class which is regulated may suffer economic losses not shared by others." But "that has never been a barrier to the exercise of the police power."[65] The Court's interpretation of the Constitution, as usual during national emergency, simply elevated the constitutional stipulation of governmental powers above the constitutional guarantee of individual rights.

Again Roberts dissented. "Candid appraisal of the rent control provisions of the Act in question discloses that Congress has delegated the law making power in toto to an administrative officer." The statutory standards established to guide the administrator's decisions left him "such room for disregard of specific injustices and particular circumstances that no living person could demonstrate error in his conclusion. . . . Such a 'standard' is pretense. It is a device to allow the Administrator to do anything he sees fit without accountability to anyone." The Emergency Price Control Act, Roberts concluded, "creates personal government by a petty tyrant instead of government by law."[66] Roberts was surely wrong in one respect: the Price Administrator, possessing plenary control over the prices of most civilian goods and services in the American economy, was no "petty" tyrant.

World War II witnessed the perfection of a governmental device first used on a wide scale during World War I, the indirect sanction. This is the imposition of a penalty by a governmental agent other than the one legislatively authorized to penalize the specific breach of law or regulation committed. For example, someone who violated an OPA regulation might be penalized not by the legislatively mandated means provided in the Emergency Price Control Act (court injunction or criminal proceedings) but by a cutoff of his raw materials by the allocators at the WPB. Throughout the war the NWLB, the WMC, the OPA, and the WPB, among others, made extensive use of indirect sanctions, which Baruch had once described as "utterly devoid of legal authority" and "nothing short of blackmail." The War Production Board relied so heavily on indirect sanctions to gain compliance with its orders that, when a congressional committee considered suppressing their use, the WPB protested that such a restriction "would destroy our control completely. We might as well close up the Compliance Division."[67]

In 1944 the Supreme Court finally considered a challenge to this "administrative blackjacking." But the decision in *Steuart* v. *Bowles*, a case involving the use of indirect sanctions by the OPA to punish a fuel-oil dealer who had violated rationing regulations, found no constitutional defect in the government's actions. "In times of war," Justice Douglas announced impatiently, "the national interest cannot wait on individual claims to preference." But what had "individual claims to preference" to do with the question at issue, namely, whether the OPA could lawfully punish the violator by suspending his access to fuel-oil supplies instead of by the legal proceedings stipulated in the Emergency Price Control Act? Straining to construct an apology for the government's suspension orders, Douglas fashioned a chain of argument with the following links: (1) the war powers justify economic controls to promote "efficient" economic conduct on the home front; (2) an unscrupulous dealer in fuel oil is "an inefficient and wasteful conduit" in the economy's distributional system; therefore, (3) to promote greater "efficiency" the government properly may divert fuel oil away from a dealer who handles a "scarce and vital commodity . . . in an inefficient, inequitable and wasteful way."[68] The argument is so nonsensical as economics and so spurious as law—so substandard even by the abysmally low standards of the Supreme Court—that, unless Douglas is assumed to have been a complete fool, one must regard it as disingenuous. The most plausible explanation of the decision is simply that the Court lacked the motivation or courage to impede the government's use of an important and widely employed administrative club for beating the economy into the desired shape. Only Roberts dissented.

Perfected in wartime, indirect sanctions were destined to become deeply embedded in governmental administration during the postwar era. (Jimmy Carter's wage-price guidelines program during 1978–1980, for example, relied entirely on indirect sanctions.) As Rossiter noted soon after the end of the war, the Court had "acquiesced in an exercise of presidential war power that would seem to have infinite and explosive possibilities."[69] Vastly enlarged yet almost invisible—and essentially lawless—governmental control over private economic activities was one of the possibilities.

Soon after the explosion of procurement orders early in 1942 some congressmen became concerned that in its haste the government might be bidding too high; hence the Renegotiation Act of 1942 and its several amendments during the war. These statutes looked suspiciously like devices to permit the government to back out of valid contracts or even to set aside the terms of valid contracts between private parties, such as prime contractors and subcontractors. After recounting how he had bargained with the head of Alcoa to fix the price of the aluminum to be made in government-constructed plants, Jesse Jones added revealingly: "As a matter of fact, because of excess profits taxes and renegotiations *later authorized* by Congress it did not make too much difference what price Mr. Davis and I agreed upon."[70]

Naturally court challenges arose. Again, however, the plaintiffs challenged not the statutes themselves but merely their implementation, especially certain alleged abuses of discretion by the administrators of the laws. Not until 1948 did the Supreme Court get around to ruling on these questions. The challengers lost on every point. The Court could find no unconstitutional delegation by omission of clear standards, no uncompensated taking of private property for public use, no deprivation of due process of law. It reached these conclusions even though the original Renegotiation Act had failed to define "excessive profits" at all and a subsequent amendment defined them tautologically as "any amount of a contract or subcontract price which is found as a result of renegotiation to represent excessive profits." Miraculously "a statutory definition was not necessary in order to give effect to the congressional intent." Again the Court clothed its empty-headed abdication of the judicial function in the familiar uniform: "In total war it is necessary that a civilian make sacrifices of his property and profits with at least the same fortitude as that with which a drafted soldier makes his traditional sacrifices of comfort, security and life itself."[71]

The most notorious capitulation of the Supreme Court to the war powers had to do not with the government's economic controls but with its herding of some 110,000 innocent men, women, and children of Japanese descent—two-thirds of them U.S. citizens—into concentration camps. Corwin called it "the most drastic invasion of the rights of citizens of the United States by their own government . . . in the history of our nation." The Court ruled, however, that in the circumstances the judgment of the military authorities must prevail and "it is not for any court to sit in review of the wisdom of their action or substitute its judgment for theirs." If the military authorities found racial discrimination desirable, then such discrimination "in the crisis of war . . . is not wholly beyond the limits of the Constitution."[72] Thus did the United States government, at war against Hitler and his hoard of racist fanatics, demonstrate that it differed from the enemy only in degree.

Historians typically consider the Japanese-American internment, which they almost universally regard as the most egregious episode in the twentieth-century history of American civil liberties, separately from the military draft and the government's imposition of economic controls during the war. Many applaud the draft and the economic controls while deploring the internment. In fact, all were forged from the same metal: governmental suppression of private property rights, including the right of innocent persons to control the use of their own bodies. Hence no one should be surprised that the Supreme Court allowed all these invasions of individual rights to stand. During total war, wrote Corwin, "The restrictive clauses of the Constitution are not . . . automatically suspended, but the scope of the rights to which they extend is capable of being reduced in the face of the urgencies of war, sometimes even to the vanishing point. . . . [T]he Court will not intrude its veto while war is flagrant." As Rossiter recognized, "the people with their overt or silent resistance, not the Court with its power of judicial review, will set the only practical limits to arrogance and abuse."[73] The Supreme Court is part of the government, and the government had committed itself above everything else to the prosecution of war.

LEGACIES, INSTITUTIONAL AND IDEOLOGICAL

In 1945, as in 1918, most people longed to lay down the burdens of war. And again the government quickly surrendered most of its wartime powers. On August 18, 1945, President Truman ordered his subordinates "to move as rapidly as possible without endangering the stability of the economy toward the removal of price, wage, production, and other controls and toward the restoration of collective bargaining and the free market." By the end of the year much of the administrative machinery of the wartime command economy had been dismantled: the WMC's manpower controls, all but one (involving sugar) of the OPA's rationing programs and many of its price controls, most of the WPB's priorities and almost all of its materials allocations, almost all the travel restrictions of the Office of Defense Transportation, many of the controls affecting exports and ocean shipping. By the end of 1945 several agencies had gone out of business, including the WMC, the OES, the Foreign Economic Administration, the WPB, the Smaller War Plants Corporation, the NWLB, and the War Food Administration.[74]

But not all the emergency activities of the government disappeared; some functions migrated from an emergency agency to a regular governmental department or to a newly created agency. When the WPB shut down, the newly created Civilian Production Administration absorbed some of its powers to allocate resources. The Labor Department took over the Employment Service and the Reemployment and Retraining Administration. The State Department received jurisdiction where previously the Foreign Economic Administration had operated. The Commerce Department assumed the functions previously exercised by the Smaller War Plants Corporation. The OWM, now designated the Office of War Mobilization and Reconversion, took the responsibility for overseeing the remaining price controls from the OES.[75] Thus, part of the immediate dismantling of the command economy was spurious, being mere consolidation and relocation of powers, some of which became permanently lodged in the government. Some price controls continued until late 1946; some "wartime" subsidies were paid until the summer of 1947; rent controls persisted even longer.[76]

The war had taught the American people many lessons, some true, some false. Of the latter sort, a leading example was the Keynesian illusion, the belief that the federal government's management of the economy, primarily by its fiscal policies, can prevent business declines and stabilize the economy as it grows. Herbert Stein has noted that "[t]he great weight assigned to full employment as a postwar goal certainly resulted from the achievement of full employment during the war against the background of ten years of depression." But the notion that wartime "full employment" had resulted from the huge federal deficits was false. Quite simply, unemployment fell mainly because of the buildup of the armed forces. Between 1940 and 1945 the number of persons classified as unemployed fell by about seven million, while the number of persons in the armed forces rose by more than eleven million (see Table 9.1). Any government that can conscript prime workers by the millions can eliminate unemployment; that is the true lesson of 1940–1945.[77] The real economic miracle occurred in 1946, when nine million military personnel returned to civilian life but the much-feared postwar depression did

Table 9.1
Persons Unemployed and in the Armed Forces, 1940–1948 (in millions)

Year	Unemployed Persons	Active Personnel in Armed Forces	Total
1940	8.1	0.5	8.6
1941	5.6	1.8	7.4
1942	2.7	3.9	6.6
1943	1.1	9.0	10.1
1944	0.7	11.5	12.2
1945	1.0	12.1	13.1
1946	2.3	3.0	5.3
1947	2.3	1.6	3.9
1948	2.3	1.4	3.7

Source: U.S. Bureau of the Census, *Historical Statistics*, pp. 135, 1141.

not occur. The immediate postwar period was prosperous not because of shrewd fiscal management by the federal government but because consumers, starved by years of depression and wartime restrictions on the production of civilian durable goods and bloated with bank accounts and bonds accumulated during the war, produced an expansive market and encouraged a private investment boom.

Meanwhile, however, the war-born faith in the federal government's powers of macroeconomic management had led, on February 20, 1946, to passage of the Employment Act:

> The Congress hereby declares that it is the continuing policy and responsibility of the Federal Government to use all practicable means consistent with its needs and obligations and other essential considerations of national policy, with the assistance and cooperation of industry, agriculture, labor, and State and local governments, to coordinate and utilize all its plans, functions, and resources for the purpose of creating and maintaining, in a manner calculated to foster and promote free competitive enterprise and the general welfare, conditions under which there will be afforded useful employment opportunities, including self-employment, for those able, willing, and seeking to work, and to promote maximum employment, production, and purchasing power.[78]

Although the declaration is vague and burdened by ideological vestiges— "cooperation of industry" and "free competitive enterprise"—the import of the law was well understood at the time of its enactment and has continued to be understood in the same sense over the past four decades. It meant, in short, that the federal government was expected, and committed itself, to "do something" to prevent depressions, recessions, and other macroeconomic malfunctions. Never again could an administration excuse inaction on the

grounds that its intervention in the market is "not the proper business" of
federal authorities. As Calvin Hoover observed, "recognition of the legitimacy of this purpose [as expressed in the Employment Act] was of the
greatest importance in the development of the powers of the government over
the economy."[79]

Federal labor policies also changed in accordance with practices pioneered
during the war. In 1946, with the removal of wage controls and the disappearance of the WMC and the NWLB, labor-management relations deteriorated drastically. Strikes and assorted work stoppages plagued the economy
while managers and workers strove to convert facilities to civilian production.
Some 116 million worker-days were lost, an all-time high.[80] The conservative Congress could not stomach the disruptions. On June 23, 1947, over
Truman's veto, the Taft-Hartley Act, amending the National Labor Relations Act of 1935, was enacted. Taft-Hartley, patterned in part after the War
Labor Disputes Act of 1943, made unlawful several "unfair labor practices"
of unions. It banned the closed shop, required notice sixty days before a
strike, legalized suits against unions for breach of contract and other illegal
actions, and outlawed jurisdictional strikes, secondary boycotts, strikes by
federal employees, and union contributions to candidates for federal office.
The act empowered the Attorney General to obtain an eighty-day injunction
against strikes imperiling national health or safety.[81] Never again would labor
unions receive the immense governmental support they had enjoyed during
the years of their greatest expansion, 1933–1946. But the legal privileges and
political strength of the unions and the federal role in labor-management
affairs hardly reverted to their pre-New Deal status. In some ways the Taft-
Hartley Act embedded the government even more deeply in the regulation of
labor markets.

With the end of the war and the rapid demobilization of the armed forces
it appeared for a while that military conscription would soon end; but the
wartime precedent had entered too deeply into the experience of the American people, and the draft persisted. One "temporary, emergency" extension
followed another. Early in 1947 President Truman expressed an "earnest
desire of placing our Army and Navy on an entirely volunteer basis at the
earliest possible moment," but a year later, as Cold War tensions increased, he
requested that Congress renew the draft and establish "universal training" to
boot. Congress did not respond to the call for a national service law but did
pass the Selective Service Act of 1948, another peacetime draft. "[I]n a free
society," the act declared, "the obligations and privileges of serving in the
armed forces . . . should be shared generally, in accordance with a system of
selection which is fair and just, and which is consistent with the maintenance
of an effective national economy."

The law was not what it claimed to be. Rather, it was an inefficient tax laid on the labor services and lives of certain unfortunate young men, by no means randomly selected, at the insistence of politicians and older citizens unwilling to pay the full cost of maintaining the military establishment they desired. Congress, as Richard Gillam has observed, "remained entirely unwilling to raise military salaries to the very lowest level of attractiveness. . . . [V]oluntarism, it was feared, would simply be too expensive." In fact, the true economic cost—the market value of the most highly valued alternatives forgone—would have been lower under a voluntary system. But different people would have borne the cost. The decisive political forces preferred to shift the cost by coercion. The emergency rationale, hammered so deeply into the American psyche by four years of total war, held sway. As a congressman observed during debate on the draft act of 1948, "What we propose to do today is, under ordinary conditions, contrary to our traditions . . . yet. . . . We are not living in an ordinary time. . . . We are living in a world of fear, of chaos, of uncertainty, and to a certain extent of hopelessness."[82] In an atmosphere of crisis, American traditions of individual liberty could not survive the political onslaught.

While a volunteer armed force was bad politics, generous benefits for veterans were *de rigueur* for congressmen. Goaded by the ever-reliable American Legion and the Veterans of Foreign Wars, the lawmakers had brought forth, without a single dissenting vote and in plenty of time for the millions of voters then in the armed forces to take notice before the elections of 1944, a statute popularly known as the GI Bill of Rights. It provided counseling, readjustment allowances, job preferences, educational benefits, guarantees of mortgages and business loans, and the promise of ample medical care. The GI Bill had many consequences. As Blum notes, "All those subsistence allowances and tuitions and books for which the VA paid spawned a new, young, eager middle class." Not without cost, of course. Governmental expenditures for World War II veterans' benefits jumped to $1.5 billion in 1945 and reached $6.7 billion two years later. In 1970 they were still $3.9 billion and promised to rise much higher as the vets aged and increased their demand for medical services.[83] One may doubt whether the veterans' benefits adequately compensated the draftees of 1940–1945, especially those who never made it back alive from Salerno and Normandy and Guadalcanal and a thousand other appalling places. One thing we do know: justice deferred is justice denied. Compensation long after the fact is a poor substitute for the real thing.

That the veterans' benefits and the immense variety of other outlays of the postwar federal government could be financed owed much to the revenue machine constructed during World War II. The principal components of the machine were (1) low personal exemptions, so that many income recipients would owe taxes, (2) high rates, so that they would owe a lot, (3) a steeply progressive rate structure, so that the government would reap an ever higher return on either real economic growth or inflation, and (4) payroll withholding of taxes due, so that taxpayers would be less likely to escape paying and less aware of the total amount the government extracted from them annually (see Table 9.2). It is unlikely that without the emergency revenue "needs" of World War II the wonderful revenue machine would have been available to finance the growth of the welfare state after 1945. Before the war fewer than fifteen million individuals filed an income tax return; by 1945 about fifty million did so. And not only did most income earners have to pay; the bottom bracket had risen from 4.4 percent in 1940 to 23 percent in 1945, so they paid substantial sums. In one great wartime push the government shoved virtually the entire labor force into the hoppers of its revenue machine. In 1940 the federal government got 30 percent of its revenue from individual and corporate income taxes; by 1945 it got 69 percent. The shape of the future was now fixed. Twenty-five years later the income-tax share remained roughly the same, 64 percent.[84]

Among the novel uses of the postwar revenues was one that grew directly out of a World War II program. Lend-lease, a disingenuously named program whereby the government transferred some $50 billion of goods and services to allied nations before, during, and immediately after the war, clearly prefigured the Marshall Plan, whereby some $12.5 billion was transferred to European governments during 1948–1951. Then a permanent policy of foreign aid took hold. During 1945–1970 the U.S. government's grants and credits to foreigners accumulated to the stupendous sum of $133.8 billion.[85] Clearly lend-lease had broken a huge hole in this ice.

As soon as the Americans ceased firing at the Germans and the Japanese, they turned their silent but still loaded guns toward their former allies, the Soviets. This time, unlike all the previous times, it would not do to demobilize completely after the shooting stopped. Even in the late 1940s the government maintained a military force of some one and a half million heavily armed men.[86] To supply the Cold Warriors with an ever-more-sophisticated arsenal, many of the defense contractors of World War II—especially the aircraft companies—continued to make the development and manufacture of weapons their main business. The approximately $3 trillion spent on defense goods and services since 1945 has assured them an ample "market." (One hesitates to call these bureaucratic transactions, employing other people's money, a market. They are at best a monopsony; often a bilateral monopoly; at worst, and not infrequently, a simple conspiracy against the taxpayers. None of these forms of dealing holds much promise of bringing about a socially optimal allocation of resources, and together their potential for waste, fraud, and abuse overshadows that of all other governmental programs combined.) As Table 9.3 shows, even decades after the Big One some of

Table 9.2
Federal Income Tax Data, 1940–1946, 1950, 1960, 1970

Year	Personal Exemptions, Married Person with One Dependent	Tax Rates				Millions of Tax Collections by Payroll Withholding	Millions of Individual Income Tax Returns
		First Bracket		Top Bracket			
		Rate (%)	Income	Rate (%)	Income		
1940	$2,400	4.4	$4,000	81.1	$5,000,000	0	14.7
1941	1,900	10.0	2,000	81.0	5,000,000	0	25.9
1942	1,550	19.0	2,000	88.0	200,000	0	36.6
1943	1,550	19.0	2,000	88.0	200,000	0.7	43.7
1944	1,500	23.0	2,000	94.0	200,000	7.8	47.1
1945	1,500	23.0	2,000	94.0	200,000	10.3	49.9
1946	1,500	19.0	2,000	86.5	200,000	9.9	52.8
1950	1,800	17.4	2,000	84.4	200,000	9.9	53.1
1960	1,800	20.0	2,000	91.0	200,000	31.7	61.0
1970	1,875	14.0	500	71.8	100,000	77.4	74.3

Source: U.S. Bureau of the Census, *Historical Statistics*, pp. 1091, 1095, 1110.

Table 9.3
Leading Military Contractors, 1960–1967

Firms	Sever-Year Total of Prime Contract Awards ($ millions)	Percent of Total Sales
1. Lockheed Aircraft	10,619	88
2. General Dynamics	8,824	67
3. McDonnell Douglas	7,681	75
4. Boeing Co.	7,183	54
5. General Electric	7,066	19
6. North American-Rockwell	6,265	57
7. United Aircraft	5,311	57
8. AT&T	4,167	9
9. Martin-Marietta	3,682	62
10. Sperry-Rand	2,923	35
11. General Motors	2,818	2
12. Grumman Aircraft	2,492	67
13. General Tire	2,347	37
14. Raytheon	2,324	55
15. AVCO	2,295	75
16. Hughes	2,200	NA
17. Westinghouse Electric	2,177	13
18. Ford (Philco)	2,064	3
19. RCA	2,019	16
20. Bendix	1,915	42
21. Textron	1,798	36
22. Ling-Temco-Vought	1,744	70
23. IT&T	1,650	19
24. IBM	1,583	7
25. Raymond International	1,568	NA

Source: Clayton, ed., *Economic Impact of the Cold War*, p. 44 (Table 12).

America's leading corporations relied on the Pentagon for the greater part of their sales.

Many of these firms continued to enjoy the use of government-financed plants and equipment, just as they had enjoyed such use during the war. Of government-financed industrial facilities valued at almost $18 billion (original cost) and built during 1940–1945, about 80 percent were used by private firms after the war. Here was a hard, tangible legacy of World War II of special importance in such industries as aluminum, steel, synthetic rubber, ship building, and aircraft fabrication. Sometimes the firms occupied government-owned plants as lessees, or merely as occupants paying no rent; sometimes they acquired titles from the government. Thomas McCraw has observed that "the institutional aspects of surplus-property disposal suggest that the 'military-industrial complex' . . . is related in some degree to the purchase by lessees of so many war plants." Louis Cain and George Neumann have shown that the same handful of corporations that operated the government-built plants during 1940–1945 acquired the titles when the government disposed of (some of) its holdings after the war.[87]

Some significant constitutional legacies of World War II have been indicated above, but their great importance warrants reemphasis. As Corwin observed, after the war, for the first time in American history, the country did not return to a "peacetime Constitution." The Supreme Court's decisions during the war had embedded even deeper in the American system of government the revolutionary changes first validated during the late 1930s. Corwin noted that the Court's wartime pronouncements brought into greater prominence all of the following:

> (1) the attribution to Congress of a legislative power of indefinite scope; (2) the attribution to the President of the power and duty to stimulate constantly the positive exercise of this indefinite power for enlarged social objectives; (3) the right of Congress to delegate its powers *ad libitum* to the President for the achievement of such enlarged social objectives . . . ; (4) the attribution to the President of a broad prerogative in the meeting of "emergencies" defined by himself and in the creation of executive agencies to assist him; (5) a progressively expanding replacement of the judicial process by the administrative process in the enforcement of the law—sometimes even of constitutional law.[88]

Thus the war left the United States something far more ominous than big government, namely, Big Government in the sense of a powerful, highly arbitrary, activist government virtually unchecked by the constitutional limitations of checks and balances that had traditionally restrained the interventions if not the ambitions of governmental officials.

More fundamental than the constitutional legacy—indeed the ultimate source of that revolutionary change—was the ideological shift occasioned or accelerated by the war. As Alan Milward put it, "economic shibboleths had been much altered by the war experience." There were "important shifts in social aspirations and political opinions" and "social equality was now more widely accepted as a desirable end. The less conspicuous consumption of the wealthy, the curbs on individuals' property rights, the general antipathy to profiteering, the existence of rationing, the expectation that everyone should work, all tended to influence thought in this direction."[89] Especially important changes occurred in the attitudes of leading businessmen, many of whom had acted as unpaid governmental administrators ("dollar-a-year men") during the war. The experience, according to Calvin Hoover, "conditioned them to accept a degree of governmental intervention and control after the war which they had deeply resented prior to it." In his memoirs, published in 1951, Jesse Jones made the observation, perhaps without appreciating its full significance, that "there are among the alumni of the RFC probably more than 100 executives of big business, in industry, finance, and the railroads. Among them are men who are now directing some of the most important institutions in the United States."[90] When a pro-business Republican administration held office during 1953–1960 no real effort was made to alter the mixed economy that had assumed its enduring shape by the end of World War II. Having experienced for so many years the full-fledged command economy of the war period, most Americans now seemed to fear a return to a free-market regime more than they feared the denial of individual rights, actual and potential, under the existing politico-economic arrangements. Liberties long unexercised lost their hold on the hearts of the people.

CONCLUSIONS

Two centuries ago James Madison warned that "one legislative interference is but the first link of a long chain of repetitions, every subsequent interference being naturally produced by the effects of the preceding."[91] The development of the government's management of the economy during World War II confirmed beyond a doubt the validity of Madison's dictum. Even the official historians of the mobilization admitted that "[o]ver the war period, governmental regulations and restrictions invaded one area of economic life after another and with constantly increasing stringency."

> Freedom to operate manufacturing facilities and to use raw materials and fabricated items was severely restricted under the orders of the War Production Board; freedom to buy was sharply curtailed under the priority regulations of the War Production Board, the ration restrictions of the Office of Price Administration, and the set-aside orders of the War Food Administration. Much of the seller's freedom to ask and the buyer's freedom to offer a price vanished under the sweeping price ceilings and regulations issued by OPA. The freedom to trade with foreign countries was hemmed in by regulations on all sides. Civilian use of the transportation system was subject to the priority of military travel and transport needs. Choice of occupation and the right to change jobs suffered curtailment by action of the Selective Service System and the War Manpower Commission. The National War Labor Board intervened in the free bargaining between employers and employees whenever disputes arose or wage increases were a part of the bargain.[92]

And there were many, many more controls and constraints besides these.

Conscription of military manpower was the most important link of the Madisonian chain. The draft began early, more than a year before the declaration of war. By this means the government was able to build up an enormous armed force at a pecuniary cost far below its true free-market cost. Huge military and naval forces required correspondingly large amounts of equipment, supplies, subsistence, and transportation. When the government's procurement officers, their pockets bulging with newly created purchasing power, set in motion a bidding war that could have driven prices up to spectacular levels—thereby revealing the full cost of the government's program and provoking political reaction and resistance—the government moved to conceal the costs by price controls (and by reneging on its contracts through "renegotiation"). But price controls on goods and services could not be effectively enforced while wages remained free to rise. Hence controls of labor compensation followed in due course. The market economy, a vast and delicately interdependent system of transactions, invariably surprised and confounded the administrators of partial controls. In response the government progressively expanded and tightened the command system until, during the final two years of the war, a thoroughgoing garrison economy had been brought into operation. Fundamentally the authorities, not the market, determined what, how, and for whom the economy would produce under this regime.

If the military draft provided the crucial link in the creation of the legislative and administrative chain that the government wrapped around individual rights during the war, it served an even more fundamental purpose in giving legitimacy to the suppression of economic liberties. Virtually everyone who considered the matter, from influential economists, bureaucrats, and congressmen right up to Supreme Court justices and the President himself, used and accepted the validity of the moral argument: if A is all right, then X is certainly all right; where A was military conscription and X was any governmental suppression of individual rights whatsoever, especially any denial of private property rights. The argument is compelling. Undoubtedly it persuaded people at the time, although the evidence pertains mainly to governmental officials and one may question the extent to which the population at large accepted the argument. Most astonishing is the almost universal acceptance of the argument's premise that military conscription, a transparent example of involuntary servitude, is morally untarnished. Once the draft had been sanctioned, however, a moral and constitutional objection to any other measure of governmental control seemed manifestly inconsistent. (Of course, many people somehow managed to contain both their consciences and their concern for logical consistency, resisting certain governmental intrusions [notably, universal national service] even while upholding the desirability of the military draft.)

As victory came into view almost everyone demanded an end to the galling restraints of the garrison economy, and a rapid if incomplete dismantling of the administrative apparatus of control ensued. But a host of legacies remained: all the government-financed plants and equipment and the military-industrial complex to continue operating them; important postwar legislation inspired by wartime practices, including the Employment Act, the

Taft-Hartley Act, and the Selective Service Act of 1948; the GI Bill and the new middle class it fostered; a voracious and effective federal income-tax system; a massive foreign-aid program. More importantly the war left the constitutional structure of the country deeply altered in the direction of judicial abdication and executive autonomy; the nation no longer possessed a "peacetime Constitution" to which it could return. Most significantly the war moved the prevailing ideology markedly toward acceptance of an enlarged governmental presence in the economy. At last even the majority of businessmen had come to accept, and often to demand, Big Government.

.

CHAPTER TEN

Crisis and Leviathan: From World War II to the 1980s

> This is the one song everyone
> would like to learn: the song
> that is irresistible:
> the song that forces men
> to leap overboard in squadrons
> even though they see the beached skulls.
>
> MARGARET ATWOOD

By the end of World War II, as Jonathan Hughes has written, "the balance of economic power had been altered for good, away from the primacy of private decision making and into the arena of government and politics."[1] Three decades of crisis after crisis had left the free-market system, once the predominant national institution for the pricing and allocation of resources, constrained and corrupted almost beyond recognition. Strangely, economics textbooks continued to be written and many people continued to talk as if the American economy remained essentially a free-market system. Left-wing radicals continued to castigate American "capitalism," something that certainly had not existed since the 1920s, perhaps not since before World War I. One could for various reasons dislike the socioeconomic regime of the post–World War II era, but what one was disliking was by the standard criteria surely not capitalism.

To recognize that capitalism no longer existed and that some kind of "mixed economy" had come fully into sway does not conclude the story. The great transformation that had been completed by the late 1940s entailed not only that governmental officials henceforth would either make or effectively constrain many of the economic decisions previously made by autonomous private citizens. It entailed also, and more portentously, that the dynamics of the political economy from that time forward would take a different shape. Under the new rules the game would be played differently, and its sequence of outcomes would differ as well. Most significantly the new regime possessed no enduringly effective checks on the continuing growth of government. Once the fundamental barriers of a restrictive ideology and the old Constitution had been battered down, persistent political forces pushing toward Bigger Government could exert themselves virtually without limit.

Added to the now unchecked "normal" growth of government were the effects of recurring postwar crises and, even more fundamentally, the consequences of that permanent emergency known as the Cold War. First in Korea, then in Vietnam, massive military adventures gave the usual fillip to the powers of government. Concurrently with the Vietnam War a violent unraveling of the civil-rights movement, marked by large-scale riots, arson, and other disturbances in cities across the nation, prompted new governmental programs to deal with the so-called urban crisis. Partisans of other causes—environmentalists, "consumerists," egalitarian redistributionists, and those dedicated to eliminating a variety of workaday risks to life and health— organized to exploit the potential created by the more significant political forces opposing the war or promoting the interests of blacks and other ethnic minority groups.

Throughout the post–World War II era, in war and peace, in storms of international conflict and lulls of détente, the military-industrial complex consumed a variable but always substantial portion of the nation's resources. The planning, production, and deployment of armaments occupied an exceptionally large proportion of the technical and scientific work force, at the heavy cost of forgone opportunities for innovation in civilian production. Comprising an enormous coalition of military officers, politicians, contractors, labor unions, universities, and research organizations, all financed on a grand scale by citizens whose natural fears were kept chronically aroused by Pentagon propaganda, this huge nonmarket system directed hundreds upon hundreds of billions of dollars into the pockets of its privileged participants.[2] Never did so many prosper so much by feeding on fear.

In an atmosphere of unending crisis the emergency game became one of the most common gambits in the political economy. No grasping interest-group proposal was complete without the claim that it ought to be carried out because "an emergency exists." Many people eventually grew jaded, having heard the bogus claim so often, but its continued assertion suggests that the emergency game still promises a positive payoff. Sometimes, most notably with the wage-price controls and the energy controls of the 1970s, the game was played with huge stakes. Even under the Tory administration of Ronald Reagan, emergency claims continued to be pressed, and honored. Special farm loans, international travel restrictions, and export controls exemplify the recent emergency actions taken by the "conservative" American government.[3]

THE MIXED ECONOMY:
MARCH INTO SOCIALISM OR FASCISM?

Joseph Schumpeter, one of the most celebrated social scientists of the twentieth century, delivered his final public address on December 30, 1949, just nine days before he died. He entitled the talk, which dealt with the probable future of the American economy, "The March into Socialism." Forswearing any pretense of absolute knowledge of the future, Schumpeter claimed only a vision based on past tendencies and the logic by which one might reasonably expect the tendencies to work themselves out. While his analysis of the politico-economic dynamics of Western countries pointed to socialism as the "likely heir apparent," he recognized several other possibilities, including one in which the political economy would become lodged in a "halfway house" short of full-fledged socialism.[4]

The Schumpeterian model of politico-economic dynamics, which indicates a probable transition from capitalism to socialism, rests on four central propositions: (1) Large corporate firms, bureaucratically managed and routinely innovative, displace the entrepreneurs and owner-managers of classic capitalism, thereby shrinking the size, attenuating the economic function, and diminishing the social and political standing of the business class. (2) As capitalism matures, society grows ever more "rational," which causes a loss of respect for and allegiance to such extra-rational institutions as private property rights and freedom of contract. (3) Capitalism nurtures a growing intellectual class that, ironically, is inherently hostile toward the system that makes possible its existence. (4) As the opposition of intellectuals, labor unionists, and their allies mounts, the bourgeoisie loses faith in its traditional values and ideals; its defense of the free-market system grows steadily weaker as it accommodates itself to a political environment that gives ever greater priority to social security, equality, and governmental regulation and planning. While Schumpeter recognized at the end of the 1940s a residual capitalist vitality in the American economic order, he emphasized that "we have traveled far indeed from the principles of laissez-faire capitalism."[5]

Although he conceded that crises such as war or depression would accelerate the secular tendencies, he denied that "any mere 'events,' even events of the importance of 'total wars,' or the political situations created thereby, or any attitudes or feelings entertained by individuals or groups on the subject of these situations, dominate the long-run contours of social history—these are a matter of much deeper forces." Mere events could only "remove obstacles from the path of the more fundamental tendencies. . . . Evolution toward socialism would be slower" in the absence of social crises "but also steadier."[6] In the long run, Schumpeter concluded, chronic inflation plays a crucial role in the process by which the capitalist order breaks down: the economy will pass through a succession of wage-price controls into complete socialism.[7]

Schumpeter's ideas have been evaluated and reevaluated in great detail. While almost everyone acknowledges his penetrating insights into politico-economic dynamics, critics generally have concluded that Schumpeter's vision harbors unsolved problems and unwarranted inferences and suffers from considerable vagueness in critical components of the analysis. For present purposes several questions are pertinent, all relating to ideas Schumpeter seems to have derived from Marxism.[8]

First, is the growth of government that has occurred in the United States since Schumpeter issued his final forecast really a march into socialism? Certainly many conservatives have characterized it as "creeping socialism." Social scientists generally presume that extensions of the government's control over the economy constitute in effect moves toward socialism. One may seriously question, however, whether this characterization is the most descriptively accurate one available in the terminology of social science. As William Fellner pointed out, Schumpeter's analysis "leaves the question open why the decomposition of Western-type systems could not lead to a non-socialist variety of 'fascism.'" Schumpeter himself only hinted at the possibility in passing remarks, as when he observed that the future is unlikely to bring "the advent of the civilization of which orthodox socialists dream. It is much more likely to present fascist features."[9]

If by socialism one understands, as Schumpeter in his celebrated book generally did, a high degree of outright public ownership and management by governmental planners of industry, agriculture, and public utilities, then the United States since 1945 clearly has not marched far into socialism.[10] As the American mixed economy has developed, the tendency has been to destroy the substance more than the form of private ownership. The most common methods of governmental control have been not explicit takeovers but rather heavy taxation and subsidization (often in hidden forms) and, especially, extensive regulation of ostensibly private activities. Although critics decry the pervasive governmental intrusion in the economy as "socialistic," it clearly has not produced an economic order resembling any standard form of socialism.

Has it instead produced "fascism"? The term unfortunately has been abused by Americans in at least two distinct ways. On the one hand, "fascist" serves merely as a loose term of opprobrium by which radical leftists characterize anything they dislike about the present political economy. On the other hand, and more commonly, it simply brings to mind the regimes of Mussolini and Hitler, which are generally considered to have nothing in common with the postwar political economy of the United States. Indeed most Americans find the mere suggestion of such similarities offensive and repellent—did Americans not spill their blood to destroy the fascist regimes?—and refuse to consider seriously the possibility that the United States may be fascist in some respects.

The term *fascism*, however, has a definite meaning; and one may employ it as an analytical concept independent of distasteful historical exemplars. As Charlotte Twight has shown, the essence of fascism is nationalistic collectivism, the affirmation that the "national interest" should take precedence over the rights of individuals. So deeply has the presumption of individual subservience to the state entered into the thinking of modern Americans that few people have noticed—and no doubt many would be offended by the suggestion—that fascism has colored countless declarations by public officials during the past fifty years. Unfortunately, as Friedrich Hayek noted during World War II, "many who think themselves infinitely superior to the aberrations of naziism, and sincerely hate all its manifestations, work at the same time for ideals whose realization would lead straight to the abhorred tyranny."[11]

More than anything else, the peacetime military draft signaled the triumph of fascist sentiment in the post–World War II era. "There existed," wrote Richard Gillam, "a state of quiet consensus that America had entered a period of perpetual national emergency which demanded and justified creation of a garrison state based on peacetime military conscription." For more than twenty years, periodic extensions of the draft law took place with little or no debate. No one in Congress stood up in favor of voluntarism or an individual right of ownership over one's own body and one's own life. "Gone was any sense that conscription itself violated ideals which were once themselves seen as vital" to the American way of life.[12] When Richard Nixon ended the draft in the early 1970s he acted not so much to restore a traditional individual liberty as for reasons of political expediency, hoping to diminish the troublesome opposition of students and others to the administration's conduct of the war in Vietnam.[13] Even in the mid-1980s the fascist idea that the government has a superior claim to the lives of innocent citizens whenever political leaders deem military conscription necessary retains its grip on the thinking of elites and masses alike. Young men are required by law to register for a draft—and sent to federal prison for conspicuous failure to comply—even though no conscription is presently authorized. Only the absence of an emergency prompting a large increase in the number of people under arms permits the volunteer military system to survive.

Alone among collectivist systems, fascism preserves private property, but "capitalism is turned inside out in this unlikely union." Fascism recognizes people's desire to possess private property and admires the strength of the profit motive, but it "uses these features of capitalism [only] *insofar as they do not conflict with the national interest as formulated by fascism's political authori-*

ties." Every part of economic life is ideologically, constitutionally, and legally vulnerable to governmental control. Hence "fascism tolerates the *form* of private ownership at the government's pleasure, but it eliminates any meaningful *right* of private property." It is "a bogus capitalism indeed, a sham deferral to individual economic rights readily nullified whenever political leaders deem it expedient."[14]

Twight argues that this abstract description of fascist economic policy matches in detail not only the actions of the regimes of Hitler and Mussolini but the practice of the government of the United States since World War II. Of course the fanatical hero worship, the general suppression of civil and political rights, and the mass murders that marked the fascism of Germany and Italy have not characterized the American case. But the similarities of economic policy are striking. All fascist systems have imposed the same sweeping controls over such "vital" industries as agriculture, energy, transportation, communications, and armaments whenever the political authorities deemed the controls appropriate; all have heavily regulated the labor markets and union-management relations; all have captured the financial and money-supply mechanisms and used them to promote "national" objectives; all have resorted, at least episodically, to wage-price controls and physical allocations; all have extensively controlled international travel and international exchanges of goods, financial capital, and currencies; all have employed a huge administrative corps to monitor private activities and to formulate and enforce governmental directives. In all cases a coalition of big business and the government has emerged, as "fascism's abrogation of the market in favor of political control over the economy inherently favors big business at the expense of the small entrepreneur." Characteristically there has been an "extensive interchange of positions between ranking civil servants and high corporate executives"—the revolving door familiar at the highest levels of American government, especially but by no means exclusively between the Pentagon and the major defense contractors.[15]

In recognition of the apparent openness of the American political system and the "care and attention . . . devoted to the formal trappings of due process," Twight calls the political economy of the United States "participatory fascism." There is an "ostensible inclusion of all potential dissident parties within the government's decision-making process." This "provides the appearance of fairness"; it placates the losers in the policy struggles, who settle for having had their views considered. Thus "the bright facade of fair procedure blinds the public to the system's fundamental abrogation of individual economic freedom."[16] Evidently Schumpeter missed the mark: America's political economy has marched not into socialism as he understood it but rather into an arrangement more accurately described as participatory fascism.

Schumpeter's vision of the future political economy went awry in part because he misperceived the character of the individuals and groups effectively contending over it and thereby determining its form. Adopting a modified Marxian two-class scheme, he viewed the major contending parties as on one side the bourgeoisie or "business class," the only potential defenders of capitalism, and on the other side the labor unionists and intellectuals and governmental bureaucrats, who seek to tear down capitalism and replace it with socialism or at least with what he sometimes called "laborism." For one who constantly espoused taking the long view, Schumpeter appears in retrospect to have been too much impressed by the rise of organized labor and by the disaffection of big business from the Roosevelt administration after 1935. He failed to appreciate how much the abandonment of traditional economic liberties over the long run had resulted not from the acquiescence or defeat of businessmen but from their enthusiastic sponsorship. As Douglass North has pointed out, "conflicts amongst propertied groups . . . set off the growth of government regulation." Businessmen have done more than their full share to foster the active regulatory state from its very inception.[17]

Consider William Simon's recent description of the relation of business and government as he witnessed it during his tenure as Secretary of the Treasury in the 1970s:

> I watched with incredulity as businessmen ran to the government in every crisis, whining for handouts or protection from the very competition that has made this system so productive. I saw Texas ranchers, hit by drought, demanding government-guaranteed loans; giant milk cooperatives lobbying for higher price supports; major airlines fighting deregulation to preserve their monopoly status; giant companies like Lockheed seeking federal assistance to rescue them from sheer inefficiency; bankers, like David Rockefeller, demanding government bailouts to protect them from their ill-conceived investments; network executives, like William Paley of CBS, fighting to preserve regulatory restrictions and to block the emergence of competitive cable and pay TV. And always, such gentlemen proclaimed their devotion to free enterprise and their opposition to the arbitrary intervention into our economic life by the state. Except, of course, for their own case, which was always unique and which was justified by their immense concern for the public interest.[18]

One wonders whether anyone—with the possible exception of a few right-wing ideologues—any longer supports the free-market system as an inviolable desideratum; whether anyone is willing to bear its costs in order to preserve its benefits. Talk is cheap, and accordingly business people often talk as if they favor capitalism. But the blatant hypocrisy of their rhetoric suggests that it is either a political device, deliberately employed as part of a "public relations" strategy, or a mindless reflex inherited from the past and readily abandoned when it seems incompatible with short-run gain.

Leland Yeager has argued that business people "as such" have no strong interest in limiting governmental activism. Business interests frequently profit from constraints on the market economy. Firms can usually cope with regulation, even when it is not immediately beneficial. Indeed "[t]he prospects for businessmen of ordinary ability relative to the prospects of the most dynamic entrepreneurs may even be better in a highly regulated economy than under substantial laissez faire." Leftist ideology notwithstanding, "Businessmen as such, rather than simply as human beings, are not the main beneficiaries of a free economy."[19] They know this and act accordingly.

Besides misconstruing the relation of the business class to the preservation of capitalism, Schumpeter persistently underestimated how much governmental authorities would act not as an executive committee of the bourgeoisie, or of any other group, but as interested parties in their own right, especially during crises. By accepting the classic Marxian formulation of socioeconomic change propelled by "the" class struggle as his point of departure, he failed to appreciate the emergence of a separate "class," neither bourgeoise nor proletarian, possessing sufficient autonomy to pursue interests exclusively its own, whether material or ideological.

Finally the Marxian foundations of Schumpeter's thought served him poorly in his assessment of crises. As I have argued above in some detail, what he called "mere events" played a supremely important part in the historical breakdown of the free-market regime. In his insistence on the preeminence of so-called more fundamental tendencies, he disregarded his own observation that "the very concept of historical sequence implies the occurrence of irreversible changes in the economic structure which must be expected to affect the law of any given economic quantity"—*a fortiori* the evolution of any politico-economic system.[20] Such irreversibilities, giving "mere events" magnified and enduring significance, marked American historical development after 1950, too.

CRISIS AND LEVIATHAN:
THE RECENT EPISODES

Not long after the Truman administration committed the armed forces of the United States to fight in Korea the government greatly expanded its powers over the American economy. A leader in moving public opinion to favor the strong controls was—*mirabile dictu*—Bernard Baruch, the gray eminence still going strong at age eighty-one in his performances before news reporters and congressional committees. On September 8, 1950, the Baruch-inspired Defense Production Act became law, empowering the President to mobilize resources for the war. Under authority granted him by this act, Harry Truman issued Executive Order 10161, delegating his economic war powers to various administrators and creating such agencies as the National Production Authority, which set up rules for a priority system, and the Economic Stabilization Agency, which arranged for wage-price controls.[21]

On December 16, 1950, in response to "the increasing menace of the forces of communist aggression," Truman proclaimed a national emergency. Urging that individuals lay aside their own interests in favor of the "national interest" as he and his political pals had defined it, he summoned

> all citizens to make a united effort for the security and well-being of our beloved country and to place its needs foremost in thought and action . . . our farmers, our workers in industry, and our businessmen to make a mighty production effort . . . and to subordinate all lesser interests to the common good . . . every person and every community to make . . . whatever sacrifices are necessary for the welfare of the Nation . . . all state and local leaders and officials to cooperate fully with the military and civilian defense agencies of the United States in the national defense program.[22]

The President established the Office of Defense Mobilization to coordinate the war program and the Defense Production Agency to oversee the production controls. On January 26, 1951, the ESA issued regulations to control wages and prices. In July 1951 a Controlled Materials Plan patterned after that used in World War II was initiated; it became fully effective three months later. Additional controls were imposed on shipping, credit, and the production of consumer durable goods.[23]

Despite the many controls imposed, the government's mobilization of the economy during the Korean War never reached the extremes experienced during the Big One. It was simply a much smaller war, only about one-third (5.8 million military personnel) or one-sixth (1.6 million draftees) or one-eighth (54,000 total deaths) as big. Adjusted for changes in the price index for federal purchases, the $54 billion original cost of the Korean War is about one-eighth as much as the corresponding outlay during World War II.[24] Although the controls were imposed quicker than before —"evidence that the American public was growing accustomed to the type of action that must be taken in economic mobilization"—the limited scale of the war meant that the government did not need to divert resources from civilian to military uses so forcefully as before.[25] To a greater extent, ordinary fiscal and market devices could serve the government's purposes satisfactorily. Because much smaller costs had to be borne, the government had less incentive to adopt cost-concealing methods of capturing resources. As an expert on the economics of war described it, the mobilization for the Korean War was "part way between the methods of free enterprise and the strong governmental control and regulation of World War II."[26]

The limitations of the government's program became clear in the steel seizure episode. Placed in an uncomfortable political position by a deadlocked union-management dispute that threatened a nationwide strike, Truman directed the Secretary of Commerce to seize and operate the steel industry in April 1952. The owners obtained an injunction to prevent the seizure. The Supreme Court upheld the injunction by a 6 to 3 vote in the *Youngstown* case decided June 2, 1952. Although the Court thereby denied Truman—by that time a very unpopular President—a power previously exercised freely by Wilson and FDR, the decision did not impose a restriction on the government's power to take private property. It restrained only a presidential taking without specific statutory authorization. As Justice Hugo Black said in announcing the majority's opinion, "This is a job for the Nation's lawmakers, not for its military authorities." Justice Robert Jackson, in a concurring opinion, emphasized "the ease, expedition and safety with which Congress can grant and has granted large emergency powers." Neither the majority nor the minority gave any weight to private property rights. While the majority objected only to Truman's presidential high-handedness, the minority grumbled that "such a [presidential] power of seizure has been accepted throughout our history."[27] The Constitution was read in this case, as in many others, not as a bulwark against governmental oppression of private citizens but rather as the institutional setting within which high officials in the different branches of government conduct their internecine struggles for supremacy.

After cessation of the fighting in Korea the United States enjoyed a decade of respite from the growth of governmental authority over economic affairs. The wartime wage-price and production controls lapsed, although the authority to reinstitute the production controls remained. No major extensions of the government's economic controls were enacted. Big Government did not disappear; virtually all the controls that had been created before 1950 remained in force. But businessmen, according to Herbert Stein, "had learned to live with and accept most of the regulations." Disturbed only by new and unfamiliar regulations, "they regard the regulations they are used to as being freedom."[28] Governmental spending, especially for Social Security benefits, crept upward. All in all, however, the administrations of Eisenhower and Kennedy were remarkably placid in comparison with those that preceded and followed them.

Under LBJ and Nixon the federal government's intrusion in the economy took another leap. As Table 10.1 shows, many major regulatory laws were enacted during 1964–1976. The bulk of the legislation belongs to five broad areas: (1) protection of consumers from dangerous, defective, or misrepresented products; (2) protection of employees and consumers from discrimination based on race, sex, age, or handicap; (3) protection of the natural environment from various kinds of pollution; (4) protection of employees from workplace risks of injury or disease; (5) wage-price controls and

Table 10.1
Major Federal Regulatory Legislation, 1964–1976

1964	Civil Rights Act
1966	Traffic Safety Act
	Coal Mine Safety Amendments
1967	Flammable Fabrics Act
	Age Discrimination in Employment Act
1968	Consumer Credit Protection (Truth-in-Lending) Act
1969	National Environmental Policy Act
1970	Economic Stabilization Act
	Clean Air Act Amendments
	Occupational Safety and Health Act
1972	Consumer Product Safety Act
	Water Pollution Control Act
	Equal Employment Opportunity Act
1973	Emergency Petroleum Allocation Act
1974	Federal Energy Administration Act
	Employee Retirement Income Security Act
1975	Energy Policy and Conservation Act
1976	Energy Conservation and Production Act
	Toxic Substances Control Act

physical allocations, either across the board or specifically in energy markets. Taken together, these regulatory measures raised the governmental presence in the economy to a considerably higher level—one is tempted to compare them to the New Deal. Though the comparison would show the New Deal to be the more significant episode, the surge of new regulatory programs between 1964 and 1976 was unquestionably of great consequence.

What accounts for the interventionist outburst? Perhaps the most revealing answer requires that one consider each new regulatory program separately. A large literature taking such a piecemeal approach has come into being. From it one learns, not surprisingly, that the explanation of why regulatory program *x* was created generally differs somewhat from the explanation of why regulatory program *y* was created. No doubt the Consumer Product Safety Act and the Equal Employment Opportunity Act do have quite different backgrounds. One ought not to dismiss such distinctions or to depreciate the efforts of the scholars who have illuminated them. Still, from this literature one cannot learn, except by additional investigation and inference, why so many distinct regulatory programs appeared simultaneously during the late sixties and early seventies.

Some scholars have attempted to find a common denominator in the diverse regulatory measures. Stein, for example, argues that an important influence was exerted by an intellectual development that he dubs, after its leading popularizer, Galbraithianism: a loose collection of socioeconomic analysis and evaluation hostile toward the free-market system and favorably inclined toward more sweeping governmental controls. "There was," says Stein, "no demand for a new and different economic system" in the Galbraithian view. Rather "[t]he ideological case for the old system, the free market, capitalist system, was punctured by the demonstration of exceptions to its general rules and claims, and this opened the way for specific policy interventions and measures of income redistribution without any visible limits." The arguments and attitudes of Galbraithianism gained strength from a spreading conviction that the American economy would continue to grow forever at a high rate, thereby insuring that new and costly governmental programs could easily be financed by drawing from the so-called growth dividend.[29] Henry Aaron's description of the climate of opinion in the sixties essentially agrees with Stein's. Aaron traces the roots of Galbraithianism back to previous crises: "The faith in government action, long embraced by reformers and spread to the mass of the population by depression and war, achieved political expression in the 1960s. This faith was applied to social and economic problems, the perceptions of which were determined by simplistic and naive popular attitudes and by crude analyses of social scientists."[30] As the observations of the conservative Stein and the liberal Aaron illustrate, scholars of diverse ideological persuasions agree that prevailing attitudes among both elites and masses in the mid-1960s favored increased governmental intervention in the market economy. Ideological postures engendered by past crises had come once again into political prominence.

Some scholars, especially those former radicals and liberals now known as neoconservatives, associate the ideological trends of the sixties and seventies with the growing ascendancy of an alleged New Class. According to Irving Kristol, who has popularized the notion, this class comprises scientists, lawyers and judges, city planners, social workers, professors, criminologists, public health doctors, reporters, editors, and commentators in the news media, and others. Many of these people work for the government or in the not-for-profit sector; they are "idealistic" and denigrate profit-seeking activities. Ostensibly reformist, they harbor, in Kristol's view, a "hidden agenda: to propel the nation from that modified version of capitalism we call 'the welfare state' toward an economic system so stringently regulated in detail as to fulfill many of the traditional anti-capitalist aspirations of the Left."[31] One may question whether the individuals implicated by Kristol constitute a class in the sense that sociological theorists employ the concept of class, but no one can deny that a multitude of left-leaning intellectuals and quasi intellectuals gave prominent leadership and support to the regulatory outburst of 1964–1976.

Questions remain about the specific timing of the outburst and about how the New Class and others who shared its values and aspirations succeeded in transforming their ideals into concrete regulatory measures. To answer the questions, one must consider some more prosaic political developments.

Presidential and congressional changes in the mid-sixties loom large in this story. The accession of Lyndon B. Johnson from the vice presidency and his subsequent landslide election placed in the highest office a man driven by an ambition to leave an indelible mark on history, to carry forward the political programs of his hero and mentor, Franklin D. Roosevelt. Formerly a powerful senator, LBJ knew well how to work with Congress, and he had compliant members of Congress to work with. Not only did the Democrats have enormous majorities in both houses of Congress—an advantage they would continue to enjoy until the 1980s—but the election of 1964 brought into office on Johnson's coattails an extraordinarily liberal group of legislators. No longer did the traditionalist "conservative" Democrats, mainly Southerners, dominate the lawmaking branch of government. According to Aaron, "No administration since Franklin Roosevelt's first had operated subject to fewer political constraints than President Johnson's."[32] Under such favorable political conditions the proponents of collectivist programs had enormous room to maneuver.

But what determined the specific forms the regulatory programs took? To which constituencies did the activist Presidents (Johnson *and* Nixon) and the left-leaning Congress cater most during the decade after 1963?

In considering these questions one must recognize the unprecedented proliferation of animals in the American political jungle during the 1960s. None of the old factions disappeared—big business, labor unions, middle-class professional and trade groups, farmers, and many other longstanding interest groups remained well entrenched—but a plethora of new groups emerged. The civil-rights movement first spawned a number of politically organized and active groups seeking to promote better economic and social conditions for blacks, then spun off "by way of osmosis and highly contagious analogical thinking" various groups to promote the political aims of other "oppressed minorities": women, Indians, Chicanos, white ethnic groups, students, homosexuals, the handicapped, the elderly, and many others, all previously not directly represented as such to an important extent in American politics. The newly potent groups demanded that the federal government solve diverse racial, urban, employment, and consumer problems, real and imagined. Similarly the antiwar movement spilled over into "a spreading interest in an assortment of 'general publics' and 'public goods' supposedly in need of the protection that organized political action brings." Agitation in support of environmentalist, consumerist, and zero-risk regulations reached unprecedented levels. By the early seventies "the universe of political organizations was handsomely populated by groups widely discounted before as unorganizable."[33]

That all these groups organized and began to flex their political muscles precisely when they did was no accident: once again social crisis had substantially enlarged the domain of political feasibility. The turmoil of the sixties, with its acrimonious divisions on a scale not witnessed in the United States since the Civil War era, created two critical preconditions for a burst of regulatory legislation. First, it got the attention of many people who in normal times would have remained uninterested in politics. The promise—or the threat—of massive changes in race relations awakened millions of politically dormant citizens. Troubling questions about the aims, methods, risks, and costs of American military actions in Vietnam gained the attention of even more people; virtually no one could ignore or stand aloof from a conflict that claimed the lives of fifty-eight thousand U.S. servicemen, 86 percent of them white men, in a distant land of doubtful strategic importance. Second, the socially divisive crises of race relations and the war, widely felt as overriding moral issues, provoked massive participation in protests, demonstrations, and more conventional political activities: that is, ideologically motivated actions swept aside the free-rider problem.[34]

Once masses of people had been politically motivated, activated, and organized, their solidarity greatly heightened in many instances by hostile encounters with ideological opponents or police, they readily extended their interests and energies in directions that seemed to them parallel to their original aims and actions. Many—especially among the students—came to believe that a ruling politico-corporate establishment, which they mistakenly identified with capitalism or the free-market system, was responsible for the unjust racial relations and the savage, pointless war. "War-related dissent had been the catalyst for unusually acerbic political divisions and had created a large cadre of radicalized political activists disposed to continue their struggle against other aspects of the system once the war was over."[35]

Galbraithianism and other varieties of critical socioeconomic analysis helped to justify the displacement of antiwar and pro-civil-rights enthusiasms onto a diversity of antimarket causes. Sensing an enlarged opportunity, members of the New Class strove to realize their cherished regulatory aspirations, drawing strength from the errantly anticapitalist climate of opinion and, not wholly by accident, doing well while doing good. After Johnson was driven from office, the Nixon administration, only mildly reactionary, dared not resist the leftists too much, and the regulatory mania born in the mid-sixties carried into the seventies before a conservative reaction—and a severe, inflationary recession—finally began to restrain it.[36]

While under modern ideological conditions almost any kind of crisis promotes expanded governmental activity, some do so more than others. Lawrence Brown has advanced the provocative idea of a "good" crisis. In such an event "simple causes seem to be evident for all to see, . . . simplistic solutions lie near at hand and command consensus, and . . . the upper and middle classes of the population can identify with efforts to solve someone else's problems." In Brown's view the urban crisis of the sixties exemplifies a good crisis: its causes were taken to be poverty and racism; a "war" on poverty and racial discrimination would eliminate them once and for all; both the legislators and the poverty fighters liked this kind of war.[37] (By such criteria World War II was an even "better" crisis.) Whether one views the twin crises of the mid-sixties as especially "good" or not, they were clearly fundamental in the creation of sociopolitical conditions favorable to the regulatory outburst that began then.

Like FDR, Richard Nixon had a crisis mentality. In 1962, unhappily out of public office, he wrote an autobiographical account entitled *Six Crises.* But whereas Roosevelt's crises were real, Nixon's were more the product of his personal sense of siege. As President, Nixon twice declared a state of national emergency, once on March 23, 1970, in response to a strike by postal workers, and again on August 15, 1971, when balance-of-payments problems led him to impose a 10 percent surcharge on dutiable imports.[38] Had the declarations done nothing more than facilitate the President's handling of the problem at hand, they would not have been particularly noteworthy. At that time, however, Nixon's declarations—along with FDR's of 1933 and Truman's of 1950, which remained in effect—gave force to 470 provisions of federal law delegating extraordinary powers to the President.

As a congressional committee report described them, the emergency powers conferred "enough authority to rule the country without reference to normal constitutional processes."

> Under the powers delegated by these statutes, the President may: seize property; organize and control the means of production; seize commodities; assign military forces abroad; institute martial law; seize and control all transportation and communication; regulate the operation of private enterprise; restrict travel; and, in a plethora of particular ways, control the lives of all American citizens.[39]

Not until the passage of the National Emergencies Act of 1976 did Congress provide for the termination of existing declared national emergencies and for the systematic oversight and termination of future declared national emergencies. Still, the law stopped short of withdrawing past statutory delegations of emergency power to the President. In particular the emergency presidential authority to control international financial and property transactions, first authorized by the Trading with the Enemy Act of 1917, was kept in force. In 1977 Congress further clarified that authority, by no means eliminating it, in the International Emergency Economic Powers Act.[40]

Nixon, like most incumbent politicians, gladly took advantage of crises to augment his power, but he did not just sit waiting for an emergency to come along. For him the risk that he might not be reelected was crisis enough. According to his economic adviser Stein, he "tended to worry exceedingly about his reelection prospects and so to feel impelled to extreme measures to assure his reelection." Years before the election of 1972 Nixon and his aides began to scheme how they could manipulate the economy to maximize the likelihood of his reelection. The economic policies they implemented epitomize those that generate so-called political business cycles. (Whether such cycles have actually occurred is a separate, more complicated, and controversial question.)[41]

Nothing illustrates Nixon's political opportunism better than his imposition of mandatory wage-price controls in August 1971. The President, who had served as a low-level functionary in the OPA during World War II, had often expressed an aversion to price controls. Such controls, he declared during the campaign of 1968, "can never be administered equitably and are not compatible with a free economy." Yet, as James Reichley has observed, he was "not prepared to take extreme political risks for the sake of economic dogmas." Having convinced himself that his defeat in 1960 had resulted from the Eisenhower administration's failure to generate favorable macroeconomic conditions on the eve of the election, Nixon was determined not to suffer again from the same kind of mistake. His latent fears were sharply aroused in 1970–1971, when the new administration's restrictive fiscal and monetary policies had a more immediate effect in raising unemployment than in reducing inflation.

Impatient that the government's macroeconomic policies seemed to be working so slowly, many politically important people began to call for direct price controls: labor union leaders, big businessmen, members of Congress, potential presidential candidates in the next election, high-ranking economists in the Treasury Department, even Arthur Burns, now heading the Fed—all prodded the President to impose an "incomes policy" because, as Burns put it, "The rules of economics are not working in quite the way they used to." Congress, as if daring Nixon to do what he insisted he would never do, passed the Economic Stabilization Act, authorizing the President to control all prices, wages, and rents. Nixon signed the bill—which was attached as a rider to an act extending the Defense Production Act of 1950— with apparent reluctance on August 17, 1970.

Late in 1970 the appointment of the flamboyant John Connally as Secretary of the Treasury and his subsequent designation as the administration's chief economic spokesman tipped the balance toward controls. Connally had few economic scruples; he specialized in dramatic political gestures, favoring, in Nixon's football metaphor, the "big play." He supported the imposition of controls because he thought it would appeal to the public as a sweeping, take-charge action by the President.[42]

Nixon liked that aspect of the controls. As he later wrote in his memoirs, imposition of the controls "was politically necessary and immediately popular in the short run." Indeed it was. Not only did the stock markets soar and the opinion polls indicate a huge preponderance of approval of the President's action—a response that showed in Stein's view "how shallow was the general support in principle for the basic characteristics of a free market economy"— but Nixon was overwhelmingly reelected a year later, while rigorous controls remained in force.[43]

Economists, with notable exceptions, can be relied upon to testify that price controls "don't work," and in the sense that economists take to be germane—actually reducing inflation, not just temporarily suppressing its manifestations—their conclusion is valid. But in the perspective of political economy it misses the point. Price controls do work: they work to gain short-run political support for the politicians who impose them. The public never seems to learn that it is being sold a faulty political product. As Stein remarks, even after all the economic disruptions, artificial scarcities, and inequities of Nixon's price-control program, which finally ended on April 30, 1974, "the experience did not leave the country with a strong commitment to the free market, monetarist way of restraining inflation. The attraction of the direct approach remained." Just four years later the Carter administration yielded to political temptation and imposed another incomes policy, albeit a half-hearted one entirely reliant on indirect sanctions.[44]

The most important legacy of Nixon's wage-price controls was the government's energy price controls and allocations that persisted long after the comprehensive price controls had expired. When the energy crisis struck, the administration was looking forward to disengagement from its no-longer-useful incomes policy. But given the lingering presence of the price controls, the Arab oil embargo and the OPEC price hikes of late 1973 and early 1974 quickly led in many areas to shortages that were rationed mainly by the customers' waiting in the infamous gas lines. The inconvenience and uncertainty were more than the American public could bear. There immediately arose, in William Simon's words, "collective hysteria. . . . The political heat was on both Congress and the executive to solve the problem overnight."[45]

To deal with the crisis the President by executive order created the Federal Energy Office. On December 4, 1973, he named Simon, then Deputy Secretary of the Treasury, to head the FEO, which by statute later became the Federal Energy Administration and later still the Department of Energy. Overnight, Simon became the "energy czar," one of the most newsworthy people in America. Nixon authorized him "to decide everything and to decide it rapidly." The President equated the energy crisis to a wartime situation and likened Simon's job to that of Albert Speer, Hitler's

Minister of Arms and Munitions during World War II. Finding the government's energy allocation procedures tangled and ineffective, Simon and his assistants worked frantically for months to channel existing supplies to the areas with the most desperate shortages. Although eventually some improvements were made and the gas lines shortened and began to disappear by the spring of 1974, the whole arrangement remained fundamentally defective. Simon concluded: "There is nothing like becoming an economic planner oneself to learn what is desperately, stupidly wrong with such a system."[46] It got no better as Congress passed ever more complicated energy legislation in the mid-1970s (see Table 10.1). Inevitably another crisis struck; early in 1979 the gas lines reappeared. The Energy Department's erratic efforts to fix the problem just made it worse.[47] Only with Ronald Reagan's election and the scrapping of all oil price controls was the mess permitted to clean itself up through market processes. Even then, however, a complex system of price controls for natural gas lingered into the mid-1980s, a political dragon too fearful for even Sir Ronald to slay.

Notwithstanding the gas lines of 1979, the Carter years were relatively calm: no great wars, no burning cities, no masses of angry protesters in the streets. The economy grew apace, at least until 1980. The most serious economic problem of the Carter administration was one largely of its own making, the accelerating inflation that eventually reached double-digit rates not seen in the United States since the price controls lapsed after World War II. The administration tried to deflect responsibility and divert attention from the problem by embracing a weak incomes policy late in 1978, the wage-price guidelines that some corporations considered mandatory de facto even though nonexistent de jure. More significantly Carter appointed Paul Volcker to head the Fed in 1979, and thereafter a more restrictive if more erratic monetary policy was conducted. All things considered, the Reagan administration inherited an economy that was, despite the troublesome inflation and an assortment of other problems, in only moderately bad shape.

David Stockman, a congressman later to serve as Reagan's budget director, took a more excited view of the economy. After the 1980 election Stockman, in collaboration with his congressional colleague Jack Kemp, wrote a memorandum entitled "Avoiding a GOP Economic Dunkirk," which he presented to the President-elect and his chief advisers (and leaked to the press and other strategic parties).[48] After cataloging the "multiple challenges and threats lying in ambush," including an impending "credit crunch," a "double-dip recession," and a "federal budget and credit hemorrhage," Stockman proposed that the new administration act quickly, decisively, and dramatically to allay the impending risks and get the economy back on a prosperous track. His specific policy objectives included cuts in federal spending and taxing, further deregulation, and support for a steadfastly disinflationary monetary policy—nothing revolutionary or even especially radical, as every element had a clear precedent in the later phase of the Carter administration.

The remarkable aspect of the plan was how Stockman proposed that the new administration go about seeking the designated objectives. In a section of his memorandum entitled "Emergency Economic Stabilization and Recovery Program," he proposed that the new President immediately declare a national economic emergency and inform Congress and the nation that economic conditions were much worse than generally appreciated. "He should request that Congress organize quickly and clear the decks for *exclusive action* during the next hundred days on an *Emergency Economic Stabilization and Recovery Program* he would soon announce. The administration should spend the next two to three weeks in fevered consultation with Hill congressional leaders and interested private parties on the details of the package."[49] Declaration of national emergency, fevered consultation, a hundred days of legislation! Half a century after Roosevelt's New Deal the wheel had come full circle: now the conservatives would take the country by storm.

Calmer spirits prevailed. After all, it was not 1933, and there was little chance that even the Great Communicator could persuade people that it was. Though the substance of Stockman's proposal served as an influential blueprint for the administration's policy initiatives in 1981, the President decided against a declaration of national emergency. The Reaganauts did succeed in cutting income tax rates (but bracket creep and increased Social Security taxes offset much of the effect of the cuts); they carried out some additional deregulation in the communications, transportation, and financial services industries; and they supported with only occasional carping the Fed's more restrictive monetary policy, which diminished the rate of inflation much faster than anyone had thought possible, though it triggered a severe recession along the way. But much of Stockman's grandiose scheme, especially the broad cuts in federal spending and the extensive deregulation, never achieved enactment, and before long the young budget director grew sick at heart. "I have a new theory," he confided to a journalist: "There are no *real* conservatives in Congress." Indeed, after the first few hectic months, when the administration wielded the preponderance of power, politics as usual began to reassert itself. Offended constituencies rallied their troops, who dug in for a long battle or counterattacked. As always in politics there were winners and losers, but "what had changed, fundamentally, was the list of winning clients, not the nature of the game."[50]

So the heralded Reagan Revolution fizzled.[51] In part it failed because the administration never had a strong commitment to fundamental change in the first place. Witness the unyielding support for the massive transfer payments, benefitting mainly the middle class, under the Social Security system; the continued subsidies to, bailouts of, and protection from competition for farmers, timber companies, auto, steel, textile, footwear, and apparel producers, shipping companies, commercial banks, and countless others; the pervasive interference in international trade through quotas and so-called orderly marketing agreements negotiated with foreign governments. Virtually the entire hodgepodge, described by Stockman as a "coast-to-coast patchwork of dependencies, shelters, protections, and redistributions that the nation's politicians had brokered over the decades," remained intact. Political expediency reigned as supreme as ever. But even had the Reagan partisans genuinely desired to return to a free-market regime, their methods did not augur well for such a reaction. They focused not on institutional change but on altering the budget numbers, on getting income-tax rates down—particularly at the top bracket—and, with much less enthusiasm, on reducing governmental spending. Number juggling is not the stuff of revolution. Ultimately, as Stein has observed, the likelihood of a conservative revolution was slight because "even conservative governments when in office do not want to limit their own powers."[52] Conservative politicians, in short, are still politicians. And in a political system devoid of basic constitutional and ideological restraints on the scope of governmental authority, any species of politician may run amok.[53]

CONCLUSIONS

The mixed economy that has prevailed in the United States since World War II, a uniquely American form of participatory fascism, has lent itself to a substantial expansion of the scope of governmental authority over economic decision-making. Given capitalist color by the form of private property rights, the system has denied the substance of any such rights whenever governmental authorities have found it expedient to do so. No individual economic right whatever, not even the right to life, has been immune from official derogation or disallowance; besides interfering in countless economic transactions, the government has sent tens of thousands of men to their deaths bound in involuntary servitude as conscripts in the military adventures embarked upon by ruling elites. The potential for government to set aside private rights has now been plenary for over forty years, even if governments have yet to exercise the potential fully. Real reaction never materialized. Eisenhower's business-dominated administration largely accommodated itself to the legacies of the New Deal and the garrison state. Though the greatest postwar wave of new governmental powers welled forth in the 1960s under the collectivist auspices of Johnson's Great Society, the Nixon government—those "conservative men with liberal ideas"—hardly stemmed the tide. The crises, real and spurious, of the turbulent decade after 1964 fomented an unprecedented variety of influential interest groups, many of which pressed successfully for novel governmental measures on their behalf. Reagan's "conservative revolution" barely dented the enormous apparatus of governmental control. (Anyone who doubts this conclusion should look again at the appendix to Chapter 2.)

Since 1945, liberals and conservatives, Democrats and Republicans have come into and out of power as the oscillations of a pendulum, but regardless of the political swings the fixed point has remained a fundamental abrogation of private economic rights. Constantly vulnerable to unsettling governmental intervention—whether wage-price controls, energy controls, labor-market controls, environmental controls, international trade controls, or any number of other intrusions into once-private economic affairs—the postwar economy has staggered forward. All shades of politicians have preferred the powers available to them in a mixed economy to the conceivable alternatives. Without the powerful ideological and constitutional restraints that operated for over a century after the birth of the United States—restraints destroyed during the national emergencies of 1916–1945—modern governmental authorities may drink deeply and often from the heady wellsprings of political power and social control.

CHAPTER ELEVEN

Retrospect and Prospect

That which hath been is now; and that which is to be hath already been; and God requireth that which is past.

ECCLESIASTES 3:15

During the past century, most markedly between World War I and the mid-1970s, the United States developed a Big Government. One's understanding of why it developed hinges on how one conceives of it.

For every characterization, there is a different theory of its development. If Big Government is a device for repairing the "market failures" associated with monopoly power, externalities, and public goods, then its development reflects the "modernization" of the society's technical and socioeconomic structure, including such changes as urbanization, industrialization, and market concentration. If Big Government is a "safety net" to keep the helpless from starving or falling into destitution, then other economic and social changes—increased personal mobility and diminished family loyalties, perhaps—have given rise to it. Those who conceive of Big Government as essentially a coercive redistributor of wealth, responsive only to the strongest political factions, view its development in one light, while those who conceive of it as a vehicle for realizing ideological ideals or responding to national emergencies understand its history in other ways. Although none of these theories tells the whole story, each offers a useful insight.

By itself, however, each fails to depict the *process* whereby the United States developed its Big Government. No single standard explanation can account for the timing of the extension of governmental authority over economic decision-making. (The Crisis Hypothesis, which comes closest to explaining the timing of the growth of government in the twentieth century, fails to explain why crisis did not engender Big Government in the nineteenth century.) Obviously one can deepen his appreciation of the process by drawing on all the available explanations simultaneously, though that is easier to propose than to do. But even when one accepts a multicausal point of view, something is still missing. The problem with the standard explanations is not primarily their logic, though some are remarkably naive about the underlying political process. The problem is a sin of omission. None of the standard theories recognizes the extent to which the development of Big Government was a matter not of logic, however complicated and multidimensional, but of history.

RETROSPECT

To contrast a historical process with the logical linkages portrayed by the standard theories is not to assert that an illogical or irrational sequence of events generated Big Government. Instead, it is to recognize that real political and socioeconomic dynamics are "messier," more open to exogenous influences or shocks and less determinate in their outcomes than the theorists suppose. Critical events may turn on nothing more substantial than the whim of a President or the ideology of a single Supreme Court justice. In politics, important "accidents" do happen. Unanticipated consequences abound. There is no way to substitute pure theory for a knowledge of history. One must know what happens, whether it be systematic or accidental, because whatever happens alters the likelihoods of particular further developments. Historical development is a path-dependent process: where the political economy is likely to go depends on where it has been. Every "experiment," as Sumner said, enters into the life of the society and never can be removed.

Those who built the Big Government worked within an (evolving) institutional and ideological context. What they could do—even what they wanted to do—was shaped by this context. Grover Cleveland and his governmental associates could not have created a National Recovery Administration or an Agricultural Adjustment Administration; nor would they have wanted to. But Franklin Roosevelt and his governmental associates, with the wartime mobilization programs as precedents, readily established the NRA and the AAA. As another example, consider that during the Korean War extensive economic controls were quickly put in place with hardly a murmur of dissent. The ease with which the controls were imposed makes immediate sense once one appreciates what had been done along similar lines during World War II.

If the institutional and ideological context, shaped by the actual course of events, always determined how the future was most likely to unfold, it did so in part because beliefs mattered. Ideologies—telling their adherents what was going on, whether it was good or bad, what ought to be done about it, and how one could maintain his identity by solidary action with like-minded comrades—helped to determine the amount and kind of political action. Not that people failed to seek what was "in their interest"; but ideologies established what one's interest was and how one might legitimately seek it. Those who could bring about ideological change or, alternatively, shore up the ideological status quo, operated at the most fundamental sociopolitical level. Accordingly, vast efforts were exerted in ideological attack and defense. At stake was the political agenda: what questions could be decided; how the alternatives would be formulated. Elites who could manipulate the dominant ideology had already predetermined much of the outcome of the political process.

But such manipulation, notwithstanding the immense resources committed to it, did not operate in isolation. Also at work were events themselves, hence, learning from experience. Clearly, ideological changes and politico-economic changes interacted. No conceivable efforts could have prevented the Great Depression from deeply discrediting the ideas that had sustained the status quo ante. Perhaps the depression need not have discredited "capitalism" as such—the blame might have been pinned on the Fed or other inept governmental agencies—but widespread acceptance of a procapitalistic interpretation would have required more acuity from the masses than we can expect. To take another example, consider that the world wars were almost certain to leave a legacy of ideological validation of the command-and-control devices used in the mobilization programs. Post hoc, ergo propter hoc: we won; therefore the government's collectivist war policies must have been necessary and proper. How could anyone have prevented that interpretation from becoming accepted? National emergencies, and the ways they were dealt with, simply lent themselves to certain ideological changes. The world wars and the Great Depression, along with the governmental policies adopted to deal with them, virtually assured an accelerated abandonment of the free-market ideology and a corresponding acceptance of collectivist alternatives.

Events abroad continually reinforced the dialectic of politico-economic and ideological change within the United States. From the late nineteenth to the mid-twentieth century—whether one considers income taxation, central banking, nationalized retirement and health insurance, public housing, military conscription, or any number of other statist measures—the western European countries, particularly Great Britain, were always a step or two ahead of the United States, setting influential examples that appealed especially to America's most progressive ideologues. Why, Americans would be "backward," hardly civilized, to resist the adoption of such enlightened programs. During World War I the British experts bore considerable responsibility for the form taken by the mobilization program in the United States; "British experience" was the constant watchword. During and after World War II the British did much to shape American programs for postwar international monetary institutions, including heavy participation in the International Monetary Fund and the World Bank as well as the American-financed European Recovery Program, precursor of the subsequent foreign aid program. Of course Keynesianism, the main influence on U.S. macroeconomic policy for a quarter-century after 1945, may have been the most powerful ideological import of all. The United States, in short, never experienced politico-economic and ideological dynamics in a closed system. Both imported ideas and events abroad did much to shape domestic developments; and the general thrust of the foreign influences was to push the Americans further toward collectivism.

After the ideological transformation that took place during the Progressive Era, each genuine crisis has been the occasion for another ratchet toward Bigger Government. The Progressive ideological imperative that government must "do something," must take responsibility for resolving any perceived crisis, insures new actions. The actions have unavoidable costs, which governments have an incentive to conceal by substituting coercive command-and-control devices for pecuniary fiscal-and-market means of carrying out their chosen policies. Military conscription, wage-price controls, assignment of official priorities and physical allocation of selected commodities, countless economic and social regulations, import quotas and export controls—all confirm the hypothesis. Knowing how much a crisis facilitates Bigger Government, special interests always use such propitious occasions to seek whatever governmental assistance they think will promote their own ends. Once undertaken, governmental programs are hard to terminate. Interests become vested, bureaucracies entrenched, constituencies solidified. More fundamentally, each time the government expands its effective authority over economic decision-making, it sets in motion a variety of economic, institutional, and ideological adjustments whose common denominator is a diminished resistance to Bigger Government. Among the most significant of such adjustments is the Supreme Court's consistent refusal to protect individual rights from invasion by governmental officials during national emergencies. Precedents established during extraordinary times tilt the constitutional balance even during ensuing normal times.

That this institutional-ideological ratchet operated during the world wars and the Great Depression there can be little doubt. More debatable is the permanent legacy of the Great Society–Vietnam War episode. Perhaps we are still too close to this one to assess it accurately. Certainly there has been a reaction to some of its perceived excesses; a few programs, such as the oil price controls, have even been abolished. Yet the bulk of it remains intact. And the most significant elements—Medicare, Medicaid, environmental and occupational safety regulations, consumer-protection and antidiscrimination laws, and the political forces to sustain all these programs—seem solidly established. The ideology that dominated the late sixties and early seventies is presently in retreat, but far from defeated. Whatever else the so-called Reagan Revolution may have done, it certainly did not bring about an ideological revolution.

PROSPECT

In speaking of the future one must be brief. No one knows, no one can know, the future. The possibilities range from better to worse to none at all. Everyone appreciates that human society as it now exists, and perhaps human life itself, could disappear in the fires of nuclear destruction and its unthinkable aftermath.

But assuming that our luck holds and our society survives, we do know something—at least abstractly—about the future. We know that other great crises will come. Whether they will be occasioned by foreign wars, economic collapse, or rampant terrorism, no one can predict with assurance. Yet in one form or another, great crises will surely come again, as they have from time to time throughout all human history. When they do, governments almost certainly will gain new powers over economic and social affairs. Everything that I have argued and documented in the preceding chapters points toward this conclusion. For those who cherish individual liberty and a free society, the prospect is deeply disheartening.

Can such an outcome be avoided? I think not, but I hope I am wrong. Americans have been brought to their present inauspicious circumstances by, above all else, changes in the prevailing ideology. If ideologies are not mere superstructure, if ideas can gain sway through rational consideration in the light of historical evidence and moral persuasion, then there remains a hope, however slight, that the American people may rediscover the worth of individual rights, limited government, and a free society under a true rule of law.

Federal Government Agencies, Programs, and Activities (by Acronym or Abbreviation), 1983

ABMC	American Battle Monuments Commission
ACDA	Arms Control and Disarmament Agency
ACP	Agricultural Conservation Program
ACUS	Administrative Conference of the United States
ACYF	Administration for Children, Youth, and Families
ADAMHA	Alcohol, Drug Abuse, and Mental Health Administration
ADB	Asian Development Bank
ADD	Administration on Developmental Disabilities
AEDS	Atomic Energy Detection System
AFDC	Aid to Families with Dependent Children
AFIDA	Agricultural Foreign Investment Disclosure Act
AFIS	American Forces Information Service
AFPC	Armed Forces Policy Council
AFR	Air Force Reserve
AFRRI	Armed Forced Radiobiology Research Institute
AFSC	Armed Forces Staff College
AID	Agency for International Development
ALJ	Administrative Law Judge

AMS	Agricultural Marketing Service
Amtrak	National Railroad Passenger Corporation
ANA	Administration for Native Americans
AOA	Administration on Aging
APHIS	Animal and Plant Health Inspection Service
ASCS	Agricultural Stabilization and Conservation Service
ATSDR	Agency for Toxic Substances and Disease Registry
BCP	Blended Credit Program
BEA	Bureau of Economic Analysis
BIA	Bureau of Indian Affairs
BIB	Board for International Broadcasting
BJS	Bureau of Justice Statistics
BLM	Bureau of Land Management
BLS	Bureau of Labor Statistics
BPA	Bonneville Power Administration
BSC	Business Service Centers
CAB	Civil Aeronautics Board
CALS	Current Awareness Literature Service
CBO	Congressional Budget Office
CCA	Crop Condition Assessment
CCC	Commodity Credit Corporation

CCEA	Cabinet Council on Economic Affairs	DAVA	Defense Audiovisual Agency
CCR	Commission on Civil Rights	DCA	Defense Communications Agency
CDBG	Community Development Block Grant	DCAA	Defense Contract Audit Agency
CDC	Centers for Disease Control	DCASR	Defense Contract Administration Services Regions
CEA	Council of Economic Advisers	DCII	Defense Central Index of Investigations
CEQ	Council on Environmental Quality	DCS	Defense Communications System
CFA	Commission of Fine Arts		
CFC	Cooperative Finance Corporation	DEA	Drug Enforcement Administration
CFTC	Commodity Futures Trading Commission	DIA	Defense Intelligence Agency
CHAMPVA	Civilian Health and Medical Program of the Veterans Administration	DIPEC	Defense Industrial Plant Equipment Center
		DIS	Defense Investigative Service
CIA	Central Intelligence Agency	DISAM	Defense Institute of Security Assistance Management
CIC	Consumer Information Center		
COGP	Commission on Government Procurement	DLA	Defense Logistics Agency
		DLS	Defense Legal Services agency
Comcen's	Federal Communications Centers	DMA	Defense Mapping Agency
Conrail	Consolidated Rail Corporation	DMS	Defense Mapping School
CPSC	Consumer Product Safety Commission	DNA	Defense Nuclear Agency
CRS	Community Relations Service	DOD	Department of Defense
		DODCI	Department of Defense Computer Institute
CSA	Community Services Administration	DODDS	Department of Defense Dependents Schools
CSRS	Cooperative State Research Service	DOE	Department of Energy
DA	Department of the Army	DOT	Department of Transportation
DARPA	Defense Advanced Research Projects Agency	DSAA	Defense Security Assistance Agency

DSN Deep Space Network

DVOP Disabled Veterans' Outreach Program

EDA Economic Development Administration

EEOC Equal Employment Opportunity Commission

EIA Energy Information Administration

EOUSA Executive Office for United States Attorneys

EPA Environmental Protection Agency

EPIC Energy Conservation Program Guide for Industry and Commerce

ERA Economic Regulatory Administration

ERISA Employee Retirement Income Security Act

ESA Employment Standards Administration

ESF Economic Support Fund

ETA Employment and Training Administration

Eximbank Export-Import Bank of the United States

FAA Federal Aviation Administration

FAIR Fair Access to Insurance Requirements

FAR Federal Acquisition Regulations

FAS Foreign Agricultural Service

FBI Federal Bureau of Investigation

FCA Farm Credit Administration

FCC Federal Communications Commission

FCIA Foreign Credit Insurance Association

FCIC Federal Crop Insurance Corporation

FCS Foreign Commercial Service

FCU Federal credit union

FDA Food and Drug Administration

FDIC Federal Deposit Insurance Corporation

FDPC Federal Data Processing Centers

FEC Federal Election Commission

FEMA Federal Emergency Management Agency

FFB Federal Financing Bank

FGB Foster Grandparent Program

FGIS Federal Grain Inspection Service

FHA Federal Housing Administration

FHLBB Federal Home Loan Bank Board

FHWA Federal Highway Administration

FIA Federal Insurance Administration

FIC Federal Information Centers

FICC Fixed Income Consumer Counseling

FIP Forestry Incentive Program

FLETC Federal Law Enforcement Training Center

FLRA Federal Labor Relations Authority

FLITE Federal Legal Information Through Electronics

FMC Federal Maritime Commission

FMCS Federal Mediation and Conciliation Service

FmHA	Farmers Home Administration	HRSA	Health Resources and Services Administration
FNMA	Federal National Mortgage Association	HUD	Department of Housing and Urban Development
FNS	Food and Nutrition Service	IADB	Inter-American Defense Board; Inter-American Development Bank
FOMC	Federal Open Market Committee		
FPRS	Federal Property Resources Service	IAEA	International Atomic Energy Agency
FRA	Federal Railroad Administration	IAF	Inter-American Foundation
FRS	Federal Reserve System	ICAF	Industrial College of the Armed Forces
FSIS	Food Safety and Inspection Service	ICAO	International Civil Aviation Organization
FSLIC	Federal Savings and Loan Insurance Corporation	ICC	Interstate Commerce Commission
FSS	Office of Federal Supply and Services	ICM	Intergovernmental Committee for Migration
FSTS	Federal Secure Telephone Service	IDA	International Development Association; Institute for Defense Analyses
FTC	Federal Trade Commission		
FTS	Federal Telecommunications System	IDCA	United States International Development Cooperation Agency
FWS	Fish and Wildlife Service		
GAO	General Accounting Office	IFC	International Finance Corporation
GNMA	Government National Mortgage Association	IHS	Indian Health Service
		IMF	International Monetary Fund
GPO	Government Printing Office	IMS	Institute of Museum Services
GSA	General Services Administration	INS	Immigration and Naturalization Service
HCFA	Health Care Financing Administration	INTERPOL	International Criminal Police Organization
HDS	Office of Human Development Services	IRS	Internal Revenue Service
HHS	Department of Health and Human Services	ITA	International Trade Administration
HNIS	Human Nutrition Information Service	ITU	International Telecommunication Union
HRA	Health Resources Administration		

IYC	Individual Yield Coverage program
JAG	Judge Advocate General
JCS	Joint Chiefs of Staff
JFMIP	Joint Financial Management Improvement Program
JTPA	Job Training Partnership Act
LC	Library of Congress
LMRDA	Labor Management Reporting and Disclosure Act
LMSA	Labor-Management Services Administration
LSC	Legal Services Corporation
LVER	Local Veterans' Employment Representative
MA	Maritime Administration
MAC	Military Airlift Command
MBDA	Minority Business Development Agency
MDB's	Multilateral development banks
MEECN	Minimum Essential Emergency Communications Network
MILSATCOM	Military Satellite Communications Systems
MSB-COD	Minority Small Business–Capital Ownership Development program
MSC	Military Sealift Command
MSHA	Mine Safety and Health Administration
MSPB	Merit Systems Protection Board
MSSD	Model Secondary School for the Deaf
MTB	Materials Transportation Bureau
MTN	Multilateral trade negotiations
NARS	National Archives and Records Service
NASA	National Aeronautics and Space Administration
NATO	North Atlantic Treaty Organization
NBS	National Bureau of Standards
NCCB	National Consumer Cooperative Bank
NCDC	New Community Development Corporation
NCI	National Cancer Institute
NCIC	National Cartographic Information Center
NCJRS	National Criminal Justice Reference Service
NCPC	National Capital Planning Commission
NCSL	National Center for Service Learning
NCUA	National Credit Union Administration
NDU	National Defense University
NFIP	National Flood Insurance Program
NHTSA	National Highway Traffic Safety Administration
NIC	National Institute of Corrections
NIE	National Institute of Education
NIH	National Institutes of Health
NIJ	National Institute of Justice
NIS	Naval Investigative Service

NLM	National Library of Medicine	OCSE	Office of Child Support Enforcement
NLRB	National Labor Relations Board	OECD	Organization for Economic Cooperation and Development
NMB	National Mediation Board	OES	Office of Employment Security
NMCS	National Military Command System	OFCC	Office of Federal Contract Compliance
NOAA	National Oceanic and Atmospheric Administration	OFPP	Office of Federal Procurement Policy
NOS	National Ocean Survey	OFR	Office of the Federal Register
NRC	Nuclear Regulatory Commission	OGPS	Office of Grants and Programs Systems
NSA	National Security Agency	OICD	Office of International Cooperation and Development
NSC	National Security Council	OIRM	Office of Information Resources Management
NSF	National Science Foundation	OJARS	Office of Justice Assistance, Research and Statistics
NSTL	National Space Technology Laboratories	OJJDP	Office of Juvenile Justice and Delinquency Prevention
NTIA	National Telecommunications and Information Administration	OMB	Office of Management and Budget
NTID	National Technical Institute for the Deaf	OPD	Office of Policy Development
NTIS	National Technical Information Service	OPIC	Overseas Private Investment Corporation
NTS	Naval Telecommunications System	OPM	Office of Personnel Management
NTSB	National Transportation Safety Board	ORM	Office of Regional Management
NWC	National War College	ORR	Office of Refugee Relief
OA	Office of Administration	OSCE	Office of Child Support Enforcement
OAS	Organization of American States	OSHA	Occupational Safety and Health Administration
OCA	Office of Consumer Advisor	OSHRC	Occupational Safety and Health Review Commission
OCCCA	Office of Congressional, Community and Consumer Affairs	OSTP	Office of Science and Technology Policy
OCS	Office of Community Services	OT	Office of Transportation

OTA	Office of Technology Assessment		SAO	Smithsonian Astrophysical Observatory
OTAA	Office of Trade Adjustment Assistance		SBA	Small Business Administration
OVRR	Office of Veterans' Reemployment Rights		SBIC's	Small Business Investment Companies
OWBE	Office of Women's Business Enterprise		SCP	Senior Companion Program
OWP	Office of Water Policy		SCS	Soil Conservation Service
PADC	Pennsylvania Avenue Development Corporation		SCSEP	Senior Community Service Employment Program
PAHO	Pan American Health Organization		SEAN	Scientific Event Alert Network
PBGC	Pension Benefit Guaranty Corporation		SEC	Securities and Exchange Commission
PBS	Public Buildings Service		SGLI	Servicemen's Group Life Insurance
PCC	Panama Canal Commission		SIL	Smithsonian Institution Libraries
PHA's	Public Housing Agencies		SITES	Smithsonian Institution Traveling Exhibition Service
PHS	Public Health Service		SLS	Saint Lawrence Seaway Development Corporation
PIK	Payment-In-Kind program			
PRC	Postal Rate Commission		SMIDA	Small Business Innovation Development Act
PTO	Patent and Trademark Office			
RCWP	Rural Clean Water Program		SPC	South Pacific Commission
REA	Rural Electrification Administration		SRIM	Standing order microfiche service
RETRF	Rural Electrification and Telephone Revolving Fund		SRS	Statistical Reporting Service
RFE	Radio Free Europe		SSA	Social Security Administration
RL	Radio Liberty		SSI	Supplemental Security Income Program
RRB	Railroad Retirement Board		SSS	Selective Service System
RSA	Rehabilitation Services Administration		START	Strategic arms reduction talks
RSPA	Research and Special Programs Administration		TAC	Tactical Air Command
RSVP	Retired Senior Volunteer Program		TCE	Tax Counseling for the Elderly Program
RTB	Rural Telephone Bank			
SAC	Strategic Air Command			

STDN	Spaceflight Tracking and Data Network	USIA	United States Information Agency
TDP	Trade and Development Program	USICA	United States International Communication Agency
TRIMIS	Tri-Service Medical Information System	USITC	United States International Trade Commission
TRI-TAC	Joint Tactical Communications Program	USMC	United States Marine Corps
TSC	Transportation Systems Center	USN	United States Navy
TVA	Tennessee Valley Authority	USNCB	United States National Central Bureau
UCPP	Urban Crime Prevention Program	USPS	United States Postal Service
UDAG	Urban Development Action Grant	USRA	United States Railway Association
UIS	Unemployment Insurance Service	USTTA	United States Travel and Tourism Administration
UMTA	Urban Mass Transportation Administration	VA	Veterans Administration
UN	United Nations	VETS	Veterans' Employment and Training Service
UNESCO	United Nations Educational, Scientific and Cultural Organization	VGLI	Veterans Group Life Insurance
UNICEF	United Nations International Children's Emergency Fund (now United Nations Children's Fund)	VISTA	Volunteers in Service to America
		VITA	Volunteer Income Tax Assistance Program
UNICOR	Federal Prison Industries, Inc.	VMLI	Veterans Mortgage Life Insurance
UPU	Universal Postal Union	VMSP	Volunteer Management Support Program
USA	United States Army	VOA	Voice of America
USACE	United States Army Corps of Engineers	VVLP	Vietnam Veterans Leadership Program
USAF	United States Air Force	WAPA	Western Area Power Administration
USCG	United States Coast Guard	WBP	Water Bank Program
USCS	United States Commercial Service	WHO	World Health Organization
USDA	United States Department of Agriculture	WHS	Washington Headquarters Services
USES	United States Employment Service	WIC	Special supplemental food program for Women, Infants, and Children

WIN	Work Incentive Program	YCC	Youth Conservation Corps
WMO	World Meteorological Organization	YVA	Young Volunteers in ACTION
WWMCCS	Worldwide Military Command and Control System		

Source: Office of the Federal Register, *The United States Government Manual, 1983/84* (Washington, D.C.: U.S. Government Printing Office, 1983), pp. 801–807.

APPENDIX TO CHAPTER NINE
War Agencies of the Executive Branch of the Federal Government during World War II

Advisory Board on Just Compensation (WSA)

Alaska War Council

American Commission for the Protection and Salvage of Artistic and Historic Monuments in War Areas

Anglo-American Caribbean Commission

Army Specialist Corps

Board of Economic Warfare

Board of War Communications

British-American Joint Patent Interchange Committee

Cargoes, Inc. (FEA)

Censorship Policy Board

Central Administrative Services (OEM)

Civil Air Patrol (OCD)

Civilian Production Administration

Coal Mines Administration (Interior)

Colonial Mica Corporation

Combined Chiefs of Staff—United States and Great Britain

Combined Food Board

Combined Production and Resources Board

Combined Raw Materials Board

Combined Shipping Adjustment Board

Committee for Congested Production Areas

Committee on Fair Employment Practice

Committee on Physical Fitness (FSA)

Committee on Records of War Administration

Coordinator of Government Films

Coordinator of Information

Copper Recovery Corporation (RFC-Metals Reserve)

Defense Communications Board

Defense Homes Corporation (NHA)

Defense Housing Coordinator (NDAC)

Defense Plant Corporation (RFC)

Defense Resources Committee

Defense Supplies Corporation (RFC)

Division of Defense Aid Reports (OEM)

Division of Defense Housing Coordination (OEM)

Division of Information (OEM)

Food Distribution Administration (Agriculture)

Food Production Administration (Agriculture)

Foreign Broadcast Intelligence Service (FCC)

Foreign Economic Administration (OEM)

Foreign Funds Control (Treasury)

Government Information Service (Budget)

Institute of Inter-American Affairs (OIAA)

Institute of Inter-American Transportation (OIAA)

Inter-American Defense Board

Inter-American Educational Foundation, Inc. (OIAA)

Inter-American Financial and Economic Advisory Committee

Inter-American Navigation Corporation (OIAA)

Interdepartmental Committee for Coordination of Foreign and Domestic Military Purchases

Interdepartmental Committee to Consider Cases of Subversive Activities on the Part of Federal Employees

Interdepartmental Committee for the Voluntary Pay-Roll Savings Plan for the Purchase of War Bonds

Interim International Information Service (State)

Interim Research and Intelligence Service (State)

Joint Aircraft Committee

Joint Brazil–United States Defense Commission

Joint chiefs of Staff

Joint Contract Termination Board

272

Joint Economic Committees—United States and Canada

Joint Mexican–United States Defense Commission

Joint War Production Committee—United States and Canada

Management Labor Policy Committee (Labor)

Material Coordinating Committee—United States and Canada

Medal for Merit Board

Metals Reserve Company (RFC)

Munitions Assignment Board

National Defense Advisory Commission

National Defense Mediation Board

National Housing Agency (OEM)

National Inventor's Council

National Munitions Control Board

National Patent Planning Commission (Commerce)

National Railway Labor Panel (National Mediation Board)

National Roster of Scientific and Specialized Personnel (Labor)

National Wage Stabilization Board (Labor)

National War Labor Board

Office for Coordination of National Defense Purchases (NDAC)

Office for Emergency Management

Office of Agricultural Defense Relations

Office of Alien Property Custodian (OEM)

Office of Army-Navy Liquidation Commissioner

Office of Censorship

Office of Civilian Defense (OEM)

Office of Community War Service (FSA)

Office of Contract Settlement (OWMR)

Office of Coordinator of Inter-American Affairs (OEM)

Office of Defense Health and Welfare Service

Office of Defense Transportation (OEM)

Office of Economic Stabilization

Office of Economic Warfare (OEM)

Office of Export Control

Office of Facts and Figures

Office of Fishery Coordination (Interior)

Office of Inter-American Affairs

Office of Lend-Lease Administration (OEM)

Office of Merchant Ship Control (Coast Guard)

Office of Petroleum Coordinator for National Defense

Office of Price Administration

Office of Price Administration and Civilian Supply (OEM)

Office of Production Management (OEM)

Office of Production Research and Development (WPB)

Office of Scientific Research and Development (OEM)

Office of Solid Fuels Coordinator for National Defense

Office of Stabilization Administration (OWMR)

Office of Strategic Services

Office of Surplus Property (Commerce)

Office of War Information (OEM)

Office of War Mobilization

Office of War Mobilization and Reconversion

Pacific War Council

Petroleum Administration for War

Petroleum Reserves Corporation (RFC)

Prencinradio, Inc. (OIAA)

President's Committee on Deferment of Federal Employees

President's Committee on War Relief Agencies

President's Soviet Protocol Committee

President's War Relief Control Board

Priorities Board (NDAC)

Publications Board (OWMR)

Reconstruction Finance Corporation

Retraining and Reemployment Administration (Labor)

Rubber Development Corporation

Rubber Reserve Company (RFC)

Salary Stabilization Unit (Treasury)

Selective Service System

Shipbuilding Stabilization Committee (Labor)

Smaller War Plants Corporation

Solid Fuels Administration for War (Interior)

Southwestern Power Administration (Interior)

Steel Recovery Corporation (RFC-Metals Reserve)

Supply Priorities and Allocations Board (OEM)

Surplus Property Administration (OWMR)

Surplus Property Board (OWMR)

Surplus War Property Administration (OWM)

United States Commercial Company (RFC)

United States Emergency Court of Appeals

United States of America Typhus Commission

Wage Adjustment Board for the Construction Industry (Labor)

War Assets Corporation (RFC)

War Ballots Commission

War Contracts Price Adjustment Board

War Damage Corporation (RFC)

War Emergency Pipe Lines, Inc. (RFC)

War Food Administration (Agriculture)

War Forwarding Corporation (WSA)

War Hemp Industries, Inc. (Agriculture)

War Insurance Corporation (RFC)

War Manpower Commission (OEM)

War Materials, Inc. (RFC)

War Production Board (OEM)

War Refugee Board

War Relocation Authority (Interior)

War Resources Board (ANMB)

War Resources Council (Interior)

War Shipping Administration (OEM)

Source: U.S. Bureau of the Budget, *The United States at War: Development and Administration of the War Program by the Federal Government* (Washington, D.C.: U.S. Government Printing Office, 1946), pp. 521–535.

Notes

CHAPTER ONE

1. Ludwig von Mises, *The Ultimate Foundation of Economic Science: An Essay on Method* (Kansas City, Kans: Sheed Andrews and McMeel, 1978), p. 98. Also Frank H. Knight, *Freedom and Reform: Essays in Economics and Social Philosophy* (Indianapolis: Liberty Press, 1982), p. 232.

2. James Willard Hurst, *Law and the Conditions of Freedom in the Nineteenth-Century United States* (Madison: University of Wisconsin Press, 1956), pp. 3–32 and passim. Also idem, *Law and Markets in United States History: Different Modes of Bargaining Among Interests* (Madison: University of Wisconsin Press, 1982), pp. 96, 124–125; Lawrence M. Friedman, *A History of American Law* (New York: Simon & Schuster, 1973).

3. G. Warren Nutter, *Political Economy and Freedom: A Collection of Essays* (Indianapolis: Liberty Fund, 1983), pp. 51–52. Useful general accounts of the growth of American government in the twentieth century include Solomon Fabricant, *The Trend of Government Activity in the United States since 1900* (New York: National Bureau of Economic Research, 1952) and Jonathan R. T. Hughes, *The Governmental Habit: Economic Controls from Colonial Times to the Present* (New York: Basic Books, 1977), pp. 126–242. The most revealing descriptions of the vast scope of modern government have been produced not by scholars but unwittingly by the authors of "helpful guides" for citizens seeking governmental benefits, for example, William Ruder and Raymond Nathan, *The Businessman's Guide to Washington* (New York: Collier Books, 1975) and *The Encyclopedia of U.S. Government Benefits*, ed. Roy A. Grisham, Jr., and Paul D. McConaughy (New York: Avon Books, 1975). For a straightforward agency-by-agency description of the contemporary federal government, see Office of the Federal Register, *The United States Government Manual, 1983/84* (Washington, D.C.: U.S. Government Printing Office, 1983).

4. James E. Alt and K. Alec Chrystal, *Political Economics* (Berkeley: University of California Press, 1983), pp. 190, 243. In a recent econometric study, David Lowery and William D. Berry tested nine different explanations of the growth of governmental spending in the postwar United States and found that, considered separately, only one "receive[d] even a minimal degree of support"—and even that one, because of econometric problems in the test, was questionable. "The Growth of Government in the United States: An Empirical Assessment of Competing Explanations," *American Journal of Political Science* 27 (Nov. 1983): 665–694 (quotation from 686).

5. José Ortega y Gasset, *The Revolt of the Masses* (New York: Norton, 1957), pp. 119–121. Ortega y Gasset recognized (p. 122) that "for all that the State is still composed of the members of that society," but few lines later he wrote of "what State intervention leads to: the people are converted into fuel to feed the mere machine which is the State." I agree with John R. Commons that "the officials-in-action- . . . constitute the state-in-action . . . [whereas] the legal relations . . . are formal statements of ideals, wishes and hopes which may or may not be realized when the officials come to act." *Legal Foundations of Capitalism* (Madison: University of Wisconsin Press, 1959), p. 123.

6. Thomas R. Dye and L. Harmon Zeigler, *The Irony of Democracy: An Uncommon Introduction to American Politics*, 5th ed. (Monterey, Calif.: Duxbury Press, 1981), pp. 327, 431; Graham K. Wilson, *Interest Groups in the United States* (Oxford: Clarendon Press, 1981), pp. 132–133.

7. Two (highly partisan) blow-by-blow accounts of recent governmental infighting are Paul Craig Roberts, *The Supply-Side Revolution: An Insider's Account of Policymaking in Washington* (Cambridge, Mass.: Harvard University Press, 1984) and David A. Stockman, *The Triumph of Politics: How the Reagan Revolution Failed* (New York: Harper & Row, 1986).

8. Eric A. Nordlinger, *On the Autonomy of the Democratic State* (Cambridge, Mass.: Harvard University Press, 1981), p. 15; Lance T. LeLoup, *Budgetary Politics* (Brunswick, Ohio: King's Court Communications, 1980), p. 21.

9. Calvin B. Hoover, *The Economy, Liberty, and the State* (New York: Twentieth Century Fund, 1959), p. 373. Echoing this refrain, Morton Keller recently declared: "A complex and ever changing economy requires a dense and flexible regulatory system." See "The Pluralist State: American Economic Regulation In Comparative Perspective, 1900–1930," in *Regulation in Perspective: Historical Essays*, ed. Thomas K. McCraw (Cambridge, Mass.: Harvard University Press, 1981), p. 94. Among economists the Modernization Hypothesis often appears in the form of Wagner's Law. For a sensible critique of this vague notion, see Alan T. Peacock and Jack Wiseman, *The Growth of Public Expenditure in the United Kingdom* (Princeton, N.J.: Princeton University Press, 1961), pp. 16–20, 24–28.

10. Adam Smith, *An Inquiry into the Nature and Causes of the Wealth of Nations* (New York: Modern Library, 1937); F. A. Hayek, *Law, Legislation and Liberty: A New Statement of the Liberal Principles of Justice and Political Economy, Vol. I. Rules and Order* (Chicago: University of Chicago Press, 1973), pp. 35–54, esp. pp. 50–51. Also Thomas Sowell, *Knowledge and Decisions* (New York: Basic Books, 1980), esp. pp. 214–223; Israel M. Kirzner, "Economic Planning and the Knowledge Problem," *Cato Journal* 4 (Fall 1984): 407–418. Compare Leonid Hurwicz, "Economic Planning and the Knowledge Problem': A Comment," ibid., pp. 419–425.

11. The thesis is developed by John Kenneth Galbraith, *American Capitalism: The Concept of Countervailing Power*, 2nd ed. (Boston: Houghton Mifflin, 1956), esp. pp. 135–153 on "Countervailing Power and the State." Lenin's statement from *Imperialism: The Highest Stage of Capitalism*, new rev. trans. (New York: International Publishers, 1939), p. 17.

12. Joseph A. Schumpeter, *Capitalism, Socialism, and Democracy*, 3rd ed. (New York: Harper & Row, 1950), pp. 81–106; Israel M. Kirzner, *Competition and Entrepreneurship* (Chicago: University of Chicago Press, 1973), esp. pp. 125–131. Also Thomas K. McCraw, "Rethinking the Trust Question," in *Regulation in Perspective*, ed. McCraw, pp. 1–24. J. R. T. Hughes has suggested to me that even if the threat actually posed by big business was not genuine, people might still have (mistakenly) feared it and therefore sought governmental protection from it.

13. George J. Stigler, *The Citizen and the State: Essays on Regulation* (Chicago: University of Chicago Press, 1975), p. 183. For surveys of studies of a wide variety of regulatory programs, see Thomas K. McCraw, "Regulation in America: A Re-

view Article," *Business History Review* 49 (Summer 1975): 159–183, and Bernard H. Siegan, *Economic Liberties and the Constitution* (Chicago: University of Chicago Press, 1980), pp. 283–303. In "Rethinking the Trust Question," McCraw concludes (p. 55) that "economic regulation typically has not been the ally but the enemy of competition."

14. McCraw, "Regulation in America," p. 171.

15. Leland B. Yeager, "Is There a Bias Toward Overregulation?" in *Rights and Regulation: Ethical, Political, and Economic Issues*, ed. Tibor R. Machan and M. Bruce Johnson (Cambridge, Mass.: Ballinger, 1983), p. 125.

16. Edward Meeker, "The Social Rate of Return on Investment in Public Health, 1880–1910," *Journal of Economic History* 34 (June 1974): 392–431; Robert Higgs, *The Transformation of the American Economy, 1865–1914: An Essay in Interpretation* (New York: Wiley, 1971), pp. 67–72; idem, "Cycles and Trends of Mortality in 18 Large American Cities, 1871–1900, "*Explorations in Economic History* 16 (Oct. 1979): 396–398.

17. Murray L. Weidenbaum, *Business, Government, and the Public*, 2nd ed. (Englewood Cliffs, N.J.: Prentice-Hall, 1981), pp. 92–113; Douglas F. Greer, *Business, Government, and Society* (New York: Macmillan, 1983), pp. 463–489.

18. Thomas E. Borcherding, "The Sources of Growth of Public Expenditures in the United States, 1902–1970," in *Budgets and Bureaucrats: The Sources of Government Growth*, ed. Thomas E. Borcherding (Durham, N.C.: Duke University Press, 1977), p. 53; Willliam A. Niskanen, "The Growth of Government," *Cato Policy Report* 7 (July/Aug. 1985): 8–10; Edgar K. Browning and Jacquelene M. Browning, *Public Finance and the Price System*, 2nd ed. (New York: Macmillan, 1983), pp. 93, 98. Also the sources cited in note 3 above, especially the "helpful guides."

19. Because national defense so often exemplifies the concept of a public good, it is well to note that "[d]efense spending also confers private benefits in significant amounts, and those considerations often cloud the issues concerning defense as a public good. . . . The amount of defense spending does not translate into a certain level of capability. But as long as defense spending also provides substantial private benefits, there will be strong pressures to continue to increase expenditures." LeLoup, *Budgetary Politics*, pp. 253, 255. Milton and Rose Friedman have observed that "[t]he iron triangle"—in this case consisting of the Pentagon, the defense contractors, and the pertinent congressmen—"is as powerful in the military area as it is in the civilian area." Milton Friedman and Rose Friedman, *Tyranny of the Status Quo* (New York: Harcourt Brace Jovanovich, 1984), p. 78.

20. Browning and Browning, *Public Finance*, pp. 29–34, 42–44, 49–50; Joseph P. Kalt, "Public Goods and the Theory of Government," *Cato Journal* 1 (Fall 1981): 565–584; Russell D. Roberts, "A Taxonomy of Public Provision," *Public Choice* 47 (1985): 267–303. Compare E. C. Pasour, Jr., "The Free Rider as a Basis for Government Intervention," *Journal of Libertarian Studies* 5 (Fall 1981): 453–464.

21. Victor R. Fuchs, "The Economics of Health in a Post-Industrial Society," *Public Interest* (Summer 1979): 19, 13. For provocative variations on the theme, see Robert Nisbet, *Twilight of Authority* (New York: Oxford University Press, 1975), esp. pp. 230–287.

22. Wilhelm Ropke, *A Humane Economy: The Social Framework of the Free Market*, trans. Elizabeth Henderson (Chicago: Henry Regnery, 1971), pp. 156, 164–165. Also Mancur Olson, *The Rise and Decline of Nations: Economic Growth, Stagflation, and Social Rigidities* (New Haven, Conn.: Yale University Press, 1982), p. 174.

23. Allan H. Meltzer and Scott F. Richard, "Why Government Grows (and Grows) in a Democracy," *Public Interest* (Summer 1978): 116. Also, by the same authors, "A Rational Theory of the Size of Government," *Journal of Political Economy* 89 (Oct. 1981): 914–927. The latter article measures the size of government by the share of income redistributed. Given the multitude of indirect as well as direct ways

that governmental policies effect redistributions, the measure is not operational and hence the hypothesis cannot be tested empirically. A subsequent paper by Meltzer and Richard fails to recognize the problem and its test of the authors' hypothesis is therefore unpersuasive. "Tests of a Rational Theory of the Size of Government," *Public Choice* 41 (1983): 403–418.

24. Olson, *Rise and Decline*, p. 174.

25. Sam Peltzman, "The Growth of Government," *Journal of Law and Economics* 23 (Oct. 1980): 285, emphasis in original.

26. Ibid., pp. 221–223, 233–234. Political scientist Morris P. Fiorina has aptly remarked that "most economists receive a tolerably good training in statistical method, so they are capable of producing analyses which have the appearance of thoroughness and sophistication, but . . . their lack of contextual knowledge leads them to rely on naive model specification. Often, too, public choice empirical studies utilize outrageous indicators for crucial theoretical variables." Fiorina's "Comments," in *Collective Decision Making: Applications from Public Choice Theory*, ed. Clifford S. Russell (Baltimore: Johns Hopkins University Press, 1979), p. 48. Unrepentant, Peltzman has recently provided another example of what Fiorina was criticizing: "An Economic Interpretation of the History of Congressional Voting in the Twentieth Century," *American Economic Review* 75 (Sept. 1985): 656–675.

27. On the Supreme Court, see Siegan, *Economic Liberties*, and Paul L. Murphy, *The Constitution in Crisis Times, 1918–1969* (New York: Harper Torchbooks, 1972). On conservative (and other) public opinion, see Chapters 3 and 4 below and sources cited there. On the bureaucracy, see Browning and Browning, *Public Finance*, pp. 72–75; Dye and Zeigler, *Irony of Democracy*, pp. 323–324, 335; Samuel P. Hays, "Political Choice in Regulatory Administration," in *Regulation in Perspective*, ed. McCraw, pp. 124–154; Francis E. Rourke, *Bureaucracy, Politics, and Public Policy*, 2nd ed. (Boston: Little, Brown, 1976), pp. 179–184 and passim. For a clever if less than compelling argument that the bureaucracy is actually more subservient to the legislature than it appears to be, see Barry R. Weingast, "The Congressional-Bureaucratic System: A Principal Agent Perspective (with applications to the SEC)," *Public Choice* 44 (1984): 147–191.

28. W. Lance Bennett, *Public Opinion in American Politics* (New York: Harcourt Brace Jovanovich, 1980), pp. 43–45, 122–123, 350, 384–390 (quotation from p. 44); James M. Buchanan, "Why Does Government Grow?" in *Budgets and Bureaucrats*, ed. Borcherding, p. 13. Also James M. Buchanan, *The Limits of Liberty: Between Anarchy and Leviathan* (Chicago: University of Chicago Press, 1975), pp. 156–161; Browning and Browning, *Public Finance*, pp. 54–72; Alt and Chrystal, *Political Economics*, pp. 154, 155, 161; Siegan, *Economic Liberties and the Constitution*, pp. 91, 265–282; Olson, *Rise and Decline*, p. 52; Nordlinger, *Autonomy*, pp. 87, 96, 209; Graham K. Wilson, *Interest Groups*, pp. 110, 117, 125; Dye and Zeigler, *Irony of Democracy*, pp. 193, 196, 362, 364, 367; Brian Barry, *Sociologists, Economists and Democracy* (Chicago: University of Chicago Press, 1978), pp. 127, 135; Joseph D. Reid, Jr., "Understanding Political Events in the New Economic History," *Journal of Economic History* 37 (June 1977): 308, 313–314; Leland B. Yeager, "Rights, Contract, and Utility in Policy Espousal," *Cato Journal* 5 (Spring/Summer 1985): pp. 284–285.

29. Wilson, *Interest Groups*, p. 117 (also pp. 110, 125). The economists' typical presumption appears starkly in Gary Becker's recent contribution, where "politicians and bureaucrats [are] assumed to be hired to further the collective interests of pressure groups, who fire or repudiate them by elections and impeachment when they deviate excessively from those interests." See "A Theory of Competition among Pressure Groups for Political Influence," *Quarterly Journal of Economics* 98 (Aug. 1983): 396. Does this tight control include firing a civil service bureaucrat or impeaching a Supreme Court justice? If so, some intractable problems are assumed away; if not, some important actors are left out of the model.

30. William Greider, "The Education of David Stockman," *Atlantic Monthly* 248 (Dec. 1981): 30; "Pete McCloskey: Trying to Run on the Issues," *Wall Street Journal*, June 3, 1982, p. 22.

31. Joseph A. Schumpeter, *History of Economic Analysis* (New York: Oxford University Press, 1954), p. 429.

32. John Maynard Keynes, *The General Theory of Employment, Interest and Money* (New York: Harcourt, Brace & World, 1936), pp. 383–384.

33. Friedrich A. Hayek, *The Constitution of Liberty* (Chicago: University of Chicago Press, 1960), pp. 231–232.

34. Midway between Keynes and Hayek on the political spectrum, the Friedmans also espouse an ideological-change explanation of the growth of government (*Tyranny of the Status Quo*, pp. 37–38). On ideology in relation to the changing role of government, see Chapters 3 and 4 below and the sources cited there.

35. Ortega y Gasset, *The Revolt of the Masses*, p. 128 (also p. 126). Also Knight, *Freedom and Reform*, pp. 235, 414.

36. Herbert McClosky and John Zaller, *The American Ethos: Public Attitudes toward Capitalism and Democracy* (Cambridge, Mass: Harvard University Press, 1984), p. 159.

37. Wilson, *Interest Groups*, p. 11; Ropke, *A Humane Economy*, p. 142. Ortega y Gasset agreed that "[t]he majority of men have no opinions, and these have to be pumped into them from outside." Also, "Under universal suffrage, the masses do not decide, their role consists in supporting the decision of one minority or another" (*The Revolt of the Masses*, pp. 128–129, 48). Also Schumpeter, *Capitalism, Socialism, and Democracy*, p. 263; Becker, "Competition among Pressure Groups," p. 392; Bennett, *Public Opinion*, pp. 230–232, 240–241, 306, 311; McClosky and Zaller, *American Ethos*, pp. 11–12, 152, 234.

38. William Letwin, *Law and Economic Policy in America: The Evolution of the Sherman Antitrust Act* (Chicago: University of Chicago Presss, 1965), p. 54. Thomas Dye cites a study by Warren E. Miller and Donald Stokes that "found very low correlations between the voting records of Congressmen and the attitudes of their constituents on social welfare issues, and even lower correlations on foreign policy issues. Only in the area of civil rights did Congressmen appear to vote according to the views of a majority of their constituents." *Understanding Public Policy*, 2nd ed. (Englewood Cliffs, N.J.: Prentice-Hall, 1975), p. 309. For opposing conclusions on the relation of ideology to congressional voting, see Sam Peltzman, "Constituent Interest and Congressional Voting," *Journal of Law and Economics* 27 (April 1984): 181–210, and Keith T. Poole and R. Steven Daniels, "Ideology, Party, and Voting in the U.S. Congress, 1959–1980," *American Political Science Review* 79 (June 1985): 373–399. Mismatches between the actions of legislators and the preferences of their constituents may reflect what voting theorists call the "cyclical majority phenomenon." In this case, "No matter what is chosen, something else is preferred by a majority." For a comprehensible explanation of this phenomenon, see Browning and Browning, *Public Finance*, pp. 62–65 (quotation from p. 62).

39. Nordlinger, *Autonomy*, p. 35. Also Joseph P. Kalt and M. A. Zupan, "Capture and Ideology in the Economic Theory of Politics," *American Economic Review* 74 (June 1984): 279–300.

40. Alvin W. Gouldner, *The Dialectic of Ideology and Technology: The Origins, Grammar, and Future of Ideology* (New York: Oxford University Press, 1976), pp. 234–235; Peter Navarro, *The Policy Game: How Special Interests and Ideologues Are Stealing America* (New York: Wiley, 1984), p. 100. Compare John Kenneth Galbraith, *The Anatomy of Power* (Boston: Houghton Mifflin, 1983), pp. 48–49, 84–85.

41. Schumpeter, *Capitalism, Socialism, and Democracy*, p. 129–130.

42. Hendrik Wilm Lambers, "The Vision," in *Schumpeter's Vision*: Capitalism, Socialism and Democracy *after 40 years*, ed. Arnold Heertje (New York: Praeger,

1981), p. 120; Herbert K. Zassenhaus, "Capitalism, Socialism and Democracy: the 'Vision' and the 'Theories,' " ibid., pp. 189–191; K. R. Popper, *The Open Society and Its Enemies* (New York: Harper Torchbooks, 1963), II, pp. 212–223.

43. Hoover, *The Economy, Liberty, and the State*, pp. 326–327. Also Peacock and Wiseman, *Growth of Public Expenditures*, pp. 27–28, 66–67, and passim; Knight, *Freedom and Reform*, p. 404; Friedman and Friedman, *Tyranny of the Status Quo*, p. 8; Robert Higgs, "The Effect of National Emergency," *Pathfinder* 4 (April 1982): 1–2; Peter Temin, "Government Actions in Times of Crisis: Lessons from the History of Drug Regulation," *Journal of Social History* 18 (Spring 1985): 433–438; Stephen Skowronek, *Building a New American State: The Expansion of National Administrative Capacities, 1877–1920* (New York: Cambridge University Press, 1982), p. 10. For an excellent development of the Crisis Hypothesis by a political scientist, emphasizing the governmental consequences but not neglecting the economic aspect, see Clinton L. Rossiter, *Constitutional Dictatorship: Crisis Government in the Modern Democracies* (Princeton, N.J.: Princeton University Press, 1948). Impressive econometric support for a version of the Crisis Hypothesis has recently been presented by Karen A. Rasler and William R. Thompson, "War Making and State Making: Governmental Expenditures, Tax Revenues, and Global Wars," *American Political Science Review* 79 (June 1985): 491–507.

CHAPTER TWO

1. George F. Break, "Issues in Measuring the Level of Government Activity," *American Economic Review* 72 (May 1982): 288–295; idem, "The Role of Government: Taxes, Transfers, and Spending," in *The American Economy in Transition*, ed. Martin Feldstein (Chicago: University of Chicago Press, 1980), pp. 617–656; Michael J. Boskin, "Federal Government Deficits: Some Myths and Realities," *American Economic Review* 72 (May 1982): 296–303; James E. Alt and K. Alec Chrystal, *Political Economics* (Berkeley: University of California Press, 1983), pp. 185–187.

2. Lance T. LeLoup, *Budgetary Politics* (Brunswick, Ohio: King's Court Communications, 1980), p. 41.

3. John L. Palmer and Isabel V. Sawhill, eds., *The Reagan Record: An Assessment of America's Changing Domestic Priorities* (Cambridge, Mass.: Ballinger, 1984), pp. 76, 182; Edgar K. Browning and Jacquelene M. Browning, *Public Finance and the Price System* (New York: Macmillan, 1983), pp. 189–190, 232–233.

4. Michael R. Darby, "Three-and-a-Half Million U.S. Employees Have Been Mislaid: Or, an Explanation of Unemployment, 1934–1941," *Journal of Political Economy* 84 (Feb. 1976): 1–16; J. R. Kesselman and N. E. Savin, "Three-and-a-Half Million Workers Never Were Lost," *Economic Inquiry* 16 (April 1978): 205–225; John Joseph Wallis and Daniel K. Benjamin, "Public Relief and Private Employment in the Great Depression," *Journal of Economic History* 41 (March 1981): 97–102; Gene Smiley, "Recent Unemployment Rate Estimates for the 1920s and 1930s," ibid. 43 (June 1983): 487–493.

5. James T. Bennett and Manuel H. Johnson, *The Political Economy of Federal Government Growth, 1959–1978* (College Station, Tex.: Center for Education and Research in Free Enterprise, 1980), p. 54.

6. A tremendous amount of such information appears in U.S. Bureau of the Census, *Historical Statistics of the United States, Colonial Times to 1970* (Washington, D.C.: U.S. Government Printing Office, 1975), pp. 1086–1134 on "Government Employment and Finances," which may be brought up to date by consulting the Census Bureau's annual *Statistical Abstract of the United States*.

7. Eric A. Nordlinger, *On the Autonomy of the Democratic State* (Cambridge, Mass.: Harvard University Press, 1981), p. 21.

8. James Willard Hurst, *Law and Markets in United States History: Different Modes of Bargaining Among Interests* (Madison: University of Wisconsin Press, 1982), pp. 122–123. Also Joseph D. Reid, Jr., "Tax Revolts in Historical Perspective," *National Tax Journal* 32 (June 1979): 69; John F. Witte, *The Politics and Development of the Federal Income Tax* (Madison: University of Wisconsin Press, 1985), passim. On tax incidence and the various costs associated with taxation, see Browning and Browning, *Public Finance*, pp. 291–451.

9. James M. Buchanan, *The Limits of Liberty: Between Anarchy and Leviathan* (Chicago: University of Chicago Press, 1975), pp. 163–164.

10. Murray L. Weidenbaum, *Business, Government, and the Public*, 2nd ed. (Englewood Cliffs, N.J.: Prentice-Hall, 1981), pp. 25–26.

11. Edward S. Herman, *Corporate Control, Corporate Power* (New York: Cambridge University Press, 1981), pp. 166–168; Douglas F. Greer, *Business, Government, and Society* (New York: Macmillan, 1983), pp. 531–534.

12. Richard B. McKenzie, *Bound To Be Free* (Stanford, Calif.: Hoover Institution Press, 1982), p. 18: "Through regulation, the government . . . induces private businesses and citizens to spend their dollars on accomplishing government objectives." Also Lawrence Brown, *New Policies, New Politics: Government's Response to Government's Growth* (Washington, D.C.: Brookings Institution, 1983), p. 40; Warren Nutter, *Political Economy and Freedom: A Collection of Essays* (Indianapolis: Liberty Press, 1983), p. 104.

13. Lawrence Brown draws a similar distinction between the government's share of GNP or employment and what he calls its "scope" ("the number of distinct activities government pursues") or its "scale" ("the number of citizens and groups these activities affect"); he notes that these scope and scale concepts are unrelated to the standard measures of the size of government. *New Policies, New Politics*, pp. 5–6, 40. For a heroic but unsuccessful attempt to measure the total allocational influence of government, see Bernard P. Herber and Paul U. Pawlik, "Measuring Government's Role in the Mixed Economy: A New Approach," *National Tax Journal* 36 (March 1983): 45–56. Herber and Pawlik's indices are hopelessly subjective, rigid, and arbitrary.

14. Richard Rose, "Are Laws a Cause, a Constraint, or Irrelevant to the Growth of Government?" *Studies in Public Policy Number 124* (Glasgow: Center for the Study of Public Policy, University of Strathclyde, 1984), pp. 5, 23. Also W. Mark Crain, Robert D. Tollison, Brian L. Goff, and Dick Carlson, "Legislator Specialization and the Size of Government," *Public Choice* 46 (1985): 314: "Before government can spend, tax, or grow, a law has to be passed."

15. LeLoup, *Budgetary Politics*, p. 91. Also Rose, "Are Laws a Cause," p. 27: "The coalition of interests that promotes more spending is even more formidable in defense of existing statutory entitlements."

16. As late as 1955, Social Security outlays under the Old-Age, Survivors, and Disability Insurance program were only $4.3 billion. In 1984 they were $178.2 billion. James R. Storey, "Income Security," in *The Reagan Experiment*, ed. John L. Palmer and Isabel V. Sawhill (Washington, D.C.: The Urban Institute Press, 1982), pp. 364–365; U.S. Office of Management and Budget, *The United States Budget in Brief, Fiscal Year 1986* (Washington, D.C.: U.S. Government Printing Office, 1985), p. 71. For detailed data on the period before 1971, see U.S. Bureau of the Census, *Historical Statistics*, pp. 340–351.

17. For a recent study motivated largely by such econometric concerns, see Karen A. Rasler and William R. Thompson, "War Making and State Making: Governmental Expenditures, Tax Revenues, and Global Wars," *American Political Science Review* 79 (June 1985): esp. 496–499.

18. Jacob Metzer, "How New Was the New Era? The Public Sector in the 1920's," *Journal of Economic History* 45 (March 1985): 119–126. Also the similar but

much more extensive investigation by John Maurice Clark, *The Costs of the World War to the American People* (New Haven, Conn.: Yale University Press, 1931). For a sensible consideration of this question, with reference to British data, see Alan T. Peacock and Jack Wiseman, *The Growth of Public Expenditure in the United Kingdom* (Princeton, N.J.: Princeton University Press, 1961), pp. 52–61.

19. Bennett and Johnson, *Federal Government Growth*, pp. 70–76. Combining the ratchet and the concentration hypothesis can usually be traced to Peacock and Wiseman's study of British government spending (*Growth of Public Expenditure*, esp. pp. 30, 118–120), a cautious and highly qualified study.

20. Browning and Browning, *Public Finance*, pp. 475–483; Wallace E. Oates, "Searching for Leviathan: An Empirical Study," *American Economic Review* 75 (Sept. 1985): 752. Oates also concludes (p. 756) that "there does not exist a strong, systematic relationship between the size of government and the degree of centralization of the public sector."

21. John Joseph Wallis argues that "[t]he fundamental change in government structure during the 1930s was the shift in expenditures from local to state and federal levels . . . [which] can be explained by financial provisions of the federal government programs." See "The Birth of the Old Federalism: Financing the New Deal, 1932–1940," *Journal of Economic History* 44 (March 1984): 139. Also idem, "Why 1933? The Origins and Timing of National Government Growth," in *Emergence of the Modern Political Economy*, ed. Robert Higgs (Greenwich, Conn.: JAI Press, 1985).

22. Sam Peltzman, "The Growth of Government," *Journal of Law and Economics* 23 (Oct. 1980): 209.

23. Rose, "Are Laws a Cause," p. 13. Also B. Guy Peters and Martin O. Heisler, "Thinking About Public Sector Growth: Conceptual, Operational, Theoretical, and Policy Considerations," in *Why Governments Grow: Measuring Public Sector Size*, ed. Charles Lewis Taylor (Beverly Hills, Calif.: Sage, 1983), pp. 178–181.

CHAPTER THREE

1. Thomas Sowell, *Knowledge and Decisions* (New York: Basic Books, 1980).

2. Douglass C. North, *Structure and Change in Economic History* (New York: Norton, 1981), pp. 45–58; James B. Kau and Paul H. Rubin, *Congressmen, Constituents, and Contributors: Determinants of Roll Call Voting in the House of Representatives* (Boston: Nijhoff, 1982); Joseph P. Kalt and M. A. Zupan, "Capture and Ideology in the Economic Theory of Politics," *American Economic Review* 74 (June 1984): 279–300; idem, "The Ideological Behavior of Legislators: Rational On-the-Job Consumption or Just a Residual?" Harvard Institute for Economic Research, Discussion Paper Number 1043, March 1984. Compare Sam Peltzman, "Constituent Interest and Congressional Voting," *Journal of Law and Economics* 27 (April 1984): 181–210.

3. Giovanni Sartori, "Politics, Ideology, and Belief Systems," *American Political Science Review* 63 (June 1969): 398. Also Homa Katouzian, *Ideology and Method in Economics* (New York: New York University Press, 1980), pp. 147–148; Herbert McClosky and John Zaller, *The American Ethos: Public Attitudes toward Capitalism and Democracy* (Cambridge, Mass.: Harvard University Press, 1984), p. 189.

4. A. James Reichley, *Conservatives in an Age of Change: The Nixon and Ford Administrations* (Washington, D.C.: The Brookings Institution, 1981), p. 3.

5. George C. Lodge, *The New American Ideology* (New York: Knopf, 1976), p. 7.

6. North, *Structure and Change*, p. 49.

7. Roy C. Macridis, *Contemporary Political Ideologies: Movements and Regimes* (Cambridge, Mass.: Winthrop 1980), p. 4.

8. David Joravsky, *The Lysenko Affair* (Cambridge, Mass.: Harvard University Press, 1970), p. 3.

9. G. William Domhoff, *Who Rules America Now?* (Englewood Cliffs, N.J.: Prentice-Hall, 1983), p. 99.

10. M. Seliger, *Ideology and Politics* (New York: Free Press, 1976), pp. 119–120.

11. Edward Shils, "Ideology. I. The Concept and Function of Ideology," *International Encyclopedia of the Social Sciences* 7 (1968): 66–76.

12. Aileen S. Kraditor, "Introduction" [to a special issue on Conservatism and History], *Continuity* 4–5 (1982): 1–9; idem, *The Radical Persuasion, 1890–1917: Aspects of the Intellectual History and the Historiography of Three American Radical Organizations* (Baton Rouge: Louisiana State University Press, 1981), p. 102. Also Robert Higgs, "When Ideological Worlds Collide: Reflections on Kraditor's 'Radical Persuasion,'" *Continuity* (Fall 1983): 99–112, and Aileen Kraditor, "Robert Higgs on 'The Radical Persuasion,'" ibid., pp. 113–123.

13. Seliger, *Ideology and Politics*; idem, *The Marxist Conception of Ideology: A Critical Essay* (Cambridge: Cambridge University Press, 1977). Also Alvin W. Gouldner, *The Dialectic of Ideology and Technology: The Origins, Grammar, and Future of Ideology* (New York: Oxford University Press, 1982), pp. 9, 13, 44, 211 and passim.

14. Clifford Geertz, "Ideology as a Cultural System," in *Ideology and Discontent*, ed. David E. Apter (New York: Free Press, 1964), pp. 52–64. Also W. Lance Bennett, *Public Opinion in American Politics* (New York: Harcourt Brace Jovanovich, 1980), pp. 158–184, 216–218, 410–412.

15. Seliger, *Marxist Conception*, p. 56. Alvin W. Gouldner retorts that Marxism itself is "the false consciousness of cultural bourgeoisie who have been radicalized." *The Future of Intellectuals and the Rise of the New Class* (New York: Seabury Press, 1979), p. 75.

16. Seliger, *Marxist Conception*, p. 57.

17. Kraditor, *Radical Persuasion*. Also Robert E. Lane, "Personality, Political: I. The Study of Political Personality," *International Encyclopedia of the Social Sciences* 12 (1968): 19.

18. Mancur Olson, *The Logic of Collective Action: Public Goods and the Theory of Groups* (Cambridge, Mass.: Harvard University Press, 1965), p. 127. Also Russell Hardin, *Collective Action* (Baltimore: Johns Hopkins Press, 1982), p. 2 and passim.

19. Olson, *Logic of Collective Action*, pp. 2, 51, 60–65, 133–134; Bruno S. Frey, *Modern Political Economy* (Oxford: Martin Robertson, 1978), pp. 92–93, 97–98. Compare John Mark Hansen, "The Political Economy of Group Membership," *American Political Science Review* 79 (March 1985): esp. 93. Gary Becker observes that "the emphasis on free riding in many discussions of the effectiveness of pressure groups is a little excessive because political success is determined by relative, not absolute, degree of control over free riding." See "A Theory of Competition among Pressure Groups for Political Influence," *Quarterly Journal of Economics* 98 (Aug. 1983): 380. But the question remains: How does a large political action group exercise *any* control over free riding? The means Becker mentions (p. 377) all fall within Olson's two categories (selective material incentives or coercion) and hence apply little if at all to many forms of large-scale collective action.

20. For an elaborate model of political behavior based on the assumption of such a utility function, see Becker, "Competition among Pressure Groups," esp. pp. 372, 374. For an excellent discussion of the conventional neoclassical utility function and an argument that it is inadequate for the analysis of political action, see Howard Margolis, *Selfishness, Altruism, and Rationality: A Theory of Social Choice* (Chicago: University of Chicago Press, 1982), esp. pp. 6–11, 66–69. Despite Margolis's keen insight into problems of social choice, his solution, a "Darwinian" model, seems contrived.

21. G. Warren Nutter, *Political Economy and Freedom: A Collection of Essays* (Indianapolis: Liberty Press, 1983), p. xiii. Nutter added (p. xiv) that "[n]o theory of social behavior is complete unless it allows for the passion of the mob, the zeal of the martyr, the loyalty of the palace guard, the insatiability of the egomaniac."

22. Amartya K. Sen, "Rational Fools: A Critique of the Behavioral Foundations of Economic Theory," *Philosophy & Public Affairs* 6 (Summer 1977): 336; North, *Structure and Change*, p. 46. Amyra Grossbard-Shechtman observes that "[e]conomists generally recognize that utility functions are based on biological and cultural factors, but they tend to leave the study of these factors to scholars from other disciplines such as psychology, biology or anthropology. Although such division of labor could in principle be efficient, in practice the study of any particular subject rarely combines insights from the various perspectives." Review of *Microeconomics and Human Behavior: Toward a New Synthesis of Economics and Psychology* by David A. Alhadeff, *Journal of Economic Literature* 21 (June 1983): 553–554. Also Robert Dorfman's review of *The Economist as Preacher and Other Essays* by George Stigler, *Journal of Economic Literature* 22 (March 1984): 105; James E. Alt and K. Alec Chrystal, *Political Economics* (Berkeley: University of California Press, 1983), p. 7.

23. North, *Structure and Change*, p. 53. Sartori makes virtually the same point when he describes "ideological politics" as "a situation in which the utility scale of each actor is altered by an ideological scale. Hence . . . the logic of interest no longer suffices to explain, and even less to predict, political behavior." See "Politics, Ideology, and Belief Systems," p. 410. Similar points are made by Brian Barry, *Sociologists, Economists, and Democracy* (Chicago: University of Chicago Press, 1978), pp. 39–40; Albert O. Hirschman, *Essays in Trespassing: Economics to Politics and Beyond* (New York: Cambridge University Press, 1981), pp. 239–240; idem, *Shifting Involvements: Private Interest and Public Action* (Princeton, N.J.: Princeton University Press, 1982), pp. 85–90.

24. Russell Hardin argues against this approach, which he calls the "modified theory of collective action." *Collective Action*, p. 14. But after dismissing it at the outset, he admits it in midstream in his excellent Chapter 7 (pp. 101–124), which bears the unnecessarily defensive title "Extrarational Motivations." There is no good argument for taking people's interest in so-called noneconomic ends to be either irrational or extrarational. To be rational is to suit means to ends. The nature of the ends reveals nothing about whether people are rational in seeking them. For sophisticated observations on rationality, see Sen, "Rational Fools," pp. 342–344; Jon Elster, *Sour Grapes: Studies in the Subversion of Rationality* (Cambridge: Cambridge University Press, 1983), esp. pp. 1–42. What I call rationality corresponds to Elster's "thin" rationality. What Elster calls "broad" rationality would be better called something else.

25. Hardin, *Collective Action*, p. 109; Richard D. Auster and Morris Silver, *The State as a Firm: Economic Forces in Political Development* (Boston: Nijhoff, 1979), p. 50.

26. Jon Elster writes that "[m]y self-image is not a benefit: it is what defines what counts as a benefit." He adds, however, that this conceptualization is "treacherous ground where it is best to shun any pretension to false precision" as we lack "an adequate conceptual scheme to deal with these matters." See "Rationality, Morality and Collective Action," unpublished George Lurcy Lecture, University of Chicago, May 1984, p. 29. Compare his suggestion that identity may be only a "by-product" in *Sour Grapes*, pp. 93, 100, 107–108. An interesting analytical proposal (Sen, "Rational Fools," pp. 337–341) involves meta-rankings—that is, rankings of preference rankings (or utility functions), perhaps associated with particular group memberships or ideological convictions. Also Albert O. Hirschman, "Against Parsimony: Three Easy Ways of Complicating Some Categories of Economic Discourse," *American Economic Review* 74 (May 1984): 89–96. Hirschman (p. 92) refers to a proposal by Alessandro Pizzorno that an individual's participation in collective action be viewed

as "an investment in individual and group identity." Additional discussion of meta-preferences appears in Hirschman, *Shifting Involvements*, pp. 68–71.

27. Murray Webster, Jr., *Actions and Actors: Principles of Social Psychology* (Cambridge, Mass.: Winthrop, 1975), pp. 377–396; Elisha Y. Babad, Max Birnbaum, and Kenneth D. Benne, *The Social Self: Group Influences on Personal Identity* (Beverly Hills, Calif.: Sage, 1983); Peter L. Berger and Thomas Luckmann, *The Social Construction of Reality: A Treatise in the Sociology of Knowledge* (Garden City, N.Y.: Anchor Books, 1967), pp. 131–132, 173–174; Erik H. Erikson, "Identity, Psychosocial," *International Encyclopedia of the Social Sciences* 7 (1968): 61–63; Muzafer Sherif, "Self Concept," ibid. 14: 150–159; Tamotsu Shibutani, "Mead, George Herbert," ibid. 10: esp. p. 86; Lane, "Political Personality," ibid. 12: 17; Murray Edelman, *The Symbolic Uses of Politics* (Urbana: University of Illinois Press, 1964), pp. 84–87.

28. Tibor Scitovsky, *The Joyless Economy: An Inquiry into Human Satisfaction and Consumer Dissatisfaction* (New York: Oxford University Press, 1976), p. 115. Also Wilhelm Ropke, *A Humane Economy: The Social Framework of the Free Market* (Chicago: Henry Regnery, 1971), p. 91. According to the sociologist Amitai Etzioni, "Individuals function as members of social groups, which means that they have emotional ties to each other that are supplemented by cognitive and normative bonds. . . . The impact of an organization on its members tends to grow in extent and depth the broader its scope" [scope denotes "the number of social spheres into which an organization penetrates"]. "Societal Turnability: A Theoretical Treatment," in *The Economic Consequences of Reduced Military Spending*, ed, Bernard Udis (Lexington, Mass.: Lexington Books, 1972), p. 362.

29. Sherif, "Self Concept," p. 154; Babad, Birnbaum, and Benne, *Social Self*, esp. pp. 236–237; Peter L. Berger, Brigitte Berger, and Hansfried Kellner, *The Homeless Mind: Modernization and Consciousness* (New York: Vintage Books, 1974), esp. pp. 74–79.

30. Bennett, *Public Opinion*, p. 107; David Satter, "Soviet Threat Is One of Ideas More than Arms," *Wall Street Journal* (May 23, 1983). For perceptive observations on the relation of identity and ideology, see Gouldner, *Dialectic of Ideology and Technology*, pp. 31, 47, 56–57, 68, 84, 176.

31. Samuel Bowles, "State Structures and Political Practices: A Reconsideration of the Liberal Democratic Conception of Politics and Accountability," in *Capitalism and Democracy: Schumpeter Revisited*, ed. Richard D. Coe and Charles K. Wilber (Notre Dame, Ind.: University of Notre Dame Press, 1985), p. 164. Compare Mancur Olson, *The Rise and Decline of Nations: Economic Growth, Stagflation, and Social Rigidities* (New Haven, Conn.: Yale University Press, 1982), pp. 19–25, 85; Gouldner, *Dialectic of Ideology and Technology*, p. 211; Amartya Sen, "Goals, Commitments, and Identity," *Journal of Law, Economics, and Organization* 1 (Fall 1985): 348–349; and Robert Higgs, "Identity and Cooperation: A Comment on Sen's Alternative Program," ibid. 3 (Spring 1987). Hansen distinguishes "solidarity benefits," gained by associating with comrades, and "expressive benefits," gained by publicly contributing to a worthy cause. "The Political Economy of Group Membership," pp. 79–80. Obviously the two often go together.

32. Robert Cameron Mitchell, "National Environmental Lobbies and the Apparent Illogic of Collective Action," in *Collective Decision Making: Applications from Public Choice Theory*, ed. Clifford S. Russell (Baltimore: Johns Hopkins University Press, 1979), pp. 110–111; Karl-Dieter Opp, "Economics, Sociology, and Political Protest," in *Theoretical Models and Empirical Analyses: Contributions to the Explanation of Individual Actions and Collective Phenomena*, ed. Werner Raub (Utrecht: E.S.-Publications, 1982), pp. 166–185. Opp notes (p. 180) that "acting in accordance with internalized norms is intrinsically beneficial and deviating from such norms is intrinsically costly." The question remains: What determines the extent to which an individual will allow moral norms to dictate his participation in collective action? For an

insightful analysis of this question, see Michael Hechter, "A Theory of Group Solidarity," in *The Micro-foundations of Macrosociology*, ed. Michael Hechter (Philadelphia: Temple University Press, 1983), pp. 16–57.

33. Steven Kelman interviewed "the most active Washington-based participants in environmental policy formation outside the Environmental Protection Agency" and discovered "a liberal-conservative ideological division in the reactions of respondents": "The economists say, 'Use the market,' and both supporters and opponents go on automatic pilot and react generally either for or against 'the market'—not really ever hearing the narrower efficiency argument the economists are making." See "Economists and the Environmental Muddle," *Public Interest* (Summer 1981): 107, 109, 122. More generally, see Henry J. Aaron, *Politics and the Professors: The Great Society in Perspective* (Washington, D.C.: The Brookings Institution, 1978), esp. pp. 146–167.

34. Sartori, "Politics, Ideology, and Belief Systems," p. 409.

35. Reichley, *Conservatives*, p. 4.

36. Sartori, "Politics, Ideology, and Belief Systems," p. 407. Also Seliger, *Ideology and Politics*, p. 275; McClosky and Zaller, *American Ethos*, pp. 11–12, 152–153, 234; Thomas R. Dye and L. Harmon Zeigler, *The Irony of Democracy: An Uncommon Introduction to American Politics*, 5th ed. (Monterey, Calif.: Duxbury Press, 1981), pp. 154, 178, 305.

37. Larry G. Gerber, *The Limits of Liberalism: Josephus Daniels, Henry Stimson, Bernard Baruch, Donald Richberg, Felix Frankfurter and the Development of the Modern American Political Economy* (New York: New York University Press, 1983), p. 11. Taking the same approach is Thomas K. McCraw, *Prophets of Regulation: Charles Francis Adams, Louis D. Brandeis, James M. Landis, and Alfred E. Kahn* (Cambridge, Mass.: Belknap Press, 1984) as well as countless political biographers. Also Daniel J. Levinson, "Personality, Political: II. Conservatism and Radicalism," *International Encyclopedia of the Social Sciences* 12 (1968): 13.

38. Robert A. Dahl, *Democracy in the United States: Promise and Performance*, 3rd ed. (Chicago: Rand McNally, 1976), pp. 364, 370.

39. Dye and Zeigler, *Irony of Democracy*, pp. 194–195; Philip E. Converse, "The Nature of Belief Systems in Mass Publics," in *Ideology and Discontent*, ed. Apter, pp. 206–261; Herbert McClosky, "Consensus and Ideology in American Politics," *American Political Science Review* 58 (June 1964): 361–382.

40. Dahl, *Democracy*, p. 371. Domhoff, *Who Rules America Now?*, p. 128, refers to "the self-deceiving ideology that the country has no ideology."

41. William S. Maddox and Stuart A. Lilie, *Beyond Liberal and Conservative: Reassessing the Political Spectrum* (Washington, D.C.: Cato Institute, 1984), p. 179. Compare the fourfold classifications of McClosky and Zaller, *American Ethos*, pp. 245–258.

42. For an extensive survey of the literature and discussion of the issues, see Bennett, *Public Opinion*, pp. 48–56.

43. Sartori, "Politics, Ideology, and Belief Systems," p. 411; Gouldner, *Dialectic of Ideology and Technology*, p. 28.

44. Richard Hofstadter, *The American Political Tradition, And the Men Who Made It* (New York: Vintage, 1974), p. 178. Also Shils, "Ideology," p. 75; Olson, *Rise and Decline*, p. 77; Kevin P. Phillips, *Post-Conservative America: People, Politics and Ideology in a Time of Crisis* (New York: Random House, 1982), pp. 4, 240; Alt and Chrystal, *Political Economics*, p. 159; Gouldner, *Dialectic of Ideology and Technology*, pp. 244–247; Stephen Skowronek, *Building a New American State: The Expansion of National Administrative Capacities, 1877–1920* (New York: Cambridge University Press, 1982), p. 31; William A. Schambra, "Progressive Liberalism and American 'Community,'" *Public Interest* (Summer 1985): 42.

45. Sartori, "Politics, Ideology, and Belief Systems," pp. 410–411.

46. Vicente Navarro, "The Labor Process and Health: A Historical Materialist Interpretation," *International Journal of Health Services* 12 (1982): 8.

47. Edelman, *The Symbolic Uses of Politics*, esp. pp. 114–151; idem, *Political Language: Words That Succeed and Policies That Fail* (New York: Academic Press, 1977), esp. pp. 41, 109–113; David V. J. Bell, *Power, Influence, and Authority: An Essay in Political Linguistics* (New York: Oxford University Press, 1975), esp. pp. 10, 13, 98; Eric A. Nordlinger, *On the Autonomy of the Democratic State* (Cambridge, Mass.: Harvard University Press, 1981), p. 90; Francis E. Rourke, *Bureaucracy, Politics, and Public Policy*, 2nd ed. (Boston: Little, Brown, 1976), p. 98; Bennett, *Public Opinion*, pp. 249, 252, 258.

48. Huxley as quoted in Vermont Royster, "A Matter of Words," *Wall Street Journal* (Oct. 12, 1983). Also George Orwell, *The Collected Essays, Journalism and Letters of George Orwell*, ed. Sonia Orwell and Ian Angus (New York: Harcourt, Brace & World, 1968), IV, esp. pp. 127–128, 139. George Boas declared that "nothing . . . stands in the way of ideological extension. Irrationality, nonsense, lack of evidence, nothing is strong enough to dissuade people from accepting any idea if it is couched in the proper terminology." *Johns Hopkins Magazine* 36 (Oct. 1984): 17.

49. Lenin as quoted in Paul Eidelberg, "Karl Marx and the Declaration of Independence: The Meaning of Marxism," *Intercollegiate Review* 20 (Spring/Summer 1984): 3; Viguerie and Morris Dees as quoted in John J. Fialka, "Liberals' Fund-Raisers Find Their Contributors Are Less Predictable Than Conservatives' Donors," *Wall Street Journal* (Dec. 14, 1983). Also Elizabeth Drew, *Politics and Money: The New Road to Corruption* (New York: Macmillan, 1983), pp. 130–131.

50. Geertz, "Ideology as a Cultural System," pp. 48, 64. Also Joravsky, *Lysenko Affair*, p. 6. In a discussion of a quintessential ideologue—Louis Brandeis, expounding his views in a pre–World War I article—Thomas K. McCraw notes that "[h]e brought every symbol and ideological appeal to bear, turned every conceivable argument to his advantage, and invested the whole with his distinguished moral passion. So stirring was Brandeis's rhetoric that it is difficult to keep in mind what he was in fact proposing: that small retailers be exempted from the antitrust laws and permitted, in concert with each other, to fix the prices of consumer goods." See "Rethinking the Trust Problem," in *Regulation in Perspective: Historical Essays*, ed. Thomas K. McCraw (Cambridge, Mass.: Harvard University Press, 1981), p. 49.

51. Geertz, "Ideology as a Cultural System," p. 58.

52. Ibid., p. 58. I do not mean to suggest that nonideological communication, including that of scientists and philosophers, avoids rhetoric. One sense of rhetoric is "mere words"; another is "exploring thought by conversation." Therefore, everyone who carries on reasoned conversations uses rhetoric. Donald N. McCloskey, "The Rhetoric of Economics," *Journal of Economic Literature* 21 (June 1983): 481–517, and at greater length *The Rhetoric of Economics* (Madison: University of Wisconsin Press, 1985). My point is only that ideological expression has a characteristic rhetorical style, shaped especially by the speaker's desire to provoke political mobilization. For an example of how even very good economists miss the point of ideological rhetoric, see Edgar K. Browning and Jacquelene M. Browning, *Public Finance and the Price System*, 2nd ed. (New York: Macmillan, 1983), p. 68. The Brownings assert that "rational voter ignorance accounts for the generally low level of political discourse. . . . [with its] slogans, oversimplifications, inadequate theories, and misleading facts."

53. My terms "discriminating-" and "universalistic flag words" have rough counterparts in what students of public opinion call "position" and "valence" issues. See Maddox and Lilie, *Beyond Liberal and Conservative*, p. 135.

54. See Edward Tufte's revealing analysis of the rhetoric employed in the major party platforms, the annual economic reports of the President, and the annual reports of the Council of Economic Advisers. Tufte concludes that ideology "contributed very much to the determination of economic priorities expressed" in these documents:

"Democrats were sensitive to unemployment; Republicans to inflation. . . . Furthermore, political party ideology has shaped economic priorities . . . far more than the objective economic conditions prevailing at the time of the reports." *Political Control of the Economy* (Princeton, N.J.: Princeton University Press, 1978), pp. 74–83 (quotations from pp. 82–83).

55. Karl Marx, *Capital: A Critique of Political Economy* (New York: Modern Library, n.d.), pp. 291–292.

56. Ibid., pp. 282, 291.

57. John Stuart Mill, *On Liberty* (New York: Appleton-Century-Crofts, 1947), pp. 84–85.

58. Gouldner, *Dialectic of Ideology and Technology*, p. 197.

59. Frank S. Meyer, *In Defense of Freedom: A Conservative Credo* (Chicago: Henry Regnery, 1962), p. 69.

60. Berger and Luckmann, *Social Construction of Reality*, p. 128.

61. Seliger, *Ideology and Politics*, p. 168.

62. North, *Structure and Change*, p. 51; Kraditor, *Radical Persuasion*, passim.

63. Seliger, *Marxist Conception*, pp. 99–104.

64. Seliger, *Ideology and Politics*, p. 168.

65. Ibid.

66. Tom Wolfe, "Idea Fashions of the Eighties: After Marx, What?" *Imprimis* 13 (Jan. 1984): 1–6. Wolfe views the intellectuals' susceptibility to fashion as "the key to the intellectual history of the United States in the twentieth century" (p. 1).

67. K. R. Popper, *The Open Society and Its Enemies. Vol. I. The Spell of Plato* (New York: Harper Torchbooks, 1963).

68. Seliger, *Ideology and Politics*, p. 156. Also Gouldner, *Dialectic of Ideology and Technology*, pp. 17, 19, 34–36, 112, 115.

69. Geertz, "Ideology as a Cultural System," pp. 71–72. Also Seliger, *Ideology and Politics*, pp. 154–159; North, *Structure and Change*, p. 55.

70. Joravsky, *Lysenko Affair*, p. 195 (also pp. 3, 358, n. 7).

CHAPTER FOUR

1. Joseph D. Reid, Jr., "Understanding Political Events in the New Economic History," *Journal of Economic History* 37 (June 1977): 303, 328; Jerold Waltman, "Origins of the Federal Income Tax," *Mid-America* 62 (Oct. 1980): 158. Also James E. Alt and K. Alec Chrystal, *Political Economics* (Berkeley: University of California Press, 1983), p. 126.

2. *Essays of William Graham Sumner*, ed. Albert G. Keller and Maurice R. Davie (New Haven, Conn.: Yale University Press, 1934), II, p. 473.

3. For example, Allan H. Meltzer and Scott F. Richard, studying the growth of governmental spending between 1937 and 1977, completely omit data for 1941–1945 from their "Tests of a Rational Theory of the Size of the Government," *Public Choice* 41 (1983): 403–418. Damodar Gujarati presents a list of sixty statutes to show the "Growth of Regulation in the United States" during 1932–1982, but the list shows only one act (the Taft-Hartley Act of 1947) between 1939 and 1953, the period of World War II and the Korean War. *Government and Business* (New York: McGraw-Hill, 1984), pp. 7–9.

4. In a different context Russell Hardin notes that "in many choice situations, what happened in the past matters in a fundamental way . . . because life at an earlier time . . . may have changed one's tastes." *Collective Action* (Baltimore: Johns Hopkins University Press, 1982), pp. 82–83.

5. Paul A. David, *Technical Choice, Innovation, and Economic Growth: Essays on American and British Experience in the Nineteenth Century* (New York: Cambridge

University Press, 1975), pp. 11, 15; Joseph A. Schumpeter, *Capitalism, Socialism, and Democracy*, 3rd ed. (New York: Harper & Row, 1950), p. 72. Also Paul A. David, "Clio and the Economics of QWERTY," *American Economic Review* 75 (May 1985): 332.

6. Others who have recognized the importance of path dependency include Alt and Chrystal, *Political Economics*, p. 248; G. Warren Nutter, *Political Economy and Freedom: A Collection of Essays* (Indianapolis: Liberty Press, 1983), pp. 44, 97; and Jonathan R. T. Hughes, *The Governmental Habit: Economic Controls from Colonial Times to the Present* (New York: Basic Books, 1977), passim. In a different but related context, and for rather different reasons, Gary Becker verged on this perspective when he said that sunk costs are not sunk in the political sector. See "A Theory of Competition among Pressure Groups for Political Influence," *Quarterly Journal of Economics* 98 (Aug. 1983): 383.

7. Edward S. Herman, *Corporate Control, Corporate Power* (New York: Cambridge University Press, 1981), pp. 299–300. For comparative international data on the growth of government, see Simon Kuznets, *Modern Economic Growth: Rate, Structure, and Spread* (New Haven, Conn.: Yale University Press, 1966), pp. 236–239; Leila Pathirane and Derek W. Blades, "Defining and Measuring the Public Sector: Some International Comparisons," *Review of Income and Wealth* 28 (Sept. 1982): 261–289; Alt and Chrystal, *Political Economics*, pp. 199–219.

8. James T. Bennett and Manuel H. Johnson, *The Political Economy of Federal Government Growth: 1959–1978* (College Station, Tex.: Center for Education and Research in Free Enterprise, 1980), pp. 70–72, citing Moses Abramovitz and Vera F. Eliasberg, *The Growth of Public Employment in Great Britain* (Princeton, N.J.: Princeton University Press, 1957) and Alan T. Peacock and Jack Wiseman, *The Growth of Public Expenditure in the United Kingdom* (Princeton, N.J.: Princeton University Press, 1961). Peacock and Wiseman's explanation of the spending ratchet in British history considers other elements as well; see esp. pp. 27–28, 66–67. Also Thomas R. Dye, *Understanding Public Policy*, 2nd ed. (Englewood Cliffs, N.J.: Prentice-Hall, 1975), pp. 197–199; Frances Fox Piven and Richard A. Cloward, *The New Class War* (New York: Pantheon Books, 1982), p. 133.

9. My distinction between big government and Big Government, along with my focus on the latter, explains why this book has little to say about fiscal and monetary policies, deficits, inflation, Keynesianism, and related issues that pertain to the government's macroeconomic policies, whether during crises or at other times during the twentieth century. The U.S. government possessed the authority to conduct fiscal and monetary policies, including the power to incur budgetary deficits or to inflate the money stock, from the beginning. Of course, the government did not permanently and deliberately exercise these powers for macroeconomic purposes until the 1930s, especially after the recession of 1937–1938. But that change signified only a different way of exercising a long-established power, not an increment of Big Government in my sense.

10. Peter Navarro, *The Policy Game: How Special Interests and Ideologues Are Stealing America* (New York: Wiley, 1984), p. 45; Samuel Bowles, "State Structures and Political Practices: A Reconsideration of the Liberal Democratic Conception of Politics and Accountability," in *Capitalism and Democracy: Schumpeter Revisited*, ed. Richard D. Coe and Charles K. Wilber (Notre Dame, Ind. University of Notre Dame Press, 1985), p. 178.

11. Eric A. Nordlinger, *On the Autonomy of the Democratic State* (Cambridge, Mass.: Harvard University Press, 1981), p. 8. Also Joseph P. Kalt, "Public Goods and the Theory of Government," *Cato Journal* 1 (Fall 1981): 580–583; Lawrence D. Brown, *New Policies, New Politics: Government's Response to Government's Growth* (Washington, D.C.: Brookings Institution, 1983), p. 45; Bruno S. Frey, *Modern Political Economy* (Oxford: Martin Robertson, 1978), pp. 95, 155; Gordon Tullock,

review of *The Rise and Decline of Nations* by Mancur Olson, in *Public Choice* 40 (1983): 114; Alvin W. Gouldner, *The Dialectic of Ideology and Technology: The Origins, Grammar, and Future of Ideology* (New York: Oxford University Press, 1982), pp. 238–239; Stanley Reiter and Jonathan Hughes, "A Preface on Modeling the Regulated United States Economy," *Hofstra Law Review* 9 (Summer 1981): 1404 ("the existence of costs and other difficulties of forming coalitions . . . gives to those whose hands are on the instruments of state power a degree of freedom of action which makes them true strategic players in the game"). Over forty years ago, Frank Knight observed that "in the making of laws, but more especially in their interpretation and application, the personnel of government at any moment, and particularly individuals in key positions, necessarily have considerable discretionary power." *Freedom and Reform: Essays in Economics and Social Philosophy* (Indianapolis: Liberty Press, 1982), p. 231. For an exceptionally full and careful treatment of this important issue, with a valuable survey of the related economic literature and an illuminating empirical application, see Charlotte Twight, "Government Manipulation of Constitutional-Level Transaction Costs: An Economic Theory and Its Application to Off-Budget Expenditure through the Federal Financing Bank," (Ph.D. diss., University of Washington, 1983).

12. Nordlinger, *Autonomy*, p. 76. Also Dye, *Understanding Public Policy*, pp. 197–199; W. Lance Bennett, *Public Opinion in American Politics* (New York: Harcourt Brace Jovanovich, 1980), pp. 218, 269; Barry D. Karl, *The Uneasy State: The United States from 1915 to 1945* (Chicago: University of Chicago Press, 1983), p. 211.

13. The modern imperative that government "do something" in a crisis is well established and appreciated. Brown, *New Policies, New Politics*, pp. 21, 28; Bennett, *Public Opinion*, pp. 353–354; Murray Edelman, *The Symbolic Uses of Politics* (Urbana: University of Illinois Press, 1964), pp. 78–83; Thomas R. Dye and L. Harmon Zeigler, *The Irony of Democracy: An Uncommon Introduction to American Politics*, 5th ed. (Monterey, Calif.: Duxbury Press, 1981), pp. 283–284, 296, 313; George P. Shultz and Kenneth W. Dam, *Economic Policy Beyond the Headlines* (New York: Norton 1977), pp. 2, 155, 205.

14. Frankfurter to Walter Lippmann, April 12, 1932, as quoted in Larry G. Gerber, *The Limits of Liberalism: Josephus Daniels, Henry Stimson, Bernard Baruch, Donald Richberg, Felix Frankfurter and the Development of the Modern American Political Economy* (New York: New York University Press, 1983), pp. 267–268.

15. Bertolt Brecht, "Guns Before Butter," 1939.

16. Richard D. Auster and Morris Silver, *The State as a Firm: Economic Forces in Political Development* (Boston: Martinus Nijhoff, 1979), pp. 57–62. John W. Eley speaks of "mobilization within a national mobilization," that is, "concerted efforts by affected groups to marshall their political and economic resources in order to prevent or reduce negative consequences from governmental policies." See "Management Structures for Industrial Mobilization in the 1980s: Lessons from World War II," in *Mobilization and the National Defense*, ed. Hardy L. Merritt and Luther F. Carter (Washington, D.C.: National Defense University Press, 1985), p. 33.

17. Murray Weidenbaum has observed that the federal government's use of its procurement policies to promote auxilliary social and economic objectives, which began in earnest during the New Deal and World War II, has the "advantages" of not requiring "additional, direct appropriations from the Treasury," and therefore "restrictive procurement provisions seem to be costless." The "disadvantages, being more indirect, receive less attention." *Business, Government, and the Public*, 2nd ed. (Englewood Cliffs, N.J.: Prentice-Hall, 1981), pp. 176–177.

18. Nordlinger, *Autonomy*, p. 57. Also Alt and Chrystal, *Political Economics*, p. 194; James E. Alt, "The Evolution of Tax Structures," *Public Choice* 41 (1983):

183, 208–210; Edgar K. Browning and Jacquelene M. Browning, *Public Finance and the Price System*, 2nd ed. (New York: Macmillan, 1983), p. 72.

19. Walter Y. Oi, "The Economic Cost of the Draft," *American Economic Review* 57 (May 1967): 39–62; Martin Anderson, ed., *The Military Draft: Selected Readings on Conscription* (Stanford, Calif.: Hoover Institution Press, 1982), esp. pp. 347–389; Browning and Browning, *Public Finance*, pp. 412–416.

20. Frey, *Modern Political Economy*, pp. 30, 109, 117, 120.

21. Compare Becker, "Competition among Pressure Groups," pp. 373, 381–388. In Becker's model, people are assumed not only to know about deadweight costs but to base their political behavior on such knowledge. Becker offers no empirical evidence in support of this assumption, which seems to me far-fetched.

22. Ellis Hawley, "Three Facets of Hooverian Associationalism: Lumber, Aviation, and Movies, 1921–1930," in *Regulation in Perspective: Historical Essays*, ed. Thomas K. McCraw (Cambridge, Mass.: Harvard University Press, 1981), p. 98. For a catalog of all the arguments why the market economy must be abandoned during a large-scale war, see Donald H. Wallace, *Economic Controls and Defense* (New York: Twentieth Century Fund, 1953). For a recent reaffirmation of this view, see Sir Alec Cairncross, "Economics in Theory and Practice," *American Economic Review* 75 (May 1985): 3–5.

23. J. M. Clark, "Basic Problems and Policies," in Wallace, *Economic Controls and Defense*, p. 245: "No feasible tax system . . . could possibly divert to public use as large a percentage of the country's dollar income as the percentage of its real resources which all-out war would call for."

24. On the higher costs of faster resource reallocation, see Armen A. Alchian and William R. Allen, *University Economics: Elements of Inquiry*, 3rd ed. (Belmont, Calif.: Wadsworth, 1972), pp. 265–268. The only evidence I have found that any governmental official appreciated this basic economic relationship is the statement of Jesse Jones, head of the Reconstruction Finance Corporation, that during World War II, "We had to hurry. Haste, of course, added to the cost." *Fifty Billion Dollars: My Thirteen Years with the RFC* (New York: Macmillan, 1951), p. 419. On the relation between free-market prices and risk-bearing, see J. R. Hicks, *Value and Capital: An Inquiry into Some Fundamental Principles of Economic Theory*, 2nd ed. (Oxford: At the Clarendon Press, 1946), pp. 125–126, 143, or any modern textbook in the economics of finance.

25. Francis E. Rourke, *Bureaucracy, Politics, and Public Policy*, 2nd ed. (Boston: Little, Brown, 1976), p. 30; Bruce D. Porter, "Parkinson's Law Revisited: War and the Growth of American Government," *Public Interest* (Summer 1980): 68; Jack Hirshleifer, *Price Theory and Its Applications* (Englewood Cliffs, N.J.: Prentice-Hall, 1976), p. 486; F. A. Hayek, *The Constitution of Liberty* (Chicago: Henry Regnery, 1972), pp. 290–291. With respect to the "technical context of regulation," Samuel Hays has written that "[t]he mass of detail constitutes a barrier to ferreting out the choices and frustrates a wide range of interested parties, including legislators, judges, other administrators, professionals, and the general public." "Political Choice in Regulatory Administration," in *Regulation in Perspective*, ed. McCraw, p. 145. Reiter and Hughes, "A Preface," p. 1417, make a similar point. For a beautiful example, see David A. Stockman's account of how the bureaucrats of the Department of Health and Human Services "cooperated" when asked to prepare options for cutting Social Security benefits. *The Triumph of Politics: How the Reagan Revolution Failed* (New York: Harper & Row, 1986), p. 186.

26. Rourke, *Bureaucracy*, passim; Richard B. McKenzie and Gordon Tullock, *The New World of Economics: Explorations into the Human Experience* (Homewood, Ill.: Richard D. Irwin, 1975), pp. 204–207.

27. Bernard H. Siegan, *Economic Liberties and the Constitution* (Chicago: Univer-

sity of Chicago Press, 1980); Paul L. Murphy, *The Constitution in Crisis Times, 1918–1969* (New York: Harper Torchbooks, 1972).

28. Navarro provides other examples of political entrepreneurs who have "helped to overcome the well-known inertia of American consumers, taxpayers, and citizens." *Policy Game*, pp. 48, 164–165, 207 (quotation from p. 164). Also Theodore E. Keeler, "Theories of Regulation and the Deregulation Movement," *Public Choice* 44 (1984): 130; Hardin, *Collective Action*, pp. 35–37. Lately even the mighty Pentagon has suffered defeat at the hands of a determined congressman. John J. Fialka, "Oregon Congressman Outflanks the Pentagon In Single-Minded, Single-Handed Weapon War," *Wall Street Journal* (Sept. 13, 1985): 54.

29. Victor R. Fuchs, "The Economics of Health in a Post-Industrial Society," *Public Interest* (Summer 1979): 16; Shultz and Dam, *Economic Policy Beyond the Headlines*, pp. 51–52; John Mark Hansen, "The Political Economy of Group Membership," *American Political Science Review* 79 (March 1985): 81.

30. See the related discussions of the "endowment effect" by Richard H. Thaler, "Illusions and Mirages in Public Policy," *Public Interest* (Fall 1983): 64–65; of "hysteresis" by Hardin, *Collective Action*, pp. 82–83; of "universalism and reciprocity" by Alt and Chrystal, *Political Economics*, pp. 196–197.

31. Nordlinger, *Autonomy*, p. 38; Dye and Zeigler, *The Irony of Democracy*, pp. 98–99, 101–102; Dye, *Understanding Public Policy*, p. 199; Karl, *Uneasy State*, p. 226; Mancur Olson, *The Rise and Decline of Nations: Economic Growth, Stagflation and Social Rigidities* (New Haven, Conn.: Yale University Press, 1982), p. 71; Karen A. Rasler and William R. Thompson, "War Making and State Making: Governmental Expenditures, Tax Revenues, and Global Wars," *American Political Science Review* 79 (June 1985): 494; and Brown, *New Policies, New Politics*, p. 58. Also Herbert McClosky and John Zaller, *The American Ethos: Popular Attitudes toward Capitalism and Democracy* (Cambridge, Mass.: Harvard University Press, 1984), pp. 292–293, 298–299.

32. Edwin Mansfield, *The Economics of Technological Change* (New York: Norton, 1968); Nathan Rosenberg, ed., *The Economics of Technological Change: Selected Readings* (Harmondsworth, Middlesex: Penguin, 1971); idem, *Perspectives on Technology* (New York: Cambridge University Press, 1976).

33. On technological change as a residual, see M. Ishaq Nadiri, "Some Approaches to the Theory and Measurement of Total Factor Productivity: A Survey," *Journal of Economic Literature* 8 (Dec. 1970): 1137–1177. On ideological change as a residual, see Douglass C. North, "Structure and Performance: The Task of Economic History," ibid. 16 (Sept. 1978): 973; Joseph P. Kalt and M. A. Zupan, "Capture and Ideology in the Economic Theory of Politics," *American Economic Review* 74 (June 1984): 291–295.

34. Karl R. Popper, *The Poverty of Historicism* (New York: Harper Torchbooks, 1964); Ronald A. Heiner, "The Origin of Predictable Behavior," *American Economic Review* 83 (Sept. 1983): 560–595.

35. David, *Technical Choice*, pp. 60–86; Nadiri, "Some Approaches," p. 1148.

36. Carl Sandburg, *The People, Yes*, 1936.

37. B. Guy Peters and Martin O. Heisler, in different language, present a similar argument:

> The response to a conditioning of many of the expectations of citizens by the governments of modern welfare state have [*sic*] legitimized interventions by those governments into the market economy for several generations now. These interventions often began as temporary measures, or as the ad hoc responses to crisis, or politically instigated redistribution of income. The beneficiaries of such interventions, however, associate them not with a particular situation or a government of a particular political complexion,

but rather with the state. In this sense the fundamental compact has been altered, such
that a government that sought to roll back benefits or programs of long standing would
probably not be tolerated as legitimate by citizens.

See "Thinking about Public Sector Growth: Conceptual, Operational, Theoretical,
and Policy Considerations," in *Why Governments Grow: Measuring Public Sector Size*,
ed. Charles Lewis Taylor (Beverly Hills, Calif.: Sage, 1983), pp. 181–182. Essentially the same interpretation appears in the classic anarchistic polemic of Albert Jay
Nock, *Our Enemy, The State* (New York: Free Life Editions, 1973), esp. pp. 3–6.
Also Wallace, *Economic Controls and Defense*, p. 46; Olson, *Rise and Decline*, pp. 69,
71, 73. Some psychologists maintain that "[t]he conforming *behavior* of others,
especially those in one's own peer group, and even one's own conforming behavior,
may tend to generate the appropriate approving *attitude*." Samuel Mermin, *Law and
the Legal System*, 2nd ed. (Boston: Little, Brown, 1982), p. 55.
  38. Robinson Jeffers, "Cassandra," 1948 (with apologies for my rearrangement
of lines and capitalization).
  39. Knight, *Freedom and Reform*, p. 236; Karl, *Uneasy State*, pp. 39–40, 106–107,
114, 172, 216.

CHAPTER FIVE

  1. Godkin as quoted in Samuel Rezneck, "Unemployment, Unrest, and Relief in
the United States during the Depression of 1893–97," *Journal of Political Economy* 61
(August 1953): 339; Frederick Jackson Turner, "The Problem of the West," *Atlantic
Monthly* 78 (September 1896): 296. John Tipple describes the Populists as "a political
faction made up chiefly of farmers but having significant support from industrial
workers, social reformers, and intellectuals." *The Capitalist Revolution: A History of
American Social Thought, 1890–1919* (New York: Pegasus, 1970), p. 21. James
Turner concludes that, among farmers, Populists "tended to live out of the social and
economic mainstream. [They were] not merely rural folk, but rural folk outside of the
orbit of towns." See "Understanding the Populists," *Journal of American History* 67
(September 1980): 359. Also Jeffrey C. Williams, "Economics and Politics: Voting
Behavior in Kansas during the Populist Decade," *Explorations in Economic History* 18
(July 1981): 233–256.
  2. White as quoted in Rezneck, "Unemployment," p. 344. For the Populist and
Democratic platforms and Bryan's famous Cross of Gold speech, see *Documents of
American History*, ed. Henry Steele Commager (New York: Appleton-Century-
Crofts, 1948), II, pp. 143–146, 174–180.
  3. Andrew Carnegie, *Triumphant Democracy: Sixty Years' March of the Republic*,
rev. ed. (New York: Charles Scribner's Sons, 1893), p. 494; Henry George, *Progress
and Poverty* (New York: Modern Library, n.d.), p. 7.
  4. Simon Kuznets, *Capital in the American Economy, Its Formation and Financing*
(Princeton, N.J.: Princeton University Press, 1961), p. 64; Stanley Lebergott,
"Labor Force and Employment, 1800–1960," in National Bureau of Economic
Research, Conference on Research in Income and Wealth, *Output, Employment, and
Productivity in the United States after 1800* (New York: Columbia University Press,
1966), p. 118.
  5. Robert E. Gallman, "Gross National Product in the United States, 1834–
1909," in National Bureau of Economic Research, *Output, Employment, and Produc-
tivity*, p. 30; Robert Higgs, *The Transformation of the American Economy, 1865–1914:
An Essay in Interpretation* (New York: Wiley, 1971), pp. 18–47.

6. Lebergott, "Labor Force and Employment," p. 119; Higgs, *The Transformation*, pp. 47–49, 58–67; idem, "Urbanization and Invention in the Process of Economic Growth: Simultaneous-Equations Estimates for the United States, 1880–1920," *Research in Population Economics* 2 (1980): 3–20; Robert Gallman, "Commodity Output, 1839–1899," in National Bureau of Economic Research, Conference on Research in Income and Wealth, *Trends in the American Economy in the Nineteenth Century* (Princeton, N.J.: Princeton University Press, 1960), p. 26.

7. On the giant corporations the definitive treatise is Alfred D. Chandler, *The Visible Hand: The Managerial Revolution in American Business* (Cambridge, Mass.: Belknap Press, 1977). On the pervasiveness of the "trust question" as a political issue in the 1880s, see William Letwin, *Law and Economic Policy in America: The Evolution of the Sherman Antitrust Act* (Chicago: University of Chicago Press, 1965), pp. 58–59, 69–70.

8. The common law was not uniformly hostile toward every aspect of monopoly. For clarification of the legal details, see Letwin, *Law and Economic Policy*, pp. 77–85.

9. Thomas K. McCraw, "Rethinking the Trust Question," in *Regulation in Perspective: Historical Essays*, ed. Thomas K. McCraw (Cambridge, Mass.: Harvard University Press, 1981), pp. 1–55.

10. *Documents*, ed. Commager, II, p. 113; "Justice Brown on the Social Outlook," *Public Opinion* 19 (1895): 78. On the pervasiveness of corruption in late nineteenth-century politics, see Morton Keller, *Affairs of State: Public Life in Late Nineteenth Century America* (Cambridge, Mass.: Belknap Press, 1977), pp. 524–530, 542–543. Keller notes (p. 543) that "[t]his was a mutually exploitative relationship. The politicians extorted money from the companies by threats of hostile legislation, the companies sought favors and services from the politicos." Also Edmund Morris, *The Rise of Theodore Roosevelt* (New York: Ballantine Books, 1979), pp. 171–172, 261–262, 434–435, 485–487, 499–500. Morris says (p. 171) that "blackmail, not bribery, was the principal form of corruption in the [New York] Assembly."

11. Richard Hofstadter, *The American Political Tradition, And the Men Who Made It* (New York: Vintage, 1974), p. 219: "Between 1866 and 1872 . . . the Union Pacific spent $400,000 on bribes; between 1875 and 1885 graft cost the Central Pacific as much as $500,000 annually." In Aileen Kraditor's view, "there seems to have been a widespread conviction on the part of workers and the middle class that the capitalists performed at least some useful economic functions—gathering capital, supervising, organizing; rather, they were criticized for performing them unjustly and for illegitimately using their wealth to influence the noneconomic spheres." *The Radical Persuasion, 1890–1917: Aspects of the Intellectual History and the Historiography of Three American Radical Organizations* (Baton Rouge: Louisiana State University Press, 1981), p. 74.

12. Higgs, *The Transformation*, pp. 86–102; Robert A. McGuire, "Economic Causes of Late Nineteenth-Century Agrarian Unrest," *Journal of Economic History* 41 (December 1981): 835–852; Williams, "Economics and Politics," pp. 248–249; Bradley G. Lewis, "Economic Causes of Late Nineteenth-Century Agrarian Unrest: Comment," *Journal of Economic History* 42 (September 1982): 688–696 and the "Reply" by Robert A. McGuire, pp. 697–699.

13. George H. Miller, *Railroads and the Granger Laws* (Madison: University of Wisconsin Press, 1971).

14. Aldrich as quoted by Hofstadter, *The American Political Tradition*, p. 230. Also Gabriel Kolko, *Railroads and Regulation, 1877–1916* (Princeton, N.J.: Princeton University Press, 1965); Paul W. MacAvoy, *The Economic Effects of Regulation: The Trunk-Line Railroad Cartels and the Interstate Commerce Commission* (Cambridge, Mass.: M.I.T. Press, 1965); Stephen Skowronek, *Building a New American State: The Expansion of National Administrative Capacities, 1877–1920* (New York: Cambridge University Press, 1982), pp. 121–162, esp. 148–149.

15. *Congressional Record*, Senate, 51st Cong., 1st Sess. (1890), p. 2731.

16. Lawrence M. Friedman, *A History of American Law* (New York: Simon and Schuster, 1973), p. 466. Also Skowronek, *New American State*, pp. 16, 46, and passim.

17. Kraditor, *The Radical Persuasion*, p. 299, notes that "John Q. Worker by the millions ignored the radicals." Her statement applies specifically to the socialists, but the same thing could be said about the Populists. For a characterization of how "politically and socially effective opinion" favored a limited role for government in economic life in the late nineteenth century, see James Willard Hurst, *Law and Markets in United States History: Different Modes of Bargaining Among Interests* (Madison: University of Wisconsin Press, 1982), pp. 20–22; Herbert McClosky and John Zaller, *The American Ethos: Public Attitudes toward Capitalism and Democracy* (Cambridge, Mass.: Harvard University Press, 1984), pp. 113, 127, 144, 150.

18. James Bryce, *The American Commonwealth*, 3rd ed. (London: Macmillan, 1895), II, pp. 536–537.

19. Ibid., p. 369. Compare David McCord Wright's discussion of "The Protective Myths of Capitalism," in *Capitalism* (Chicago: Henry Regnery, 1962), esp. p. 83; Joseph A. Schumpeter's discussion of "The Civilization of Capitalism," in *Capitalism, Socialism and Democracy*, 3rd ed. (New York: Harper and Row, 1950), pp. 121–130; and Robert H. Wiebe's "catalogue of mid-nineteenth century virtues" in *The Search for Order, 1877–1920* (New York: Hill & Wang, 1967), pp. 136, 159. Kraditor, *The Radical Persuasion*, p. 64, argues that in the period 1890–1917 there was no "hegemonic *capitalist* ideology . . . although there were consensual values" (emphasis in original); also pp. 74–75, 334, n. 41. Keller, *Affairs of State*, pp. 131, 161–162, 297, 318, 409 and passim emphasizes the "widespread hostility to active government of any sort." One must recognize, however, as Bryce himself did, that the late nineteenth century was not exactly a Golden Age of laissez-faire, as the state governments were interfering more and more in economic affairs. But Bryce noted in the 1895 edition that the movement toward interventionism was occurring so gradually "that few but lawyers and economists have yet become aware of it" (*American Commonwealth*, II, p. 542). The point is that although some seeds, later to grow into important governmental controls, were planted during the late nineteenth century, the era itself witnessed quite limited interventionism.

20. "Veto Message—Distribution of Seeds," *Congressional Record*, 49th Cong., 2nd Sess., Vol. 28, Pt. II, p. 1875. Cleveland reiterated this conviction in his second inaugural speech, declaring that "[t]he lessons of paternalism ought to be unlearned." *Inaugural Addresses of the Presidents of the United States*, 89th Cong., 1st Sess., House Doc. No. 51 (1965), p. 165.

21. Wiebe, *The Search for Order*, p. 80.

22. Gerald T. White, *The United States and the Problem of Recovery after 1893* (University: University of Alabama Press, 1982), pp. 1–5; *Commercial and Financial Chronicle* 57 (Sept. 16, 1893): 446; R. Hal Williams, *Years of Decision: American Politics in the 1890's* (New York: Wiley, 1978), pp. 75–77.

23. Charles Hoffmann, *The Depression of the Nineties: An Economic History* (Westport, Conn.: Greenwood, 1970), pp. xxvi–xxxi; U.S. Bureau of the Census, *Historical Statistics of the United States, Colonial Times to 1970* (Washington, D.C.: U.S. Government Printing Office, 1975), pp. 127, 135, 224. Recent estimates of unemployment rates in the 1890s, by David R. Weir, are somewhat lower: for 1893–1898 Weir puts the overall rate at 10.5–10.7 percent on the average, with a peak in 1896 at 12 percent; for the nonfarm labor force, 17 percent on the average, with peaks in 1894 and 1896 at more than 19 percent. "Okun's Law and the Curious Stability of Historical Unemployment Estimates," paper presented at the meetings of the Economic History Association, New York, Sept. 20, 1985. Another recent reestimation, by Christina Romer, puts the overall rate at about 12 percent throughout the period

1894–1898. "Spurious Volatility in Historical Unemployment Data," *Journal of Political Economy* 94 (Feb. 1986): 31.

24. U.S. Bureau of the Census, *Historical Statistics*, p. 224.

25. Rezneck, "Unemployment," pp. 333–334; Carl N. Degler, *The Age of the Economic Revolution, 1876–1900*, 2nd ed. (Glenview, Ill.: Scott, Foresman, 1977), pp. 123–124; Stetson as quoted in Ray Ginger, *Age of Excess: The United States from 1877 to 1914*, 2nd ed. (New York: Macmillan, 1975), p. 164.

26. Rezneck, "Unemployment," pp. 332–333; White, *Recovery after 1893*, pp. 23–25; B. O. Flower, "Emergency Measures Which Would Have Maintained Self-Respecting Manhood," *Arena* 9 (May 1894): 823.

27. Quoted in William Nelson Black, "The Coxey Crusade and Its Meaning: A Menace to Republican Institutions," *Engineering Magazine* 7 (June 1894): 313. Black added (p. 309) that "[w]e are a commonplace people in the United States, and do not take kindly to the magnificent and helpful conceptions of governmental paternalism."

28. State of New York, *Public Papers of Roswell P. Flower, Governor, 1893* (Albany, N.Y.: Argus, 1894), pp. 346, 451.

29. *Congressional Record*, Senate, 53rd Cong., 2nd Sess., January 18, 1894, p. 979. Berry's remarks become even more striking when one appreciates the occasion: a trifling proposal to build in the state of New Hampshire a monument to two heroes of the revolutionary war.

30. U.S. Bureau of the Census, *Historical Statistics*, pp. 512, 518.

31. Williams, "Economics and Politics," pp. 247–251; *Documents*, ed. Commager, II, pp. 144–145.

32. Morton to Olney, November 5, 1896, printed in J. D. Whelpley, "An International Wheat Corner," *McClure's Magazine* 15 (August 1900): 364. Whelpley observed (pp. 368, 367) that "[t]he agrarian party in the United States has already demanded government aid for the farmers as some compensation for the protective tariff levied for the benefit of manufacturers." However, "It is unlikely that the United States, within the life of the present generation at least, will seriously consider such a plan [as that proposed by the Russians]. It is contrary to the recognized principles of a republic which, theoretically at least, does not interfere with the business of the individual, fights shy of paternalism, and as a government of the people by all the people, denies that any one industry can hope for such specialized effort on its behalf."

33. Milton Friedman and Anna Jacobson Schwartz, *A Monetary History of the United States, 1867–1960* (Princeton, N.J.: Princeton University Press, 1963), p. 133.

34. *Inaugural Addresses of the Presidents*, p. 164.

35. Allan Nevins, *Grover Cleveland: A Study in Courage* (New York: Dodd, Mead, 1932), p. 599.

36. Ibid., p. 658; White, *Recovery after 1893*, p. 49; Friedman and Schwartz, *Monetary History*, pp. 111–112.

37. Nevins, *Grover Cleveland*, pp. 665–666.

38. *Evening Post*, Feb. 21, 1895, as cited ibid., p. 664.

39. *Documents*, ed. Commager, II, pp. 174–178. Bryan was consistently the ideologue. According to William G. McAdoo, who later served with him in Wilson's cabinet, "He turned every public question into a moral issue. . . . He thought in terms of people bearing burdens, of the wicked in high places, of the altars of sacrifice." *Crowded Years* (Boston: Houghton Mifflin, 1931), p. 338. McAdoo also declared (p. 337) in 1931 that Bryan "had more to do with the shaping of the public policies of the last forty years than any other American citizen"—a strong but plausible claim. For further substantiation, see Hofstadter, *The American Political Tradition*, pp. 256–257.

40. Wiebe, *Search for Order*, pp. 94–99. Also Keller, *Affairs of State*, p. 383; Williams, *Years of Decision*, pp. 78–86, 96.

41. Kraditor, *The Radical Persuasion*, p. 310, refers to "[t]he increased conspicuousness of class divisions in the post–Civil War period."

42. Robert W. Smuts, *European Impressions of the American Worker* (1953), pp. 26–28, as quoted in Kraditor, *The Radical Persuasion*, p. 334, n. 41.

43. Kraditor, *The Radical Persuasion*, p. 79. Skowronek speaks of "an era [1877–1898] of labor violence unparalleled in any other industrial nation." *New American State*, p. 87.

44. Minneapolis *Times* as reproduced in *Public Opinion* 14 (1893): 620. Kraditor refers to turn-of-the-century "public opinion's fear of the one form of social disorder it would not tolerate—violence" and considers it "likely that if the authorities had not suppressed those who violated conventions of law and order, the majority of politically active people, including workers, would have punished such officials at the next election." *The Radical Persuasion*, pp. 82, 97; also pp. 101–103.

45. Kraditor, *The Radical Persuasion*, pp. 80–81.

46. Ricks, Brewer, and Walker as quoted in *Public Opinion* 15 (1893): 128–129.

47. Arnold M. Paul, *Conservative Crisis and the Rule of Law: Attitudes of Bar and Bench, 1887–1895* (New York: Harper Torchbooks, 1969), pp. 104–130.

48. Ibid., p. 136.

49. Judge Jenkins' statement from his opinion of April 6, 1894, in *Farmers' Loan and Trust Co.* v. *Northern Pac. R. Co. et al.*, 60 Fed. 803 (E. D. Wisc.) at 821.

50. Quoted in Nevins, *Grover Cleveland*, p. 617.

51. As quoted in *In re Debs*, 158 U.S. 564 (1895) at 570–572.

52. Nevins, *Grover Cleveland*, pp. 620–621.

53. Altgeld's and Cleveland's messages as quoted in *Public Opinion* 17 (1894): 330–331. The governors of Missouri and Colorado also protested Cleveland's dispatching federal troops without their requesting them.

54. Olney and Debs as quoted in Nevins, *Grover Cleveland*, pp. 622–623.

55. Taft to Helen H. Taft, July 7, 1894, as quoted in Henry F. Pringle, *The Life and Times of William Howard Taft: A Biography* (New York: Farrar and Rinehart, 1939), p. 128.

56. See the large sample of press reactions reproduced in *Public Opinion* 17 (1894): 331–332.

57. "President Cleveland and 'President Debs,'" *American Law Review* 28 (July–August 1894): 592, and "Cogley on Strikes and Boycotts [a book review]," ibid., p. 633.

58. *In re Debs*, 158 U.S. 564 (1895) at 582. For additional expression of the emergency doctrine, see p. 592.

59. Paul, *Conservative Crisis*, pp. 139, 227–230, 235–237.

60. *Voice* and *Nation* as reproduced in *Public Opinion* 18 (1895): 629.

61. Keller, *Affairs of State*, p. 311.

62. James D. Richardson, ed. and comp., *Messages and Papers of the Presidents* (Washington, D.C.: Government Printing Office, 1898), IX, p. 460.

63. George Tunell, "The Legislative History of the Second Income-Tax Law," *Journal of Political Economy* 3 (June 1985): 314. Also Jerold Waltman, "Origins of the Federal Income Tax," *Mid-America* 62 (Oct. 1980): 151–154.

64. Tunell, "Legislative History," p. 333; John F. Witte, *The Politics and Development of the Federal Income Tax* (Madison: University of Wisconsin Press, 1985), p. 73. Also Bennett D. Baack and Edward John Ray, "Special Interests and the Adoption of the Income Tax in the United States," *Journal of Economic History* 45 (Sept. 1985): 608–610.

65. Nevins, *Grover Cleveland*, p. 649.

66. Quoted in Paul, *Conservative Crisis*, p. 164. W. H. Mallock wrote that "[s]uch a tax might indeed be loosely called socialistic, in the sense that it might theoretically be used as a means toward accomplishing that economic transition, which Socialists hope to accomplish, from the existing system to Socialism; but it is a tax which, so levied, would be in its nature temporary, as its object and result would be to extinguish the very sources from which it was derived—that is to say, large private incomes." See "Is an Income Tax Socialistic?" *Public Opinion* 19 (1895): 239–240.

67. Tunell, "Legislative History," pp. 324–325; Paul, *Conservative Crisis*, p. 163.

68. *Pollock* v. *Farmers' Loan and Trust Company*, 157 U.S. 429 (1895).

69. Nevins, *Grover Cleveland*, p. 666; Robert T. Swaine, *The Cravath Firm and Its Predecessors* (1946), I, p. 522, as quoted in Paul, *Conservative Crisis*, p. 185.

70. 157 U.S. at 502, 513.

71. Ibid. at 518, 533.

72. Ibid. at 532–533.

73. Ibid. at 553.

74. Ibid. at 596, 600, 607.

75. Ibid. at 650–651.

76. *Pollock* v. *Farmers' Loan and Trust Company* (rehearing), 158 U.S. (1895) at 617.

77. Ibid. at 663, 671, 684.

78. Ibid. at 685, 695, 706.

79. Douglass C. North, *Structure and Change in Economic History* (New York: Norton, 1981), p. 56. Also Harry N. Scheiber, "Public Economic Policy and the American Legal System: Historical Perspectives," *Wisconsin Law Review* (1980): 1166.

80. Skowronek observes that Cleveland "virtually committed political suicide." *New American State*, p. 170.

81. 60 Fed. (E. D. Wisc.) at 809 (also 823).

CHAPTER SIX

1. David M. Kennedy remarks that "[m]ost American academic historians have thought of themselves as the political heirs of the Progressive tradition." See the Introduction to *Progressivism: The Critical Issues*, ed. David M. Kennedy (Boston: Little, Brown, 1971), p. xiii.

2. U.S. Department of Commerce, *Long Term Economic Growth, 1860–1970* (Washington, D.C.: U.S. Government Printing Office, 1973), pp. 107, 182–183.

3. Ibid., p. 105.

4. U.S. Bureau of the Census, *Historical Statistics of the United States, Colonial Times to 1970* (Washington, D.C.: U.S. Government Printing Office, 1975), pp. 127, 177–178.

5. Quoted in Graham Adams, Jr., *Age of Industrial Violence, 1910–15: The Activities and Findings of the United States Commission on Industrial Relations* (New York: Columbia University Press, 1966), p. 38. Accounts of the casualties at Ludlow disagree. Deaths of six men, two women, and eleven children are reported by Harold U. Faulkner, *The Quest for Social Justice, 1898–1914* (Chicago: Quadrangle Books, 1971), p. 75. Adams, *Age of Industrial Violence*, pp. 146–161, indicates that many others died or sustained wounds in the violent events preceding and following the Ludlow massacre itself.

6. Woodrow Wilson, "The Lawyer and the Community," *North American Re-*

view 192 (Nov. 1910): 618. Of all the articles published in America's leading economics journals between 1900 and 1909, fully one-fourth dealt with monopoly or public regulation. George J. Stigler, "The Economists and the Problem of Monopoly," *American Economic Review* 72 (May 1982): 8.

7. Quoted by William A. Schambra, "The Roots of American Public Philosophy," *Public Interest* (Spring 1982): 42. Robert Wiebe described Roosevelt as "[a] man of unlovely traits who relished killing human beings, nursed harsh personal prejudices, and juggled facts to enhance his fame. . . . Behind the flashing teeth and flailing arms lay a keen-edged intelligence and an insatiable ambition for power within the framework of popular acclaim." *The Search for Order, 1877–1920* (New York: Hill & Wang, 1967), p. 189. For ample documentation of TR's bloodthirst and many insights into other aspects of his character, see Edmund Morris, *The Rise of Theodore Roosevelt* (New York: Ballantine Books, 1979), passim, esp. p. 850, n. 119.

8. Woodrow Wilson, *The New Freedom*, 3rd ed. (Garden City, N.Y.: Doubleday, Page, 1921; originally published 1913), p. 284.

9. Mary Cornelia Porter, "That Commerce Shall Be Free: A New Look at the Old Laissez-Faire Court," *Supreme Court Review* (1976): esp. 151–154. Porter's special insight is her recognition of the great frequency with which the rulings of the Court in the era of economic substantive due process (c. 1897–1936) pertained to public utilities. On the concept of natural monopoly, see Fritz Machlup, *The Political Economy of Monopoly: Business, Labor and Government Policies* (Baltimore: Johns Hopkins Press, 1952), pp. 48, 294.

10. Lincoln Steffens, *The Shame of the Cities* (New York: Hill & Wang, 1957; originally published 1904), pp. 3, 17. Also idem, "IT: An Exposition of the Sovereign Political Power of Organized Business," *Everybody's Magazine* 23 (Sept. 1910): 291–298. On the extent to which the trust problem was perceived as, and indeed *was*, more political than economic, see Thomas K. McCraw, "Rethinking the Trust Problem," in *Regulation in Perspective: Historical Essays*, ed. Thomas K. McCraw (Cambridge, Mass.: Harvard University Press, 1981), pp. 19–20, 37.

11. Gabriel Kolko, *The Triumph of Conservatism: A Reinterpretation of American History, 1900–1916* (Chicago: Quadrangle Books, 1967), passim, esp. pp. 98–110 on "Meat Inspection: Theory and Reality." Producers, not consumers, also provided the driving force behind the Pure Food and Drug Act. David Vogel, "The 'New' Social Regulation in Historical and Comparative Perspective," in *Regulation in Perspective*, ed. McCraw, pp. 166–167. Compare Peter Temin, "Government Actions in Times of Crisis: Lessons from the History of Drug Regulation," *Journal of Social History* 18 (Spring 1985): 433–435. Temin emphasizes the actions of Harvey W. Wiley, an eccentric crusader who headed the Division of Chemistry in the U.S. Department of Agriculture.

12. As an antidote to Kolko's interpretation, see Robert H. Wiebe, *Businessmen and Reform: A Study of the Progressive Movement* (Chicago: Quadrangle Books, 1968). Though he stresses the political disunity of the various business interests, Wiebe (p. 217) agrees with Kolko that "the business community was the most important single factor—or set of factors—in the development of economic regulation." Also John Tipple, *The Capitalist Revolution: A History of American Social Thought, 1890–1919* (New York: Pegasus, 1970), pp. 142–147; Arthur S. Link and Richard L. McCormick, *Progressivism* (Arlington Heights, Ill.: Harland Davidson, 1983), pp. 64–66; Daniel T. Rodgers, "In Search of Progressivism," *Reviews in American History* (Dec. 1982): 120–121.

13. The only genuine solution to this fundamental social problem requires that everyone accept the legitimacy of the socioeconomic *process* that generates (and changes over time) the distributions of income and wealth, abjuring any concern for the specific *outcomes* produced by the process. Although one can conceive of a

society's attaining such consensus, empirical examples do not come readily to mind. As Samuels and Mercuro have noted, "There are no *correct* rights, price, and rent structure and attendant distribution. There is, rather, a contest over rights. . . . [T]he process of determining the legal change of economic interests to be protected as legal rights is *the* critical legal-economic process." Warren J. Samuels and Nicholas Mercuro, "A Critique of Rent-Seeking Theory," in *Neoclassical Political Economy*, ed. David C. Colander (Cambridge, Mass.: Ballinger, 1984), pp. 59, 65, emphasis in original.

14. Quoted by Jerold Waltman, "Origins of the Federal Income Tax," *Mid-America* 62 (Oct. 1980): 155. According to John F. Witte, Aldrich's proposals originated in the Taft administration, which sought to "defuse a potential constitutional crisis between Congress and the Supreme Court." *The Politics and Development of the Federal Income Tax* (Madison: University of Wisconsin Press, 1985), pp. 74–75.

15. *Flint* v. *Stone Tracy Co.*, 220 U.S. 107 (1911). The Court had been edging away from its *Pollock* decision ever since 1899, upholding taxes on sales in business exchanges, on inheritances, and on sales of stock, all of which differed only technically from income taxes. Loren P. Beth, *The Development of the American Constitution, 1877–1917* (New York: Harper Torchbooks, 1971), p. 159.

16. For a novel explanation of how a winning coalition was formed in support of the Sixteenth Amendment, see Ben Baack and Edward John Ray, "The Political Economy of the Origin and Development of the Federal Income Tax," in *Emergence of the Modern Political Economy*, ed. Robert Higgs (Greenwich, Conn.: JAI Press, 1985), pp. 121–138 and idem, "Special Interests and the Adoption of the Income Tax in the United States," *Journal of Economic History* 45 (Sept. 1985): 607–625.

17. Witte, *Federal Income Tax*, pp. 76–79 (quotation from p. 77); U.S Bureau of the Census, *Historical Statistics*, p. 1095.

18. Introduction to *Progressivism*, ed. Kennedy, pp. vii, xiii. Compare Rodgers, "In Search of Progressivism," pp. 123, 127.

19. Wiebe, *The Search for Order*, p. 159. On the Progressive Era as an ideological watershed, see also Frank Tariello, Jr., *The Reconstruction of American Political Ideology, 1865–1917* (Charlottesville: University of Virginia Press, 1982), esp. pp. 48, 161; Arthur A. Ekirch, Jr., *Progressivism in America* (New York: New Viewpoints, 1974); Herbert McClosky and John Zaller, *The American Ethos: Public Attitudes toward Capitalism and Democracy* (Cambridge, Mass.: Harvard University Press, 1984), pp. 87, 221, 269–270.

20. Charles Whiting Baker, *Government Control and Operation of Industry in Great Britain and the United States during the World War* (New York: Oxford University Press, 1921), p. 3; George W. Perkins, "Business: The Moral Question," *World's Work* 22 (June 1911): 14469. Ekirch (*Progressivism*, p. 166) describes Perkins as an admirer "of a strong administrative state and of German nationalism"; Rodgers ("In Search of Progressivism," p. 115) calls him "an archetypical 'corporate liberal.'"

21. Quoted in Tipple, *The Capitalist Revolution*, p. 5. Much of big business's support for federal regulation sprang from a desire to avoid the likely alternative: diverse regulations at the state level. Richard Sylla, in an unpublished paper (1986), makes this relation the central explanation of Progressivism in general.

22. U.S. Bureau of the Census, *Historical Statistics*, p. 140.

23. Joseph A. Schumpeter, *Capitalism, Socialism, and Democracy*, 3rd ed. (New York: Harper & Row, 1950), p. 145.

24. On Ross, see Tipple, *The Capitalist Revolution*, pp. 338–339. Ross's "wise minority" has counterparts in Galbraith's "technostructure" and his "educational and scientific estate." John Kenneth Galbraith, *The New Industrial State* (Boston: Houghton Mifflin, 1967), pp. 60–71, 282–295, 378–387 and passim. Compare Alvin W. Gouldner, *The Dialectic of Ideology and Technology: The Origins, Grammar, and*

Future of Ideology (New York: Oxford University Press, 1982), pp. 255–257 ("a fantasy, a utopia, an ideal type").

25. Tipple, *The Capitalist Revolution*, p. 275. Also Wiebe, *The Search for Order*, pp. 159–163; James Gilbert, *Designing the Industrial State: The Intellectual Pursuit of Collectivism in America, 1880–1940* (Chicago: Quadrangle Books, 1972); Charles Forcey, *The Crossroads of Liberalism: Croly, Weyl, Lippmann, and the Progressive Era, 1900–1925* (New York: Oxford University Press, 1961); Ronald Steel, *Walter Lippmann and the American Century* (Boston: Little, Brown, 1980), pp. 23–44; Tariello, *The Reconstruction*, esp. pp. 118–119. Ekirch has emphasized that to a large extent American Progressives took their ideals and programs from the more advanced statism of western Europe. *Progressivism*, esp. pp. 3–15, and idem, *The Decline of American Liberalism* (New York: Atheneum, 1980), pp. 171–196. Barry D. Karl says that "[a]lthough such aspects of socialism as government ownership of railroads and utilities were attractive to some progressives and populists, they were attractive more as methods than as parts of a revolutionary ideology." *The Uneasy State: The United States from 1915 to 1945* (Chicago: University of Chicago Press, 1983), p. 24.

26. Four national labor unions representing engineers, firemen, conductors, and trainmen constituted the combined operating brotherhoods. *No*noperating railroad workers comprised those involved in construction, maintenance, station management, etc.

27. For detailed accounts of the railroad labor troubles of 1916–1917, see K. Austin Kerr, *American Railroad Politics, 1914–1920: Rates, Wages, and Efficiency* (Pittsburgh: University of Pittsburgh Press, 1968), pp. 31–35; Albro Martin, *Enterprise Denied: Origins of the Decline of American Railroads, 1897–1917* (New York: Columbia University Press, 1971), pp. 319–335; and the Supreme Court case cited in note 32 below.

28. U.S. Bureau of the Census, *Historical Statistics*, p. 740.

29. Phrases employed by the *Literary Digest* and the New York *Call* as quoted in Martin, *Enterprise Denied*, p. 325.

30. Quoted in Martin, *Enterprise Denied*, p. 328.

31. "An Act to establish an eight-hour day for employees of carriers engaged in interstate and foreign commerce, and for other purposes," 39 *Stat.* 721, c. 436 (Sept. 3, 5, 1916), known unofficially as the Adamson Act.

32. *Wilson, United States Attorney for the Western District of Missouri* v. *New et al., Receivers of the Missouri, Oklahoma & Gulf Railway Company*, 243 U.S 332 (1917).

33. Michael E. Parrish, *Felix Frankfurter and His Times: The Reform Years* (New York: Free Press, 1982), p. 75.

34. 243 U.S. at 350–351, 356–357.

35. Ibid. at 348, 352.

36. *Adair* v. *United States*, 208 U.S. 161 (1908); *Coppage* v. *Kansas*, 236 U.S. 1 (1915). For a refreshing discussion of these famous cases, see Bernard H. Siegan, *Economic Liberties and the Constitution* (Chicago: University of Chicago Press, 1980), pp. 122–125.

37. 243 U.S. at 370, 372.

38. Ibid. at 377. The conclusion that emergency cannot alter constitutional guarantees in any respect goes back to a landmark case of the Civil War era, *Ex parte Milligan*, 4 Wallace 2 (1866).

39. 243 U.S. at 378.

40. Ibid. at 382.

41. Ibid. at 386.

42. Ibid. at 387.

43. Jonathan R. T. Hughes, *The Governmental Habit: Economic Controls from Colonial Times to the Present* (New York: Basic Books, 1977), pp. 138–139.

CHAPTER SEVEN

1. Benjamin M. Anderson, *Economics and the Public Welfare: A Financial and Economic History of the United States, 1914–46* (Indianapolis: Liberty Press, 1979), pp. 25–43; U.S. Bureau of the Census, *Historical Statistics of the United States, Colonial Times to 1970* (Washington, D.C.: U.S. Government Printing Office, 1975), pp. 884, 135, 224.

2. U.S. House of Representatives, 64th Cong., 1st Sess., *Report No. 659*, May 9, 1916, pp. 43, 45 (see pp. 46–66 for rates on various routes for various commodities).

3. William Gibbs McAdoo, *Crowded Years* (Boston: Houghton Mifflin, 1931), pp. 296–297, 304–309.

4. Ibid., pp. 311–312.

5. Ibid., p. 314; *News* and *Herald* as quoted in the *Literary Digest* 52 (May 27, 1916), p. 1522. "Dread vision" was the *Digest*'s characterization of the views of the bill's opponents.

6. *Post* and *World* as quoted in the *Literary Digest* 52 (May 27, 1916), p. 1523; U.S. House, *Report No. 659*, pp. 73–74.

7. McAdoo, *Crowded Years*, pp. 314–315; David M. Kennedy, *Over Here: The First World War and American Society* (New York: Oxford University Press, 1980), p. 305.

8. Waldo G. Leland and Newton D. Mereness, comp., *Introduction to the American Official Sources for the Economic and Social History of the World War* (New Haven, Conn.: Yale University Press, 1926), p. 280); Edmund E. Day, "The American Merchant Fleet: A War Achievement, A Peace Problem," *Quarterly Journal of Economics* 34 (August 1920): 567–606 (quotation from 591), esp. pp. 579–591 on extensions of the authority in the original Shipping Act.

9. Hurley as quoted in Frederick Palmer, *Newton D. Baker: America at War* (New York: Dodd, Mead, 1931), I, p. 403. The phrase with "leaping costs" is Palmer's.

10. George Soule, *Prosperity Decade: From War to Depression, 1917–1929* (New York: Holt, Rinehart & Winston, 1947), p. 32.

11. Carl Sandburg, "Killers," 1916.

12. "Official drillmaster" from Robert D. Cuff, *The War Industries Board: Business-Government Relations during World War I* (Baltimore: Johns Hopkins Press, 1973), p. 29; "mostly preparedness" from Robert H. Ferrell, *Woodrow Wilson and World War I, 1917–1921* (New York: Harper & Row, 1985), p. 103. On the preparedness controversy, see Kennedy, *Over Here*, pp. 30–33; Arthur S. Link and William B. Catton, *American Epoch*, 4th ed. (New York: Knopf, 1973), I, pp. 169–171; Arthur A. Ekirch, Jr., *Progressivism in America* (New York: New Viewpoints, 1974), pp. 238–259; Stephen Skowronek, *Building a New American State: The Expansion of National Administrative Capacities, 1877–1920* (New York: Cambridge University Press, 1982), pp. 228–229.

13. Cuff, *War Industries Board*, pp. 13–42; Grosvenor B. Clarkson, *Industrial America in the World War: The Strategy Behind the Line, 1917–1918* (Boston: Houghton Mifflin, 1923), pp. 15–19; Bernard M. Baruch, *Baruch: The Public Years* (New York: Holt, Rinehart & Winston, 1960), pp. 23–25. Sources disagree about the exact number of Americans killed or injured in the sinking of the *Sussex*; they agree that American casualties occurred.

14. Skowronek, *New American State*, p. 232; 39 Stat. 166 (June 3, 1916) at 213. Similar powers of requisition were later granted with respect to shipyards and naval supply facilities by the Naval Emergency Fund Act of March 4, 1917. Clarence A. Berdahl, *War Powers of the Executive in the United States* (Urbana: University of Illinois, 1921), p. 210.

15. 39 Stat. at 214.

16. 39 Stat. 619 (August 29, 1916) at 645. According to Jonathan R. T. Hughes, some of the senators who promoted this provision did so on the understanding that it would assist the government in defending the border with Mexico, where notable skirmishes had occurred earlier in 1916. *The Governmental Habit: Economic Controls from Colonial Times to the Present* (New York: Basic Books, 1977), p. 142.

17. 39 Stat. at 649.

18. Jordan A. Schwarz, *The Speculator: Bernard M. Baruch in Washington, 1917–1965* (Chapel Hill: University of North Carolina Press, 1981), p. 59; Soule, *Prosperity Decade*, pp. 13–14. For a brief account of the vast extensions of governmental control in Europe during the war, see Shepard B. Clough, *European Economic History*, 2nd ed. (New York: McGraw-Hill, 1968), pp. 433–435.

19. John Maurice Clark, *The Costs of the World War to the American People* (New Haven, Conn.: Yale University Press, 1931), p. 29.

20. Clarkson, *Industrial America in the World War*, p. 97. A photocopy of the original signed declaration of war appears in Palmer, *Newton D. Baker*, I, facing p. 90.

21. U.S. Bureau of the Census, *Historical Statistics*, p. 1140; Palmer, *Newton D. Baker*, I, pp. 144–145.

22. Scott's statement from Annual Report of the War Department for 1916, as reprinted in *The Military Draft: Selected Readings on Conscription*, ed. Martin Anderson (Stanford, Calif.: Hoover Institution Press, 1982), p. 518. On the events that caused the administration to support the draft, see Palmer, *Newton D. Baker*, I, pp. 184–185; Mark Sullivan, "Conscription," in *The Military Draft*, ed. Anderson, pp. 26–27, 33; Kennedy, *Over Here*, pp. 145–147; Seward W. Livermore, *Politics Is Adjourned: Woodrow Wilson and the War Congress, 1916–1918* (Middletown, Conn.: Wesleyan University Press, 1966), pp. 16–17.

23. Sullivan, "Conscription," pp. 29–30; Livermore, *Politics Is Adjourned*, pp. 17–18.

24. Livermore, *Politics Is Adjourned*, pp. 19, 26–29; Kennedy, *Over Here*, pp. 148–149.

25. Palmer, *Newton D. Baker*, I, pp. 216–217. Also Sullivan, "Conscription," pp. 30–31; Kennedy, *Over Here*, p. 150. Wilson's statement superbly exemplifies Alvin N. Gouldner's observation: "Ideological discourse is aimed continually at denying the legitimacy of partisan interests; sometimes it even denies the *reality* of partisanship." *The Dialectic of Ideology and Technology: The Origins, Grammar, and Future of Ideology* (New York: Oxford University Press, 1982), p. 278, emphasis in original.

26. Palmer, *Newton D. Baker*, I, facing p. 214.

27. Ibid., p. 217; Frederic L. Paxson, "The American War Government, 1917–1918," *American Historical Review* 26 (October 1920): 64; Berdahl, *War Powers*, p. 202.

28. Kennedy, *Over Here*, pp. 152–167 (quotations from pp. 155, 163). Also Livermore, *Politics Is Adjourned*, p. 41. John Hope Franklin notes that 31 percent of the blacks who registered were drafted as against 26 percent of the whites. He attributes the difference to "the inclination of some draft boards to discriminate against Negroes in the matter of exemptions." *From Slavery to Freedom: A History of Negro Americans*, 3rd ed. (New York: Vintage Books, 1969), p. 456. Also Ferrell, *Wilson and World War I*, p. 213.

29. Second Report of the Provost Marshal General as quoted in Kennedy, *Over Here*, p. 152.

30. U.S. Bureau of the Census, *Historical Statistics*, p. 1140; Ferrell, *Wilson and World War I*, pp. 18–19, 206. Some 65,000 men refused combat service because of scruple against fighting.

31. Sullivan, "Conscription," pp. 31–32.

32. Kennedy, *Over Here*, p. 106 (also pp. 99–106 on the resort to cost-concealing inflationary finance and emotion-driven bond sales). Also McAdoo, *Crowded Years*, pp. 378–381.

33. Herbert Hoover, *The Memoirs of Herbert Hoover: Years of Adventure, 1874–1920* (New York: Macmillan, 1952), p. 243; Soule, *Prosperity Decade*, p. 21; Kennedy, *Over Here*, p. 117.

34. Kennedy, *Over Here*, pp. 117–119. Also Hoover, *Memoirs*, p. 240; Livermore, *Politics Is Adjourned*, pp. 48–49.

35. Quoted in Hoover, *Memoirs*, pp. 251–252.

36. Ibid., p. 248. Also Soule, *Prosperity Decade*, pp. 22–23; Kennedy, *Over Here*, p. 123; Livermore, *Politics Is Adjourned*, pp. 49–52; Simon Litman, *Prices and Price Control in Great Britain and the United States during the World War* (New York: Oxford University Press, 1920), pp. 206–207.

37. 40 Stat. 276 (August 10, 1917).

38. Lewis H. Haney, "Price Fixing in the United States during the War. I," *Political Science Quarterly* 34 (March 1919): 117, 123. Price fixing, not only by the Food Administration but by the Fuel Administration and the War Industries Board, is discussed in Haney's article, pp. 104–126, and in his two sequels in the same volume, pp. 262–289, 434–453. Also F. W. Taussig, "Price-Fixing as Seen by a Price-Fixer," *Quarterly Journal of Economics* 33 (Feb. 1919): 205–241, esp. 205–208; Litman, *Prices and Price Control*, pp. 209–236; Hugh Rockoff, *Drastic Measures: A History of Wage and Price Controls in the United States* (New York: Cambridge University Press, 1984), pp. 43–84.

39. Livermore, *Politics Is Adjourned*, pp. 170–175, 244.

40. Newspaper as quoted in Gilbert C. Fite and Jim E. Reese, *An Economic History of the United States*, 3rd ed. (Boston: Houghton Mifflin, 1973), p. 454; Ferrell, *Wilson and World War I*, pp. 92–95. According to a contemporary writer, "A real stigma was placed upon the person who was not loyal to Food Administration edicts through pressure by the schools, churches, women's clubs, public libraries, merchants' associations, fraternal organizations, and other social groups." Paul Willard Garrett as quoted in Murray N. Rothbard, "War Collectivism in World War I," in *A New History of Leviathan: Essays on the Rise of the American Corporate State*, ed. Ronald Radosh and Murray N. Rothbard (New York: Dutton, 1972), p. 84.

41. Paxson, "American War Government," p. 64.

42. Charles Whiting Baker, *Government Control and Operation of Industry in Great Britain and the United States during the World War* (New York: Oxford University Press, 1921), p. 108.

43. Ibid., p. 109; Leland and Mereness, *American Official Sources*, p. 411.

44. Anderson, *Economics and the Public Welfare*, p. 53; Baker, *Government Control*, p. 114; Soule, *Prosperity Decade*, p. 39; Kennedy, *Over Here*, p. 124; Rockoff, *Drastic Measures*, pp. 59–63.

45. Clarkson, *Industrial America in the World War*, pp. 43, 138–139 (also pp. 8, 112–113, 235). Also Cuff, *War Industries Board*, pp. 86, 138; Paul A. C. Koistinen, "The 'Industrial-Military Complex' in Historical Perspective: World War I," *Business History Review* 41 (Winter 1967): 386–375; Skowronek, *New American State*, p. 237; Ferrell, *Wilson and World War I*, pp. 25, 104, 245; Daniel R. Beaver, "The Problem of American Military Supply, 1890–1920," in *War, Business, and American Society: Historical Perspectives on the Military-Industrial Complex*, ed. Benjamin Franklin Cooling (Port Washington, N.Y.: Kennikat Press, 1977), pp. 79, 83–84.

46. Berdahl, *War Powers*, pp. 172–173; Baruch, *Public Years*, pp. 46–47.

47. Berdahl, *War Powers*, pp. 173–175. Also Livermore, *Politics Is Adjourned*, p. 98; Palmer, *Newton D. Baker*, II, p. 200; Barry D. Karl, *The Uneasy State: The United States from 1915 to 1945* (Chicago: University of Chicago Press, 1983), p. 44.

48. Curtice N. Hitchcock, "The War Industries Board: Its Development, Orga-

nization, and Functions," *Journal of Political Economy* 26 (June 1918): 557; Clarkson, *Industrial America in the World War*, pp. 100–103 ("inspector-general" from p. 101, "tired, bored" from p. 59).

49. The notion that Baruch acted as an "industrial dictator" is deeply embedded in the historical literature. See the numerous citations compiled by Cuff, *War Industries Board*, p. 271. Baruch himself explicitly denied it in his memoirs, *The Public Years*, p. 53: "Such a view of my power is overwrought." But he seems to have enjoyed having people think he had been an economic dictator, his denial notwithstanding. Clarkson's book, which did much to create the myth, was checked by one of Baruch's top aides and subsidized by the Speculator himself. Clarkson said while his work was still in progress that "Baruch seems to be happy over the book. . . . I sincerely tried to please him, to get his point of view, and to give him the place in the sun he so richly deserves." Schwarz, *The Speculator*, pp. 200, 212; Rothbard, "War Collectivism," p. 70.

50. The entire text of Wilson's letter is reproduced in Clarkson, *Industrial America in the World War*, pp. 49–50.

51. Ibid., p. 49.

52. Thanks in large part to Baruch's desire to memorialize his own services, the WIB is extensively documented. In addition to the standard work by Clarkson, see Richard H. Hippelheuser, ed., *American Industry in the War: A Report of the War Industries Board* (New York: Prentice-Hall, 1941), esp. the organizational chart facing p. 14. For authoritative recent accounts, see Cuff, *War Industries Board*, and Schwarz, *The Speculator*, pp. 50–108.

53. Baruch, *The Public Years*, p. 63.

54. Clarkson, *Industrial America in the World War*, p. 177 (also pp. 103–104); Baruch, *The Public Years*, p. 58.

55. Baruch, *The Public Years*, pp. 55–56.

56. Cuff, *War Industries Board*, pp. 220–240; Rothbard, "War Collectivism," pp. 73–82. For a list of the products subjected to formal price control, with dates, see Litman, *Prices and Price Control*, p. 323. For a somewhat longer list that includes commodities subjected to less formal price controls, see Haney, "Price Fixing, I," pp. 105–106.

57. Baruch, *The Public Years*, p. 54, emphasis added.

58. Ferrell, *Wilson and World War I*, p. 87; Leland and Mereness, *American Official Sources*, p. 423; McAdoo, *Crowded Years*, pp. 441–442; Merlo J. Pusey, *Eugene Meyer* (New York: Knopf, 1974), pp. 157–163 ("rescue mission" from p. 163).

59. Leland and Mereness, *American Official Sources*, p. 425; Anderson, *Economics and the Public Welfare*, p. 51; McAdoo, *Crowded Years*, p. 443.

60. Albert A. Blum and J. Douglas Smyth, "Who Should Serve: Pre–World War II Planning for Selective Service," *Journal of Economic History* 30 (June 1970): 391.

61. U.S. Bureau of the Census, *Historical Statistics*, pp. 178–179; Wilson as quoted in Kennedy, *Over Here*, p. 269. In May 1918, General Crowder issued his famous "work-or-fight" order, instructing the draft boards to give priority in induction to the unemployed and those in certain occupations the government considered nonessential.

62. Michael E. Parrish, *Felix Frankfurter and His Times: The Reform Years* (New York: Free Press, 1982), pp. 87–97. Also Louis B. Wehle, "Labor Problems in the United States during the War," *Quarterly Journal of Economics* 32 (Feb. 1918): 333–392; L. C. Marshall, "The War Labor Program and Its Administration," *Journal of Political Economy* 26 (May 1918): 425–460.

63. Parrish, *Frankfurter*, pp. 102–117 (quotations from pp. 110, 82). Also Kennedy, *Over Here*, pp. 258–270; Leland and Mereness, *American Official Sources*, pp. 227–228, 241–242, 245–246.

64. K. Austin Kerr, *American Railroad Politics, 1914–1920: Rates, Wages, and*

Efficiency (Pittsburgh: University of Pittsburgh Press, 1968), pp. 36–63; Marshall, "War Labor Program," p. 427 (half of all contracts, excepting those of the Shipping Board, went to Ohio, Pennsylvania, and New York); Frank Haigh Dixon, "Federal Operation of the Railroads during the War," *Quarterly Journal of Economics* 33 (Aug. 1919): 580; Soule, *Prosperity Decade*, p. 33; McAdoo, *Crowded Years*, pp. 448–458 (quotation from p. 458). Skowronek says "The Government was simply too incoherent to support the private remedy." *New American State*, p. 275.

65. McAdoo, *Crowded Years*, p. 458.

66. Ibid., pp. 458–461 (quotation from p. 447); Kennedy, *Over Here*, p. 253. Also Kerr, *American Railroad Politics*, pp. 63–71.

67. McAdoo, *Crowded Years*, p. 482; Dixon, "Federal Operation," p. 602.

68. McAdoo, *Crowded Years*, pp. 489–490; Dixon, "Federal Operation," pp. 602–606.

69. Clark, *Costs of the World War*, p. 237. Also McAdoo, *Crowded Years*, p. 494; Dixon, "Federal Operation," pp. 606–607; Kerr, *American Railroad Politics*, pp. 111–119.

70. 40 Stat. 451 (March 21, 1918) at 452.

71. U.S. Bureau of the Census, *Historical Statistics*, p. 211; Clark, *Costs of the World War*, pp. 153–154.

72. McAdoo, *Crowded Years*, p. 495; Clark, *Costs of the World War*, p. 242.

73. Dixon, "Federal Operation," p. 618; Kerr, *American Railroad Politics*, pp. 128–203.

74. 40 Stat. at 458.

75. Zechariah Chafee as quoted in Kennedy, *Over Here*, p. 84. According to Rossiter, "the single important case in which any part of the vast body of regulatory legislation enacted in World War I was held unconstitutional" was *United States* v. *Cohen Grocery Co.*, 255 U.S. 81 (1921), which concerned the power of the government under the Lever Act to regulate the rates or charges of dealers in necessities. Notice, however, that the decision was handed down on February 28, 1921, long after the end of the war. Clinton Rossiter and Richard P. Longaker, *The Supreme Court and the Commander in Chief*, exp. ed. (Ithaca, N.Y.: Cornell University Press, 1976), pp. 96–97.

76. *Arver* v. *United States*, 245 U.S. 366 (1918): *Goldman* v. *United States*, 245 U.S. 474 (1918); *Ruthenberg* v. *United States*, 245 U.S. 480 (1918). Quotations that follow in the text are from *Arver*, the leading case.

77. Leon Friedman, "Conscription and the Constitution: The Original Understanding," *Michigan Law Review* 67 (May 1969): 1493–1552, as reprinted in *The Military Draft*, ed. Anderson, pp. 233, 281. Also Paul L. Murphy, *The Constitution in Crisis Times, 1918–1969* (New York: Harper Torchbooks, 1972), pp. 12–13. On the American Protective League, see Herbert McClosky and John Zaller, *The American Ethos: Public Attitudes toward Capitalism and Democracy* (Cambridge, Mass.: Harvard University Press, 1984), p. 40.

78. Murphy, *Constitution*, p. 22. See also Kennedy, *Over Here*, pp. 79–86.

79. Holmes as quoted in Murphy, *Constitution*, p. 24. Also Kennedy, *Over Here*, pp. 84–86. In Holmes' opinions in the Espionage Act cases, wrote H. L. Mencken, "one finds a clear statement of the doctrine that, in war time, the rights guaranteed by the First Amendment cease to have any substance, and may be set aside summarily by any jury that has been sufficiently inflamed by a district attorney itching for higher office." See "Mr. Justice Holmes," in *The Vintage Mencken*, comp. Alistair Cooke (New York: Knopf, 1955), p. 189.

80. Murphy, *Constitution*, p. 27. Also Ferrell, *Wilson and World War I*, pp. 200–218.

81. *Northern Pacific Railway Company et al.* v. *State of North Dakota on the Relation of Langer, Attorney General*, 250 U.S. 135 (1919) at 149. Also Murphy, *Constitution*, p. 21.

82. *Block, Trading Under the Name of Whites,* v. *Hirsh,* 256 U.S. 135 (1921) at 136, 168–169. Also *Marcus Brown Holding Company, Inc.* v. *Feldman et al.,* 256 U.S. 170 (1921). Not until 1923 did the Supreme Court decide that the emergency had passed and refuse to validate a 1921 extension of the 1919 rent-control act in the District of Columbia. *Chastleton Corp.* v. *Sinclair,* 264 U.S. 543 (1924). Commenting on this decision, Edward S. Corwin wrote: "The power of the Court to take notice of an emergency is, it appears, a two-edged sword, but its anti-government edge descends only after the emergency is over." *Total War and the Constitution* (New York: Knopf, 1947), p. 83. Fifty years after the court ruled on *Block* and *Marcus Brown,* these decisions were employed to establish the constitutionality of a Rent Control Enabling Act when the government of Cambridge, Massachusetts, declared a "housing emergency" and imposed local rent controls. Peter Navarro, *The Policy Game: How Special Interests and Ideologues Are Stealing America* (New York: Wiley, 1984), pp. 14, 302.

83. Clark, *Costs of the World War,* p. 290.

84. John F. Witte, *The Politics and Development of the Federal Income Tax* (Madison: University of Wisconsin Press, 1985), pp. 79–87 (quotation from p. 86); U.S. Bureau of the Census, *Historical Statistics,* p. 1104; Kennedy, *Over Here,* p. 112.

85. Frederick Lewis Allen, *Only Yesterday: An Informal History of the Nineteen-Twenties* (New York: Blue Ribbon Books, 1931), p. 247 ("the war gave the dry leaders their great opportunity"); Edward L. Schaub, "The Regulation of Rentals during the War Period," *Journal of Political Economy* 28 (Jan. 1920): 1–36; Rockoff, *Drastic Measures,* pp. 63–64; quotations from Clark, *Costs of the World War,* pp. 51, 58.

86. Herbert Hoover, *The Memoirs of Herbert Hoover: The Cabinet and the Presidency, 1920–1933* (New York: Macmillan, 1952), p. 16; Ferrell, *Wilson and World War I,* p. 45; Leland and Mereness, *American Official Sources,* pp. 398–399, 411, 377.

87. Murphy, *Constitution,* pp. 6–7; Kerr, *American Railroad Politics,* pp. 204–227; Skowronek, *New American State,* p. 282.

88. Murphy, *Constitution,* p. 7; Clark, *Costs of the World War,* pp. 55, 111, 250–252 (quotation from p. 251).

89. Pusey, *Eugene Meyer,* pp. 164–183 ("distressed farmers" from p. 178). Evidently, most of the lending for "war purposes" occurred after the armistice; hence the discrepancy with the figure ($71 million) for lending "during the war," given above.

90. Kennedy, *Over Here,* p. 141. For a recent survey that stresses the pervasive associationalist trends of the period, see Ellis W. Hawley, *The Great War and the Search for a Modern Order, A History of the American People and Their Institutions, 1917–1933* (New York: St. Martin's Press, 1979).

91. Soule, *Prosperity Decade,* pp. 62–63.

92. Clarkson, *Industrial America in the World War,* p. 312.

93. Baruch, *The Public Years,* pp. 2–3, 74. For a much earlier report that "government operation and control of industry . . . [had] driven the last nail into the coffin containing the defunct *laissez faire* theory of government," see Baker, *Government Controls,* p. 5.

94. Kennedy, *Over Here,* p. 246; Daniels and Frankfurter as quoted in Larry G. Gerber, *The Limits of Liberalism: Josephus Daniels, Henry Stimson, Bernard Baruch, Donald Richberg, Felix Frankfurter and the Development of the Modern American Political Economy* (New York: New York University Press, 1983), pp. 172–173. The Progressives and their liberal descendants "would never forget the lessons of 1917–18, and would thereafter search constantly for the 'moral equivalent of war.'" William A. Schambra, "Progressive Liberalism and the American 'Community,'" *Public Interest* (Summer 1985): 36.

95. Clark, *Costs of the World War,* p. 290.

96. Ferrell quotes from a letter written by Senator Reed Smoot of Utah on April 6, 1917: "This war is a very unpopular one. I believe a majority of the people are opposed to it. I am still receiving many protests from all parts of the country."

Ferrell himself observes: "To have paid all the cost of participation in the war out of tax revenues would have required a steep rise in the income tax, and many other new taxes. In the spring of 1917, pushing new taxes through Congress was very unattractive. The government also feared the effect of taxes upon businessmen, whom it could not safely discourage." *Wilson and World War I*, pp. 8, 84.

97. J. M. Clark, "The Basis of War-Time Collectivism," *American Economic Review* 7 (Dec. 1917): 786. See also a similar analysis by Harold G. Moulton, "Industrial Conscription," *Journal of Political Economy* 25 (Nov. 1917): 917–945. Moulton distinguished two methods of mobilization, which he called "the financial method" and "industrial conscription." Like Clark, he favored the latter because (p. 939) "the volunteer system is hopelessly slow and uncertain where speed and certainty are indispensable," never recognizing that more rapid resource reallocation and greater risk-bearing are both socially more costly but can be induced through markets if sufficient rewards are proffered.

98. Kennedy, *Over Here*, p. 143.

99. Taussig, "Price-Fixing," p. 210. For corroboration of Taussig's explanation, see Haney, "Price Fixing, III," pp. 434–437, 453; Litman, *Prices and Price Controls*, pp. 318–319. Rockoff, *Drastic Measures*, p. 67, agrees that "[t]he authorities sought to bring under control [the prices of] . . . the commodities critical to the war effort and which therefore faced the strongest and most persistent demand. . . . After controls were imposed, uncontrolled prices continued to rise at about the same rate as before."

CHAPTER EIGHT

1. Jonathan Hughes, *American Economic History* (Glenview, Ill.: Scott, Foresman, 1983), pp. 467–474; Gene Smiley, "Did Incomes for Most of the Population Fall from 1923 Through 1929?" *Journal of Economic History* 43 (March 1983): 209–216.

2. Alistair Cooke, comp., *The Vintage Mencken* (New York: Knopf, 1955), p. 233. Mencken also said: "Counting out Harding as a cypher only, Dr. Coolidge was preceded by one World Saver and followed by two more."

3. Excellent economic accounts include Lester V. Chandler, *America's Greatest Depression, 1929–1941* (New York: Harper & Row, 1970) and Milton Friedman and Anna Jacobson Schwartz, *A Monetary History of the United States, 1867–1960* (Princeton: Princeton University Press, 1963), pp. 229–419. For poignant portraits of the human face of the tragedy, see David A. Shannon, ed., *The Great Depression* (Englewood Cliffs, N.J.: Prentice-Hall, 1960).

4. Hughes, *American Economic History*, pp. 490–491; Chandler, *Greatest Depression*, pp. 6–7, 22; Friedman and Schwartz, *Monetary History*, p. 301.

5. Friedman and Schwartz, *Monetary History*, p. 351; Chandler, *Greatest Depression*, p. 62.

6. Chandler, *Greatest Depression*, pp. 18, 26–27; U.S. Bureau of the Census, *Historical Statistics of the United States, Colonial Times to 1970* (Washington, D.C.: U.S. Government Printing Office, 1975), pp. 235–236.

7. Chandler, *Greatest Depression*, pp. 58–59, 64–65; Lee J. Alston, "Farm Foreclosures in the United States during the Interwar Period," *Journal of Economic History* 43 (Dec. 1983): 885–903; idem, "Farm Foreclosure Moratorium Legislation: A Lesson from the Past," *American Economic Review* 74 (June 1984): 445–457.

8. Herbert Hoover, *The Memoirs of Herbert Hoover: The Great Depression, 1929–1941* (New York: Macmillan, 1952), pp. 30–31.

9. "Far too little, much too late" is the verdict of Chandler, *Greatest Depression*, p. 87. He recognizes, however, that Hoover's actions "seemed bold indeed to the President and to the many others who shared his views concerning the proper role of government." For extensive documentation of the Hoover administration's relief,

credit, and fiscal policies to combat the depression, see Ray Lyman Wilbur and Arthur Mastick Hyde, *The Hoover Policies* (New York: Charles Scribner's Sons, 1937), pp. 359–534.

10. John Kenneth Galbraith, *The Great Crash, 1929* (Boston: Houghton Mifflin, 1961), pp. 142–145.

11. Chandler, *Greatest Depression*, pp. 33–34; Hoover, *Memoirs*, pp. 43–46; Murray N. Rothbard, "Herbert Hoover and the Myth of Laissez-Faire," in *A New History of Leviathan: Essays on the Rise of the American Corporate State*, ed. Ronald Radosh and Murray N. Rothbard (New York: E. P. Dutton, 1972), pp. 128–131; Robert E. Lucas, Jr., and Leonard A. Rapping, "Unemployment in the Great Depression: Is There a Full Explanation?" *Journal of Political Economy* 80 (Jan./Feb. 1972): 186–191; Albert Rees, "Real Wages and Inflation: Rejoinder," ibid., p. 192.

12. Hoover, *Memoirs*, pp. 47–48, 88, 114, 143–144, 156, 162–163; Herbert Stein, *The Fiscal Revolution in America* (Chicago: University of Chicago Press, 1969), pp. 6–24. The Glass-Steagall Act of 1932 should not be confused with the better remembered Glass-Steagall Act of 1933. The latter, also known as the Banking Act of 1933, mandated inter alia the separation of investment and commercial banking and the establishment of the Federal Deposit Insurance Corporation.

13. Hoover, *Memoirs*, pp. 140–141, 118 (also pp. 258–259). On Hoover's use of martial imagery, see Arthur A. Ekirch, Jr., *Ideologies and Utopias: The Impact of the New Deal on American Thought* (Chicago: Quadrangle Books, 1969), p. 50.

14. 47 Stat. 5 (January 22, 1932).

15. Ibid. at 8; Jesse H. Jones, *Fifty Billion Dollars: My Thirteen Years with the RFC* (New York: Macmillan, 1951), pp. 514, 516.

16. Merlo J. Pusey, *Eugene Meyer* (New York: Knopf, 1974), pp. 216–226 (quotation from p. 226); Hoover, *Memoirs*, pp. 98, 107–111, 168–169; Chandler, *Greatest Depression*, pp. 88–90. On the ill-fated National Credit Corporation and its connection with monetary policy-making in 1931, see Gerald Epstein and Thomas Ferguson, "Monetary Policy, Loan Liquidation, and Industrial Conflict: The Federal Reserve and the Open Market Operations of 1932," *Journal of Economic History* 44 (Dec. 1984): 966. On recent proposals for revival of the RFC, see Richard B. McKenzie, "A New Reconstruction Finance Corp.: No Cure for U.S. Economic Ills." *Heritage Foundation Backgrounder*, No. 316 (Dec. 20, 1983). According to Thomas J. DiLorenzo, there are presently "about $30 billion in direct loans . . . [plus] more than 150 federal loan guarantee programs administered by federal agencies that guide the allocation of more than $100 billion in loans annually," all constituting "part of the legacy of the original RFC." See "The Political Economy of National Industrial Policy," *Cato Journal* 4 (Fall 1984): 595. See also pp. 597–600 for an evaluation of the RFC.

17. Hoover as quoted in Broadus Mitchell, *Depression Decade: From New Era through New Deal, 1929–1941* (New York: Harper Torchbooks, 1969), pp. 87–88; "detested politics" from Richard Hofstadter, *The American Political Tradition, And the Men Who Made It* (New York: Vintage, 1974), p. 382.

18. *News* as quoted in William E. Leuchtenburg, *Franklin D. Roosevelt and the New Deal, 1932–1940* (New York: Harper Colophon Books, 1963), p. 15 (also pp. 14–16); Hoover, *Memoirs*, pp. 225–232.

19. Leuchtenburg, *Roosevelt and the New Deal*, p. 13.

20. The splendidly expressive phrase "interregnum of despair" is taken from Jordan A. Schwarz, *The Interregnum of Despair: Hoover, Congress, and the Depression* (Urbana: University of Illinois Press, 1970).

21. Johnson as quoted in Leuchtenburg, *Roosevelt and the New Deal*, p. 28; Schwarz, *Interregnum*, pp. 205–229.

22. Quoted in Schwarz, *Interregnum*, p. 206. Also Barry D. Karl, *The Uneasy State: The United States from 1915 to 1945* (Chicago: University of Chicago Press, 1983), p. 99.

23. Hoover, *Memoirs*, pp. 176–216; Frank Freidel, *Franklin D. Roosevelt: Launching the New Deal* (Boston: Little, Brown, 1973), pp. 18–45, 175–195; Edgar Eugene Robinson, *The Roosevelt Leadership, 1933–1945* (Philadelphia: Lippincott, 1955), pp. 81–103.

24. Friedman and Schwartz, *Monetary History*, pp. 324–327, 331–332, 349–350; Hoover, *Memoirs*, p. 213; Freidel, *Launching the New Deal*, pp. 187–195; Benjamin M. Anderson, *Economics and the Public Welfare: A Financial and Economic History of the United States, 1914–46* (Indianapolis: Liberty Press, 1979), pp. 279–289.

25. 48 Stat. 1689 (March 6, 1933).

26. Ibid. (March 9, 1933) at 1691.

27. Hoover, *Memoirs*, pp. 214–215 (includes quotation of Moley); Freidel, *Launching the New Deal*, pp. 181, 195; Clinton Rossiter, *Constitutional Dictatorship: Crisis Government in the Modern Democracies* (Princeton, N.J.: Princeton University Press, 1948), p. 299 (Rossiter credits Professor Friedrich for the idea expressed).

28. Leuchtenburg, *Roosevelt and the New Deal*, p. 30. Herbert McClosky and John Zaller report that "[e]ven during the Great Depression, 91 percent of the American public opposed dictatorship as a solution to the nation's problems, while only 3 percent endorsed the idea." But the evidence they cite comes from a Gallup poll taken in 1937, when, after four years of recovery, public opinion was far different from what it had been in 1932–1933. *The American Ethos: Public Attitudes toward Capitalism and Democracy* (Cambridge, Mass: Harvard University Press, 1984), p. 74).

29. John A. Garraty, "The New Deal, National Socialism, and the Great Depression," *American Historical Review* 78 (Oct. 1973): 932. Also Ellis W. Hawley, *The Great War and the Search for a Modern Order, A History of the American People and Their Institutions* (New York: St. Martin's Press, 1979), p. 222. Another historian observed that any account of the events of 1933 "will be false to the truth . . . if it does not convey the sense of emergency, the feeling of desperate need, the determination that the will to live should be expressed in ceaseless activity." Robinson, *The Roosevelt Leadership*, p. 114. Karl, *Uneasy State*, p. 111, says that "a sense of crisis had built like the head of steam in a calliope."

30. Lippmann as quoted in Ronald Steel, *Walter Lippmann and the American Century* (Boston: Little, Brown, 1980), pp. 291–292. Also Leuchtenburg, *Roosevelt and the New Deal*, pp. 10–11.

31. Roosevelt's First Inaugural Address, reproduced in *Documents of American History*, 4th ed., ed. Henry Steele Commager (New York: Appleton-Century-Crofts, 1948), II, pp. 420–422; Freidel, *Launching the New Deal*, p. 205.

32. *New State Ice Company* v. *Liebmann*, 285 U.S. 262 (1932), reprinted in *Documents*, ed. Commager, p. 411; Hoover, *Memoirs*, p. 357; 48 Stat. 1 (March 9, 1933); Leuchtenburg, *Roosevelt and the New Deal*, pp. 42–44; Jones, *Fifty Billion Dollars*, p. 22.

33. Hawley, *Great War*, pp. 222–226; Garraty, "The New Deal," pp. 914, 924–925; Robinson, *The Roosevelt Leadership*, pp. 155–156; Murray Edelman, *The Symbolic Uses of Politics* (Urbana: University of Illinois Press, 1964), pp. 78–83. Rossiter described the Congress of the Hundred Days as "practically a wartime legislature" and FDR as "the most crisis-minded public figure in American history, a man who thrived on crises, emergencies, dangers, perils, and panics. . . . The resort to extraordinary power in extraordinary circumstances was instinct for this extraordinary man, and his character is not to be overlooked in any estimate of the crisis government of 1933." *Constitutional Dictatorship*, pp. 256, 259–260.

34. Quoted in Leuchtenburg, *Roosevelt and the New Deal*, p. 62. Freidel observes: "There can be no shred of doubt that Roosevelt was well aware of the unique nature of his opportunity. Not for long could the nation remain at such an emotional pitch or feel that desperate emergency justified Roosevelt's measures. As soon as conditions

improved, the acute pressure for action would slacken. Not for long could he expect heavy majorities in both houses of Congress so speedily to pass bill after bill." *Launching the New Deal*, pp. 301–302.

35. Freidel, *Launching the New Deal*, p. 307.

36. James F. Byrnes, *All in One Lifetime* (New York: Harper and Brothers, 1958), p. 70.

37. William E. Leuchtenburg, "The New Deal and the Analogue of War," in *Change and Continuity in Twentieth-Century America*, ed. John Braeman, Robert H. Bremner, and Everett Walters (Columbus: Ohio State University Press, 1964), pp. 109, 122–123.

38. Freidel, *Launching the New Deal*, pp. 88, 320–339; Chandler, *Greatest Depression*, pp. 164–168; Friedman and Schwartz, *Monetary History*, pp. 462–483; Jones, *Fifty Billion Dollars*, pp. 245–254; U.S. Bureau of the Census, *Historical Statistics*, p. 197; Anderson, *Economics and the Public Welfare*, pp. 314–318, 338–348 (quotations from pp. 316–317). According to Friedman and Schwartz (p. 466), "The aim of the gold policy to raise prices of farm products and raw materials was . . . largely achieved."

39. 48 Stat. 31 (May 12, 1933).

40. Freidel, *Launching the New Deal*, pp. 83–101, 299–319 (quotations from pp. 90, 311). On the sharecroppers, see Warren C. Whatley, "Labor for the Picking: The New Deal in the South," *Journal of Economic History* 43 (Dec. 1983): 905–929.

41. Leuchtenburg, *Roosevelt and the New Deal*, p. 50; 48 Stat. at 51–54.

42. 48 Stat. at 35, 39; Bernard Baruch, *Baruch: The Public Years* (New York: Holt, Rinehart & Winston, 1960), pp. 250–251; Leuchtenburg, "The New Deal," pp. 112–113; Mitchell, *Depression Decade*, p. 187; Chandler, *Greatest Depression*, pp. 215–219.

43. 48 Stat. 195 (June 16, 1933) at 195–196.

44. Ellis W. Hawley, *The New Deal and the Problem of Monopoly: A Study in Economic Ambivalence* (Princeton, N.J.: Princeton University Press, 1966), pp. 35–52; Chamber's Committee as quoted by Hofstadter, *The American Political Tradition*, p. 431; Byrnes, *All in One Lifetime*, p. 79.

45. Hawley, *Problem of Monopoly*, pp. 21–31.

46. 48 Stat. at 198–199; Freidel, *Launching the New Deal*, p. 447.

47. Hawley, *Problem of Monopoly*, pp. 54–55.

48. Garraty, "The New Deal," pp. 925–932 (quotations from pp. 930, 932); Hawley, *Problem of Monopoly*, pp. 53–54. For a survey of contemporary comment on the New Deal's fascistic aspect, see Ekirch, *Ideologies and Utopias*, pp. 180, 183, 188–190.

49. Hawley, *Problem of Monopoly*; Chandler, *Greatest Depression*, pp. 223–236; Hoover, *Memoirs*, pp. 420–432 entitled "Fascism Comes to Business—with Dire Consequences."

50. Robert H. Jackson, *The Struggle for Judicial Supremacy: A Study of a Crisis in American Power Politics* (New York: Knopf, 1941), pp. 75, 115.

51. *Home Building and Loan Association* v. *Blaisdell et al.*, 290 U.S. 398 (1934). For an econometric analysis of the causes and effects of the moratoria, see Alston, "Farm Foreclosure Moratorium Legislation," pp. 445–457.

52. Archibald M. Woodruff, Jr., *Farm Mortgage Loans of Life Insurance Companies* (New Haven, Conn.: Yale University Press, 1937), pp. 108–111; William L. Prosser, "The Minnesota Mortgage Moratorium," *Southern California Law Review* 7 (1934), as reprinted in *Selected Essays on Constitutional Law: Book 2. Limitations on Governmental Power*, comp. and ed. Committee of the Association of American Law Schools (Chicago: Foundation Press, 1938), pp. 359–371.

53. Prosser, "Minnesota Mortgage Moratorium," p. 367; 290 U.S. at 409; Holmes's "very verge" from *Pennsylvania Coal Company* v. *Mahon*, 260 U.S. 393

(1921). Also Jane Perry Clark, "Emergencies and the Law," *Political Science Quarterly* 49 (June 1934): 268–283. For a recent study of the emergency powers doctrine, which is far more comprehensive than its title suggests, see Michal R. Belknap, "The New Deal and the Emergency Powers Doctrine," *Texas Law Review* 62 (1983): 67–109.

54. 290 U.S. at 425, 426, 428, 437, 440–441, 444.

55. Paul L. Murphy, *The Constitution in Crisis Times, 1918–1969* (New York: Harper Torchbooks, 1972), p. 110; Prosser, "Minnesota Mortgage Moratorium," p. 373.

56. 290 U.S. at 448, 465, 471, emphasis in original.

57. Ibid. at 473–474.

58. *Nebbia* v. *New York*, 291 U.S. 502 (1934).

59. Murphy, *Constitution*, p. 113.

60. Bernard H. Siegan, *Economic Liberties and the Constitution* (Chicago: University of Chicago Press, 1980), p. 143.

61. 291 U.S. as reprinted in *Documents*, ed. Commager, II, pp. 479–481.

62. 291 U.S. as quoted in Siegan, *Economic Liberties*, pp. 140–141.

63. Murphy, *Constitution*, pp. 114–115; Siegan, *Economic Liberties*, pp. 145–150; Norman Karlin, "Substantive Due Process: A Doctrine for Regulatory Control," in *Rights and Regulations: Ethical, Political, and Economic Issues*, ed. Tibor R. Machan and M. Bruce Johnson (Cambridge: Ballinger, 1983), pp. 43–70.

64. *Norman C. Norman* v. *Baltimore and Ohio Railroad Company* and *U.S.* v. *Bankers Trust Company*, 294 U.S. 240 (1935); *F. Eugene Nortz* v. *U.S.*, 294 U.S. 317 (1935); *John M. Perry* v. *U.S.*, 294 U.S. 330 (1935).

65. 48 Stat. 113 (June 5, 1933).

66. Murphy, *Constitution*, p. 137 (the phrase "masterpiece" belongs to Arthur M. Schlesinger, Jr.); Jackson, *Struggle*, p. 102, says "Chinese puzzle."

67. 294 U.S. at 311, 307–310.

68. Ibid. at 353–354, 355, 357.

69. Murphy, *Constitution*, pp. 137–138.

70. 294 U.S. at 361, 369, 372, 377, 378, 381.

71. *Panama Refining Co.* v. *Ryan*, 293 U.S. 388 (1935); Murphy, *Constitution*, pp. 136–137. "Political realist" is the description of William O. Douglas, *Go East, Young Man: The Early Years. The Autobiography of William O. Douglas* (New York: Vintage, 1983), p. 401.

72. *U.S.* v. *A. L. A. Schechter Poultry Corporation*, 295 U.S. 495 (1935).

73. Ibid. at 528, 537–538, 553, 548.

74. *U.S.* v. *William M. Butler et al., Receivers of Hoosac Mills Corporation*, 297 U.S. 1 (1936) at 68, 75, 87, 80.

75. Arthur S. Link and William B. Catton, *American Epoch: A History of the United States since 1900*, 4th ed. (New York: Knopf, 1973), II, pp. 124, 148.

76. Leuchtenburg, *Roosevelt and the New Deal*, p. 163; Larry G. Gerber, *The Limits of Liberalism: Josephus Daniels, Henry Stimson, Bernard Baruch, Donald Richberg, Felix Frankfurter, and the Development of the Modern American Political Economy* (New York: New York University Press, 1983), p. 306.

77. Jesse H. Jones, *Fifty Billion Dollars*; U.S. Council of Economic Advisers, *Annual Report, 1979* (Washington, D.C.: U.S. Government Printing Office, 1979), pp. 106–108.

78. Chandler, *Greatest Depression*, pp. 219–222 (quotation from p. 222).

79. Ibid., pp. 236–237; Leuchtenburg, *Roosevelt and the New Deal*, pp. 161–163, 261–263; Mitchell, *Depression Decade*, pp. 278, 332–333; Gary D. Libecap, "The Political Economy of the Establishment of the Interstate Oil Cartel, 1933–1940," in *Emergence of the Modern Political Economy*, ed. Robert Higgs (Greenwich, Conn.: JAI Press, 1985). More generally, Rossiter observed that "the emergency practices of the

Year of Crisis wrought several lasting alterations in the constitutional structure," including "important permanent delegations of crisis power . . . ; a greatly expanded administration; a marked breakdown of the federal principle; and a general increase of presidential power based on executive leadership in the lawmaking process and the delegation of power." *Constitutional Dictatorship*, p. 264.

80. Hawley, *Problem of Monopoly*, p. 189 (pp. 149–280 for an excellent extended discussion of how much was salvaged from the NRA experiment after the *Schechter* decision). Also Otis L. Graham, Jr., *Toward a Planned Society: From Roosevelt to Nixon* (New York: Oxford University Press, 1976), pp. 1–68.

81. Anderson, *Economics and the Public Welfare*, p. 430 ("naked bid"); Murphy, *Constitution*, pp. 156–169 (quotations from pp. 157, 166); Douglas, *Go East, Young Man*, pp. 318–327, 457–459; Robinson, *The Roosevelt Leadership*, pp. 195–212; Siegan, *Economic Liberties*, pp. 184–203; Karlin, "Substantive Due Process," pp. 62–63, 68; Michael Conant, *The Constitution and Capitalism* (St. Paul, Minn.: West Publishing Co., 1974), pp. 137–147; Edward S. Corwin, *Total War and the Constitution* (New York: Knopf, 1947), p. 170.

82. Link and Catton, *American Epoch*, II, p. 183; Leuchtenburg, *Roosevelt and the New Deal*, p. 340; Freidel, *Launching the New Deal*, pp. 60–82; Michael E. Parrish, *Felix Frankfurter and His Times: The Reform Years* (New York: Free Press, 1982), pp. 238–251; Richard H. Pels, *Radical Visions and American Dreams: Culture and Social Thought in the Depression Years* (New York: Harper & Row, 1973), esp. pp. 43–95 on "Political and Economic Thought, 1929–1935"; Ekirch, *Ideologies and Utopias*, passim.

83. Herbert Stein, *Presidential Economics: The Making of Economic Policy from Roosevelt to Reagan and Beyond* (New York: Simon & Schuster, 1984), p. 63; Nathan Glazer, "The Social Policy of the Reagan Administration: A Review," *Public Interest* (Spring 1984): 97. For ample confirmation by a leading figure in the Reagan administration, see David A. Stockman, *The Triumph of Politics: Why the Reagan Revolution Failed* (New York: Harper & Row, 1986), passim: "a drastic shrinking of the welfare state was not [President Reagan's] conception of the Reagan Revolution" (p. 276); "The Reaganites were, in the final analysis, just plain welfare state politicians like everybody else" (p. 385).

84. Frank H. Knight, *Freedom and Reform: Essays in Economics and Social Philosophy* (Indianapolis: Liberty Press, 1982), p. 73; Leuchtenburg, *Roosevelt and the New Deal*, p. 333; Link and Catton, *American Epoch*, II, p. 184. Also Stein, *Presidential Economics*, pp. 29, 32. According to Karlyn Keene, the editor of *Public Opinion* magazine, many students have found that people who reached political maturity during the 1930s "have carried throughout their adult lives different attitudes than those who came before and after them. They tend to be more sympathetic to government involvement in the economy." See "What We Know of Baby-Boomer Beliefs," *Wall Street Journal*, Oct. 3, 1984.

CHAPTER NINE

1. U.S. Council of Economic Advisers, *Annual Report* (Washington, D.C.: U.S. Government Printing Office, 1984), pp. 220–221; War Records Section, U.S. Bureau of the Budget, *The United States at War: Development and Administration of the War Program by the Federal Government* (Washington, D.C.: U.S. Government Printing Office, 1946), p. 104.

2. Luther Gulick, *Administrative Reflections from World War II* (University: University of Alabama Press, 1948), p. 110. Also Roland Young, *Congressional Politics in the Second World War* (New York: Columbia University Press, 1956), p. 11.

3. W. H. Auden, "In Memory of W. B. Yeats," 1939.

4. Roosevelt as quoted in Edgar Eugene Robinson, *Roosevelt Leadership, 1933–1945* (Philadelphia: Lippincott, 1955), p. 242.

5. Arthur S. Link and William B. Catton, *American Epoch: A History of the United States since 1900*, 4th ed. (New York: Knopf, 1973), p. 223.

6. Alonzo L. Hamby, *Liberalism and Its Challengers: FDR to Reagan* (New York: Oxford University Press, 1985), pp. 37–43 (quotation from p. 40). Also Link and Catton, *American Epoch*, pp. 214–247; Barry D. Karl, *The Uneasy State: The United States from 1915 to 1945* (Chicago: University of Chicago Press, 1983), pp. 182–204; James MacGregor Burns, *Roosevelt: The Soldier of Freedom* New York: Harcourt Brace Jovanovich, 1970), p. 6; Clinton L. Rossiter, *Constitutional Dictatorship: Crisis Government in the Modern Democracies* (Princeton, N.J.: Princeton University Press, 1948), pp. 266–268. After noting "the unedifying spectacle of President Roosevelt and Wendell Willkie both giving and the country assurances [in the 1940 campaign] that our young men would not have to fight on foreign soil," Benjamin M. Anderson asked in disgust: "Shall we never again have presidential candidates who will tell the people the truth?" *Economics and the Public Welfare: A Financial and Economic History of the United States, 1914–46* (Indianapolis: Liberty Press, 1979), p. 505.

7. U.S. Bureau of the Census, *Historical Statistics of the United States, Colonial Times to 1970* (Washington, D.C.: U.S. Government Printing Office, 1975), p. 1141; Henry L. Stimson and McGeorge Bundy, *On Active Service in Peace and War* (London: Hutchinson, 1947), pp. 161–162; Albert A. Blum and J. Douglas Smyth, "Who Should Serve: Pre–World War II Planning for Selective Service," *Journal of Economic History* 30 (June 1970): 379–404. A notable exception: Senator Robert A. Taft proposed that "the army should be composed of volunteers, not conscripts. If the pay for soldiers were increased to $1000 per year and if a $40 per month food and clothing allowance were added, the army could easily attract 750,000 men. . . . In the frightening late summer of 1940 the Senate rejected, 55 to 32, Taft's amendment limiting the peacetime army to 500,000 volunteers and 1,500,000 reservists." James T. Patterson, *Mr. Republican: A Biography of Robert A. Taft* (Boston: Houghton Mifflin, 1972), p. 241.

8. Vandenberg as quoted by Richard Gillam, "The Peacetime Draft: Voluntarism to Coercion," in *The Military Draft: Selected Readings on Conscription*, ed. Martin Anderson (Stanford, Calif.: Hoover Institution Press, 1982), p. 100 (also pp. 101–104); Ashhurst and George as quoted in War Records Section, *United States at War*, p. 36 (also p. 37 for changes in public opinion on the draft in 1940).

9. 54 Stat. 885 (Sept. 16, 1940), emphasis added.

10. Ibid. p. 892.

11. U.S. Bureau of the Census, *Historical Statistics*, p. 1141.

12. Burns, *Roosevelt*, p. 120; Stimson and Bundy, *On Active Service*, pp. 184–186.

13. U.S. Bureau of the Census, *Historical Statistics*, p. 1140; Stimson and Bundy, *On Active Service*, p. 162; War Records Section, *United States at War*, pp. 38–41.

14. Arthur A. Ekirch, Jr., *Ideologies and Utopias: The Impact of the New Deal on American Thought* (Chicago: Quadrangle Books, 1969), p. 254. After passage of the Tydings Amendment to the Selective Service Act, which gave a blanket deferment to virtually all farm workers, agriculture became early in 1943 "a haven for draft-dodgers." Jacob J. Kaufman, "Farm Labor during World War II," *Journal of Farm Economics* 31 (Feb. 1949): 134–137.

15. Wesley C. Mitchell, "Wartime 'Prosperity' and the Future," National Bureau of Economic Research *Occasional Paper 9* (March 1943), pp. 2–3. Also Jordan A. Schwarz, *The Speculator: Bernard M. Baruch in Washington, 1917–1956* (Chapel Hill: University of North Carolina Press, 1981), pp. 332–333.

16. On the War Resources Board, see Albert A. Blum, "Birth and Death of the M-Day Plan," in *American Civil-Military Decisions*, ed. Harold Stein (Birmingham:

University of Alabama Press, 1962), pp. 61–96, and R. Elberton Smith, *The Army and Economic Mobilization* (Washington, D.C.: U.S. Army, 1959), pp. 99–105. "Mismanaged, confused" from Robert Sobel, *The Age of Giant Corporations: A Microeconomic History of American Business, 1914–1970* (Westport, Conn.: Greenwood Press, 1972), p. 158; Richard Polenberg, *War and Society: The United States, 1941–1945* (New York: Lippincott, 1972), pp. 6–7; Bernard M. Baruch, *Baruch: The Public Years* (New York: Holt, Rinehart & Winston, 1960), p. 284 (also pp. 264, 280–283); Schwarz, *The Speculator*, pp. 358–388. For a detailed account of the development of the government's administrative apparatus for mobilization before the attack on Pearl Harbor, see War Records Section, *United States at War*, pp. 50–63, 73–89.

17. 54 Stat. 573 (June 25, 1940).

18. Jesse H. Jones, *Fifty Billion Dollars: My Thirteen Years with the RFC* (New York: Macmillan, 1951), pp. 315–484 (quotation from p. 9). At the end of 1941, Jones was described as "the second most powerful man in the government." See "The War Goes to Mr. Jesse Jones," *Fortune* 24 (Dec. 1941): 91.

19. "President Roosevelt's Broadcast on the War with Japan," in *Documents of American History*, ed. Henry Steele Commager (New York: Appleton-Century-Crofts, 1948), II, pp. 637–639. Students of rhetoric may find FDR's use of the "gangster" metaphor especially interesting.

20. Young, *Congressional Politics*, pp. 29–30; 55 Stat. 838 (December 18, 1941) at 838–841.

21. 56 Stat. 176 (March 27, 1942) at 176–180, emphasis added. Also Edward S. Corwin, *Total War and the Constitution* (New York: Knopf, 1947), pp. 41–43.

22. War production goals from War Records Section, *United States at War*, p. 103.

23. Ibid., pp. 235–239; Hugh Rockoff, *Drastic Measures: A History of Wage and Price Controls in the United States* (New York: Cambridge University Press, 1984), pp. 87–90; Chester Bowles, *Promises to Keep: My Years in Public Life, 1941–1969* (New York: Harper & Row, 1971), pp. 49–50; John Kenneth Galbraith, *A Life in Our Times; Memoirs* (New York: Ballantine Books, 1981), pp. 139–143 (quotation from p. 139).

24. War Records Section, *United States at War*, pp. 239–248; Burns, *Roosevelt*, pp. 196–197.

25. Public Law 421, 77th Cong., 2nd Sess., Chap. 26 (Jan. 30, 1942).

26. Explanation: provision (1) was most favorable for wheat, corn, oats, barley, sweet potatoes, soybeans, peanuts, and flaxseed; provision (2) was most favorable for cottonseed and certain types of tobacco; provision (3) was most favorable for rice, eggs, beef cattle, veal calves, and wool; and provision (4) was most favorable for potatoes, edible dry beans, cotton, live chickens, and lambs. War Records Section, *United States at War*, p. 247, fn. 26. One is reminded of Mencken's characterization of the American farmer: "No more grasping, selfish and dishonest mammal, indeed, is known to students of the Anthropoidea." H. L. Mencken, *Prejudices: A Selection*, ed. James T. Farrell (New York: Vintage Books, 1955), pp. 159–160.

27. War Records Section, *United States at War*, p. 105.

28. Ibid., pp. 254–257; Polenberg, *War and Society*, pp. 31–33 (quotation from pp. 32–33).

29. Bowles, *Promises to Keep*, p. 62.

30. La Guardia as quoted in Polenberg, *War and Society*, p. 33. Also Seymour E. Harris, *Price and Related Controls in the United States* (New York: McGraw-Hill, 1945), p. 28. Bowles (*Promises to Keep*, p. 42) noted that after the congressional elections of 1942 the OPA "was gradually becoming a haven for defeated [Democratic] politicians."

31. War Records Section, *United States at War*, pp. 259–267; Harris, *Price and Related Controls*, pp. 111–112, 130; Bowles, *Promises to Keep*, p. 40.

32. Burns, *Roosevelt*, pp. 260–262 (quotation from p. 261); War Records Sec-

tion, *United States at War*, pp. 267–270. Corwin noted that Roosevelt's ultimatum of September 7 "can only be interpreted as a claim of power on the part of the President to suspend the Constitution in a situation deemed by him to make such a step necessary." Crown, *Total War and the Constitution*, p. 64.

33. 56 Stat. 765 (October 2, 1942).

34. War Records Section, *United States at War*, pp. 271–272, 388.

35. Hugh Rockoff, "Indirect Price Increases and Real Wages during World War II," *Explorations in Economic History* 15 (October 1978): 407–420; idem, "The Response of the Giant Corporations to Wage and Price Controls in World War II, *Journal of Economic History* 41 (March 1981): 123–128; idem, "Price and Wage Controls in Four Wartime Periods," *Journal of Economic History* 41 (June 1981): 381–401; idem, *Drastic Measures*, pp. 127–176; Paul Evans, "The Effects of General Price Controls in the United States during World War II," *Journal of Political Economy* 90 (Oct. 1982): 944–966.

36. Harris, *Price and Related Controls*, pp. 29–30, 58.

37. Stimson and Bundy, *On Active Service*, p. 269; Samuel P. Huntington, *The Soldier and the State: The Theory and Politics of Civil-Military Relations* (Cambridge, Mass.: Belknap Press, 1957), p. 316; John W. Eley, "Management Structures for Industrial Mobilization in the 1980s: Lessons from World War II," in *Mobilization and the National Defense*, ed. Hardy L. Merritt and Luther F. Carter (Washington, D.C.: National Defense University Press, 1985), pp. 25–36; Smith, *Army and Economic Mobilization*, passim.

38. Sobel, *Age of Giant Corporations*, pp. 166, 168; Burns, *Roosevelt*, p. 246. A total of $303.7 billion computed from data in U.S. Council of Economic Advisers, *Annual Report*, p. 221. The figure would of course be much larger—seven or eight times larger—if expressed in dollars of present-day purchasing power.

39. Burns, *Roosevelt*, p. 191; Huntington, *Soldier and the State*, p. 340.

40. War Records Section, *United States at War*, pp. 113–114. Also Burns, *Roosevelt*, pp. 246–247; Smith, *Army and Economic Mobilization*, pp. 154–158.

41. Huntington, *Soldier and the State*, pp. 340–342; Polenberg, *War and Society*, pp. 219–227; Paul A. C. Koistinen, "Mobilizing the World War II Economy: Labor and the Industrial-Military Alliance," *Pacific Historical Review* 42 (Nov. 1973): 454; Schwarz, *The Speculator*, pp. 427–441. For a detailed account, see War Records Section, *United States at War*, chaps. 5, 10, 12, esp. pp. 129–131, 280–281.

42. War Records Section, *United States at War*, p. 281. Also Koistinen, "Mobilizing," p. 449.

43. Polenberg, *War and Society*, pp. 218–219; Harris, *Price and Related Controls*, pp. 248–249, 259–264; Koistinen, "Mobilizing," p. 446; John Morton Blum, *V Was for Victory: Politics and American Culture During World War II* (New York: Harcourt Brace Jovanovich, 1976), pp. 117–146; Louis Cain and George Neumann, "Planning for Peace: The Surplus Property Act of 1944," *Journal of Economic History* 41 (March 1981): 129–135; Jones, *Fifty Billion Dollars*, pp. 338–339; Roger A. Beaumont, "Quantum Increase: The MIC [military-industrial complex] in the Second World War," in *War, Business, and American Society: Historical Perspectives on the Military-Industrial Complex*, ed. Benjamin Franklin Cooling (Port Washington, N.Y.: Kennikat Press, 1977), pp. 127–128; Smaller War Plants Corporation, *Economic Concentration and World War II* (Washington, D.C.: U.S. Government Printing Office, 1946), pp. 21–54; Smith, *Army and Economic Mobilization*, pp. 262–266 and passim.

44. Sobel, *Age of Giant Corporations*, p. 165; Blum, *V Was for Victory*, p. 115. Jones (*Fifty Billion Dollars*, p. 331) remarked that Kaiser "was ready to try anything if the government would put up the money."

45. Anderson, *Economics and the Public Welfare*, p. 555; Beaumont, "Quantum Increase," p. 132. The figure of $3 trillion computed from data in U.S. Council of Economic Advisers, *Annual Report*, p. 221 and U.S. Office of Management and Budget, *The United States Budget in Brief; Fiscal Year 1986* (1985), p. 65. For a good

selection of information and opinion on the military-industrial complex, see James L. Clayton, ed., *The Economic Impact of the Cold War: Sources and Readings* (New York: Harcourt, Brace & World, 1970). Also Jacques S. Gansler, *The Defense Industry* (Cambridge, Mass.: MIT Press, 1980).

46. War Records Section, *United States at War*, pp. 195–201.

47. Ibid., pp. 190–191; Polenberg, *War and Society*, pp. 155–156.

48. War Records Section, *United States at War*, pp. 192–194; Polenberg, *War and Society*, pp. 156–158. See the marvelously informative compilation of seizures attached to Justice Frankfurter's concurring opinion in *Youngstown Sheet & Tube Co. et al. v. Sawyer*, 343 U.S. 579 (1952) at 621–628. According to Rockoff, "The Response of the Giant Corporations," p. 127, fn. 15, citing John L. Blackman's *Presidential Seizure in Labor Disputes*, "At least a third of the top 100 corporations experienced seizure, either the whole firm or at least a plant or subsidiary." Also Rockoff, *Drastic Measures*, pp. 119–120.

49. War Records Section, *United States at War*, pp. 194–195; Polenberg, *War and Society*, pp. 158–159; U.S. Bureau of the Census, *Historical Statistics*, p. 178.

50. Polenberg, *War and Society*, pp. 161–170; Burns, *Roosevelt*, pp. 335–337; James F. Byrnes, *All in One Lifetime* (New York: Harper & Brothers, 1958), p. 182.

51. *War Labor Disputes Act*, Chapter 144, Public Law 89, 78th Cong., 1st Sess., June 25, 1943; Young, *Congressional Politics*, pp. 63–65; Polenberg, *War and Society*, pp. 166–169; Blum, *V Was for Victory*, p. 241.

52. Polenberg, *War and Society*, pp. 170–175; Jones, *Fifty Billion Dollars*, pp. 478–481. For the legal technicalities, see Corwin, *Total War and the Constitution*, pp. 66–70.

53. War Records Section, *United States at War*, pp. 182–189.

54. Polenberg, *War and Society*, pp. 20–22; War Records Section, *United States at War*, pp. 429–447.

55. Polenberg, *War and Society*, pp. 176–177; War Records Section, *United States at War*, pp. 188–189; Stimson and Bundy, *On Active Service*, pp. 261–263; Koistinen, "Mobilizing," pp. 456–457; Byrnes, *All in One Lifetime*, pp. 206–207.

56. War Records Section, *United States at War*, pp. 450–455; Polenberg, *War and Society*, pp. 177–183; Stimson and Bundy, *On Active Service*, pp. 264–266; Koistinen, "Mobilizing," pp. 457–460; Corwin, *Total War and the Constitution*, pp. 88–91.

57. Polenberg, *War and Society*, p. 25 (also pp. 179–181); Schwarz, *The Speculator*, p. 452.

58. Corwin, *Total War and the Constitution*, pp. 83–84.

59. Clinton Rossiter and Richard P. Longaker, *The Supreme Court and the Commander in Chief*, exp. ed. (Ithaca, N.Y.: Cornell University Press, 1976), p. 97. Also Paul L. Murphy, *The Constitution in Crisis Times, 1918–1969* (New York: Harper Torchbooks, 1972), pp. 222–224, 246.

60. Rossiter and Longaker, *The Supreme Court and the Commander in Chief*, p. 91; Corwin, *Total War and the Constitution*, p. 177; *United States of America v. Bethlehem Steel Corporation*, 315 U.S. 289 (1942) at 305.

61. Rossiter and Longaker, *The Supreme Court and the Commander in Chief*, p. 100.

62. *Albert Yakus v. United States of America*, 321 U.S. 414 (1944).

63. Ibid. at 451, 458–460.

64. Ibid. at 481.

65. *Chester Bowles v. Mrs. Kate C. Willingham and J. R. Hicks, Jr.*, 321 U.S. 503 (1944) at 514–521.

66. Ibid. at 529–541.

67. Corwin, *Total War and the Constitution*, pp. 56–61 (quotations from pp. 56, 59).

68. *L. P. Steuart & Bro., Inc. v. Chester Bowles*, 322 U.S. 398 (1944) at 405–406. "Administrative blackjacking" from Corwin, *Total War and the Constitution*, p. 60.

69. Rossiter and Longaker, *The Supreme Court and the Commander in Chief*, p. 99.

On the indirect sanctions under Carter's program, see Robert Higgs, "Carter's Wage-Price Guidelines: A Review of the First Year," *Policy Review* (Winter 1980): 97–113, and idem, "Wage-Price Guidelines: Retreat and Defeat," *Freeman* 31 (Nov. 1981): 643–652.

70. Jones, *Fifty Billion Dollars*, pp. 325–326, emphasis added.

71. *Jacob Lichter* v. *United States of America, A. V. Pownall* v. *United States of America, Alexander Wool Combing Company* v. *United States of America*, 334 U.S. 742 (1948) at 754, 776–777, 784.

72. *Gordon Kiyoshi Hirabayashi* v. *United States of America*, 320 U.S. 81 (1943) at 93, 101. Related cases were *Fred Toyosaburo Korematsu* v. *United States of America*, 323 U.S. 214 (1944) and *Ex Parte Mitsuye Endo*, 323 U.S. 283 (1944). For a succinct account of the Japanese-American internment, see Murphy, *Constitution*, pp. 232–242 or William Petersen, *Japanese Americans: Oppression and Success* (New York: Random House, 1971), pp. 66–100. For a complete and highly detailed account, see Jacobus tenBroek, Edward N. Barnhart, and Floyd W. Matson, *Prejudice, War and the Constitution* (Berkeley: University of California Press, 1954).

73. Corwin, *Total War and the Constitution*, p. 131; Rossiter and Longaker, *The Supreme Court and the Commander in Chief*, p. 100.

74. War Records Section, *United States at War*, pp. 491–492, 499–500 (quotation from p. 491); Polenberg, *War and Society*, p. 235.

75. War Records Section, *United States at War*, pp. 495, 500.

76. Robert J. Donovan, *Conflict and Crisis: The Presidency of Harry S. Truman, 1945–1948* (New York: Norton, 1977), pp. 236–237, 239; Jones, *Fifty Billion Dollars*, p. 373; Rockoff, *Drastic Measures*, pp. 98–108, 155; Bowles, *Promises to Keep*, pp. 166–191; Rossiter, *Constitutional Dictatorship*, p. 285. Rent controls migrated after the war to the state and local levels of government, the outstanding case being New York, later said to have experienced a "30-year rent control emergency." Peter Navarro, *The Policy Game: How Special Interests and Ideologues Are Stealing America* (New York: Wiley, 1984), pp. 13, 25.

77. Herbert Stein, *The Fiscal Revolution in America* (Chicago: University of Chicago Press, 1969), p. 171. The correct view is succinctly stated (with no more than the usual hyperbole) by Jonathan R. T. Hughes, "Stagnation Without 'Flation: The 1930s Again," in *Money in Crisis: The Federal Reserve, the Economy, and Monetary Reform*, ed. Barry N. Siegal (Cambridge, Mass.: Ballinger, 1984), pp. 154–155: "It is no problem to solve unemployment if you put the unemployed into military service, cut civilian output of durables to the bone, and create a military force big enough to conquer the world. . . . We did that in 1942–45."

78. "Employment Act of 1946," as reproduced in *Documents*, 9th ed., ed. Commager, II, pp. 514–516.

79. Calvin B. Hoover, *The Economy, Liberty and the State* (New York: Twentieth Century Fund, 1959), p. 240.

80. U.S. Bureau of the Census, *Historical Statistics*, p. 179.

81. "Taft-Hartley Act," 80th Cong., Public Law 101, partially reproduced in *Documents*, 9th ed., ed. Commager, II, pp. 537–541.

82. *Selective Service Act of 1948*, 80th Cong., 2nd Sess., Chapter 625, Public Law 759, June 24, 1948; Gillam, "The Peacetime Draft," pp. 105–110. On the economics of the draft, see Edgar K. Browning and Jacquelene M. Browning, *Public Finance and the Price System*, 2nd ed. (New York: Macmillan, 1983), pp. 412–416.

83. Young, *Congressional Politics*, pp. 213–217; Polenberg, *War and Society*, pp. 96–97; Blum, *V Was for Victory*, pp. 248–250, 337 (quotation from p. 337); U.S. Bureau of the Census, *Historical Statistics*, pp. 1145–1146. Thomas Sowell notes that the GI Bill "had an almost revolutionary effect on the ability of blacks to attend college." *Civil Rights: Rhetoric or Reality?* (New York: William Morrow, 1984), p. 86. Davis R. B. Ross concludes that the veterans' benefits "acted as a flywheel, so

to speak, to continue the impetus of the Federal Government's expanding promotion of the general welfare. Thus, when the steam appeared to have escaped from the engine of the New Deal by 1945, the World War II nondisabled veterans' benefits— by design and by chance—provided new sources of energy." *Preparing for Ulysses: Politics and Veterans During World War II* (New York: Columbia University Press, 1969), p. 290.

84. U.S. Bureau of the Census, *Historical Statistics*, p. 1105. Also Ben Baack and Edward John Ray, "The Political Economy of the Origin and Development of the Federal Income Tax," in *Emergence of the Modern Political Economy*, ed. Robert Higgs (Greenwich, Conn.: JAI Press, 1985), pp. 132–133; John F. Witte, *The Politics and Development of the Federal Income Tax* (Madison: University of Wisconsin Press, 1985), pp. 110–130. Witte notes (p. 128) that "1944 and 1945 were the most progressive tax years in U.S history."

85. U.S. Bureau of the Census, *Historical Statistics*, p. 872.

86. Ibid., p. 1141.

87. Robert J. Gordon, "$45 Billion of U.S. Private Investment Has Been Mislaid," *American Economic Review* 69 (June 1969): 221–238 (esp. the table on p. 227); Cain and Neumann, "Planning for Peace," pp. 129–135 and "Discussion" by Thomas K. McCraw, p. 137. Also Gansler, *The Defense Industry*, pp. 54–57, 284, 288, 292.

88. Corwin, *Total War and the Constitution*, p. 179 (also pp. 172, 174, and passim).

89. Alan S. Milward, *War, Economy and Society, 1939–1945* (Berkeley: University of California Press, 1977), pp. 128, 244, 343.

90. Hoover, *Economy, Liberty and the State*, p. 212; Jones, *Fifty Billion Dollars*, p. 546 (for a list of names, see the appendix to Jones's book entitled "Some RFC Alumni Who Have Done Well," pp. 602–608). Also Herbert Stein, *Presidential Economics: The Making of Economic Policy from Roosevelt to Reagan and Beyond* (New York: Simon and Schuster, 1984), pp. 65–67.

91. James Madison, "The Federalist No. 44," in *The Federalist* (New York: Modern Library, n.d.), p. 291.

92. War Records Section, *United States at War*, pp. 462–463.

CHAPTER TEN

1. Jonathan Hughes, *American Economic History* (Glenview, Ill.: Scott, Foresman, 1983), p. 450. Also Otis L. Graham, Jr., *Toward a Planned Society: From Roosevelt to Nixon* (New York: Oxford University Press, 1976), esp. pp. 79–82.

2. The literature on the military-industrial complex is voluminous. See, for example, James L. Clayton, ed., *The Economic Impact of the Cold War: Sources and Readings* (New York: Harcourt, Brace & World, 1970); Steven Rosen, ed., *Testing the Theory of the Military-Industrial Complex* (Lexington, Mass.: Lexington Books, 1973); Paul A. C. Koistinen, *The Military-Industrial Complex: A Historical Perspective* (New York: Praeger, 1980); Jacques S. Gansler, *The Defense Industry* (Cambridge, Mass.: MIT Press, 1980); J. William Fulbright, *The Pentagon Propaganda Machine* (New York: Vintage Books, 1971). According to recent reports, the Pentagon employs 1,066 full-time public relations people and spends over $25 million per year on public relations. Tom G. Palmer, "Uncle Sam's Ever-Expanding P.R. Machine," *Wall Street Journal*, January 10, 1985; Peter Navarro, *The Policy Game: How Special Interests and Ideologues Are Stealing America* (New York: Wiley, 1984), p. 254 (the uniformed services add another $25 million).

3. "FmHA to make emergency loans to farmers in '84," Easton (Pa.) *Express*, Dec. 28, 1983; "U.S. Extends Deadline to Seek Price Supports," New York *Times*,

Feb. 19, 1984; "Cuba-travel ban is reimposed until high court gets more facts," Seattle *Times,* June 25, 1983; "Reagan Extends Law on Export Authority of Commerce Agency," *Wall Street Journal,* April 2, 1984; "Crop loans help farmers, but more is needed," Easton (Pa.) *Express,* July 26, 1985, reporting a "$1 billion emergency measure signed by Reagan." Also Robert Higgs, "To Deal with a Crisis: Governmental Program or Free Market?" *Freeman* 36 (Sept. 1986): 331–335.

 4. Joseph A. Schumpeter, *Capitalism, Socialism and Democracy,* 3rd ed. (New York: Harper & Row, 1950), pp. 415–417.

 5. Ibid., pp. 417–418.

 6. Ibid., pp. 420–421.

 7. Ibid., pp. 421–424. For an analytical extension and updating of Schumpeter's argument about the role of inflation, see Robert Higgs, "Inflation and the Destruction of the Free Market Economy," *Intercollegiate Review* 14 (Spring 1979): 67–76.

 8. Seymour E. Harris, ed., *Schumpeter, Social Scientist* (Cambridge, Mass.: Harvard University Press, 1951); Arnold Heertje, ed., *Schumpeter's Vision* (New York: Praeger, 1981); John E. Elliott, "Marx and Schumpeter on Capitalism's Creative Destruction: A Comparative Restatement," *Quarterly Journal of Economics* 95 (August 1980): 45–68; Richard D. Coe and Charles K. Wilber, eds., *Capitalism and Democracy: Schumpeter Revisited* (Notre Dame, Ind.: University of Notre Dame Press, 1985).

 9. William Fellner, "March into Socialism, or Viable Postwar Stage of Capitalism?" in *Schumpeter's Vision,* ed. Heertje, p. 52; Schumpeter, *Capitalism, Socialism and Democracy,* p. 375.

 10. Douglas F. Greer, *Business, Government, and Society* (New York: Macmillan, 1983), pp. 531–533; Edward S. Herman, *Corporate Control, Corporate Power* (New York: Cambridge University Press, 1981), pp. 164–172. Every major industrial economy has relatively more government ownership of industry than the United States; and the extent of government ownership has not changed markedly during the post–World War II era in the United States.

 11. Charlotte Twight, *America's Emerging Fascist Economy* (New Rochelle, N.Y.: Arlington House, 1975), Chap. 1; Friedrich A. Hayek, *The Road to Serfdom* (Chicago: University of Chicago Press, 1944), p. 4.

 12. Richard Gillam, "The Peacetime Draft: Voluntarism to Coercion," *Yale Review* 57 (June 1968), reprinted in *The Military Draft: Selected Readings on Conscription,* ed. Martin Anderson (Stanford: Hoover Institution Press, 1982), p. 113.

 13. Alonzo L. Hamby, *Liberalism and Its Challengers: FDR to Reagan* (New York: Oxford University Press, 1985), p. 307; Frank Freidel, *America in the Twentieth Century,* 4th ed. (New York: Knopf, 1976), pp. 381–392. According to Herbert Stein, "The free market economists of the Nixon administration, and the President himself, regarded the draft for military service in peacetime as an intolerable infringement of personal liberty and an extremely unfair tax." *Presidential Economics: The Making of Economic Policy from Roosevelt to Reagan and Beyond* (New York: Simon and Schuster, 1984), p. 195; Richard M. Nixon, *RN: The Memoirs of Richard Nixon* (New York: Grosset & Dunlap, 1978), p. 522. My judgment that Nixon ended the draft expediently rather than ideologically rests on my belief that he almost invariably acted as an unprincipled political animal. In this case the principle came very cheap, so he upheld it. For some evidence, including the testimony of his aides, that Nixon "had no convictions . . . but did what was feasible and tactically shrewd," see Graham, *Toward a Planned Society,* pp. 247–258 (quotation from p. 255).

 14. Twight, *America's Emerging Fascist Economy,* pp. 14–17, emphasis in original.

 15. Ibid., pp. 17–29 (quotations from pp. 21–22). For data on the revolving door between the Pentagon and the contractors, see William Proxmire, "Retired High-Ranking Military Officers," in *The Military-Industrial Complex,* ed. Carroll W. Pursell, Jr. (New York: Harper & Row, 1972), pp. 253–262. In 1969, for example, the one

hundred largest prime military contractors employed 2,072 former military officers of the rank of colonel, navy captain, or higher. A New York *Times* editorial ("A War Machine Mired in Sleaze," March 31, 1985) reported that during 1981–1983, "at least 1,900 high-ranking officers retired from the military and went to work for contractors." Also Navarro, *Policy Game*, pp. 257–258. For extensive discussions of the personal nexus between big business and big government, see Thomas R. Dye, *Who's Running America?* (Englewood Cliffs, N.J.: Prentice-Hall, 1983) and G. William Domhoff, *Who Rules America Now?* (Englewood Cliffs, N.J.: Prentice-Hall, 1983). After an extensive survey of the evidence, Domhoff (p. 143) concludes that "the highest levels of the executive branch, especially in the State, Defense, and Treasury departments, are interlocked constantly with the corporate community through the movement of executives and lawyers in and out of government. . . . [T]here is enough continuity for the relationship to be described as one of 'revolving interlocks.'"

16. Twight, *America's Emerging Fascist Economy*, pp. 279–280.

17. Douglass C. North, "Structure and Performance: The Task of Economic History," *Journal of Economic Literature* 16 (September 1978): 967 (pp. 966–967 present an excellent short critique of the Schumpeterian framework as applied to American history). Also Thomas K. McCraw, *Prophets of Regulation: Charles Francis Adams, Louis D. Brandeis, James M. Landis, Alfred E. Kahn* (Cambridge, Mass.: Belknap Press, 1984), p. 67: "The most conspicuous political warfare" of the late nineteenth century "matched *one group of businessmen against another*" (emphasis in original).

18. William E. Simon, *A Time for Truth* (New York: Berkley Books, 1979), pp. 210–211.

19. Leland B. Yeager, "Is There a Bias Toward Overregulation?" in *Rights and Regulation: Ethical, Political, and Economic Issues*, ed. Tibor R. Machan and M. Bruce Johnson (Cambridge, Mass.: Ballinger, 1983), pp. 106–107. Herman, *Corporate Control, Corporate Power*, Chap. 5, emphasizes the ambiguous relationship—half master, half servant—of big business to the government. Compare Warren J. Samuels, "A Critique of *Capitalism, Socialism, and Democracy*," in *Capitalism and Democracy*, ed. Coe and Wilber, esp. pp. 90–93, 107–108.

20. Schumpeter, *Capitalism, Socialism and Democracy*, p. 72.

21. Jordan A. Schwarz, *The Speculator: Bernard M. Baruch in Washington, 1917–1965* (Chapel Hill: University of North Carolina Press, 1981), pp. 526–534; Benjamin H. Williams, *Emergency Management of the National Economy. Vol. 21. Reconversion and Partial Mobilization* (Washington, D.C.: Industrial College of the Armed Forces, 1956), pp. 61–62; Hugh Rockoff, *Drastic Measures: A History of Wage and Price Controls in the United States* (New York: Cambridge University Press, 1984), pp. 177–178. The Defense Production Act was patterned after a draft "Emergency Powers Act" produced by the National Security Resources Board, an agency created by the National Security Act of 1947. Leon N. Karadbil and Roderick L. Vawter, "The Defense Production Act: Crucial Component of Mobilization Preparedness," in *Mobilization and the National Defense*, ed. Hardy L. Merritt and Luther F. Carter (Washington, D.C.: National Defense University Press, 1985), pp. 37–41.

22. Proclamation Number 2914, 15 Fed. Reg. 9029 (December 16, 1950).

23. Williams, *Emergency Management*, pp. 62–64; Rockoff, *Drastic Measures*, pp. 179–184.

24. U.S. Bureau of the Census, *Historical Statistics of the United States, Colonial Times to 1970* (Washington, D.C.: U.S. Government Printing Office, 1975), pp. 198, 1140.

25. Quotation from Williams, *Emergency Management*, pp. 64–65.

26. Ibid., p. 66.

27. *Youngstown Sheet & Tube Co. et al.* v. *Sawyer*, 343 U.S. 579 (1952) at 587, 653, 700. See Paul L. Murphy, *The Constitution in Crisis Times, 1918–1969* (New York: Harper Torchbooks, 1972), pp. 288–290.

28. Stein, *Presidential Economics*, p. 84. Also Graham, *Toward a Planned Society*, pp. 99–101, 114–125; Hamby, *Liberalism*, pp. 121–123.

29. Stein, *Presidential Economics*, pp. 97–100 (quotation from p. 98).

30. Henry J. Aaron, *Politics and the Professors: The Great Society in Perspective* (Washington, D.C.: Brookings Institution, 1978), p. 151. Also Samuel P. Huntington, "The Democratic Distemper," in *The American Commonwealth, 1976*, ed. Nathan Glazer and Irving Kristol (New York: Basic Books, 1976), pp. 13–16. For survey data corroborating the mass allegiance to the mixed economy, see Herbert McClosky and John Zaller, *The American Ethos: Public Attitudes toward Capitalism and Democracy* (Cambridge, Mass.: Harvary University Press, 1984), esp. pp. 148, 157, 271, 291, 300–301.

31. Irving Kristol, "On Corporate Capitalism in America," in *The American Commonwealth*, ed. Glazer and Kristol, p. 134. Also Seymour Martin Lipset, "The Paradox of American Politics," ibid., pp. 161–163; Paul H. Weaver, "Regulation, Social Policy, and Class Conflict," *Public Interest* (Winter 1978): 56–62. For a critique of the New Class theory, see Peter Steinfels, *The Neoconservatives: The Men Who Are Changing America's Politics* (New York: Simon & Schuster, 1979), esp. pp. 285–290.

32. U.S. Bureau of the Census, *Statistical Abstract*, 100th ed. (Washington, D.C.: U.S. Government Printing Office, 1979), p. 507; Aaron, *Politics and the Professors*, p. 3. Also Stein, *Presidential Economics*, pp. 114–115; Lawrence D. Brown, *New Policies, New Politics: Government's Response to Government's Growth* (Washington, D.C.: Brookings Institution, 1983), p. 1; Hamby, *Liberalism*, pp. 231–232, 248–260. Keith T. Poole and R. Steven Daniels calculate that the election of 1974 produced a Congress even more liberal than the one elected in 1964. "Ideology, Party, and Voting in the U.S. Congress, 1959–1980," *American Political Science Review* 79 (June 1985): 383.

33. Brown, *New Policies, New Politics*, pp. 40–42, 52 (quotations from pp. 41–42). Also Huntington, "Democratic Distemper," pp. 10, 28.

34. Brown, *New Policies, New Politics*, p. 42; Huntington, "Democratic Distemper," p. 35; David Ignatius, "Vietnam's Legacy: A Decade after War, U.S. Leaders Still Feel Effects of the Defeat," *Wall Street Journal*, Jan. 14, 1985, p. 10. Also James Q. Wilson, "The Rise of the Bureaucratic State," in *The American Commonwealth*, ed. Glazer and Kristol, p. 97; Hamby, *Liberalism*, pp. 278–279.

35. Hamby, *Liberalism*, p. 317.

36. Stein gave his chapter on the Nixon administration, which he served as a top economic adviser, the subtitle "Conservative Men with Liberal Ideas." *Presidential Economics*, p. 133. Daniel Patrick Moynihan, Nixon's adviser on social programs, warned the President: "All the Great Society activist constituencies are lying out there in wait, poised to get you if you try to come after them: the professional welfarists, the urban planners, the day-carers, the social workers, the public housers. Frankly, I'm terrified at the thought of cutting back too fast." A. James Reichley, *Conservatives in an Age of Change: The Nixon and Ford Administrations* (Washington, D.C.: Brookings Institution, 1981), pp. 56–58, 382, and passim.

37. Brown, *New Policies, New Politics*, p. 68. Also Aaron, *Politics and the Professors*, p. 150. Half a century ago Walter Lippmann distinguished good from bad crises, the good ones being those that generate the will and the power to fashion solutions. Remarkably he regarded the Great Depression as a good crisis, as he put it "a lucky break." Arthur A. Ekirch, Jr., *Ideologies and Utopias: The Impact of the New Deal on American Thought* (Chicago: Quadrangle Books, 1969), p. 91.

38. Proclamation Number 3972 (March 23, 1970); Proclamation Number 4074

(August 15, 1971). Hamby, *Liberalism*, p. 337, describes Nixon as "envisioning his life as that of a man who moves from one extreme situation (crisis) to another."

39. U.S. Senate, 93rd Cong., 1st Sess., Special Committee on the Termination of the National Emergency, *Emergency Powers Statutes: Provisions of Federal Law Now in Effect Delegating to the Executive Extraordinary Authority in Time of National Emergency* [printed for use of the committee], September 1973, p. iii.

40. National Emergencies Act, 50 U.S.C. Sec. 1601–1651 (1976); International Emergency Economic Powers Act, 50 U.S.C. Sec. 1701–1706 (1977); Charlotte Twight, "U.S. Regulation of International Trade: A Retrospective Inquiry," in *Emergence of the Modern Political Economy*, ed. Robert Higgs (Greenwich, Conn.: JAI Press, 1985), pp. 180–182; Robert Higgs and Charlotte Twight, "National Emergency and the Erosion of Private Property Rights," *Cato Journal* 6 (Winter 1987).

41. Stein, *Presidential Economics*, p. 168; Edward R. Tufte, *Political Control of the Economy* (Princeton, N.J.: Princeton University Press, 1978), esp. pp. 29–54; Robert R. Keller and Ann Mari May, "The Presidential Political Business Cycle of 1972," *Journal of Economic History* 44 (June 1984): 265–271; James E. Alt and K. Alec Chrystal, *Political Economics* (Berkeley: University of California Press, 1983), pp. 103–125; Bruno S. Frey, *Modern Political Economy* (Oxford: Martin Robertson, 1978), pp. 125–142.

42. Reichley, *Conservatives*, pp. 205–231 (quotations from pp. 205, 206, 220); Nixon, *RN: The Memoirs*, pp. 515–522 (quotation from p. 518); Stein, *Presidential Economics*, pp. 133–187; George P. Shultz and Kenneth W. Dam, *Economic Policy Beyond the Headlines* (New York: Norton, 1977), pp. 65–85; Rockoff, *Drastic Measures*, pp. 200–233.

43. Nixon, *RN: The Memoirs*, p. 521; Stein, *Presidential Economics*, p. 180.

44. Stein, *Presidential Economics*, p. 187; Robert Higgs, "Carter's Wage-Price Guidelines: A Review of the First Year," *Policy Review* 11 (Winter 1980): 97–113. Hamby, *Liberalism*, p. 324, recognizes the sense in which Nixon's "new economic policy" was successful.

45. Simon, *A Time for Truth*, p. 54. Also Stein, *Presidential Economics*, pp. 190–194; Shultz and Dam, *Economic Policy*, pp. 179–197; Reichley, *Conservatives*, pp. 358–381. For a comprehensive analysis of the energy crises, see David Glasner, *Politics, Prices, and Petroleum* (Cambridge, Mass.: Ballinger, 1985).

46. Simon, *A Time for Truth*, pp. 50, 55.

47. Stephen Chapman, "The Gas Lines of '79," *Public Interest* (Summer 1980): 40–49; Glasner, *Politics, Prices, and Petroleum*, pp. 130–137.

48. William Greider, *The Education of David Stockman and Other Americans* (New York: E. P. Dutton, 1982), pp. 87–89. The complete text of the memorandum appears as an appendix to Greider's book, pp. 137–159. Also Leonard Silk, *Economics in the Real World* (New York: Simon & Schuster, 1984), pp. 173–176.

49. Greider, *Education of David Stockman*, pp. 150–151, emphasis in original.

50. Ibid., pp. 44, 59. Doug Bandow, who served under Reagan as Special Assistant to the President for Policy Development, wrote that "the Reagan team soon lost enthusiasm for cutting back federal jurisdiction. . . . President Reagan did virtually nothing to tear out the statutory roots of regulation. What little he did accomplish can be reversed by the stroke of a new president's pen." See "The Terrible Ten: America's Worst Regulations," *Policy Review* (Spring 1985): 42.

51. For diverse descriptions and evaluations of the Reagan adminstration's economic policies, see Stein, *Presidential Economics*, pp. 263–314; John L. Palmer and Isabel V. Sawhill, eds., *The Reagan Experiment* (Washington, D.C.: The Urban Institute, 1982); idem, *The Reagan Record* (Cambridge, Mass.: Ballinger, 1984); Milton Friedman and Rose Friedman, *Tyranny of the Status Quo* (New York: Harcourt, Brace, Jovanovich, 1984), esp. pp. 29–34, 124–129; Robert D. Hershey, Jr.,

"The Reagan Economic Legacy," New York *Times*, October 28, 1984; Leonard Silk, "Reagan's High Risk Growth Game," New York *Times*, Feb. 10, 1985; Paul Craig Roberts, *The Supply-Side Revolution: An Insider's Account of Policymaking in Washington* (Cambridge, Mass.: Harvard University Press, 1984); Paul Blustein, "Reagan's Record: Recent Budget Battles Leave the Basic Tenets of Welfare State Intact; Paring Rather Than Ending Programs Will Let Them Flourish in Another Era; The Social Security Blunder," *Wall Street Journal*, Oct. 21, 1985; David A. Stockman, *The Triumph of Politics: How the Reagan Revolution Failed* (New York: Harper & Row, 1986).

52. Stockman, *Triumph of Politics*, pp. 8–14 and passim (quotation from p. 9); Stein, *Presidential Economics*, pp. 312–313.

53. F. A. Hayek, *The Constitution of Liberty* (Chicago: University of Chicago Press, 1960), pp. 397–411 entitled "Why I Am Not a Conservative." Hayek noted (p. 401) that "the conservative does not object to coercion or arbitrary power so long as it is used for what he regards as the right purposes."

Select Bibliography

The following references indicate some of the more important works consulted by the author in the preparation of this book. They can serve as a guide for those who want to pursue in greater depth the various topics considered here. The list does not contain all the sources cited in the Notes section; in particular, statutes, standard statistical compilations, and textbooks (except a few especially useful and pertinent ones) are not listed. Anyone wishing to confirm the evidence of the text will find full publication details in the Notes section. Although the following sources are listed under headings intended to suggest their major pertinence, many apply to more than one category. In only a few instances has a work been listed more than once.

ECONOMICS, POLITICS, AND GOVERNMENT

Alt, James E. "The Evolution of Tax Structures." *Public Choice* 41 (1983).

Alt, James E., and K. Alec Chrystal. *Political Economics*. Berkeley: University of California Press, 1983.

Auster, Richard D., and Morris Silver. *The State as a Firm: Economic Factors in Political Development*. Boston: Nijhoff, 1979.

Barry, Brian. *Sociologists, Economists and Democracy*. Chicago: University of Chicago Press, 1978.

Becker, Gary. "A Theory of Competition among Pressure Groups for Political Influence." *Quarterly Journal of Economics* 98 (Aug. 1983).

Bowles, Samuel. "State Structures and Political Practices: A Reconsideration of the Liberal Democratic Conception of Politics and Accountability." In *Capitalism and Democracy: Schumpeter Revisited*, ed. Richard D. Coe and Charles K. Wilber. Notre Dame, Ind.: University of Notre Dame Press, 1985.

Break, George F. "The Role of Government: Taxes, Transfers, and Spending." In *The American Economy in Transition*, ed. Martin Feldstein. Chicago: University of Chicago Press, 1980.

Browning, Edgar K., and Jacquelene M. Browning. *Public Finance and the Price System*. 2nd ed. New York: Macmillan, 1983.

Buchanan, James M. *The Limits of Liberty: Between Anarchy and Leviathan*. Chicago: University of Chicago Press, 1975.

Drew, Elizabeth. *Politics and Money: The New Road to Corruption*. New York: Macmillan, 1983.

Dye, Thomas. *Understanding Public Policy*. 2nd ed. Englewood Cliffs, N.J.: Prentice-Hall, 1975.

Frey, Bruno S. *Modern Political Economy*. Oxford: Martin Robertson, 1978.

Friedman, Milton, and Rose Friedman. *Tyranny of the Status Quo*. New York: Harcourt Brace Jovanovich, 1984.

Galbraith, John Kenneth. *American Capitalism: The Concept of Countervailing Power*. 2nd ed. Boston: Houghton Mifflin, 1956.

———. *The Anatomy of Power*. Boston: Houghton Mifflin, 1983.

Greer, Douglas F. *Business, Government, and Society*. New York: Macmillan, 1983.

Hansen, John Mark. "The Political Economy of Group Membership." *American Political Science Review* 79 (March 1985).

Hardin, Russell. *Collective Action*. Baltimore: Johns Hopkins University Press, 1982.

Hayek, Friedrich A. *The Road to Serfdom*. Chicago: University of Chicago Press, 1944.

———. *The Constitution of Liberty*. Chicago: University of Chicago Press, 1960.

Hechter, Michael. "A Theory of Group Solidarity." In *The Micro-foundations of Macrosociology*, ed. Michael Hechter. Philadelphia: Temple University Press, 1983.

Heertje, Arnold, ed. *Schumpeter's Vision: Capitalism, Socialism and Democracy after 40 Years*. New York: Praeger, 1981.

Herman, Edward S. *Corporate Control, Corporate Power*. New York: Cambridge University Press, 1981.

Higgs, Robert. "Inflation and the Destruction of the Free Market Economy." *Intercollegiate Review* 14 (Spring 1979).

———. "To Deal with a Crisis: Governmental Program or Free Market?" *Freeman* 36 (Sept. 1986).

Hirschman, Albert O. *Essays in Trespassing: Economics to Politics and Beyond*. New York: Cambridge University Press, 1981.

———. *Shifting Involvements: Private Interest and Public Action*. Princeton, N.J.: Princeton University Press, 1982.

———. "Against Parsimony: Three Ways of Complicating Some Categories of Economic Discourse." *American Economic Review* 74 (May 1984).

Hoover, Calvin B. *The Economy, Liberty, and the State*. New York: Twentieth Century Fund, 1959.

Keeler, Theodore E. "Theories of Regulation and the Deregulation Movement." *Public Choice* 44 (1984).

Knight, Frank H. *Freedom and Reform: Essays in Economics and Social Philosophy*. Indianapolis: Liberty Press, 1982.

LeLoup, Lance T. *Budgetary Politics*. Brunswick, Ohio: King's Court Communications, 1980.

McKenzie, Richard B. *Bound To Be Free*. Stanford, Calif.: Hoover Institution Press, 1982.

Margolis, Howard. *Selfishness, Altruism, and Rationality: A Theory of Social Choice*. Chicago: University of Chicago Press, 1982.

McCraw, Thomas K. "Regulation in America: A Review Article," *Business History Review* 49 (Summer 1975).

Mitchell, Robert Cameron. "National Environmental Lobbies and the Apparent Illogic of Collective Action." In *Collective Decision Making: Applications from Public Choice Theory*, ed. Clifford S. Russell. Baltimore: Johns Hopkins University Press, 1979.

Nisbet, Robert. *Twilight of Authority*. New York: Oxford University Press, 1975.

Nordlinger, Eric. *On the Autonomy of the Democratic State.* Cambridge, Mass.: Harvard University Press, 1981.

Nutter, G. Warren. *Political Economy and Freedom: A Collection of Essays.* Indianapolis: Liberty Press, 1983.

Oates, Wallace E. "Searching for Leviathan: An Empirical Study." *American Economic Review* 75 (Sept. 1985).

Olson, Mancur. *The Logic of Collective Action: Public Goods and the Theory of Groups.* Cambridge, Mass.: Harvard University Press, 1965.

———. *The Rise and Decline of Nations: Economic Growth, Stagflation, and Social Rigidities.* New Haven, Conn.: Yale University Press, 1982.

Opp, Karl-Dieter. "Economics, Sociology, and Political Protest." In *Theoretical Models and Empirical Analyses: Contributions to the Explanation of Individual Actions and Collective Phenomena*, ed. Werner Raub. Utrecht: E.S.-Publications, 1982.

Pasour, E. C., Jr. "The Free Rider as a Basis for Government Intervention." *Journal of Libertarian Studies* 5 (Fall 1981).

Peltzman, Sam. "Constituent Interest and Congressional Voting." *Journal of Law and Economics* 27 (April 1984).

———. "An Economic Interpretation of the History of Congressional Voting in the Twentieth Century." *American Economic Review* 75 (Sept. 1985).

Reid, Joseph D., Jr. "Understanding Political Events in the New Economic History." *Journal of Economic History* 37 (June 1977).

Reiter, Stanley, and Jonathan Hughes. "A Preface on Modeling the Regulated United States Economy." *Hofstra Law Review* 9 (Summer 1981).

Roberts, Russell D. "A Taxonomy of Public Provision." *Public Choice* 47 (1985).

Rourke, Francis E. *Bureaucracy, Politics, and Public Policy.* 2nd ed. Boston: Little Brown, 1976.

Samuels, Warren J. "A Critique of *Capitalism, Socialism, and Democracy*." In *Capitalism and Democracy: Schumpeter Revisited*, ed. Richard D. Coe and Charles K. Wilber. Notre Dame, Ind.: University of Notre Dame Press, 1985.

Samuels, Warren J., and Nicholas Mercuro. "A Critique of Rent-Seeking Theory." In *Neoclassical Political Economy*, ed. David C. Colander. Cambridge, Mass.: Ballinger, 1984.

Schumpeter, Joseph A. *Capitalism, Socialism, and Democracy.* 3rd ed. New York: Harper & Row, 1950.

Sen, Amartya K. "Rational Fools: A Critique of the Behavioral Foundations of Economic Theory." *Philosophy & Public Affairs* 6 (Summer 1977).

Siegel, Barry N., ed. *Money in Crisis: The Federal Reserve, the Economy, and Monetary Reform.* Cambridge, Mass.: Ballinger, 1984.

Sowell, Thomas. *Knowledge and Decisions.* New York: Basic Books, 1980.

Stigler, George J. *The Citizen and the State: Essays on Regulation.* Chicago: University of Chicago Press, 1975.

Thaler, Richard H. "Illusions and Mirages in Public Policy." *Public Interest* (Fall 1983).

Tufte, Edward. *Political Control of the Economy.* Princeton, N.J.: Princeton University Press, 1978.

Twight, Charlotte. "Government Manipulation of Constitutional-Level Transaction Costs: An Economic Theory and Its Application to Off-Budget Expenditure through the Federal Financing Bank." Ph.D. diss., University of Washington, 1983.

Wallace, Donald H. *Economic Controls and Defense.* New York: Twentieth Century Fund, 1953.

Weidenbaum, Murray L. *Business, Government, and the Public.* 2nd ed. Englewood Cliffs, N.J.: Prentice-Hall, 1981.

Weingast, Barry R. "The Congressional-Bureaucratic System: A Principal Agent Perspective (with applications to the SEC)." *Public Choice* 44 (1984).

Wilson, Graham K. *Interest Groups in the United States.* Oxford: Clarendon Press, 1981.

Witte, John F. *The Politics and Development of the Federal Income Tax* (Madison: University of Wisconsin Press, 1985).

Yeager, Leland B. "Is There a Bias Toward Overregulation." In *Rights and Regulation: Ethical, Political, and Economic Issues,* ed. Tibor R. Machan and M. Bruce Johnson. Cambridge, Mass.: Ballinger, 1983.

GROWTH OF GOVERNMENT

Bennett, James T., and Manuel H. Johnson. *The Political Economy of Federal Government Growth, 1959–1978.* College Station, Tex.: Center for Education and Research in Free Enterprise, 1980.

Borcherding, Thomas E. "The Sources of Growth of Public Expenditures in the United States, 1902–1970." In *Budgets and Bureaucrats: The Sources of Government Growth,* ed. Thomas E. Borcherding. Durham, N.C.: Duke University Press, 1977.

Break, George F. "Issues in Measuring the Level of Government Activity." *American Economic Review* 72 (May 1982).

Brown, Lawrence. *New Policies, New Politics: Government's Response to Government's Growth.* Washington, D.C.: Brookings Institution, 1983.

Crain, W. Mark, Robert D. Tollison, Brian Goff, and Dick Carlson. "Legislator Specialization and the Size of Government. *Public Choice* 46 (1985).

Fabricant, Solomon. *The Trend of Government Activity in the United States since 1900.* New York: National Bureau of Economic Research, 1952.

Herber, Bernard P., and Paul U. Pawlik. "Measuring Government's Role in the Mixed Economy: A New Approach." *National Tax Journal* 36 (March 1983).

Hughes, Jonathan R. T. *The Governmental Habit: Economic Controls from Colonial Times to the Present.* New York: Basic Books, 1977.

Lowery, David, and William D. Berry. "The Growth of Government in the United States: An Empirical Assessment of Competing Explanations." *American Journal of Political Science* 27 (Nov. 1983).

Meltzer, Allan H., and Scott F. Richard. "Why Government Grows (and Grows) in a Democracy." *Public Interest* (Summer 1978).

———. "A Rational Theory of the Size of Government." *Journal of Political Economy* 89 (Oct. 1981).

———. "Tests of a Rational Theory of the Size of Government." *Public Choice* 41 (1983).

Niskanen, William A. "The Growth of Government." *Cato Policy Report* 7 (July/Aug. 1985).

Pathirane, Leila, and Derek W. Blades. "Defining and Measuring the Public Sector: Some International Comparisons." *Review of Income and Wealth* 28 (Sept. 1982).

Peacock, Alan T., and Jack Wiseman. *The Growth of Public Expenditure in the United Kingdom.* Princeton, N.J.: Princeton University Press, 1961.

Peltzman, Sam. "The Growth of Government." *Journal of Law and Economics* 23 (Oct. 1980).

Peters, B. Guy, and Martin O. Heisler. "Thinking About Public Sector Growth: Conceptual, Theoretical, and Policy Considerations." In *Why Governments Grow: Measuring Public Sector Size,* ed. Charles Lewis Taylor. Beverly Hills, Calif.: Sage, 1983.

Porter, Bruce D. "Parkinson's Law Revisited: War and the Growth of American Government." *Public Interest* (Summer 1980).

Rasler, Karen A., and William R. Thompson. "War Making and State Making: Governmental Expenditures, Tax Revenues, and Global Wars." *American Political Science Review* 79 (June 1985).

Rose, Richard. "Are Laws a Cause, a Constraint, or Irrelevant to the Growth of Government?" *Studies in Public Policy Number 124.* Glasgow: Center for the Study of Public Policy, University of Strathclyde, 1984.

IDEOLOGY, IDENTITY, AND RHETORIC

Babad, Elisha, Max Birnbaum, and Kenneth D. Benne. *The Social Self: Group Influences on Personal Identity.* Beverly Hills, Calif.: Sage, 1983.

Bell, David V. J. *Power, Influence, and Authority: An Essay in Political Linguistics.* New York: Oxford University Press, 1975.

Bennett, W. Lance. *Public Opinion in American Politics.* New York: Harcourt Brace Jovanovich, 1980.

Berger, Peter L., and Thomas Luckmann. *The Social Construction of Reality: A Treatise in the Sociology of Knowledge.* Garden City, N.Y.: Anchor Books, 1967.

Edelman, Murray. *The Symbolic Uses of Politics.* Urbana: University of Illinois Press, 1964.

———. *Political Language: Words That Succeed and Policies That Fail.* New York: Academic Press, 1977.

Elster, Jon. *Sour Grapes: Studies in the Subversion of Rationality.* Cambridge: Cambridge University Press, 1983.

Geertz, Clifford. "Ideology as a Cultural System." In *Ideology and Discontent,* ed. David E. Apter. New York: Free Press, 1964.

Gouldner, Alvin W. *The Dialectic of Ideology and Technology: The Origins, Grammar, and Future of Ideology.* New York: Oxford University Press, 1976.

Higgs, Robert. "Identity and Cooperation: A Comment on Sen's Alternative Program." *Journal of Law, Economics, and Organization* 3 (Spring 1987).

Kalt, Joseph P., and M. A. Zupan. "Capture and Ideology in the Economic Theory of Politics." *American Economic Review* 74 (June 1984).

Kau, James B., and Paul H. Rubin. *Congressmen, Constituents, and Contributors: Determinants of Roll Call Voting in the House of Representatives.* Boston: Nijhoff, 1982.

Maddox, William S., and Stuart A. Lilie. *Beyond Liberal and Conservative: Reassessing the Political Spectrum.* Washington, D.C.: Cato Institute, 1984.

McClosky, Herbert, and John Zaller. *The American Ethos: Public Attitudes toward Capitalism and Democracy.* Cambridge, Mass.: Harvard University Press, 1984.

Poole, Keith T., and R. Steven Daniels. "Ideology, Party, and Voting in the U.S. Congress, 1959–1980." *American Political Science Review* 79 (June 1985).

Sartori, Giovanni. "Politics, Ideology, and Belief Systems." *American Political Science Review* 63 (June 1969).

Schambra, William A. "Progressive Liberalism and American 'Community.'" *Public Interest* (Summer 1985).

Seliger, Martin. *Ideology and Politics* (New York: Free Press, 1976).

———. *The Marxist Conception of Ideology: A Critical Essay.* Cambridge: Cambridge University Press, 1977.

Sen, Amartya. "Goals, Commitments, and Identity." *Journal of Law, Economics, and Organization* 1 (Fall 1985).

THE LATE NINETEENTH CENTURY

Bryce, James. *The American Commonwealth.* 3rd ed. London: Macmillan, 1895.

Chandler, Alfred D. *The Visible Hand: The Managerial Revolution in American Business.* Cambridge, Mass.: Belknap Press, 1977.

Higgs, Robert. *The Transformation of the American Economy, 1865–1914: An Essay in Interpretation.* New York: Wiley, 1971.

Hoffman, Charles. *The Depression of the Nineties: An Economic History.* Westport, Conn.: Greenwood, 1970.

Keller, Morton. *Affairs of State: Public Life in Late Nineteenth Century America.* Cambridge, Mass.: Belknap Press, 1977.

Kolko, Gabriel. *Railroads and Regulation, 1877–1916.* Princeton, N.J.: Princeton University Press, 1965.

Kraditor, Aileen S. *The Radical Persuasion, 1890–1917: Aspects of the Intellectual History and the Historiography of Three American Radical Organizations.* Baton Rouge: Louisiana State University Press, 1981.

Letwin, William. *Law and Economic Policy in America: The Evolution of the Sherman Antitrust Act.* Chicago: University of Chicago Press, 1965.

MacAvoy, Paul W. *The Economic Effects of Regulation: The Trunk-Line Railroad Cartels and the Interstate Commerce Commission.* Cambridge, Mass.: MIT Press, 1965.

McGuire, Robert A. "Economic Causes of Late Nineteenth-Century Agrarian Unrest." *Journal of Economic History* 41 (Dec. 1981).

Meeker, Edward. "The Social Rate of Return on Investment in Public Health, 1880–1910." *Journal of Economic History* 34 (June 1974).

Miller, George H. *Railroads and the Granger Laws.* Madison: University of Wisconsin Press, 1971.

Nevins, Allan. *Grover Cleveland: A Study in Courage.* New York: Dodd, Mead, 1932.

Resneck, Samuel. "Unemployment, Unrest, and Relief in the United States during the Depression of 1893–97." *Journal of Political Economy* 61 (Aug. 1953).

Skowronek, Stephen. *Building a New American State: The Expansion of National Administrative Capacities, 1877–1920.* New York: Cambridge University Press, 1982.

Tipple, John. *The Capitalist Revolution: A History of American Social Thought, 1890–1919.* New York: Pegasus, 1970.

Tunnell, George. "The Legislative History of the Second Income-Tax Law." *Journal of Political Economy* 3 (June 1895).

Turner, James. "Understanding the Populists." *Journal of American History* 67 (Sept. 1980).

Waltman, Jerold. "Origins of the Federal Income Tax." *Mid-America* 62 (Oct. 1980).

White, Gerald T. *The United States and the Problem of Recovery after 1893.* University: University of Alabama Press, 1982.

Wiebe, Robert H. *The Search for Order, 1877–1920.* New York: Hill & Wang, 1967.

Williams, Jeffrey C. "Economics and Politics: Voting Behavior in Kansas during the Populist Decade." *Explorations in Economic History* 18 (July 1981).

Williams, R. Hal. *Years of Decision: American Politics in the 1890's.* New York: Wiley, 1978.

THE PROGRESSIVE ERA

Adams, Graham, Jr. *Age of Industrial Violence, 1910–15: The Activities and Findings of the United States Commission on Industrial Relations.* New York: Columbia University Press, 1966.

Baack, Ben[nett D.], and Edward John Ray. "The Political Economy of the Origin and Development of the Federal Income Tax." In *Emergence of the Modern Political Economy*, ed. Robert Higgs. Greenwich, Conn.: JAI Press, 1985.

——. "Special Interests and the Adoption of the Income Tax in the United States." *Journal of Economic History* 45 (Sept. 1985).

Ekirch, Arthur A., Jr. *Progressivism in America.* New York: New Viewpoints, 1974.

Forcey, Charles. *The Crossroads of Liberalism: Croly, Weyl, Lippmann, and the Progressive Era, 1900–1925.* New York: Oxford University Press, 1961.

Gilbert, James. *Designing the Industrial State: The Intellectual Pursuit of Collectivism in America, 1880–1940.* Chicago: Quadrangle Books, 1972.

Kennedy, David M., ed. *Progressivism: The Critical Issues.* Boston: Little, Brown, 1971.

Kerr, K. Austin. *American Railroad Politics, 1914–1920: Rates, Wages, and Efficiency.* Pittsburgh: University of Pittsburgh Press, 1968.

Kolko, Gabriel. *The Triumph of Conservatism: A Reinterpretation of American History, 1900–1916.* Chicago: Quadrangle Books, 1967.

Link, Arthur S., and Richard L. McCormick. *Progressivism.* Arlington Heights, Ill.: Harland Davidson, 1983.

Martin, Albro. *Enterprise Denied: Origins of the Decline of American Railroads, 1897–1917.* New York: Columbia University Press, 1971.

McCraw, Thomas K. "Rethinking the Trust Question." In *Regulation in Perspective: Historical Essays*, ed. Thomas K. McCraw. Cambridge, Mass.: Harvard University Press, 1981.

Rodgers, Daniel T. "In Search of Progressivism." *Reviews in American History* (Dec. 1982).

Skowronek, Stephen. *Building a New American State: The Expansion of National Administrative Capacities, 1877–1920.* New York: Cambridge University Press, 1982.

Steffens, Lincoln. *The Shame of the Cities.* New York: Hill & Wang, 1967; originally published 1904.

Tariello, Frank, Jr. *The Reconstruction of American Political Ideology, 1865–1917.* Charlottesville: University of Virginia Press, 1982.

Tipple, John. *The Capitalist Revolution: A History of American Social Thought, 1890–1919.* New York: Pegasus, 1970.

Waltman, Jerold. "Origins of the Federal Income Tax." *Mid-America* 62 (Oct. 1980).

Wiebe, Robert H. *Businessmen and Reform: A Study of the Progressive Movement.* Chicago: Quadrangle Books, 1968.

——. *The Search for Order, 1877–1920.* New York: Hill & Wang, 1967.

Wilson, Woodrow. *The New Freedom.* 3rd ed. Garden City, N.Y.: Doubleday Page, 1921.

WORLD WAR I

Baker, Charles Whiting. *Government Control and Operation of Industry in Great Britain and the United States during the World War.* New York: Oxford University Press, 1921.

Beaver, Daniel R. "The Problem of American Military Supply, 1890–1920." In *War, Business, and American Society: Historical Perspectives on the Military-Industrial Complex*, ed. Benjamin Franklin Cooling. Port Washington, N.Y.: Kennikat Press, 1977.

Clark, J[ohn] M[aurice]. "The Basis of War-Time Collectivism." *American Economic Review* 7 (Dec. 1917).

———. *The Costs of the World War to the American People*. New Haven, Conn.: Yale University Press, 1931.

Clarkson, Grosvenor B. *Industrial America in the World War: The Strategy Behind the Line, 1917–1918*. Boston: Houghton Mifflin, 1923.

Cuff, Robert D. *The War Industries Board: Business-Government Relations during World War I*. Baltimore: Johns Hopkins University Press, 1973.

Day, Edmund E. "The American Merchant Fleet: A War Achievement, A Peace Problem." *Quarterly Journal of Economics* 34 (Aug. 1920).

Dixon, Frank Haigh. "Federal Operation of the Railroads during the War." *Quarterly Journal of Economics* 33 (Aug. 1919).

Ferrell, Robert H. *Woodrow Wilson and World War I, 1917–1921*. New York: Harper & Row, 1985.

Haney, Lewis H. "Price Fixing in the United States during the War." *Political Science Quarterly* 34 (1919), in three parts.

Hawley, Ellis, W. *The Great War and the Search for a Modern Order, A History of the American People and Their Institutions, 1917–1933*. New York: St. Martin's Press, 1979.

Hippelheuser, Richard H., ed. *American Industry in the War: A Report of the War Industries Board*. New York: Prentice-Hall, 1941.

Hitchcock, Curtice N. "The War Industries Board: Its Development, Organization, and Functions." *Journal of Political Economy* 26 (June 1918).

Kennedy, David M. *Over Here: The First World War and American Society*. New York: Oxford University Press, 1980.

Kerr, K. Austin. *American Railroad Politics, 1914–1920: Rates, Wages, and Efficiency*. Pittsburgh: University of Pittsburgh Press, 1968.

Koistinen, Paul A. C. "The 'Industrial-Military Complex' in Historical Perspective: World War I." *Business History Review* 41 (Winter 1967).

Leland, Waldo G., and Newton D. Mereness, comp. *Introduction to the American Official Sources for the Economic and Social History of the World War*. New Haven, Conn.: Yale University Press, 1926.

Litman, Simon. *Prices and Price Control in Great Britain and the United States during the World War*. New York: Oxford University Press, 1920.

Livermore, Seward W. *Politics Is Adjourned: Woodrow Wilson and the War Congress, 1916–1918*. Middletown, Conn.: Wesleyan University Press, 1966.

Marshall, L. C. "The War Labor Program and Its Administration," *Journal of Political Economy* 26 (May 1918).

Metzer, Jacob. "How New Was the New Era? The Public Sector in the 1920's." *Journal of Economic History* 45 (March 1985).

Moulton, Harold G. "Industrial Conscription." *Journal of Political Economy* 25 (Nov. 1917).

Palmer, Frederick. *Newton D. Baker: America at War*. New York: Dodd, Mead, 1931.

Paxson, Frederic L. "The American War Government, 1917–1918." *American Historical Review* 26 (Oct. 1920).

Rothbard, Murray N. "War Collectivism in World War I." In *A New History of Leviathan: Essays on the Rise of the American Corporate State*, ed. Ronald Radosh and Murray N. Rothbard. New York: Dutton, 1972.

Schaub, Edward L. "The Regulation of Rentals during the War Period." *Journal of Political Economy* 28 (Jan. 1920).

Soule, George. *Prosperity Decade: From War to Depression, 1917–1929*. New York: Holt, Rinehart & Winston, 1947.

Taussig, F. W. "Price-Fixing as Seen by a Price Fixer." *Quarterly Journal of Economics* 33 (Feb. 1919).

Wehle, Louis B. "Labor Problems in the United States during the War." *Quarterly Journal of Economics* 32 (Feb. 1918).

THE GREAT DEPRESSION

Allen, Frederick Lewis. *Since Yesterday: The Nineteen-Thirties in America.* New York: Harper & Brothers, 1940.

Alston, Lee J. "Farm Foreclosures in the United States during the Interwar Period." *Journal of Economic History* 43 (Dec. 1983).

———. "Farm Foreclosure Moratorium Legislation: A Lesson from the Past." *American Economic Review* 74 (June 1984).

Chandler, Lester V. *America's Greatest Depression, 1929–1941.* New York: Harper & Row, 1970.

Darby, Michael R. "Three-and-a-Half Million U.S. Employees Have Been Mislaid: Or, an Explanation of Unemployment, 1934–1941." *Journal of Political Economy* 84 (Feb. 1976).

Ekirch, Arthur A., Jr. *Ideologies and Utopias: The Impact of the New Deal on American Thought.* Chicago: Quadrangle Books, 1969.

Freidel, Frank. *Franklin D. Roosevelt: Launching the New Deal.* Boston: Little, Brown, 1973.

Galbraith, John Kenneth. *The Great Crash.* Boston: Houghton Mifflin, 1961.

Garrity, John A. "The New Deal, National Socialism, and the Great Depression." *American Historical Review* 78 (Oct. 1973).

Hawley, Ellis W. *The New Deal and the Problem of Monopoly: A Study in Economic Ambivalence.* Princeton, N.J.: Princeton University Press, 1966.

———. *The Great War and the Search for a Modern Order, A History of the American People and Their Institutions, 1917–1933.* New York: St. Martin's Press, 1979.

Jones, Jesse H. *Fifty Billion Dollars: My Thirteen Years with the RFC.* New York: Macmillan, 1951.

Kesselman, J. R., and N. E. Savin. "Three-and-a-Half Million Workers Never Were Lost." *Economic Inquiry* 16 (April 1978).

Leuchtenburg, William E. *Franklin D. Roosevelt and the New Deal, 1932–1940.* New York: Harper Colophon Books, 1963.

———. "The New Deal and the Analogue of War." In *Change and Continuity in Twentieth-Century America,* ed. John Braeman, Robert H. Bremner, and Everett Walters. Columbus: Ohio State University Press, 1964.

Libecap, Gary D. "The Political Economy of the Establishment of the Interstate Oil Cartel, 1933–1940." In *Emergence of the Modern Political Economy,* ed. Robert Higgs. Greenwich, Conn.: JAI Press, 1985.

Lucas, Robert E., Jr., and Leonard A. Rapping. "Unemployment in the Great Depression: Is There a Full Explanation?" *Journal of Political Economy* 80 (Jan./Feb. 1972).

Mitchell, Broadus. *Depression Decade: From New Era through New Deal, 1929–1941.* New York: Harper Torchbooks, 1969.

Pels, Richard H. *Radical Visions and American Dreams: Culture and Social Thought in the Depression Years.* New York: Harper & Row, 1973.

Robinson, Edgar Eugene. *The Roosevelt Leadership, 1933–1945.* Philadelphia: Lippincott, 1955.

Rothbard, Murray N. "Herbert Hoover and the Myth of Laissez-Faire." In *A New History of Leviathan: Essays on the Rise of the American Corporate State,* ed. Ronald Radosh and Murray N. Rothbard. New York: E. P. Dutton, 1972.

Schwarz, Jordan A. *The Interregnum of Despair: Hoover, Congress, and the Depression.* Urbana: University of Illinois Press, 1970.

Shannon, David A., ed. *The Great Depression.* Englewood Cliffs, N.J.: Prentice-Hall, 1960.

Smiley, Gene. "Did Incomes for Most of the Population Fall from 1923 Through 1929?" *Journal of Economic History* 43 (March 1983).

———. "Recent Unemployment Rate Estimates for the 1920's and 1930's." *Journal of Economic History* 43 (June 1983).

Wallis, John Joseph. "The Birth of the Old Federalism: Financing the New Deal, 1932–1940." *Journal of Economic History* 44 (March 1984).

———. "Why 1933? The Origins and Timing of National Government Growth." In *Emergence of the Modern Political Economy*, ed. Robert Higgs. Greenwich, Conn.: JAI Press, 1985.

Wallis, John Joseph, and Daniel K. Benjamin. "Public Relief and Private Employment in the Great Depression." *Journal of Economic History* 41 (March 1981).

Whatley, Warren C. "Labor for the Picking: The New Deal in the South." *Journal of Economic History* 43 (Dec. 1983).

Wilbur, Ray Layman, and Arthur Mastick Hyde. *The Hoover Policies*. New York: Charles Scribner's Sons, 1937.

WORLD WAR II

Beaumont, Roger A. "Quantum Increase: The MIC [military-industrial complex] in the Second World War." In *War, Business, and American Society: Historical Perspectives on the Military-Industrial Complex*, ed, Benjamin Franklin Cooling. Port Washington, N.Y.: Kennikat Press, 1977.

Blum, Albert A. "Birth and Death of the M-Day Plan." In *American Civil-Military Decisions*, ed. Harold Stein. Birmingham: University of Alabama Press, 1962.

Blum, Albert A., and J. Douglas Smyth. "Who Should Serve: Pre-World War II Planning for Selective Service." *Journal of Economic History* 30 (June 1970).

Blum, John Morton. *V Was for Victory: Politics and American Culture During World War II*. New York: Harcourt Brace Jovanovich, 1976.

Burns, James McGregor. *Roosevelt: The Soldier of Freedom*. New York: Harcourt Brace Jovanovich, 1970.

Cain, Louis, and George Neumann. "Planning for Peace: The Surplus Property Act of 1944." *Journal of Economic History* 41 (March 1981).

Donovan, Robert J. *Conflict and Crisis: The Presidency of Harry S. Truman, 1945–1948*. New York: Norton, 1977.

Evans, Paul. "The Effects of General Price Controls in the United States during World War II." *Journal of Political Economy* 90 (Oct. 1982).

Gordon, Robert J. "$45 Billion of U.S. Private Investment Has Been Mislaid." *American Economic Review* 69 (June 1969).

Harris, Seymour E. *Price and Related Controls in the United States*. New York: McGraw-Hill, 1945.

Huntington, Samuel P. *The Soldier and the State: The Theory and Politics of Civil-Military Relations*. Cambridge, Mass.: Belknap Press, 1957.

Jones, Jesse H. *Fifty Billion Dollars: My Thirteen Years with the RFC*. New York: Macmillan, 1951.

Koistinen, Paul A. C. "Mobilizing the World War II Economy: Labor and the Industrial-Military Alliance." *Pacific Historical Review* 42 (Nov. 1973).

Milward, Alan S. *War, Economy and Society, 1939–1945*. Berkeley: University of California Press, 1977.

Mitchell, Wesley C. "Wartime 'Prosperity' and the Future." National Bureau of Economic Research *Occasional Paper 9* (March 1943).

Polenberg, Richard. *War and Society: The United States, 1941–1945*. New York: Lippincott, 1972.

Robinson, Edgar Eugene. *The Roosevelt Leadership, 1933–1945*. Philadelphia: Lippincott, 1955.

Rockoff, Hugh. "Indirect Price Increases and Real Wages during World War II." *Explorations in Economic History* 15 (Oct. 1978).
——. "The Response of the Giant Corporations to Wage and Price Controls in World War II." *Journal of Economic History* 41 (March 1981).
——. "Price and Wage Controls in Four Wartime Periods." *Journal of Economic History* 41 (June 1981).
Ross, Davis R. B. *Preparing for Ulysses: Politics and Veterans during World War II.* New York: Columbia University Press, 1969.
Smaller War Plants Corporation. *Economic Concentration and World War II.* Washington, D.C.: U.S. Government Printing Office, 1946.
Smith, R. Elberton. *The Army and Economic Mobilization.* Washington, D.C.: U.S. Army, 1959.
Stimson, Henry L., and McGeorge Bundy. *On Active Service in Peace and War.* London: Hutchinson, 1947.
War Records Section, U.S. Bureau of the Budget. *The United States at War: Development and Administration of the War Program by the Federal Government.* Washington, D.C.: U.S. Government Printing Office, 1946.
Young, Roland. *Congressional Politics in the Second World War.* New York: Columbia University Press, 1956.

SINCE WORLD WAR II

Aaron, Henry J. *Politics and the Professors: The Great Society in Perspective.* Washington, D.C.: Brookings Institution, 1978.
Chapman, Stephen. "The Gas Lines of '79." *Public Interest* (Summer 1980).
Clayton, James L., ed. *The Economic Impact of the Cold War: Sources and Readings.* New York: Harcourt, Brace & World, 1970.
Domhoff, William. *Who Rules America Now?* Englewood Cliffs, N.J.: Prentice-Hall, 1983.
Dye, Thomas R. *Who's Running America?* Englewood Cliffs, N.J.: Prentice-Hall, 1983.
Fulbright, J. William. *The Pentagon Propaganda Machine.* New York: Vintage Books, 1971.
Galbraith, John Kenneth. *The New Industrial State.* Boston: Houghton Mifflin, 1967.
Gansler, Jacques S. *The Defense Industry.* Cambridge, Mass.: MIT Press, 1980.
Glasner, David. *Politics, Prices, and Petroleum: The Political Economy of Energy.* Cambridge, Mass.: Ballinger, 1985.
Glazer, Nathan. "The Social Policy of the Reagan Administration: A Review." *Public Interest* (Spring 1984).
Glazer, Nathan, and Irving Kristol, eds. *The American Commonwealth, 1976.* New York: Basic Books, 1976.
Greider, William. *The Education of David Stockman and Other Americans.* New York: E. P. Dutton, 1982.
Higgs, Robert. "Carter's Wage-Price Guidelines: A Review of the First Year." *Policy Review* 11 (Winter 1980).
——. "Wage-Price Guidelines: Retreat and Defeat." *Freeman* 31 (Nov. 1981).
Karadbil, Leon N., and Roderick L. Vawter. "The Defense Production Act: Crucial Component of Mobilization Preparedness." In *Mobilization and the National Defense,* ed. Hardy L. Merritt and Luther F. Carter. Washington, D.C.: National Defense University Press, 1985.
Keller, Robert R., and Ann Mari May. "The Presidential Political Business Cycle of 1972." *Journal of Economic History* 44 (June 1984).

Koistinen, Paul A. C. *The Military-Industrial Complex: A Historical Perspective.* New York: Praeger, 1980.

Lodge, George C. *The New American Ideology.* New York: Knopf, 1976.

Navarro, Peter. *The Policy Game: How Special Interests and Ideologues Are Stealing America.* New York: Wiley, 1984.

Palmer, John [L.], and Isabel V. Sawhill, eds. *The Reagan Experiment.* Washington, D.C.: The Urban Institute, 1982.

——. *The Reagan Record.* Cambridge, Mass.: Ballinger, 1984.

Phillips, Kevin P. *Post-Conservative America: People, Politics and Ideology in a Time of Crisis.* New York: Random House, 1982.

Pursell, Carroll W., Jr., ed. *The Military-Industrial Complex.* New York: Harper & Row, 1972.

Reichley, A. James. *Conservatives in an Age of Change: The Nixon and Ford Administrations.* Washington, D.C.: Brookings Institution, 1981.

Roberts, Paul Craig. *The Supply-Side Revolution: An Insider's Account of Policymaking in Washington.* Cambridge, Mass.: Harvard University Press, 1984.

Rosen, Steven, ed. *Testing the Theory of the Military-Industrial Complex.* Lexington, Mass.: Lexington Books, 1973.

Shultz, George P., and Kenneth W. Dam. *Economic Policy Beyond the Headlines.* New York: Norton, 1977.

Silk, Leonard. *Economics in the Real World.* New York: Simon & Schuster, 1984.

Simon, William E. *A Time for Truth* New York: Berkley Books, 1979.

Stockman, David A. *The Triumph of Politics: How the Reagan Revolution Failed.* New York: Harper & Row, 1986.

Twight, Charlotte. *America's Emerging Fascist Economy.* New Rochelle, N.Y.: Arlington House, 1975.

Weaver, Paul H. "Regulation, Social Policy, and Class Conflict." *Public Interest* (Winter 1978).

Williams, Benjamin H. *Emergency Management of the National Economy. Vol. 21. Reconversion and Partial Mobilization.* Washington, D.C.: Industrial College of the Armed Forces, 1956.

BIOGRAPHICAL AND WIDER-RANGING HISTORICAL WORKS

Anderson, Benjamin M. *Economics and the Public Welfare: A Financial and Economic History of the United States, 1914–46.* Indianapolis: Liberty Press, 1979.

Baruch, Bernard, M. *Baruch: The Public Years.* New York: Holt, Rinehart & Winston, 1960.

Bowles, Chester. *Promises to Keep: My Years in Public Life, 1941–1969.* New York: Harper & Row, 1971.

Byrnes, James F. *All in One Lifetime.* New York: Harper & Brothers, 1958.

Douglas, William O. *Go East, Young Man: The Early Years. The Autobiography of William O. Douglas.* New York: Vintage, 1983.

Ekirch, Arthur A., Jr. *The Decline of American Liberalism.* New York: Atheneum, 1980.

Friedman, Milton, and Anna Jacobson Schwartz. *A Monetary History of the United States, 1867–1960.* Princeton, N.J.: Princeton University Press, 1963.

Galbraith, John Kenneth. *A Life in Our Times: Memoirs.* New York: Ballantine Books, 1981.

Gerber, Larry G. *The Limits of Liberalism: Josephus Daniels, Henry Stimson, Bernard Baruch, Donald Richberg, Felix Frankfurter and the Development of the Modern American Political Economy.* New York: New York University Press, 1983.

Graham, Otis L., Jr. *Toward a Planned Society: From Roosevelt to Nixon.* New York: Oxford University Press, 1976.

Hamby, Alonzo L. *Liberalism and Its Challenges: FDR to Reagan.* New York: Oxford University Press, 1985.

Higgs, Robert, ed. *Emergence of the Modern Political Economy.* Greenwich, Conn.: JAI Press, 1985.

Hofstadter, Richard. *The American Political Tradition, And the Men Who Made It.* New York: Vintage, 1974.

Hoover, Herbert. *The Memoirs of Herbert Hoover: Years of Adventure, 1874–1920.* New York: Macmillan, 1952.

———. *The Memoirs of Herbert Hoover: The Cabinet and the Presidency, 1920–1933.* New York: Macmillan, 1952.

———. *The Memoirs of Herbert Hoover: The Great Depression, 1929–1941.* New York: Macmillan, 1952.

Hughes, Jonathan. *American Economic History.* Glenview, Ill.: Scott, Foresman, 1983.

Karl, Barry D. *The Uneasy State: The United States from 1915 to 1945.* Chicago: University of Chicago Press, 1983.

McAdoo, William Gibbs. *Crowded Years.* Boston: Houghton Mifflin, 1931.

McCraw, Thomas K. *Prophets of Regulation: Charles Francis Adams, Louis D. Brandeis, James M. Landis, Alfred E. Kahn.* Cambridge, Mass.: Belknap Press, 1984.

Nixon, Richard M. *RN: The Memoirs of Richard Nixon.* New York: Grosset & Dunlap, 1978.

North, Douglass C. *Structure and Change in Economic History.* New York: Norton, 1981.

Parrish, Michael E. *Felix Frankfurter and His Times: The Reform Years.* New York: Free Press, 1982.

Pusey, Merlo J. *Eugene Meyer.* New York: Knopf, 1974.

Rockoff, Hugh. *Drastic Measures: A History of Wage and Price Controls in the United States.* New York: Cambridge University Press, 1984.

Schwarz, Jordan A. *The Speculator: Bernard M. Baruch in Washington, 1917–1965.* Chapel Hill: University of North Carolina Press, 1981.

Sobel, Robert. *The Age of Giant Corporations: A Mircoeconomic History of American Business, 1914–1970.* Westport, Conn.: Greenwood Press, 1972.

Steel, Ronald. *Walter Lippmann and the American Century.* Boston: Little, Brown, 1980.

Stein, Herbert. *The Fiscal Revolution in America.* Chicago: University of Chicago Press, 1969.

———. *Presidential Economics: The Making of Economic Policy from Roosevelt to Reagan and Beyond.* New York: Simon & Schuster, 1984.

Temin, Peter. "Government Actions in Times of Crisis: Lessons from the History of Drug Regulation." *Journal of Social History* 18 (Spring 1985).

Twight, Charlotte. "U.S. Regulation of International Trade: A Retrospective Inquiry." In *Emergency of the Modern Political Economy*, ed. Robert Higgs. Greenwich, Conn.: JAI Press, 1985.

LEGAL AND CONSTITUTIONAL

Anderson, Martin, ed. *The Military Draft: Selected Readings on Conscription.* Stanford, Calif.: Hoover Institution Press, 1982.

Belknap, Michal R. "The New Deal and the Emergency Powers Doctrine." *Texas Law Review* 62 (1983).

Berdahl, Clarence A. *War Powers of the Executive in the United States*. Urbana: University of Illinois, 1921.

Beth, Loren P. *The Development of the American Constitution, 1877–1917*. New York: Harper Torchbooks, 1971.

Clark, Jane Perry. "Emergencies and the Law." *Political Science Quarterly* 49 (June 1934).

Conant, Michael. *The Constitution and Capitalism*. St. Paul, Minn.: West Publishing Co., 1974.

Corwin, Edward S. *Total War and the Constitution*. New York: Knopf, 1947.

Friedman, Lawrence M. *A History of American Law*. New York: Simon & Schuster, 1973.

Friedman, Leon. "Conscription and the Constitution: The Original Understanding." *Michigan Law Review* 67 (May 1969).

Gillam, Richard. "The Peacetime Draft: Voluntarism to Coercion." *Yale Review* 57 (June 1968).

Higgs, Robert, and Charlotte Twight. "National Emergency and the Erosion of Private Property Rights." *Cato Journal* 6 (Winter 1987).

Hurst, James Willard. *Law and the Conditions of Freedom in the Nineteenth-Century United States*. Madison: University of Wisconsin Press, 1956.

——— . *Law and Markets in United States History: Different Modes of Bargaining Among Interests*. Madison: University of Wisconsin Press, 1982.

Karlin, Norman. "Substantive Due Process: A Doctrine for Regulatory Control." In *Rights and Regulation: Ethical, Political, and Economic Issues*, ed. Tibor R. Machan and M. Bruce Johnson. Cambridge, Mass.: Ballinger, 1983.

Murphy, Paul L. *The Constitution in Crisis Times, 1918–1969*. New York: Harper Torchbooks, 1972.

Paul, Arnold M. *Conservative Crisis and the Rule of Law: Attitudes of Bar and Bench, 1887–1895*. New York: Harper Torchbooks, 1969.

Porter, Mary Cornelia. "That Commerce Shall Be Free: A New Look at the Old Laissez-Faire Court." *Supreme Court Review* (1976).

Prosser, William L. "The Minnesota Mortgage Moratorium." *Southern California Law Review* 7 (1934).

Rossiter, Clinton L. *Constitutional Dictatorship: Crisis Government in the Modern Democracies*. Princeton, N.J.: Princeton University Press, 1948.

Rossiter, Clinton, and Richard P. Longaker. *The Supreme Court and the Commander in Chief*. Expanded edition. Ithaca, N.Y.: Cornell University Press, 1976.

Scheiber, Harry N. "Public Economic Policy and the American Legal System: Historical Perspectives." *Wisconsin Law Review* (1980).

Siegan, Bernard H. *Economic Liberties and the Constitution*. Chicago: University of Chicago Press, 1980.

ten Broek, Jacobus, Edward N. Barnhart, and Floyd W. Matson. *Prejudice, War and the Constitution*. Berkeley: University of California Press, 1954.

Twight, Charlotte. *America's Emerging Fascist Economy*. New Rochelle, N.Y.: Arlington House, 1975.

U.S. SUPREME COURT CASES

Adair v. United States, 208 U.S. 161 (1908).

Arver v. United States, 245 U.S. 366 (1918).

Block v. Hirsh, 256 U.S. 135 (1921).

Bowles v. Willingham, 321 U.S. 503 (1944).

Chastleton Corp. v. Sinclair, 264 U.S. 543 (1924).

Coppage v. Kansas, 236 U.S. 1 (1915).
Ex Parte Endo, 323 U.S. 283 (1944).
Flint v. Stone Tracy Co., 220 U.S. 107 (1911).
Goldman v. United States, 245 U.S. 474 (1918).
Hirabayashi v. United States, 320 U.S. 81 (1943).
Home Building and Loan Association v. Blaisdell, 290 U.S. 398 (1934).
In re Debs, 158 U.S. 564 (1895).
Korematsu v. United States, 323 U.S. 214 (1944).
Lichter v. United States, 334 U.S. 742 (1948).
Marcus Brown Holding Co. v. Feldman, 256 U.S. 170 (1921).
Nebbia v. New York, 291 U.S. 502 (1934).
New State Ice Co. v. Liebman, 285 U.S. 262 (1932).
Norman v. Baltimore and Ohio Railroad Co., 294 U.S. 240 (1935).
Northern Pacific Railway Co. v. North Dakota, 250 U.S. 135 (1919).
Nortz v. United States, 294 U.S. 317 (1935).
Panama Refining Co. v. Ryan, 293 U.S. 338 (1935).
Perry v. United States, 294 U.S. 330 (1935).
Pollock v. Farmers' Loan and Trust Co., 157 U.S. 429 (1895).
Pollock v. Farmers' Loan and Trust Co. (rehearing), 158 U.S. 601 (1895).
Ruthenberg v. United States, 245 U.S. 480 (1918).
Steuart v. Bowles, 322 U.S. 398 (1944).
United States v. Bankers Trust Co., 294 U.S. 240 (1935).
United States v. Bethlehem Steel Corp., 315 U.S. 289 (1942).
United States v. Butler, 297 U.S. 1 (1936).
United States v. Cohen Grocery Co., 255 U.S. 81 (1921).
United States v. Schechter Poultry Corp., 295 U.S. 495 (1935).
Wilson v. New, 243 U.S. 332 (1917).
Yakus v. United States, 321 U.S. 414 (1944).
Youngstown Sheet & Tube Co. v. Sawyer, 343 U.S. 579 (1952).

Index

Witte, John F., 150
Wood, Leonard, 127–128
Work-or-fight order, 218
Work relief, proposals in 1890s, 85–86
Works Progress Administration, 25, 190
World Bank, 260
World War I, 123–158, 196–198
World War II, 196–236, 245, 259

Yakus v. *United States*, 221–222
Yeager, Leland, 9, 243
Youngstown case, 246

Zaller, John, 15
Zeigler, Harman, 46, 69